CONDUCTING INTERNAL INVESTIGATIONS
GATHERING EVIDENCE AND PROTECTING YOUR COMPANY

Association of Certified Fraud Examiners

WORLD HEADQUARTERS • THE GREGOR BUILDING
716 WEST AVE • AUSTIN, TX 78701-2727 • USA

©2001, 2015 by the Association of Certified Fraud Examiners, Inc.

COURSE REVISION DATE: 1/30/15

No portion of this book may be reproduced or transmitted in any form or by any means electronic or mechanical, including photocopying, recording, or by any information storage and retrieval system without the written permission of the Association of Certified Fraud Examiners, Inc.

"Association of Certified Fraud Examiners," "Certified Fraud Examiner," "CFE," "ACFE," "Fraud Magazine," "CFE Exam Prep Course," "EthicsLine," the ACFE Seal, and the ACFE Logo are trademarks owned by the Association of Certified Fraud Examiners, Inc.

ISBN 978-1-889277-30-4

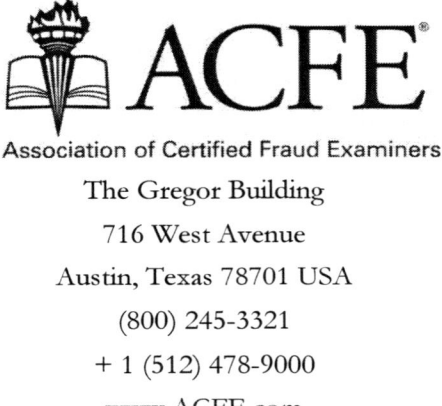

Association of Certified Fraud Examiners
The Gregor Building
716 West Avenue
Austin, Texas 78701 USA
(800) 245-3321
+ 1 (512) 478-9000
www.ACFE.com

DISCLAIMERS:

Every effort has been made to ensure that the contents of this publication are accurate and free from error. However, it is possible that errors exist, both typographical and in content. Therefore, the information provided herein should be used only as a guide and not as the only source of reference.

The author, advisors, and publishers caution that this publication is not meant to provide legal advice. The user should always consult with an attorney regarding the specific rules and regulations for your state or locality.

Printed in the United States of America.

Important Information Regarding Self-Study Continuing Professional Education Credit

This course qualifies for fraud-related continuing professional education (CPE) credit for Certified Fraud Examiners.

The Association of Certified Fraud Examiners (ACFE) is also a registered CPE sponsor with the National Association of State Boards of Accountancy (NASBA), and this course may be used in some states for self-study CPE credit for Certified Public Accountants. However, each state has the final decision as to whether to accept a particular course for CPE credit; therefore, please check with your state prior to beginning the course. Check with your state board for more information.

This course may also qualify for CPE credit for other professional designations and licenses. Please check with your licensing or certification body for more information.

IMPORTANT NOTE: This course must be completed and the exam submitted for grading <u>within one year of the date of purchase</u> in order to receive CPE credit.

Only the original purchaser of this course may obtain CPE credit. The final exam must be completed and a score of 70% or greater achieved to obtain CPE credit for this course. If you have purchased an electronic version of this workbook, please complete the exam online via the directions below, or request a Scantron through ACFE Member Services (800-245-3321 or MemberServices@ACFE.com). For hard copy versions, the exam can be completed by either of the following methods:

- <u>Online Exam</u>: To access the online exam, use the link included in your order confirmation. You can also access your exam through ACFE.com. Visit ACFE.com/OnlineCPE for additional instructions. (NOTE: If you have purchased this self-study course through a source other than the ACFE, please contact Member Services to obtain access to the online exam.)
- <u>Exam by Mail</u>: Record your answers on the original Scantron sheet included with this course. Please follow the directions on the form to make sure your answers are recorded properly and returned to the ACFE for grading. Please note that only the **original** Scantron examination form included with this workbook will be accepted for grading. Copies of the form will not be accepted. If you pass the exam, you will be e-mailed a Certificate of Completion within 5–7 business days from our receipt of your Scantron. If you prefer to receive a hard copy of your certificate, you may request one through Member Services. Individuals who score less than 70% will be notified via e-mail of their results and options for re-taking the exam.

Satisfaction is guaranteed on all ACFE products. If you are not 100% satisfied with any ACFE product, you may return it to us, provided it is in excellent condition, for a full refund.

Association of Certified Fraud Examiners is registered with the National Association of State Boards of Accountancy (NASBA) as a sponsor of continuing professional education on the National Registry of CPE Sponsors. State boards of accountancy have final authority on the acceptance of individual courses for CPE credit. Complaints regarding registered sponsors may be submitted to the National Registry of CPE Sponsors through its website: www.learningmarket.org.

CONDUCTING INTERNAL INVESTIGATIONS

TABLE OF CONTENTS

INTRODUCTION
About This Course 1
    Continuing Professional Education Credit... 3

I. PREPARING FOR AN INVESTIGATION
When Is an Investigation Necessary? 5
    Video 6
    Employer's Duty to Investigate 6
    Video 8
Statutory Disclosure Requirements 8
    Monitoring and Public Reporting Statutes 8
    Sarbanes-Oxley Act.. 11
    Video 18
    Video 19
    Video 22
    False Statement Statutes 27
    Civil Law Standard of Care and Duty to Company and Shareholders 27
    Accountants' and Auditors' Duties to Investigate 33
    External Auditors 35
    PCAOB Auditing Standard No. 5 44
Planning the Investigation 47
    Video 48
    Selecting the Investigation Team 48
    Video 49
    Investigative Strategy: Fraud Examination Methodology 50
    Video 51
    Video 55
    Video 55
Review Questions 57

II. COLLECTING DOCUMENTARY EVIDENCE
Introduction 61
Laws Governing Public Record Information 62
    Freedom of Information Act 62
    Fair Credit Reporting Act 63
    Gramm-Leach-Bliley Act 66
    Telephone Records and Privacy Protection Act of 2006 67
    Right to Financial Privacy Act 68
    Driver's Privacy Protection Act 68
    Health Insurance Portability and Accountability Act 69
Sources of Information 69
Public Sources of Information 70
    Video 71

II. COLLECTING DOCUMENTARY EVIDENCE (CONT.)

 City Government Records 71
 County Government Records 73
 Video 78
 State Government Records 78
 Federal Government Records 84

Using Databases to Find Information 93
 Locating People Using Online Records 93
 Obtaining Financial Information and Locating Assets 94
 Finding Legal Records 95
 Conducting Background Checks 96
 Public Record Database Vendors 98

Investigating with the Internet 102
 Pitfalls of the Internet 102
 Search Engines 102
 A Guide to Successful Searching 103
 Directories 104
 Meta-search Engines 105

Useful Websites 106
Review Questions 107

III. WORKPLACE SEARCHES

Introduction 109
Constitutional Privacy Rights: The Fourth Amendment 109
 Public Employers Versus Private Employers 110
 Employee Privacy Rights Under the Fourth Amendment 111
 State Constitutions 118

Effect of a Violation of an Employee's Constitutional Rights 119
 The Exclusionary Rule 119
 Civil Liability for Damages (42 U.S.C. § 1983) 119

Common Law Invasion of Privacy: Intrusion Upon Seclusion 120
 Reducing Employees' Expectation of Privacy 121
 Balancing the Need to Search or Conduct Surveillance and the Employee's Privacy Rights 122
 Other Tort Liabilities in Connection with Searches and Surveillance 122

Other Prohibitions Regarding Searches 122
 Searching an Employee's Mail 122
 Federal and State Nondiscrimination Statutes 123
 Monitoring Employee Phone Calls 123
 Pen Registers 124
 Monitoring Employees' Email 125
 Monitoring Employees' Internet Activity 126
 Monitoring Social Media 126
 Video Surveillance of Employees 127
 Searching Employees' Trash 127
 Special Privacy Rights Under Collective Bargaining Agreements 128

CONDUCTING INTERNAL INVESTIGATIONS

III. WORKPLACE SEARCHES (CONT.)
State Statutes 128
Sample Workplace Policy for Workplace Searches 128
Obtaining Evidence by Subpoena 129
Review Questions 132

IV. ANALYZING AND ORGANIZING EVIDENCE
Forensic Examination of Documents 135
    Sources for Expert Document Examinations 135
    Types of Forensic Document Examinations 136
    Handling Documents as Physical Evidence 137
    Recognizing Phony Documents 139
    Photocopies 140
Organizing Documentary Evidence 140
    Chronologies 141
    To-Do Lists 141
    Using Computer Software to Organize Documents and Other Data 141
Digital Evidence 142
    Understanding Digital Evidence 142
    Hardware 142
    Considerations When Seizing Digital Evidence 144
    Defining the Parameters of the Expert's Search 147
    Reviewing the Evidence 148
Review Questions 149

V. INTERVIEWING WITNESSES
Interview Mechanics 151
    Video 151
    Choosing a Venue for the Interview 151
    Establishing Proxemic Control over the Interview 152
    Video 152
    Taking Notes 152
    Do Not Interview More Than One Person 154
    Do Not Promise Confidentiality 154
    Handle Negotiation Attempts 154
    Do Not Discuss the Source of Allegations 155
    Common Problems Arising During the Interview 155
Types of Questions 158
    Video 159
    Introductory Questions 159
    Video 160
    Informational Questions 162
    Video 163
    Video 163
    Closing Questions 165

V. INTERVIEWING WITNESSES (CONT.)

    Assessment Questions 166
    Video 168
    Admission-Seeking Questions 176
    Video 176
    Video 178
    Video 187
    Video 193
Review Questions 194

VI. LEGAL CONSIDERATIONS IN INTERVIEWS

Employees' Duty to Cooperate 197
Employees' Rights During the Investigation 198
    Employees' Constitutional Rights 198
    Employees' Contractual Rights 206
    Employees' Statutory Rights 206
    Common Law Employee Rights and Protections 209
Presence of Corporate Attorney During Witness Interviews 216
Preserving the Confidentiality of the Investigation 217
    The Attorney-Client Privilege 218
    Attorney Work Product Doctrine 223
    The Self-Evaluation Privilege 226
Avoiding Liability for Obstruction of Justice and Witness Tampering 228
    Confidentiality Requests 229
    Witness Tampering 229
    Obstruction of Justice 230
    Spoliation of Evidence 231
    Perjury and Subornation of Perjury 231
    Misprision of a Felony 232
Recording the Results of an Interview 233
    Protect the Company's Interests in Confidentiality 233
    Factual Work Product Versus Opinion Work Product 233
    Identify the Record as Work Product 234
    Identify the Record as an Attorney-Client Communication 234
    Identify the Self-Evaluation Purpose of the Interview 235
    Identify and Treat the Record as Confidential 236
Review Questions 237

VII. WRITING REPORTS

Introduction 241
Characteristics of a Good Report 241
    Accuracy 241
    Clarity 241
    Impartiality and Relevance 242
    Timeliness 242

VII. WRITING REPORTS (CONT.)

Video 242
Legal Considerations for Written Reports 242
    Libel 242
    Privacy 243
    Privileges 244
    Disclosing the Report to Government Personnel or Other Third Parties 246
Review Questions 248

VIII. DISCHARGING EMPLOYEES

Introduction 251
The Public Policy Exception 251
Breach of Contract 252
    Types of Contracts 253
Statutory Violations 256
Common Law Causes of Action 257
    Defamation 257
    Intentional Infliction of Emotional Distress 257
    Public Disclosure of Private Facts 258
    False Imprisonment 259
Whistleblower Statutes 259
Other Considerations 259
Prosecuting Employees 259
    Video 260
    Why Prosecute an Offending Employee? 260
    Recovery of Losses in Criminal Cases 260
    Aiding the Company's Civil Remedies and Litigation 262
Malicious Prosecution 263
Review Questions 264

IX. CONCLUSION 267

X. PRACTICAL PROBLEMS

Practical Problem 1 270
Practical Problem 2 271
Practical Problem 3 272
Practical Problem 4 274
Practical Problem 5 275
Practical Problem 6 277
Practical Problem 7 279
Practical Problem 8 280

XI: APPENDIX: VIDEO TRANSCRIPTS 281

XII. SOLUTIONS TO REVIEW QUESTIONS
I. Preparing for an Investigation 299
II. Collecting Documentary Evidence 305
III. Workplace Searches 309
IV. Analyzing Documentary Evidence 314
V. Interviewing Witnesses 318
VI. Legal Considerations in Interviews 324
VII. Writing Reports 330
VIII. Discharging Employees 333

XIII. SOLUTIONS TO PRACTICAL PROBLEMS
Practical Problem 1 337
Practical Problem 2 339
Practical Problem 3 341
Practical Problem 4 345
Practical Problem 5 346
Practical Problem 6 349
Practical Problem 7 351
Practical Problem 8 353

XIV. FINAL EXAMINATION E-1

XV. INDEX I-1

ABOUT THE AUTHORS

Craig A. Starr, J.D., CFE

Craig A. Starr, J.D., CFE, is a former senior litigator and partner with the insurance defense firm of Bledsoe, Cathcart, Leahy, Starr and Diestel in San Francisco, California, where his caseload included fraud and other complex, multi-party cases in state and federal courts. He also spent a substantial part of his practice advising and assisting insurance companies in the investigation and disposition of suspected fraudulent claims and instructing claims handlers on civil litigation and claims investigation. Before joining the Bledsoe firm in 1982, he was a prosecutor for more than eight years with the U.S. Justice Department's Organized Crime Strike Force, where he investigated and tried numerous criminal organized crime cases and gained considerable experience with the Federal Racketeer Influenced and Corrupt Organizations Act (RICO). Mr. Starr currently has his own litigation and legal consulting practice in Eugene, Oregon.

In his present practice, as well as throughout his career, Mr. Starr has devoted substantial time and effort to teaching and writing about legal topics, such as litigation, evidence, fraud, and fraud investigation. He has written and taught courses and lectured for the ACFE and for other professional organizations on investigating insurance fraud, litigating fraud cases, fraud remedies, and workplace investigations. He was an adjunct professor at Hastings School of Law in San Francisco, where he taught seminars on evidence handling and advanced trial advocacy skills, and he continues to serve as a part-time instructor in trial advocacy at the University of Oregon Law School in Eugene. While in private practice in San Francisco, he wrote periodically for the *CEB (Continuing Education of the Bar) Civil Litigation Reporter*, and he served as a judicial arbitrator and as a judge *pro tem* for different courts in the San Francisco Bay Area.

Mr. Starr is a Certified Fraud Examiner and is a member of the California (inactive) and Oregon bars, as well as the bars of several federal courts, where he has practiced regularly. He graduated summa cum laude from the University of California at San Diego with a degree in history, and he received his J.D. degree, cum laude, from the University of Michigan School of Law in 1974.

John Warren, J.D., CFE

John Warren has served as general counsel of the Association of Certified Fraud Examiners since September 2004. Mr. Warren is chief legal officer of the ACFE, responsible for providing guidance, oversight, and direction to ACFE management and staff on all legal issues that affect the association. In 2006, Mr. Warren was appointed as an advisory member of the ACFE Board of Regents, and in 2009, he was appointed the vice president of the ACFE.

Aside from his legal responsibilities, Mr. Warren also contributes to the production of the Report to the Nations on Occupational Fraud and Abuse, a bi-annual report issued by the ACFE on the costs and effects of occupational fraud.

Prior to becoming general counsel, Mr. Warren served for eight years as associate general counsel and senior researcher of the ACFE. He contributed works on occupational fraud, courtroom procedure, corporate espionage, and embezzlement to the ACFE's training program, and he served as a guest author for the "Fraud and the Law" column in The White Paper. Mr. Warren worked with Chairman Joseph T. Wells to develop the ACFE's Higher Education Initiative, which provides free educational materials to colleges and universities that teach courses in fraud examination. He also has worked on behalf of ACFE to develop the Institute for Fraud Prevention, a multidisciplinary academic research center and consortium of universities dedicated to preventing and deterring fraud and corruption through research and education.

Mr. Warren received Bachelor of Science degrees in Political Science and Economics from the University of South Dakota in 1992, and a J.D. from Baylor Law School in 1995. He is a licensed member of the State Bar of Texas.

Acknowledgements

The authors and the Association of Certified Fraud Examiners would like to acknowledge the following individuals and thank them for their editorial assistance in developing this course: John D. Gill, J.D., CFE; DeAnn Holzman; and Jeanette LeVie, CFE.

INTRODUCTION

About This Course

Conducting an internal investigation can be one of the most difficult tasks a business organization will ever undertake. Internal investigations, by their very nature, tend to involve accusations or insinuations of wrongdoing against employees within the organization. As a result, these investigations are frequently divisive and disruptive to an organization's workforce. Furthermore, internal investigations are often costly, distracting, and time-consuming, drawing resources away from more traditional business functions and inhibiting productivity. In addition, internal investigations can lead to a wide variety of legal problems and other unexpected complications for the host organization if they are not conducted with the utmost care. Add to all this the fact that internal investigations are usually conducted without much advance notice and during periods of stress within the organization—after fraud losses have been discovered or allegations of wrongdoing by an employee have surfaced—and it becomes apparent that an internal investigation can be a challenging, complicated, and generally unpleasant affair.

Nevertheless, internal investigations are often absolutely necessary for the well-being of the organization in question. A well-run investigation can help an organization detect not only the source of lost funds, but also help it recover its losses. It can prevent future losses and save the organization untold dollars as a result. It can also help the organization successfully defend itself against legal charges by terminated or disgruntled employees.

The goal of this workbook is to train the reader to understand when an internal investigation is necessary, how it should be conducted, and how to avoid mistakes that can end up subjecting the organization to legal liability and possibly cost it more than the source of the problem for which the investigation was initiated.

You will learn how to:
- Ascertain effective methods to organize and plan your investigation.
- Determine fraud examination methodology.
- Identify documentary and electronic evidence.
- Recognize an employee's legal rights in an investigation.
- Devise an effective approach to conducting a successful admission-seeking interview.
- Determine the best practices to use while composing the investigation report.

The workbook has been divided into eight sections that address the major issues involved in the typical investigation.

Introduction

Chapter 1, "Preparing for an Investigation," is intended to provide the reader with an overview of the issues that an organization should consider before undertaking an internal investigation. This includes the company's legal duty to conduct an investigation and its potential liability for failing to do so. In addition, this chapter addresses basic pre-investigative strategies such as selecting the investigative team and developing an investigative strategy.

Chapter 2, "Collecting Documentary Evidence," focuses on how investigators can assemble the documents and background information that will provide the basic structure for an internal investigation.

Chapter 3, "Workplace Searches," addresses the legal considerations that accompany any effort at collecting documentary evidence, particularly the organization's right to access information and the employees' privacy rights in connection with workplace searches and monitoring.

Chapter 4, "Analyzing Documentary Evidence," explains how investigators should handle and organize documentary evidence to preserve it for trial and protect its confidentiality.

Chapter 5, "Interviewing Witnesses," gives the practitioner an overview of interview techniques that should be used during an internal investigation to help gather as much information as possible and to enable the investigator to obtain valid confessions.

Chapter 6, "Legal Considerations in Interviews," explains the potential legal liability that a company faces in connection with employee interviews and how to avoid that liability. This chapter also explains how to guard the confidentiality of the internal investigation and protect the results of the investigation from unwanted disclosure to outside parties.

Chapter 7, "Writing Reports," provides insight for the investigator on how to draft a well-written investigative report. This chapter also addresses the key legal considerations for investigative reports and explains how a company can avoid legal liability in connection with the results of an internal investigation, as well as how to keep the report confidential.

Chapter 8, "Discharging Employees," addresses a frequent outcome of internal investigations—the discharge of employees for wrongdoing. This chapter explains the potential legal liability that exists when an organization fires one of its employees, and how to avoid creating a cause of action for an employee who has been terminated. It concludes by discussing the advantages and disadvantages of referring a case of internal misconduct to government prosecutors.

Following each chapter is a set of review questions. We encourage you to take the time to answer each question thoroughly. When you have answered the questions, you may review the correct answers near the end of the workbook. Following the concluding chapter is a set of practical problems that will provide an opportunity to apply the knowledge gained from this workbook to a real-life scenario. Suggested answers to the practical problems are included.

This course is supplemented by exclusive online video content intended to enhance your understanding of the material. While working through the course, you will occasionally be directed to www.acfe.com/internalinvestigations to view a video associated with the corresponding section of the workbook. The videos, featuring insights from convicted fraudsters and subject matter experts, are optional and not required to successfully complete the review questions or final exam.

Continuing Professional Education Credit

Individuals who complete this course and score at least 70 percent on the final examination will earn continuing professional education (CPE) credit.

I. PREPARING FOR AN INVESTIGATION

When Is an Investigation Necessary?

The need for an internal investigation can arise in a number of circumstances. Obviously, internal investigations may be necessary to determine the source of losses caused by fraud. A thorough investigation in these circumstances can enable a company to reduce its losses, identify the perpetrator, gather evidence for a criminal prosecution or civil trial, and recapture some or all of its losses. It can also shed light on weaknesses in the company's control structure, thereby helping to shore up the company's internal defenses against future employee misconduct.

In addition to preventing losses due to fraud, an organization or its officers may have legal duties to investigate alleged misconduct. Certain federal statutes, such as the Foreign Corrupt Practices Act (FCPA), are specifically aimed at detecting wrongful conduct and require that companies report specific instances of misconduct. Obviously, to make an accurate report of misconduct, the management will need to conduct an investigation into alleged wrongdoing. Regulatory agencies such as the Securities and Exchange Commission (SEC) require accurate financial reporting by the companies they oversee, and they have the power to impose penalties for reports that are inaccurate or omit facts that could affect the accuracy of the reported information. An investigation can ensure that all relevant facts are known and reported.

Officers and directors of companies are also bound by duties of loyalty and reasonable care in overseeing the operations of their companies. This means they must act in the best interests of the company and take reasonable steps to prevent harm that the company might suffer as a result of employee misconduct. The failure to investigate reliable allegations of misconduct can amount to a violation of this duty, thereby subjecting the director or officer to civil liability for any damages that the company incurs as a result of the failure to investigate.

In many situations, companies must also conduct an internal investigation before they can dismiss an employee who has committed fraud or otherwise violated company rules and policies. A thoroughly documented investigation will help insulate the company from charges that it discriminated against the employee or otherwise wrongfully terminated him.

Where an organization might be liable for the conduct of one of its employees, an internal investigation can help mitigate the company's liability by cutting off the wrongful conduct before it is allowed to grow, and by demonstrating that the company has an effective program to detect and prevent criminal misconduct by its employees—a factor that provides for the diminishment of fines under the Organizational Sentencing Guidelines.

Preparing for an Investigation

These are only some of the reasons that a company may choose or be compelled to conduct an internal investigation. The remainder of this section will be devoted to explaining exactly when an investigation is called for, and how an organization can prepare itself to not only uncover the facts and evidence that are necessary to fulfill the purpose of the investigation, but also avoid the numerous legal pitfalls that await the unprepared company.

Video

In the video titled "Chapter I: Know Your Objective," fraud investigation expert Meric Bloch, J.D., CFE, explains the importance of knowing your objective when beginning a fraud investigation. Mr. Bloch has served as an expert consultant for the United States Secret Service and is the compliance officer for Adecco Group, a Fortune 500 company, where he has conducted more than 300 internal fraud investigations. (Go to www.acfe.com/internalinvestigations to view the video.)

Employer's Duty to Investigate

When there are signs or suspicions of employee wrongdoing, the employer—and the fraud examiner—face two related questions: (1) whether to conduct an internal investigation of the alleged wrongdoing and (2) whether to voluntarily disclose the results of that investigation to law enforcement or other government agencies. The decision to disclose the results of an investigation is not always voluntary. In many circumstances, companies are required by law to report wrongdoing by their employees or officers. This section will address some of the statutory and common-law duties and other factors that companies should take into account in deciding whether to conduct an internal investigation. Issues relating to voluntary disclosure of the results of an internal investigation and the employer's right to keep an investigative report confidential will be covered later in this workbook.

It may seem incongruous to speak of an employer's duty to investigate. After all, if an employee is stealing or otherwise behaving dishonestly, why would an employer need to be compelled to investigate? Would the company not want to conduct an investigation so that it could stop the thefts, possibly recover its losses, and take steps to prevent the illegal conduct from recurring? It is true conducting a thorough internal investigation results in several obvious benefits, but adverse consequences can arise as well. When a company is a victim of employee misconduct, and when that misconduct becomes public, it can potentially harm the company beyond the immediate losses from the theft itself.

As a result of public disclosure, the company may face its own criminal or civil liability or administrative fines because of an employee's misconduct for which it is legally responsible. Even if the misconduct is already public knowledge and a criminal or civil proceeding has begun, the internal investigation may have an adverse effect on the victim company. The results of the internal investigation may be subject to discovery in a civil or criminal case. Thus, by conducting an internal investigation, a company may unintentionally provide outside investigators with previously unknown evidence that could be used against the company.

> EXAMPLE
>
> *Acme is under FBI criminal investigation for offenses in connection with corrupt payments to foreign officials. Acme is conducting its own internal investigation, which has focused on Larson, a clerk in the accounts payable department. Larson has refused to answer the FBI's questions, asserting his Fifth Amendment right against self-incrimination. However, Larson has responded to questions from his own company's investigators because he understands that he could be fired for refusing to comply with Acme's internal investigation. (Acme is a private employer and its employees, therefore, do not enjoy constitutional protections in connection with internal investigations.) Furthermore, Larson hopes that the internal investigation will remain confidential and that his cooperation will help him avoid more serious discipline.*
>
> *However, if the FBI can obtain Larson's statements to the company or the internal report that reflects Larson's information, it would have access to information that it could not otherwise obtain from Larson due to his Fifth Amendment protections. Moreover, the government prosecutors then could contend that Larson had waived his privilege against self-incrimination by voluntarily making a statement to the company's investigator. This might enable the government to force Larson to testify. (See Chapter 6, "Legal Considerations in Interviews," for further discussion of these Fifth Amendment issues.)*

Public disclosure of internal fraud can subject a company to a number of additional adverse financial consequences, such as the loss of collateral business or trading partners, the loss of government licenses necessary for certain regulated activities, or a decline in the value of publicly traded equities. The directors of a corporation might face liability to their shareholders for the losses resulting from the misconduct or for any collateral consequences that result (e.g., fines or other civil liability imposed on the company). These are all factors that can incline a company toward avoiding knowledge of harmful facts.

Conversely, there are a number of legal duties and requirements that might outweigh a company's desire to ignore an employee or managerial offense. Many companies are required to monitor and report specific kinds of regulated transactions to various government agencies. For instance, financial institutions must file a report with the Financial Crimes Enforcement Network (FinCEN) when they suspect insider abuse by an employee. Furthermore, the officers and directors of all corporations are bound by statutory and common law standards of due care and loyalty in conducting company business.

Preparing for an Investigation

A company's managers may find that the best way to fulfill these legal duties and requirements is to conduct an internal investigation of known or suspected misconduct. Put another way, by failing to adequately investigate, a company may not be complying with the law. Note that the decision of whether to investigate is often very fact specific, and whether an investigation is compelled by some other legal duty or requirement is best answered by the company's lawyer(s) in consultation with senior management and after a consideration of all the relevant facts.

In the remainder of this section, we will review the most common legal duties and requirements that may compel or motivate a company to conduct an internal investigation.

Video

In the video titled "Chapter I: Fraud Awareness," fraud investigation expert Meric Bloch, J.D., CFE, explains the importance of both fraud awareness and effective monitoring. (Go to www.acfe.com/internalinvestigations to view the video.)

Statutory Disclosure Requirements

As mentioned earlier, several factors go into determining whether a fraud investigation should be performed. One of the most deciding factors is whether an applicable law would require an inquiry into the fraud or a disclosure of known fraud to a government agency. If a law imposes such a duty and the company fails to comply, severe penalties may result. Several laws impose disclosure requirements on businesses, including:

- Monitoring and public reporting statutes
- The Sarbanes-Oxley Act
- False statement statutes
- Civil law duties to a company and its shareholders
- Accountants' and internal auditors' duties to investigate
- External auditors' duty to investigate

Monitoring and Public Reporting Statutes

There are a number of statutes and regulations that impose on companies the duty to monitor themselves, file accurate reports and statements, and keep accurate records. These laws do not explicitly require companies to conduct internal investigations; however, there may be an implied duty to investigate internal wrongdoing in order to ensure that a company meets its disclosure requirements (i.e., that its filings are accurate or that it has taken appropriate steps to self-monitor).

For example, public companies are required to file accurate financial information with the SEC. Assume that after a company files its annual report it determines that a massive fraud may have significantly overstated the company's revenues. Since management has now learned that it filed inaccurate information, it may be required to do whatever is necessary to correct the inaccurate information. This would generally require the company to conduct an investigation of the fraud and file corrected reports. Therefore, the company is, in effect, required to conduct an inquiry or investigation even though the law may not specifically state so.

There are a number of statutes and related administrative regulations that impose monitoring, recordkeeping, and reporting requirements on companies. Under these statutes, a company might have an express or implied duty to investigate internal wrongdoing.

Some statutes, such as the FCPA[1] and the Anti-Kickback Act of 1986,[2] are aimed at detecting and disclosing specific wrongful conduct (e.g., bribery of foreign officials or bribery in connection with federal contracts). Besides specifically prohibiting corrupt payments, these statutes require that companies:
- Keep accurate recordkeeping concerning subject transactions.
- Report findings of specific misconduct.
- Establish appropriate procedures to prevent and limit the offending conduct.

Other statutes, such as federal and state securities and banking statutes, do not mandate reporting of specific forms of misconduct, but instead require companies in certain regulated industries and activities to prepare and file accurate financial statements and public reports (such as prospectuses, proxy statements, and annual reports) concerning a company's affairs. These reporting requirements carry with them an implied duty to report certain forms of wrongdoing.

Companies subject to such monitoring and reporting statutes must take steps to avoid omitting or inaccurately reporting facts (including incidents of internal misconduct) that might affect a statement's accuracy. Violations of these public reporting statutes do not always require fraudulent intent or willful falsification. Furthermore, these statutes may be violated not just when management knows of reportable misconduct and fails to report it, but also when it has indications of possible wrongdoing which it does not disclose.

---

[1] 15 U.S.C. §§ 78dd(1) and (2) and 78m, among other Sections.
[2] Title 41, U.S. Code, §§ 51–58

For example, the SEC enforces the FCPA and other federal securities laws through administrative rules such as:

- Rule 10b-5(b), which prohibits untrue statements or omissions of material facts in the sale of securities
- Rule 13b-2(1), which prohibits falsification of "books, records, and accounts" subject to federal securities laws
- Rule 13b-2(2), which prohibits an officer or director from making a materially false or misleading statement or omission to an accountant in connection with an audit or examination, or a submission to the SEC required by federal securities laws

The SEC takes the position that senior management and corporate counsel who fail to investigate alleged misconduct and fail to establish appropriate procedures for limiting the prohibited conduct may be held liable for violating the FCPA. Similarly, directors and others specified in reporting statutes are responsible for ensuring the accuracy of required corporate public filings, such as prospectuses, proxy statements, and annual reports. The SEC has held directors liable, among other things, for insufficient efforts to ensure adequate information and reporting systems are in place and for ignoring weaknesses in those systems. Moreover, in the SEC's view, liability for reporting violations may exist not only when responsible individuals actually know of misconduct, but also where they know of facts that indicate possible wrongdoing. The SEC has stated that it will not tolerate "benign indifference" to employee misconduct.

Thus, an internal investigation may be appropriate or necessary under some circumstances to ensure that public statements and reports are accurate and, where required, to establish adequate procedures to prevent and limit the illegal conduct. The failure to investigate can lead a company to include inaccurate or misleading facts in public filings, for which the company and its directors and other senior management may be held liable even absent fraudulent intent or actual knowledge of the falsehoods.

Management also can incur liability if it fails to inform outside auditors of misconduct that could cause material contingent liabilities or loss of income. By failing to disclose such liabilities or losses, the organization's required financial statements may not meet generally accepted accounting principles (GAAP) and may be considered inaccurate or misleading, which is a violation of federal and state securities statutes and regulations. In those cases, using an internal investigation to discover—and report—accurate facts about the misconduct may be the most appropriate action that senior management can take to ensure that financials are accurate and in compliance with GAAP.

The Private Securities Litigation Reform Act of 1995 underscores the importance of an appropriate company response to facts that suggest employee or management misconduct. Under this Act (which is an amendment to the 1934 Securities and Exchange Act), an outside accountant who learns of material illegal acts by the audited company or its employees may be required to inform the SEC of those illegal acts if the audited company's management fails to take corrective action after it is notified of the illegal acts. Thus, in this scenario, the audited company may be required to initiate an internal investigation in order to determine if the allegations are true, and, if so, what actions are required to correct the situation.

Under these monitoring and disclosure statutes, a subject company's duty to disclose—and therefore to investigate—typically pertains to facts that are material to the financial statement or other public report. Determining what is material for purposes of these statutes can be complex and is beyond the scope of this course. Legal counsel should be consulted in such cases. However, by way of example, the SEC has found employee or management misconduct to be material in each of the following circumstances:
- The misconduct causes a contingent liability or loss of income or other adverse financial impact that must be shown in the financial statements under GAAP.
- The misconduct reflects on management's integrity.
- A significant amount of the company's business depends on the misconduct.

Sarbanes-Oxley Act
On July 30, 2002, President Bush signed into law the Sarbanes-Oxley Act (SOX). This law, which was triggered in large part by several corporate accounting scandals in 2001 and 2002, significantly changed the laws of corporate governance and the rules and regulations under which accounting firms must operate. The Sarbanes-Oxley Act was designed to restore investor confidence in capital markets and help eliminate financial statement fraud in publicly traded companies, while at the same time significantly increasing the penalties for corporate accounting fraud. The most significant changes brought on by the Act include:
- The creation of the Public Company Accounting Oversight Board (PCAOB)
- Requirements for senior financial officers to certify SEC filings
- New standards for audit committee independence
- New standards for auditor independence
- Enhanced financial disclosure requirements
- New protections for corporate whistleblowers
- Enhanced penalties for white-collar crime

Since the enactment of Sarbanes-Oxley, the SEC has issued numerous rules and interpretations that support and expand the Act's requirements. Below is a summary of some of the most important provisions of Sarbanes-Oxley and the corresponding SEC Releases that relate to fraud detection and prevention. Because these rules are extensive and ever-changing, auditors should periodically review the SEC's website for updates and new rules at sec.gov/rules/final.shtml.

Public Company Accounting Oversight Board

Section 101 of the Sarbanes-Oxley Act establishes the PCAOB, whose purpose is:

> *[T]o oversee the audit of public companies that are subject to the securities laws, and related matters, in order to protect the interests of investors and further the public interest in the preparation of informative, accurate, and independent audit reports for companies the securities of which are sold to, and held by and for, public investors.*

In short, the PCAOB is charged with overseeing public company audits, setting audit standards, and investigating acts of noncompliance by auditors or audit firms. The PCAOB is appointed and overseen by the SEC, which is part of the executive branch. It is to be made up of five individuals—two who are or have been Certified Public Accountants (CPAs) and three who have never been CPAs. The PCAOB members are appointed by the SEC. Until recently, the members could only be removed for cause by the SEC. However, the Supreme Court held in *Free Enterprise Fund v. Public Accounting Oversight Board* that this policy impeded the President's authority under the separation of powers doctrine. Rather than find the PCAOB totally unconstitutional, the court simply excised the for cause provision, leaving it unnecessary for the SEC to have cause to remove members.

The Act lists the PCAOB's duties, which include:
- Registering public accounting firms that audit publicly traded companies
- Establishing or adopting auditing, quality control, ethics, independence, and other standards relating to audits of publicly traded companies
- Inspecting registered public accounting firms
- Investigating registered public accounting firms and their employees, conducting disciplinary hearings, and imposing sanctions where justified
- Performing such other duties as are necessary to promote high professional standards among registered accounting firms, to improve the quality of audit services offered by those firms, and to protect investors
- Enforcing compliance with the Sarbanes-Oxley Act, the rules of the PCAOB, professional standards, and securities laws relating to public company audits

REGISTRATION WITH THE BOARD

Public accounting firms must be registered with the PCAOB to legally prepare or issue an audit report on a publicly traded company. To become registered, accounting firms must disclose, among other things, the names of all public companies they audited in the preceding year; the names of all public companies they expect to audit in the current year; and the annual fees they received from each of their public audit clients for audit, accounting, and non-audit services.

AUDITING, QUALITY CONTROL, AND INDEPENDENCE STANDARDS AND RULES

Section 103 of the Act requires the PCAOB to establish standards for auditing, quality control, ethics, independence, and other issues relating to audits of publicly traded companies. Although the Act places the responsibility on the PCAOB to establish audit standards, it also sets forth certain rules that the PCAOB is required to include in those auditing standards. These rules are:

- Audit work papers must be maintained for at least seven years.
- Auditing firms must include a concurring or second-partner review and approval of audit reports, as well as concurring approval in the issuance of the audit report by a qualified person other than the person in charge of the audit.
- All audit reports must describe the scope of testing of the company's internal control structure and must present the auditor's findings from the testing, including an evaluation of whether the internal control structure is acceptable and a description of material weaknesses in internal controls and any material noncompliance.

INSPECTIONS OF REGISTERED PUBLIC ACCOUNTING FIRMS

The Act also authorizes the PCAOB to conduct regular inspections of public accounting firms to assess their degree of compliance with laws, rules, and professional standards regarding audits. Inspections are to be conducted once a year for firms that regularly audit more than 100 public companies, and at least once every three years for firms that regularly audit between 100 or fewer public companies.

INVESTIGATIONS AND DISCIPLINARY PROCEEDINGS

The PCAOB has the authority to investigate registered public accounting firms (or their employees) for potential violations of the Sarbanes-Oxley Act, professional standards, any rules established by the board, or any securities laws relating to the preparation and issuance of audit reports. During an investigation, the PCAOB has the power to compel testimony and document production.

Additionally, the PCAOB has the power to issue sanctions for violations or for non-cooperation with an investigation. Sanctions can include temporary or permanent suspension of a firm's registration with the board (which would mean that the firm could no longer legally audit publicly traded companies), temporary or permanent suspension of a person's right to be associated with a registered public accounting firm, prohibition from auditing public companies, and civil monetary penalties of up to $750,000 for an individual and up to $15 million for a firm.

Certification Obligations for CEOs and CFOs

One of the most significant changes affected by the Sarbanes-Oxley Act is the requirement that the Chief Executive Officer (CEO) and the Chief Financial Officer (CFO) of public companies personally certify annual and quarterly SEC filings. These certifications essentially require CEOs and CFOs to take responsibility for their companies' financial statements and prevent them from delegating this responsibility to their subordinates and then claiming ignorance when fraud is uncovered in the financial statements.

There are two types of officer certifications mandated by Sarbanes-Oxley: criminal certifications, which are set forth in Sarbanes-Oxley Section 906 and codified in 18 U.S.C. § 1350, and civil certifications, which are set forth in Sarbanes-Oxley Section 302.

CRIMINAL CERTIFICATIONS (SOX § 906)

Under Section 906, all periodic filings with the SEC must be accompanied by a statement, signed by the CEO and CFO, which certifies that the report fully complies with the SEC's periodic reporting requirements and that the information in the report fairly presents, in all material respects, the financial condition and results of operation of the company.

These certifications are known as "criminal certifications" because the Act imposes criminal penalties on officers who violate the certification requirements.

- Corporate officers who *knowingly* violate the certification requirements are subject to fines of up to $1 million and up to 10 years imprisonment, or both.
- Corporate officers who *willfully* violate the certification requirements are subject to fines of up to $5 million and up to 20 years imprisonment, or both.

CIVIL CERTIFICATIONS (SOX § 302)

Sarbanes-Oxley Section 302 requires the CEO and CFO to personally certify the following six items in every annual and quarterly report:

1. They have personally reviewed the report.
2. Based on their knowledge, the report does not contain any material misstatement that would render the financials misleading.
3. Based on their knowledge, the financial information in the report fairly presents in all material respects the financial condition, results of operations, and cash flow of the company.
4. They are responsible for designing, maintaining, and evaluating the company's internal controls; they have evaluated the controls within 90 days prior to the report; and they have presented their conclusions about the effectiveness of those controls in the report.
5. They have disclosed to the auditors and the audit committee any material weaknesses in the controls and any fraud, whether material or not, that involves management or other employees who have a significant role in the company's internal controls.
6. They have indicated in their report whether there have been significant changes in the company's internal controls since the filing of the last report.

INTERNAL CONTROLS

Under Section 404 of the Sarbanes-Oxley Act and SEC Release Nos. 33-8238 and 34-47986, management's responsibility pertaining to the company's internal control over financial reporting has been increased substantially.

<u>DEFINING INTERNAL CONTROL</u>

Internal control over financial reporting (ICOFR) is defined as: "A process designed ... to provide reasonable assurance regarding the reliability of financial reporting and the preparation of financial statements for external purposes in accordance with generally accepted accounting principles …."

Additionally, ICOFR is deemed to include all policies and procedures that:
- "Pertain to the maintenance of records that in reasonable detail accurately and fairly reflect the transactions and dispositions of the assets of the [company];
- Provide reasonable assurance that transactions are recorded as necessary to permit preparation of financial statements in accordance with generally accepted accounting principles, and that receipts and expenditures of the [company] are being made only in accordance with authorizations of management and directors of the [company]; and
- Provide reasonable assurance regarding prevention or timely detection of unauthorized acquisition, use, or disposition of the [company's] assets that could have a material effect on the financial statements."

Examples of internal controls covered by Section 404 and the related Releases and Standards include, but are not limited to:
- Controls over initiating, authorizing, recording, processing, reconciling, and reporting significant account balances, transactions, and disclosures included in the financial statements
- Controls related to the prevention, identification, and detection of fraud
- Controls related to the initiating and processing of non-routine and non-systematic transactions
- Controls related to the selection and application of appropriate accounting policies

<u>MANAGEMENT'S REPORT ON INTERNAL CONTROL</u>

The provisions of Section 404 require management to acknowledge its responsibility for the ICOFR of the company and to assess the operating effectiveness of those controls. As a result, public companies must issue an additional internal control report within their annual report. The report on internal control should contain the following information:
- A statement of management's responsibility for establishing and maintaining adequate ICOFR
- A statement identifying the framework that management used in conducting the assessment of the effectiveness of the company's ICOFR

Preparing for an Investigation

- Management's assessment of the effectiveness of the company's ICOFR as of the end of the company's most recent fiscal year, including disclosure of any material weaknesses identified in the company's ICOFR and an explicit statement as to whether the ICOFR is effective
- A statement that the company's independent auditor has issued an attestation report, which must also be filed with the annual report, covering management's assessment of the company's ICOFR

MANAGEMENT'S ASSESSMENT OF INTERNAL CONTROL

In performing the ICOFR assessment, management must choose a suitable internal control framework against which to evaluate the design and effectiveness of the company's ICOFR. The most commonly used model in the United States is the Internal Control—Integrated Framework established by the Committee of Sponsoring Organizations (COSO) of the Treadway Commission, which provides five components of effective internal controls:

- Control environment
- Control activities
- Risk assessment
- Information and communication
- Monitoring

Further detail on the Internal Control—Integrated Framework is available at the COSO website (www.coso.org).

Additionally, management must carry out the following tasks:
- Determine which internal controls to test in performing the assessment, considering the significance of each control both individually and in the aggregate.
- Evaluate whether the failure of a control could result in a misstatement to the financial statements, the likelihood and magnitude of any resulting misstatement, and whether other controls are in place to mitigate this occurrence.
- Determine which locations or business units to include in the assessment, if applicable.
- Evaluate the design and operating effectiveness of the internal controls using the internal control framework chosen as a guide.
- Evaluate the probability of occurrence and the size of potential misstatements resulting from the internal control deficiencies identified and determine whether they, either individually or in the aggregate, constitute material weaknesses (any deficiency where the likelihood of potential misstatement is more than remote) or significant deficiencies (any deficiency where the likelihood of potential misstatement is more than remote and the magnitude is more than inconsequential).
- Provide sufficient documentation to support the assessment of ICOFR, including documenting the design of the internal controls and the results of management's testing and evaluation.
- Communicate the assessment findings to the independent auditor and any other applicable parties.

Recognizing that each company differs with regard to internal control structure, the rules state that the nature of the testing performed by management will depend on the specific circumstances of the company and the significance of the control being tested. However, the rules also assert that inquiries alone are generally not a sufficient basis for management's assessment.

In July 2007, the SEC issued guidance specifically addressed to management about fulfilling its responsibilities pertaining to reporting on internal control over financial reporting. The guidance emphasizes a top-down, risk-based approach to management's evaluation of ICOFR and explicitly states that an evaluation performed in compliance with the guidance is one way that management can satisfy the internal control requirements established by Sarbanes-Oxley. In providing direction to assist companies' management in evaluating and assessing the ICOFR, the guidance addresses the following topics:
- Identifying Financial Reporting Risks and Controls
- Evaluating Evidence of the Operating Effectiveness of ICOFR
- Reporting Considerations

The full text of the SEC interpretive guidance can be found at www.sec.gov/rules/interp/interparchive/interparch2007.shtml.

CODE OF ETHICS

As required by Section 406 of the Act and SEC Release No. 33-8177, public companies must disclose in their annual report whether they have adopted a code of ethics for senior financial officers, and if they have not, they must explain their reasoning.

DEFINING CODE OF ETHICS

The rules define a *code of ethics* as a set of written standards that are designed to deter wrongdoing and to promote:
- Honest and ethical conduct, including the ethical treatment of actual or apparent conflicts of interest between personal and professional interests
- Full, fair, accurate, timely, and understandable disclosure in all documents filed with the SEC and all other public communications
- Compliance with all applicable governmental laws, rules, and regulations
- The prompt reporting to the appropriate person or persons within the company of violations of the code
- Accountability for adherence to the code

The SEC believes that the establishment of provisions beyond this definitional outline is best left to the discretion of the company. Therefore, the rules do not specify any detailed requirements, particular language, compliance procedures, or sanctions for violations that must be included in the code of ethics. The SEC does, however, explicitly encourage the adoption of codes that are broader and more comprehensive than necessary to meet the new disclosure requirements.

Video

In the video titled "Chapter I: Ethics Policy," fraud investigation expert Meric Bloch, J.D., CFE, explains the importance of implementing an ethics policy. (Go to www.acfe.com/internalinvestigations to view the video.)

SENIOR FINANCIAL OFFICERS

The senior financial officers who must be covered by the company's code of ethics include the principal executive officer, principal financial officer, principal accounting officer or controller, and persons performing similar functions. While the rules state that a company must have a specialized code of ethics that applies to senior financial officers, the company does not need to adopt a separate code of ethics for these officers. However, if it does not, the company's general code of ethics should expressly state that it applies to all senior financial officers.

DISCLOSURE REQUIREMENTS

In addition to the disclosure of the existence of the code of ethics in the annual report, the rules require that companies make publicly available the portions of their code of ethics that address the ethical considerations contained within the definition of *code of ethics* and that apply to the senior financial officers. To do so, the SEC permits companies to employ one of three alternative methods:

- Filing the code of ethics that applies to the senior financial officers as an exhibit in the company's annual report
- Posting the code of ethics that is relevant to the senior financial officers on its website, and disclosing the Internet address and the fact that the code is posted in this manner within the annual report
- Providing a copy of the code of ethics to any person upon request and without charge, assuming that the annual report contains an undertaking to do so and an explanation of how a person can make such a request.

Public companies must also make known, either on a Form 8-K or on their website, any changes in and any waivers of the code of ethics relating to the senior financial officers. The nature of the change or waiver must be disclosed within five business days of its occurrence and, if disclosed on a website, must remain posted for 12 months.

Preparing for an Investigation

EXAMPLES OF CODES OF ETHICS

The following are examples of organizations that have adopted codes of ethics that meet the SEC's guidelines.
- FEI (http://files.shareholder.com/downloads/FEIC/3775079482x0x353508/A07A9B0F-238C-4D41-99A9-A067EDF0DED1/FEI_Code_of_Conduct_090903_as_amended_022410_.pdf)
- Neiman Marcus (media.corporate-ir.net/media_files/nys/nmg.a/reports/nmg_coefp.pdf)

Video

In the video titled "Chapter I: Code of Ethics," convicted securities fraudster Justin Paperny explains how the lack of an instilled ethics policy, and lax compliance monitoring, contribute to an atmosphere ripe for fraud. (Go to www.acfe.com/internalinvestigations to view the video.)

Audit Committee

The audit committee of a company is a committee established by the board of directors for the purpose of overseeing the accounting, financial reporting, and auditing processes. Sections 301 and 407 of the Act and SEC Release Nos. 33-8177, 33-8220, 34-47235, and 34-47654 set out specific requirements for audit committees of public companies.

COMPOSITION OF THE AUDIT COMMITTEE

INDEPENDENCE

Each member of the audit committee must be a member of the board of directors and must be "independent," as evaluated by two criteria:
- Fees—Audit committee members may only be compensated for their services on the board and any board committee. They cannot be paid by the company, or any of its subsidiaries, for any other consulting or advisory work, including indirect payments made by the company to a party related to the committee member. Audit committee members may receive any fixed retirement benefits they are entitled to for prior service with the company without violating this provision, as long as the benefits are not contingent upon the member's continued service.
- Affiliation—Audit committee members cannot be "affiliated persons" of the company or any other company related to it. This precludes executive officers, director-employees, general partners, and managing members of the company, or its parent, subsidiary, or sister company, from serving on the audit committee. There is a safe-harbor provision that excludes members from being considered an affiliated person as long as they are not an executive officer of the company or any of its subsidiaries, and they are not a shareholder of 10 percent or more of any class of voting stock of the company or any of its subsidiaries.

The SEC permits three exemptions from the independence standards. The first provides a one-year phase-in period for public non-investment companies, whereby there must be at least one fully independent member when the company goes public, a majority of independent members within 90 days, and a fully independent committee within one year. The second exemption allows a committee member to simultaneously sit on the board of directors of the company and the board of an affiliated company (i.e., a parent, subsidiary, or sister company) without being considered an affiliated person, provided that the member otherwise meets the independence criteria. The final exemption exists to provide a number of accommodations for "foreign private issuers," or listed companies that are incorporated outside of the United States. The SEC has stated that beyond these three exemptions, no additional exemptions will be granted, nor will it consider exemptions or waivers for particular relationships on a case-by-case basis.

FINANCIAL EXPERT

The board of directors must include a disclosure in the company's annual report stating whether there is at least one member of its audit committee who qualifies as an "audit committee financial expert." If there is, the company must also include the name of the expert and whether the expert is independent from management. If there is not, an explanation must be given as to why the committee does not have such an expert. Additionally, the board is permitted, but not required, to disclose that it has more than one audit committee financial expert on its audit committee.

To qualify as an *audit committee financial expert*, an individual must possess all of the following characteristics:
- An understanding of generally accepted accounting principles and of financial statements
- The ability to evaluate the application of accounting principles used in accounting for estimates, accruals, and reserves
- Experience in preparing, auditing, analyzing, or evaluating financial statements containing accounting issues that are "generally comparable" to those expected to be raised in the company's financial statements, or experience supervising someone engaged in such activities
- An understanding of internal controls and financial reporting procedures
- An understanding of the functions of an audit committee

The rules state that the audit committee financial expert must have acquired these attributes through education and experience from serving as or actively supervising a principal financial officer, principal accounting officer, controller, public accountant or auditor, or other similar position, or through the oversight or assessment of companies or public accountants regarding the preparation, audit, or evaluation of financial statements. The SEC also recognizes that individuals that do not meet any of these requirements but have "other relevant experience" may qualify as an audit committee financial expert. However, any board of directors that qualifies an expert under this category is required to provide a brief listing of that person's experience with the disclosure in the annual report.

In determining whether an individual qualifies as an audit committee financial expert, the board of directors should consider all relevant facts and circumstances including, but not limited to, certain qualitative factors such as the level of the person's accounting or financial education, whether the person is a CPA, whether the person has previously served as a CFO or controller of a public company, the person's past or current membership on other audit committees, and any other relevant qualifications or experience that would assist in understanding and evaluating the company's financial statements. The SEC emphasizes that such factors are merely examples and should be considered only as part of an evaluation of the person's knowledge and experience as a whole.

To dissuade hesitancy to serve as an audit committee financial expert, the SEC has expressly stated that the duties, obligations, and liabilities of the member serving as the expert are no greater than the duties, obligations, and liabilities of all other members of the audit committee. Similarly, the designation of an audit committee member as a financial expert does not change the duties, obligations, or liabilities of any other board or audit committee members.

RESPONSIBILITIES RELATING TO EXTERNAL AUDITORS

The audit committee has sole responsibility for hiring, paying, retaining, overseeing, and, if necessary, firing the company's outside auditors, as well as the ultimate authority to approve all audit engagement fees and terms. As a result, the external auditors must report directly to the audit committee. The committee is also charged with resolving any disputes that arise between the external auditors and management regarding financial reporting issues.

All audit and permitted non-audit services, other than *de minimis* services (those too insignificant to be of concern), provided by the external auditor must be pre-approved by the audit committee. The audit committee can accomplish this either by approving all services separately prior to each engagement or by establishing a detailed set of pre-approval policies and procedures covering all engagements, as long as the audit committee is informed on a timely basis of each service. The responsibility of pre-approval also cannot be shifted to management. If the committee chooses to implement a set of pre-approval policies and procedures, then a clear description or a copy of those policies and procedures must be included with the company's proxy statement.

Preparing for an Investigation

PROCEDURES FOR HANDLING COMPLAINTS

The audit committee is required to establish procedures (such as a hotline) for receiving, retaining, and dealing with complaints—including confidential or anonymous employee tips—regarding irregularities in the company's accounting methods, internal controls, or auditing matters.

The SEC does not require any specific procedures for handling complaints, but rather allows the audit committee to determine the most appropriate procedures for the company's circumstances. Included in this flexibility is the ability of the audit committee to defer the receipt and screening of the complaints to another party, such as a messaging service. However, when complaints are received by a party outside of the audit committee, the procedures should dictate that the tips are ultimately directed to the audit committee for resolution. Further, the procedures should be designed such that management is not exclusively responsible for receiving and screening the complaints to prevent unscrupulous managers from mishandling complaints or retaliating against employee complainants. Ultimately, the enactment of formal procedures should encourage the disclosure of concerns and promote proper conduct throughout the organization. The established procedures should also allow the audit committee to be alerted to potential problems before serious consequences arise.

AUTHORITY TO ENGAGE OUTSIDE ADVISORS

In certain situations, audit committees may want to consult experts other than those hired by management, especially when faced with possible conflicts of management interests. The rules provide that audit committees are allowed to engage outside advisors, such as experts in specific accounting issues, who might be necessary to properly carry out their duties.

FUNDING

The audit committee is entitled to receive appropriate funding from the company for the following items:
- Fees paid to the external auditors for performance of any audit, review, or attestation engagements
- Payments to any outside advisors retained by the audit committee
- Any administrative expenses necessary for the audit committee to carry out its duties

Video

In the video titled "Chapter I: Audit Committee," fraud investigation expert Meric Bloch, J.D., CFE, further explains the role of a company's audit committee. (Go to www.acfe.com/internalinvestigations to view the video.)

Additional Sarbanes-Oxley Provisions

CONFLICT OF INTEREST PROVISIONS

Another provision of Sarbanes-Oxley aimed at improving auditor independence is Section 206, which seeks to limit conflicts or potential conflicts that arise when auditors cross over to work for their former clients. The Act now makes it unlawful for a public accounting firm to audit a company if, within the prior year, the client's CEO, CFO, controller, or chief accounting officer worked for the accounting firm and participated in the company's audit.

IMPROPER INFLUENCE ON AUDITS

The Sarbanes-Oxley Act also makes it unlawful for any officer or director of a public company to take any action to fraudulently influence, coerce, manipulate, or mislead an auditor in the performance of an audit of the company's financial statements. This is yet another attempt by Congress to ensure the independence and objectivity of audits to prevent accounting fraud and strengthen investor confidence in the reliability of public company financial statements.

OFF-BALANCE SHEET TRANSACTIONS

The Sarbanes-Oxley Act directed the SEC to issue rules that require the disclosure of all material off-balance sheet transactions by publicly traded companies. The rules require disclosure of "all material off-balance sheet transactions, arrangements, obligations (including contingent obligations), and other relationships the company may have with unconsolidated entities or persons that may have a material current or future effect on the company's financial condition, changes in financial condition, liquidity, capital expenditures, capital resources, or significant components of revenues or expenses." These disclosures are required in all annual and quarterly SEC reports.

PRO FORMA FINANCIAL INFORMATION

Sarbanes-Oxley Section 401 increases the type and extent of disclosures in periodic reports filed with the SEC. Under section 401, pro forma financials that are filed with the SEC or that are included in any public disclosure or press release must not contain any untrue statements or omissions that would make them misleading, and they must be reconciled to GAAP.

PROHIBITIONS ON PERSONAL LOANS TO EXECUTIVES

Sarbanes-Oxley Section 402 makes it illegal for public companies to make personal loans or otherwise extend credit, either directly or indirectly, to or for any director or executive officer. There is an exception that applies to consumer lenders if the loans are consumer loans of the type the company normally makes to the public and are on the same terms.

RESTRICTIONS ON INSIDER TRADING

Sarbanes-Oxley Section 403 established disclosure requirements for stock transactions by directors and officers of public companies, or by persons who own more than 10 percent of a publicly traded company's stock. SEC rules further specify content and timing requirements of blackout-period notices that must be provided to directors and officers. Reports of changes in beneficial ownership by these persons must now be filed with the SEC by the end of the second business day following the transaction.

Under Sarbanes-Oxley Section 306, directors and officers are also prohibited from trading in the company's securities during any pension fund blackout periods. This restriction only applies to securities that were acquired as a result of their employment or service to the company. A blackout period is defined as any period of more than three consecutive business days in which at least 50 percent of the participants in the company's retirement plan are restricted from trading in the company's securities. If a director or officer violates this provision, he can be forced to disgorge all profits received from the sale of securities during the blackout period to the company.

ENHANCED REVIEW OF PERIODIC FILINGS

Sarbanes-Oxley Section 408 requires the SEC to make regular and systematic reviews of disclosures made by public companies in their periodic reports to the SEC. Reviews of a company's disclosures, including its financial statements, must be made at least once every three years. Prior to this enactment, reviews were typically minimal and tended to coincide with registered offerings.

REAL-TIME DISCLOSURES

Under Sarbanes-Oxley Section 409, public companies must publicly disclose information concerning material changes in their financial condition or operations. These disclosures must be in plain English and must be made "on a rapid and current basis."

Restrictions on Non-Audit Activity

Perhaps the greatest concern arising out of the public accounting scandals of 2001 and 2002 was the fear that public accounting firms that received multimillion-dollar consulting fees from their public company clients could not maintain an appropriate level of objectivity in conducting audits for those clients. To address this concern, Sarbanes-Oxley Section 201 provides a list of activities that public accounting firms are now prohibited from performing on behalf of their audit clients. The prohibited services include:

- Bookkeeping services
- Financial information systems design and implementation
- Appraisal or valuation services, fairness opinions, or contribution-in-kind reports
- Actuarial services

- Internal audit outsource services
- Management functions or human resources
- Broker or dealer, investment advisor, or investment banking services
- Legal services and expert services unrelated to the audit
- Any other service that the Public Company Accounting Oversight Board proscribes

There are certain other non-audit services—most notably tax services—that are not expressly prohibited by Sarbanes-Oxley. However, in order for a public accounting firm to perform these services on behalf of an audit client, the service must be approved in advance by the client's audit committee. This approval must be disclosed in the client's periodic SEC reports. Furthermore, regarding non-audit services, the SEC prevents firms from providing audit clients with expert opinions and services, as well as legal representation, for advocating the audit client's litigation, regulatory, or administrative interests.

External Auditors
REPORTS TO THE AUDIT COMMITTEE
Sarbanes-Oxley section 301 requires that auditors report directly to the audit committee—not management—and must make timely reports on the following items:
- All critical accounting policies and other policies used
- Alternative GAAP methods that were discussed with management, the ramifications of the use of those alternative treatments, and the treatment preferred by the auditors
- Any other material written communications between the auditors and management, such as any management letter or the schedule of unadjusted audit differences

REPORT OVER INTERNAL CONTROLS
Auditors must also now attest to and issue a report on management's assessment of internal control over financial reporting under Section 404 of Sarbanes-Oxley. This requirement is covered in more detail in the previous section on PCAOB Auditing Standard No. 5—*An Audit of Internal Control Over Financial Reporting That Is Integrated with An Audit of Financial Statements*.

Whistleblower Protection
The Sarbanes-Oxley Act establishes broad new protections for corporate whistleblowers. There are two sections of the Act that address whistleblower protections: Section 806 deals with civil protections, and Section 1107 establishes criminal liability for those who retaliate against whistleblowers.

CIVIL LIABILITY WHISTLEBLOWER PROTECTION
Sarbanes-Oxley Section 806, which is codified at 18 U.S.C. Section 1514A, creates civil liability for companies that retaliate against whistleblowers. It should be noted that this provision does not provide universal whistleblower protection; it only protects employees of publicly traded companies. Section 806

makes it unlawful to fire, demote, suspend, threaten, harass, or in any other manner discriminate against an employee for providing information or aiding in an investigation of securities fraud. To trigger Section 806 protections, the employee must report the suspected misconduct to a federal regulatory or law enforcement agency, a member of Congress or a committee of Congress, or a supervisor. Employees are also protected against retaliation for filing, testifying in, participating in, or otherwise assisting in a proceeding filed or about to be filed relating to an alleged violation of securities laws or SEC rules.

The whistleblower protections apply even if the company is ultimately found not to have committed securities fraud. As long as the employee reasonably believes he is reporting conduct that constitutes a violation of various federal securities laws, then he is protected. The protections not only cover retaliatory acts by the company, but also by any officer, employee, contractor, subcontractor, or agent of the company.

If a public company is found to have violated Sarbanes-Oxley Section 806, the Act provides for an award of compensatory damages sufficient to "make the employee whole." Penalties include reinstatement; back pay with interest; and compensation for special damages, including litigation costs, expert witness fees, and attorney's fees.

CRIMINAL SANCTION WHISTLEBLOWER PROTECTION
Sarbanes-Oxley Section 1107—codified at 18 U.S.C. § 1513—makes it a crime to knowingly, with the intent to retaliate, take any harmful action against a person for providing truthful information relating to the commission or possible commission of any federal offense. This protection is only triggered when information is provided to a law enforcement officer; it does not apply to reports made to supervisors or to members of Congress, as is the case under Sarbanes-Oxley Section 806.

In general, the coverage of Sarbanes-Oxley Section 1107 is much broader than the civil liability whistleblower protections of Sarbanes-Oxley Section 806. While the Sarbanes-Oxley Section 806 protections apply only to employees of publicly traded companies, Sarbanes-Oxley Section 1107's criminal whistleblower protections cover all individuals (and organizations) regardless of where they work. Also, Sarbanes-Oxley Section 806 only applies to violations of securities laws or SEC rules and regulations. Sarbanes-Oxley Section 1107 protects individuals who provide truthful information about the commission or possible commission of *any federal offense.*

Violations of Sarbanes-Oxley Section 1107 can be punished by fines of up to $250,000 and up to ten years in prison for individuals. Corporations that violate the Act can be fined up to $500,000.

False Statement Statutes

There are many federal and state statutes that outlaw the submission of false or fraudulent statements in connection with regulated activities. Examples include:

- *18 U.S.C. § 1035*: Section 1035 prohibits false statements in health care claims.
- *15 U.S.C. § 77k*: Section 77k provides damages for individuals injured as a result of the purchase of a security whose required registration statement contains untrue or misleading material facts.
- *15 U.S.C. § 78r*: Section 78r prohibits false or misleading statements in any application, report, or other document required to be filed in connection with the sale or offer for sale of a security.
- *SEC Rule 10b-5(b)* (Title 17, Code of Federal Regulations, § 240.10b-5(b)): Rule 10b-5 prohibits false or misleading statements in connection with securities transactions.
- *18 U.S.C. § 1001*: Section 1001 prohibits false or fraudulent statements, orally or in writing, to federal agencies and departments, which are material to a matter within federal jurisdiction.
- *18 U.S.C. § 1005*: Section 1005 prohibits any officer, director, agent, or employee of a federally insured or chartered bank from making any false entries on the bank's books with the intent to injure or defraud the bank or third parties, or to deceive any bank officer, examiner, or government agency.
- *18 U.S.C. § 1014*: Section 1014 prohibits false statements or reports on any credit application or related document submitted to a federally insured bank or credit institution for the purpose of influencing the institution's action in any way.
- *18 U.S.C. § 1031*: Section 1031 prohibits any scheme to defraud the United States or obtain money or property from the United States by means of false or fraudulent pretenses in the procurement of a contract with the federal government worth $1 million or more.

Most of these statutes require proof of fraudulent intent or a knowing or willful falsehood. Typically, an inadvertent or careless misstatement or omission, even if material, will not cause the company to be criminally liable. Nevertheless, a court could conclude that willfully ignoring strong indications of employee or management misconduct, which results in false or misleading representations, is evidence of criminal intent. Accordingly, when faced with a reasonable indication of possible misconduct by an employee, it might be advisable to investigate the incident to avoid potential liability.

Civil Law Standard of Care and Duty to Company and Shareholders

Statutory Standards

A duty to investigate may also arise from state statutes that set forth the duties that directors and officers owe to their corporations. (These statutes frequently derive from common law duties of reasonable care and loyalty, but some may expand or limit the duties required under common law. Consult applicable statutes in your jurisdiction to determine exactly what duties and responsibilities apply in any particular case.) An internal investigation of known or suspected employee misconduct may be required to fulfill a director's or officer's duty to act in the company's best interests. For example, if financial losses to the company could be avoided or minimized by an investigation, then the director or officer would be required to investigate under the duty of care he owes to the company. Similarly, if an investigation would have enabled the director or officer to implement measures to prevent the wrongdoing, or to realize a substantial recovery of the losses, a duty to investigate could be inferred.

A director or officer who violates these statutory standards of conduct may incur liability to the corporation. Furthermore, directors who fail to investigate possible wrongdoing—and therefore fail to detect and prevent or mitigate the wrongdoing—have been held personally liable to their corporations for losses or fines that were incurred by the corporations as a result of the wrongdoing.

Finally, failing to investigate known or possible wrongdoing within the company can lead indirectly to violations of other statutes. For example, the Internal Revenue Code prohibits deduction of illegal expenses, such as payments to foreign officials that violate the Foreign Corrupt Practices Act (FCPA). If a company deducts payments to foreign officials and those payments turn out to be prohibited by the FCPA, the company could incur liability for IRS Code violations. Similarly, if an employee makes corrupt payments to government officials that give the company an unfair competitive advantage, this could subject the company to liability for antitrust violations. These potential liabilities can be avoided by investigating known and suspected wrongdoing when it occurs so that managing officers and directors are fully informed of all relevant facts.

Other Civil Law Standards of Care

Courts have come closest to finding an express duty to investigate in the area of sexual harassment. Faced with a complaint or evidence of sexual harassment, the company is obliged to respond adequately and effectively to deal with the offender and prevent future recurrences. In many cases, a thorough investigation is seen as a necessary component of that response if the company is to avoid liability.

In some jurisdictions, a company also may find itself obliged to conduct an internal investigation before it can terminate an employee for theft, fraud, or other misconduct. In the view of some courts, a company must demonstrate evidence of an employee's wrongdoing to terminate that employee; it is not enough to rely on the company's own good faith belief that the employee has acted improperly. To gather the requisite proof, the company in this scenario will need to conduct an adequate investigation into the suspected misconduct. (These cases tend to concern contract employees, who cannot be fired without "good cause." However, under modern court trends, an increasingly larger number of employees are qualifying for good cause treatment. See Chapter 8, "Discharging Employees," for more information.)

COMMON LAW DUTY TO INVESTIGATE

Common law refers to traditional judge-made law, as opposed to law that comes from statutes. Common law varies from state to state. As noted earlier, common law imposes duties of care and loyalty on directors and officers of corporations. Similar duties exist for other fiduciaries, such as trustees, lawyers, and accountants. In short, these standards require directors, officers, and other fiduciaries to use the same reasonable care in conducting the affairs of a company that they would in their own affairs, and to always put the interests of the company ahead of their own interests. Therefore, a director, officer, or other fiduciary may be required to conduct an internal investigation of known or suspected employee misconduct when it is reasonable to do so to prevent, reverse, or minimize harm to the company. A director who refuses to investigate a known case of employee fraud or does too little to uncover and correct internal misconduct may be personally liable to the company or its shareholders for the losses caused by the misconduct, for the amount of fines assessed and paid by the company because of the conduct, or for the costs of recovering those losses.

COMPANY'S VICARIOUS LIABILITY FOR CIVIL AND CRIMINAL MISCONDUCT OF EMPLOYEES

Under some circumstances, an internal investigation may help a company avoid criminal or civil liability for an employee's misconduct. At the federal level, and in many states, corporate civil and criminal liability is *vicarious liability* (i.e., the absolute liability of one party for the misconduct of another party) that is imposed under the doctrine of respondeat superior. Under respondeat superior, an employer is liable for any misconduct committed by an agent or employee if those acts occur in the course and scope of his employment. Within the *course and scope* means that the agent or employee performed acts of the kind he was authorized to perform and that his acts were intended, at least in some part, to benefit the company. The fact that the particular conduct was wrongful or criminal does not necessarily mean that it was outside of the course and scope of employment. Thus, a company can be liable for the illegal acts of its employees.

However, if an employer has clearly established policies and standards that prohibit employees from engaging in a particular kind of illegal conduct, and if the employer shows that it regularly enforces those policies and standards, then a judge or jury may conclude that the employee's conduct was not within the course and scope of employment. In other words, the company would not be vicariously liable for the misdeeds. Realistic efforts to enforce such policies would require, at a minimum, that management thoroughly investigate alleged violations whenever they occur and that it enforces the policies through appropriate consequences to wrongdoers.

EXAMPLE

The fact that there is no sales tax in Oregon attracted a large number of purchasers from California and Washington to the state to buy recreational vehicles. At one RV dealership, sales employees knowingly helped these purchasers submit false Oregon residence addresses to the DMV in order to avoid the sales tax in their home states. After prosecuting the salespeople for federal mail fraud charges, federal authorities charged the dealership on the grounds that the salespeople acted within the course and scope of their employment. The salespeople were doing what they were authorized to do—complete and submit vehicle registration and licensing forms to the state DMV offices—and the dealership benefited to the extent that it sold the vehicles to the out-of-state purchasers. Although the dealership's management protested that it prohibited employee falsification of a purchaser's residence address on DMV licensing and registration forms, there apparently was insufficient evidence that the dealership investigated the alleged incidents or otherwise enforced the policy. The dealership eventually settled the charges for what was reported to be a record fine.

Other Factors to Consider
ORGANIZATIONAL SENTENCING GUIDELINES

Even where company liability cannot be avoided, it may be mitigated by efforts that include an effective internal investigation of the misconduct that caused the liability. Since 1991, federal courts have used a prescribed formula to determine fines for organizations that have committed (or are vicariously liable for) felonies as per the Organizational Sentencing Guidelines. Fines under the guidelines were based on two factors: the seriousness of the offense and the level of culpability by the organization. The seriousness of the offense determined the base fine to be imposed. Essentially, under the guidelines, the organization's culpability was a measure of the actions taken by the organization that either mitigated or aggravated the situation. Depending on the culpability of the organization, the base fine could be increased by as much as 400 percent, or reduced by as much as 95 percent.

In January 2005, the U.S. Supreme Court ruled that the Sixth Amendment right to a jury trial requires that federal sentencing guidelines be advisory, rather than mandatory. As set forth below, the guidelines were (and remain) significant to corporate executives because an entity that found itself in court for behaving badly could seek mitigation of punishment if it had a properly implemented an effective compliance and ethics program. The Court's ruling suggested that federal judges are to continue to take into account the guidelines—thus having an effective compliance and ethics program is still very beneficial to companies. According to the guidelines, judges are still required to examine the adequacy of a company's compliance and ethics program. Furthermore, judges may now mitigate punishment beyond the mandated level of mitigation given under the guidelines.

An *effective compliance program* is one that is reasonably designed, implemented, and enforced so that it will generally be effective in preventing and detecting criminal conduct. The guidelines encourage organizations to exercise due diligence in seeking to prevent and detect criminal conduct by their officers, directors, employees, and agents. At a minimum, due diligence requires the following eight steps:

- The organization must have established compliance standards and procedures to be followed by its employees and other agents who are reasonably capable of reducing the prospect of criminal conduct.
- Specific individual(s) within an organization's high-level personnel must be knowledgeable about the content and operation of the compliance and ethics program and have assigned overall responsibility to oversee compliance with such standards and procedures to other individuals. Additionally, where the day-to-day operational responsibility has been delegated, the governing authority must have received, at a minimum, annual reports regarding the implementation and effectiveness of such programs.
- The organization must have used reasonable efforts to refrain from delegating substantial discretionary authority to individuals whom the organization knew, or should have known through the exercise of due diligence, had engaged in illegal activities or other conduct inconsistent with an effective compliance and ethics program.
- The organization must conduct an "effective training program," as well as periodically and appropriately communicate the program's compliance requirements and procedures to all employees affected by the program.
- The organization must have periodically taken steps to effectively communicate its standards and procedures to all employees and other agents by requiring participation in training programs and disseminating publications that explain in an appropriate manner what is required of each individual—including high-level personnel and substantial authority personnel.
- The organization must have taken reasonable steps to achieve compliance with its standards by 1) using monitoring and auditing systems reasonably designed to detect criminal conduct by its employees and other agents; 2) periodically evaluating the program's effectiveness; and 3) having in place and publicizing a reporting system whereby employees and other agents can report, or seek guidance regarding, actual or potential criminal conduct by others within the organization while retaining anonymity or confidentiality without fear of retribution.
- The standards must have been consistently promoted and enforced through 1) suitable incentives to perform in accordance with the organization's program; and 2) appropriate disciplinary mechanisms, often including the discipline of individuals responsible for the failure to detect an offense. Adequate discipline of individuals responsible for an offense is a necessary component of enforcement; however, the appropriate form of discipline is case specific.
- After an offense has been detected, the organization must have taken all reasonable steps to respond appropriately and to prevent further similar offenses—including any necessary modifications to its program to prevent and detect violations of law.
- Organizations must periodically assess the risk of illegal conduct and act appropriately to create, implement, or amend the above requirements as necessary.

Preparing for an Investigation

EFFECTIVE COMPLIANCE PROGRAMS

The guidelines make it clear that an effective compliance program requires organizations to be diligent in detecting and preventing criminal misconduct by their employees and agents. It is not enough to communicate a code of conduct to employees and agents; organizations must also take steps to effectively and diligently enforce these codes through:

- Adequate supervision
- Monitoring
- Enforcement
- Prevention of recurrences of misconduct that does occur

It is apparent that an internal investigation can be an important—and sometimes a necessary—element of each of these aspects of an effective compliance program.

SELF-REPORTING

Self-reporting is discussed in more detail below; however, it is obvious that an internal investigation may be necessary if a company is to make a complete and accurate self-reporting of its own internal misconduct.

COOPERATION WITH GOVERNMENT INVESTIGATORS

Similarly, although cooperation with government investigators does not necessarily mean that the company must conduct its own internal investigation, it may be better able to cooperate—and to evaluate the costs and consequences of doing so—if it conducts its own investigation, either initially or simultaneously, with the government investigation.

VOLUNTARY DISCLOSURE PROGRAMS

Self-reporting may not only mitigate an organization's sentencing, as discussed above; it might enable an organization and some individuals to avoid prosecution entirely. Several government agencies, including the Department of Defense, the Antitrust Division of the Department of Justice, and the Department of Health and Human Services, have voluntary disclosure programs. Under these programs, if a business voluntarily reports misconduct related to the agency, then the business can receive several benefits. These benefits vary, but generally, the programs provide for reduced fines and other forms of leniency. Additionally, there are several programs that provide that the agency will not recommend or seek criminal prosecution.

Even in the absence of a formal program, however, voluntary disclosure can still be advantageous. Often, criminal prosecutors will not seek prosecution of corporations that voluntarily report violations and take remedial and preventative steps. Additionally, even if the corporation is prosecuted, the Federal

Sentencing Guidelines provide for reduced penalties for corporations that voluntarily report their misconduct.

Internal investigations are not strictly required either to make a voluntary disclosure or to qualify for these programs. However, to repeat observations made earlier, an internal investigation may well be an appropriate or even necessary practical first step if a company plans a voluntary disclosure.

Accountants' and Auditors' Duties to Investigate
Internal Auditors

The Institute of Internal Auditors (IIA) has developed the *International Standards for the Professional Practice of Internal Auditing*. This section contains a description of those IIA standards that pertain to the internal auditor's responsibilities for preventing and detecting fraud within an organization. Additionally, as an organization's ethical tone is a vital component of its fraud prevention program, the IIA standards relating to responsibilities for ethical culture are discussed. More detail on these and all other IIA standards can be found at the IIA's website (www.theiia.org).

Internal auditors should be aware of the IIA's Proficiency Standard 1210 for internal auditors. The practice advisory sub-standard 1210.A2-1: *Auditor's Responsibilities Relating to Fraud Risk Assessment, Prevention, and Detection* covers the internal auditor's responsibilities to deter, detect, investigate, and report fraud. In addition to the legal duties described in the previous section, internal auditors should look to practice advisory 1210.A2-2: *Auditor's Responsibilities Relating to Fraud Investigation, Reporting, Resolution, and Communication* for guidance in dealing with fraud once evidence of it has been uncovered.

FRAUD DETECTION

Detection consists of identifying fraud indicators that warrant an examination. These indicators might arise as a result of controls established by management, tests conducted by auditors, and other sources—both within and outside the organization.

Internal auditors' responsibilities for detecting fraud during audit assignments include:
- Considering fraud risks in the assessment of control design and determination of audit steps to perform. While internal auditors are not expected to detect fraud and irregularities, internal auditors are expected to obtain reasonable assurance that business objectives for the process under review are being achieved and that material control deficiencies—whether through simple error or intentional effort—are detected.
- Having sufficient knowledge of fraud to identify red flags indicating fraud may have been committed. This knowledge includes the characteristics of fraud, the techniques used to commit fraud, and the various fraud schemes and scenarios associated with the activities being reviewed.

- Being alert to opportunities that could allow fraud, such as control weaknesses. If significant control weaknesses are detected, additional tests conducted by internal auditors should be directed at identifying other fraud indicators. Some examples of indicators are unauthorized transactions, sudden fluctuations in the volume or value of transactions, control overrides, unexplained pricing exceptions, and unusually large product losses. Internal auditors should recognize that the presence of more than one indicator at any one time increases the probability that fraud has occurred.
- Evaluating the indicators of fraud and deciding whether any further action is necessary or whether an investigation should be recommended.
- Notifying the appropriate authorities within the organization if a determination is made that fraud has occurred in order to recommend an investigation.

INVESTIGATION OF FRAUD

The role of internal audit in investigations should be defined in the internal audit charter and in the fraud policies. For example, internal audit may have the primary responsibility for fraud investigations, may act as a resource for investigations, or may be required to refrain from involving itself in investigations (because it is responsible for assessing the effectiveness of investigations). Any of these roles can be acceptable, as long as the impact of these activities on an internal audit's independence is recognized and handled appropriately.

To maintain proficiency, fraud investigation teams have a responsibility to obtain sufficient knowledge of fraud schemes, investigation techniques, and laws. There are national and international programs that provide training and certifications for investigators and forensic specialists.

If an internal audit is responsible for ensuring that investigations are conducted, an investigation may be conducted using in-house staff, outsourcing, or a combination of both. In some cases, non-audit employees of the organization may also be used to assist in the internal audit.

It is often important to assemble the investigation team without delay. If the organization needs external experts, the chief audit executive should consider pre-qualifying service providers so that the external resources are available more quickly.

In companies where the primary responsibility for the investigation function is not assigned to internal audit, auditors may still be asked to help gather information and make recommendations for internal control improvements.

REPORTING FRAUD

Fraud reporting consists of the various oral or written, interim, or final communications to senior management or the board of directors regarding the status and results of fraud investigations. Reports can be preliminary and ongoing throughout the investigation. To document the findings, a written report may follow any oral briefing made to management and the board of directors.

Section 2400 of the *International Standards for the Professional Practice of Internal Auditing* provides that internal auditors must communicate the results of their engagements. Additional interpretive guidance on reporting fraud internally follows:

- A draft of the proposed final communications on fraud should be submitted to legal counsel for review. In cases where the organization is able to invoke client privilege and has chosen to do so, the report must be addressed to legal counsel.
- When incidents of significant fraud or erosion of trust have been established to a reasonable certainty, senior management and the board of directors should be notified immediately.
- The results of a fraud investigation might indicate that fraud might have had a previously undiscovered adverse effect on the organization's financial position and its operational results for one or more years for which financial statements have already been issued. Senior management and the board of directors should be informed of such a discovery.
- A written report or other formal communication should be issued at the conclusion of the investigation phase. It should include the basis for beginning an investigation, time frames, observations, conclusions, resolutions, and corrective actions (or recommendations) taken to improve controls. Depending on how the investigation was resolved, the report might need to be written in a manner that provides confidentiality to some of the people involved. The content of the report is sensitive, and it must meet the needs of the board of directors and management while complying with legal requirements and restrictions and company policies and procedures.

External Auditors

Although this workbook focuses on internal investigations, those who investigate fraud will frequently deal with outside investigators or with external auditors. These individuals might participate in the actual investigation of internal misconduct, or, in the case of external auditors, they might be the ones who uncover the misdealing. It is therefore important to understand the implications of AU 240, *Consideration of Fraud in a Financial Statement Audit*, which governs the responsibility of external auditors to discover and report fraud, and PCAOB Auditing Standard No. 5, which addresses the independent audit of public companies' internal controls over financial reporting.

AU 240 (Source SAS Nos. 99 and 113)

In 1996, the AICPA's Auditing Standards Board issued SAS No. 82, *Considerations of Fraud in a Financial Statement Audit*, in response to questions and criticisms of the auditing and accounting professions' inadequate effort to address fraud. Following the high-profile financial frauds that occurred in 2001 and

2002, the ASB replaced SAS No. 82 with SAS No. 99, *Consideration of Fraud in a Financial Statement Audit*, to give expanded guidance to auditors for detecting material fraud. Per the AICPA, the standard was part of an effort to "restore investor confidence in U.S. capital markets and re-establish audited financial statements as a clear picture window into Corporate America." The standard became effective for audits of financial statements for periods beginning on or after December 15, 2002, and is codified in AU Section 240, *Consideration of Fraud in a Financial Statement Audit*.

AU 200, *Responsibilities and Functions of the Independent Auditor*, states: "The auditor has a responsibility to plan and perform the audit to obtain reasonable assurance about whether the financial statements are free of material misstatement, whether caused by error or fraud."

The purpose of AU 240 is to "establish standards and provide guidance to auditors in fulfilling that responsibility."

AU 240 is divided into ten main sections:
- Description and characteristics of fraud
- Importance of exercising professional skepticism
- Discussion among engagement personnel regarding risk of material misstatement due to fraud
- Obtaining information needed to identify risks of material misstatements due to fraud
- Identifying risks that may result in material misstatements due to fraud
- Assessing the identified risks after taking into account an evaluation of the entity's programs and controls
- Responding to the results of the assessment
- Evaluating audit evidence
- Communicating about fraud to management, the audit committee, and others
- Documenting the auditor's consideration of fraud

The following is a brief description of each of these sections. Practitioners in this area should review AU 240 in its entirety for more detailed information. A copy of the entire standard can be obtained from the AICPA (www.aicpa.org).

DESCRIPTION AND CHARACTERISTICS OF FRAUD
AU 240 emphasizes that while auditors do not make legal determinations about the existence of fraud, they should be interested in all acts that result in a material misstatement of the financial statements. Such misstatements can be the result of either fraud or error, depending on whether the misstatements are intentional or unintentional.

Two types of misstatements are considered relevant for audit purposes:
- Misstatements arising from fraudulent financial reporting
- Misstatements arising from misappropriation of assets

MISSTATEMENTS ARISING FROM FRAUDULENT FINANCIAL REPORTING
This category is defined as intentional misstatements or omissions of amounts or disclosures in financial statements that are "designed to deceive financial statement users."

Fraudulent financial reporting may be accomplished by using any of the following techniques:
- Manipulating, falsifying, or altering accounting records or supporting documents
- Misrepresenting or intentionally omitting events, transactions, or other significant information
- Intentionally misapplying accounting principles relating to amounts, classification, manner of presentation, or disclosure

MISSTATEMENTS ARISING FROM MISAPPROPRIATION OF ASSETS
Also referred to as theft or defalcation, this category includes the theft of an entity's assets where the effect of the theft causes the financial statements, in all material respects, not to be in conformity with GAAP.

AU 240 goes on to remind the auditor that, by definition, fraud often is concealed, and management is in a position to perpetrate fraud more easily because it is able to directly or indirectly manipulate accounting records. Auditors cannot obtain absolute assurance that material misstatements are not present, but auditors should be aware of the possibility that fraud might be concealed and that employees might be in collusion with each other or outside vendors. If the auditor notices records or activities that seem unusual, the auditor should at least consider the possibility that fraud might have occurred.

IMPORTANCE OF EXERCISING PROFESSIONAL SKEPTICISM
AU 200, *Due Professional Care in the Performance of Work*, states that due professional care requires the auditor to exercise professional skepticism. Because of the characteristics of fraud, the auditor should conduct the audit "with a mindset that recognizes the possibility that a material misstatement due to fraud could be present." AU 200 also requires an ongoing questioning of whether information the auditor obtains could suggest a material misstatement due to fraud.

DISCUSSION AMONG ENGAGEMENT PERSONNEL REGARDING RISK OF MATERIAL MISSTATEMENT DUE TO FRAUD
Prior to or in conjunction with the information-gathering procedures discussed below, the members of the audit team should discuss the potential for material misstatements due to fraud.

Preparing for an Investigation

The discussion should include brainstorming among the audit team members about the following:
- How and where they believe the entity's financial statement might be susceptible to fraud
- How management could perpetrate or conceal fraud
- How assets of the entity could be misappropriated

This discussion should also include a consideration of known external and internal factors affecting the entity that might:
- Create incentives or pressures for management and others to commit fraud
- Provide the opportunity for fraud to be perpetrated
- Indicate a culture or environment that enables management and others to rationalize committing fraud

Furthermore, the discussion should also emphasize the need to maintain "a questioning mind" in gathering and evaluating evidence throughout the audit and to obtain additional information if necessary.

OBTAINING INFORMATION NEEDED TO IDENTIFY RISKS OF MATERIAL MISSTATEMENTS DUE TO FRAUD

AU 315, *Understanding the Entity and Its Environment and Assessing the Risks of Material Misstatement*, provides guidance on how the auditor obtains knowledge about the entity and its environment, including its internal controls. As part of that process, the auditor should perform the following procedures to obtain information to use in identifying the risks of material misstatement due to fraud:
- Make inquiries of management and others within the entity to obtain their views on the risks of fraud and how those risks are addressed
- Consider any unusual or unexpected relationships that have been identified in performing analytical procedures in planning the audit
- Consider whether one or more fraud risk factors exist
- Consider other information that might be helpful in the identification of risks of material misstatement due to fraud

<u>MAKING INQUIRIES OF MANAGEMENT AND OTHERS WITHIN THE ENTITY TO OBTAIN THEIR VIEWS ABOUT THE RISKS OF FRAUD AND HOW THOSE RISKS ARE ADDRESSED</u>

This step involves asking management about a number of issues, including:
- Whether management has knowledge of fraud or suspected fraud
- Management's understanding of the risk of fraud
- Programs and controls the entity has established to help prevent, deter, or detect fraud
- Whether and how management communicates to employees its views on business practices and ethical behavior

The auditor should also question the audit committee directly about its views concerning the risk of fraud and whether the committee has knowledge of fraud or suspected fraud. The same should be done with the company's internal audit department.

Additionally, the auditor may need to conduct similar inquiries of the entity's other personnel if the auditor believes they may have additional information about the risks of fraud.

CONSIDERING THE RESULTS OF ANALYTICAL PROCEDURES PERFORMED IN PLANNING THE AUDIT
AU 520, *Analytical Procedures*, requires that analytical procedures be performed in planning the audit with the objective of identifying the existence of unusual transactions or events, and amounts, ratios, and trends that might indicate matters "that have financial statement and audit planning implications." If the results of these procedures yield unusual or unexpected relationships, the auditor should consider the results in identifying the risks of material misstatement due to fraud.

CONSIDERING FRAUD RISK FACTORS
As discussed above, even though fraud is concealed, the auditor may identify events or conditions that indicate incentives or pressures to commit fraud, opportunities to carry out fraud, or attitudes and rationalizations to justify that fraudulent conduct exists. These events and conditions are referred to as "fraud risk factors." The auditor should consider whether one or more fraud risk factors are present and if they should be considered in identifying and assessing the risks of material misstatement due to fraud. However, the auditor should be careful not to create a laundry list of risk factors that are only given cursory consideration. The Appendix to AU 240 contains a list of examples of fraud risk factors.

CONSIDERING OTHER INFORMATION THAT MAY BE HELPFUL IN IDENTIFYING RISKS OF MATERIAL MISSTATEMENT DUE TO FRAUD
Finally, the auditor should also consider any other information that might be helpful in identifying the risks of material misstatement due to fraud.

IDENTIFYING RISKS THAT MIGHT RESULT IN MATERIAL MISSTATEMENTS DUE TO FRAUD
After gathering the information as discussed above, the auditor should consider the information in the context of the three conditions present when fraud occurs—incentives and pressures, opportunities, and attitudes and rationalizations.

Auditors should consider all of the following matters:
- The *type* of risk that might exist (i.e., whether it involves fraudulent financial reporting or misappropriation of assets)
- The *significance* of the risk (i.e., whether it is of a magnitude that could result in a possible material misstatement)

- The *likelihood* of the risk (i.e., the likelihood that it will result in a material misstatement)
- The *pervasiveness* of the risk (i.e., whether the potential risk is pervasive to the financial statement as a whole or is specifically related to a particular assertion, account, or class of transactions)

ASSESSING THE IDENTIFIED RISKS AFTER TAKING INTO ACCOUNT AN EVALUATION OF THE ENTITY'S PROGRAMS AND CONTROLS

AU 319 requires the auditor to obtain an understanding of each of the five components of internal controls sufficient to plan the audit. As part of this requirement, the auditor should evaluate whether the programs and controls that address the entity's fraud risks have been suitably designed and implemented. These programs and controls might involve the following items:

- Specific controls designed to mitigate specific risks of fraud (e.g., controls to prevent misappropriation of particular, susceptible assets)
- Broader programs designed to prevent, deter, and detect fraud (e.g., ethics policies)

Exhibit I of AU 240 provides examples of programs and controls an entity might implement to create a culture of honesty and to prevent fraud.

RESPONDING TO THE RESULTS OF THE ASSESSMENT

Once the auditor has gathered the information and assessed the risk of fraud, he must determine what impact the assessment will have on how the audit is conducted. For example, the auditor might need to design additional or different audit procedures to obtain more reliable evidence in support of account balances, transactions, and so on, or to obtain additional corroboration of management's explanations and representations concerning material matters (e.g., third-party confirmation, documentation from independent sources, use of a specialist, and analytical procedures).

<u>OVERALL RESPONSES TO THE RISK OF MATERIAL MISSTATEMENT</u>

Judgments about the risk of material misstatement due to fraud have an overall effect on how the audit is conducted in several ways:

- *Assignment of personnel and supervision:* The auditor may need to consult with specialists in a particular field.
- *Accounting principles:* The auditor should consider management's selection and application of significant accounting principles, particularly those related to subjective measurements and complex transactions.
- *Predictability of auditing procedures:* The auditor should incorporate an "element of unpredictability" in the selection of auditing procedures to be performed, such as using differing sampling methods and performing procedures at different locations or at locations on an unannounced basis.

RESPONSES INVOLVING THE NATURE, TIMING, AND EXTENT OF PROCEDURES TO BE PERFORMED TO ADDRESS THE IDENTIFIED RISKS

This section notes that the auditing procedures performed in response to identified risks will vary depending on the type of risks identified. Such procedures may involve both substantive tests and tests of the operating effectiveness of the entity's internal controls. However, because management may have the ability to override controls that may otherwise appear to be operating effectively, it is unlikely that the audit risk can be reduced appropriately by performing only tests of controls.

Therefore, the auditor's response to specifically identified risks of fraud should include the following:
- Changing the *nature* of the auditing procedures to obtain more reliable or additional corroborative information by, for example, consulting independent sources or conducting physical inspections
- Changing the *timing* of substantive tests by, for example, conducting substantive tests at or near the end of the reporting period
- Ensuring that the *extent* of the procedures reflects the assessment of the risk of fraud by, for example, increasing the sample sizes or performing analytical procedures at a more detailed level

RESPONSES TO FURTHER ADDRESS RISK OF MANAGEMENT OVERRIDE OF CONTROLS

Because management is in a unique position to override existing controls, if such a risk is identified, the auditor might need to perform additional procedures to further address the risk of management override of controls.

EVALUATING AUDIT EVIDENCE

ASSESSING RISKS OF MATERIAL MISSTATEMENT DUE TO FRAUD THROUGHOUT THE AUDIT

During the performance of the audit, the auditor may identify conditions that either change or support a judgment regarding the assessment of risks.

Examples include:
- Discrepancies in the accounting records (e.g., transactions that are not recorded, are unsupported, are last-minute adjustments, or are unauthorized balances or transactions)
- Conflicting or missing evidential matter (e.g., missing or altered documents or records, unexplained items or reconciliations, or missing inventory)
- Problematic or unusual relationships between the auditor and management (e.g., denial of access to records, facilities, employees, customers; complaints by management about the conduct of the audit team; unusual delays in providing information; or unwillingness to add or revise disclosures)

EVALUATING WHETHER ANALYTICAL PROCEDURES PERFORMED INDICATE A PREVIOUSLY UNRECOGNIZED RISK OF FRAUD

Analytical procedures performed during the audit might result in identifying unusual or unexpected relationships that should be considered in assessing the risk of material misstatement due to fraud. Determining whether a particular trend or relationship is a fraud risk requires professional judgment. Unusual relationships involving year-end revenue and income often are particularly relevant and might include (1) uncharacteristically large amounts of income reported in the last week or two of the reporting period from unusual transactions and (2) income that is inconsistent with trends in cash flow from operations.

Analytical procedures are useful because employees or management are generally unable to manipulate all the information necessary to produce normal or expected relationships. AU 240 provides several examples, including:

- The relationship of net income to cash flows from operations might appear unusual because management recorded fictitious revenues and receivables but was unable to manipulate cash.
- Changes in inventory, accounts payable, sales, or costs of sales from the prior period to the current period might be inconsistent, indicating a possible theft of inventory because an employee was unable to manipulate all of the related accounts.
- The entity experiences unusual profitability in comparison to industry standards.
- There might be unusual bad debt write-offs when compared to industry standards, indicating a possible theft of cash receipts.
- An unexpected or unexplained relationship between sales volume as determined from the accounting records and production statistics maintained by operations personnel (which are more difficult for management to manipulate) might indicate a possible misstatement of sales.

EVALUATING RISKS OF MATERIAL MISSTATEMENT AT OR NEAR THE COMPLETION OF FIELDWORK

At or near the completion of fieldwork, the auditor should evaluate whether the accumulated results of auditing procedures and other observations affect the assessment of risk of material misstatements due to fraud made earlier. Such an evaluation might identify whether there is a need to perform further audit procedures.

RESPONDING TO MISSTATEMENTS THAT MIGHT BE THE RESULT OF FRAUD

If the auditor believes that misstatements are or might be the result of fraud, but the effect of the misstatements is not material to the financial statements, the auditor nevertheless should evaluate their implications. The auditor should be especially concerned with any implications pertaining to the "organizational position" of the person involved, as they might require a reevaluation of the assessment of the risk of material misstatement. For example, in the event of theft of cash from a small petty cash fund, the amount of the theft generally would not be of significance to the auditor; however, if the theft were perpetrated by higher-level management, it might be indicative of a more pervasive problem such as management integrity.

If the auditor believes that a misstatement is or might be the result of fraud, and either has determined that the effect of the misstatement is material to the financial statements or has been unable to evaluate whether the effect is material, the auditor should:
- Attempt to obtain additional evidence to determine whether material fraud occurred and its effect on the financial statements.
- Consider the implications for other aspects of the audit.
- Discuss the matter and the approach for further investigation with an appropriate level of management that is at least one level above those involved, and with senior management and the audit committee.
- If appropriate, suggest that the client consult with legal counsel.

COMMUNICATING ABOUT POSSIBLE FRAUD TO MANAGEMENT, THE AUDIT COMMITTEE, AND OTHERS

AU 240 states: "Whenever the auditor has determined that there is evidence that fraud may exist, the matter should be brought to the attention of an appropriate level of management." It is considered appropriate to do so even if the matter might be considered inconsequential. Fraud involving senior management and fraud (by anyone) that causes a material misstatement should be reported directly to those charged with governance.

If the auditor has identified risks of material misstatement due to fraud that have continuing control implications, the auditor should also consider whether these risks should be communicated to senior management and those charged with governance. Conversely, the auditor should also consider whether the absence of controls to deter, detect, or prevent fraud should be reported.

The disclosure of possible fraud to parties other than the client's senior management and those charged with governance is ordinarily not part of the auditor's responsibilities and might be precluded by the auditor's legal or ethical obligations of confidentiality unless the matter is reflected in the auditor's report. However, AU 240 points out that there might be a duty to disclose the information to outside parties in the following circumstances:
- To comply with certain legal and regulatory requirements (such as SEC rules)
- To a successor auditor pursuant to AU 315, *Communications Between Predecessor and Successor Auditors*
- In response to a subpoena
- To a funding agency or other specified agency in accordance with the requirements for audits of entities that receive governmental financial assistance

DOCUMENTING THE AUDITOR'S CONSIDERATION OF FRAUD

AU 240 concludes by requiring that auditors document the following:

- Discussion among engagement personnel regarding the susceptibility of the entity's financial statements to material misstatement due to fraud (including how and when the discussion occurred, the team members who participated, and the subject matter discussed)
- Procedures performed to obtain information necessary to identify and assess the risks of material misstatement due to fraud
- Specific risks of material misstatement due to fraud that were identified, and the auditor's response
- If the auditor has not identified improper revenue recognition as a risk, the reasons supporting the auditor's conclusion
- The results of the procedures performed to address the risk of management's override of controls
- Other conditions and analytical relationships that caused the auditor to believe that additional auditing procedures or other responses were required to address such risks
- The nature of the communication about fraud made to management, those charged with governance, or others

PCAOB Auditing Standard No. 5

Auditors of public companies are required to comply with auditing standards issued by the Public Company Accounting Oversight Board (PCAOB). In May 2007, the PCAOB adopted Auditing Standard No. 5, *An Audit of Internal Control Over Financial Reporting That Is Integrated with An Audit of Financial Statements*, as a replacement of Auditing Standard No. 2, *An Audit of Internal Control Over Financial Reporting Performed in Conjunction with an Audit of Financial Statements*, the previous standard governing audits of internal controls over financial reporting (ICOFR) as mandated by the Sarbanes-Oxley Act. The new auditing standard was intended to improve the efficiency and effectiveness of internal control audits while also reducing unnecessary costs, especially for smaller public companies.

Section 404 of the Sarbanes-Oxley Act mandates that management must assess and report on the effectiveness of the company's ICOFR, and the external auditor must attest to management's internal control assessment. Auditing Standard No. 5 lays out the requirements and provides guidance for auditors who are engaged to perform an audit of management's assessment of the internal controls that is integrated with an audit of the financial statements.

The following is a descriptive summary of some of the requirements laid out in the standard. Practitioners in this area should review Auditing Standard No. 5 in its entirety for more detailed information. A copy of the entire standard can be obtained from the PCAOB (pcaobus.org).

PERFORMING AN ICOFR AUDIT

INTEGRATING THE INTERNAL CONTROL AUDIT AND THE FINANCIAL STATEMENT AUDIT

Auditing Standard No. 5 states that, although the objectives of financial statement audits and audits of ICOFR are not identical, the two audits should be integrated, with the auditor planning and performing the work to achieve the objectives of both audits. The auditor should design and perform the tests of controls in a manner that yields sufficient evidence to support both the auditor's opinion at year-end and the auditor's control risk assessment for the financial statement audit.

PLANNING THE AUDIT

When planning an integrated audit of ICOFR and the financial statements, the auditor must:
- Evaluate whether the following matters are important to the financial statements and to ICOFR and, if so, how they will affect the audit procedures:
    - Knowledge of the company's ICOFR obtained during other engagements
    - Information about the company's industry, including financial reporting practices, economic conditions, laws and regulations, and technological changes
    - Information about the company's business activities, organization, operating characteristics, and capital structure
    - The existence and extent of any recent changes in the company, its operations, or its ICOFR
    - The auditor's preliminary judgments about materiality, risk, and other factors relating to the determination of material weaknesses
    - Any control deficiencies previously communicated to the audit committee, board of directors, or company management
    - Legal or regulatory issues of which the company is aware
    - The type and extent of evidence related to the effectiveness of the company's ICOFR
    - Preliminary judgments about the effectiveness of the ICOFR
    - Public information about the company related to the evaluation of the likelihood of material misstatements in the company's financial statements and the effectiveness of the company's ICOFR
    - Knowledge about the risks related to the company that were considered as part of the auditor's client acceptance and retention evaluation
    - The relative complexity of the company's operations
- Assess the risk that material weaknesses exist in areas of the company's ICOFR in order to determine which accounts, disclosures, and assertions are significant and relevant to the audit, which controls to test, and what evidence is necessary for a given control. In forming this assessment, the complexity of the organization, business unit, or process will play an important role.
- Focus the audit attention on those areas of the company's ICOFR that are assessed to have the highest risk that a material weakness exists. The auditor should keep in mind that the risk that a

Preparing for an Investigation

company's ICOFR will fail to prevent or detect a misstatement caused by fraud is usually higher than the risk of failure to prevent or detect errors.
- Scale the audit appropriately based on the ways the company meets its control objectives, with attention given to the size and complexity of the company, its business processes, and its business units.
- Evaluate the extent to which the auditor will use the work of others to reduce his own audit work.
- Use the same materiality considerations used in planning the audit of the company's financial statements.

USING A TOP-DOWN APPROACH

In an audit of ICOFR, auditors should implement a top-down approach. According to Auditing Standard No. 5, a top-down approach "begins at the financial statement level and with the auditor's understanding of the overall risks to internal control over financial reporting. The auditor then focuses on entity-level controls and works down to significant accounts and disclosures and their relevant assertions" (Paragraph 21). This approach focuses auditors on those accounts, disclosures, and assertions that are most likely to result in material misstatement of the company's financial statements. The standard makes explicit mention, however, that this approach describes the auditor's thought process when identifying risks and controls to test, which is not necessarily the order in which the auditor should perform the audit procedures.

TESTING CONTROLS

The auditor should test both the design and operating effectiveness of the company's ICOFR. In testing the design effectiveness of the controls, the auditor should determine whether the controls, if operated as prescribed, satisfy the company's control objectives and can effectively prevent or detect errors or fraud that could result in material misstatements. This testing might include inquiry of staff members, observation of operations, and examination of relevant documentation.

In testing the operating effectiveness of the controls, the auditor should determine whether the control is operating as designed, as well as whether the person operating the control has the appropriate authority and competence to perform the control effectively. An auditor may test the operations of the controls through inquiry of staff members, observation of operations, examination of relevant documentation, and re-performance of the control.

FRAUD CONSIDERATIONS

As part of an audit of ICOFR, the auditor must specifically evaluate (1) the controls enacted to address the risk of management override of other controls and (2) whether the company's internal controls adequately address the risk of material misstatement due to fraud. These controls include:
- Controls over significant, unusual transactions

- Controls over journal entries and adjustments made during the end of the period financial reporting process
- Controls over related-party transactions
- Controls related to significant management estimates
- Controls that mitigate the motivations for and pressures on management to engage in inappropriate earnings management and financial statement fraud

Further, if the auditor discovers any deficiencies in these controls, the auditor should address these deficiencies when responding to the risks of material misstatement during the financial statement audit.

FORMING AN OPINION ON THE EFFECTIVENESS OF ICOFR
In forming an opinion on the effectiveness of the company's ICOFR, the auditor must evaluate evidence from all sources. This not only includes the auditor's tests of controls, but also any misstatements detected during the financial statement audit, as well as any identified control deficiencies. The auditor should also review any reports issued during the year by the internal audit function that pertain to ICOFR and should evaluate any deficiencies identified therein.
The auditor must also evaluate management's assessment of ICOFR that is included in its annual reports filed with the SEC to ensure that all required elements in the report are complete and properly presented.

At the close of the integrated audit, the auditor may choose to issue a single report containing both an opinion on the company's financial statements and an opinion on ICOFR, or to issue separate reports for each opinion.

Planning the Investigation

The text up to this point has focused on the considerations that precede an investigation, such as the duty of auditors and accountants to seek out fraud and the duty of a company to undertake an internal investigation of suspected fraud or other wrongdoing. Once the decision has been made to pursue an investigation, the focus shifts to determining how the company can carry out the investigation in the most efficient, effective manner. The answer to this large question requires answering two smaller questions:

- Who will be involved in the investigation?
- What will be the investigative strategy?

> **Video**
>
> In the video titled "Chapter I: Planning the Investigation," fraud investigation expert Meric Bloch, J.D., CFE, explains some factors to keep in mind when planning your investigation. (Go to www.acfe.com/internalinvestigations to view the video.)

Selecting the Investigation Team

Internal investigations of fraudulent activity usually require a cooperative effort among different disciplines. Auditors, fraud examiners, line managers, attorneys, security personnel, and others are all frequently associated with internal investigations. When choosing an investigation team, it is critical to identify those who can legitimately assist in the investigation and those who have a legitimate interest in the outcome of the investigation. These persons should be included on the investigative team, and all other personnel should be segregated.

There are a number of reasons for this. First, the more people involved in the investigation, the greater the chance that one of those individuals might be somehow implicated in the fraud itself, or that one of those individuals might leak confidential information about the investigation. Second, the people involved in the investigation team might have to testify in legal proceedings, or the documents that they generate might be subject to discovery if the investigation leads to civil litigation or criminal prosecution. By limiting the number of investigators, the company can limit its exposure to discovery. In addition, any internal investigation, by its nature, can lead to harsh allegations against one or more suspects. This, in turn, can lead to charges of defamation and invasion of privacy, among others. These charges will be bolstered if it is found that the company spread information about the suspects to people who did not have a legitimate interest in that information. Therefore, by limiting the size of the investigation team, the company can limit its exposure to certain tort claims.

None of this is meant to imply that the company should exclude otherwise necessary individuals from the investigation team simply out of fear of potentially harmful legal repercussions. On the contrary, the primary goal should be to resolve the allegations of fraud as thoroughly and efficiently as possible, and that requires that all necessary individuals be involved in the effort. However, companies should guard against including extraneous personnel who add no real value to the team. A typical investigation team might include the following types of professionals.

Certified Fraud Examiners

A Certified Fraud Examiner (CFE) is trained to conduct a complex fraud examination from inception to conclusion. Fraud examinations frequently present special problems because they require an understanding of complex financial transactions, as well as traditional investigative techniques. Security personnel might be well-versed in investigative techniques, such as interviewing witnesses and collecting and preserving evidence for trial, but they might not know how to spot a fraudulent transaction on the company's books. Auditors and accountants might recognize a fraud scheme but might not have the training to conduct other aspects of an investigation. A CFE has training in all aspects of a fraud examination and therefore can serve as a valuable cornerstone of the investigation team, tying together the financial examination and the more traditional investigative techniques.

Legal Counsel

It is crucial to have counsel involved in, and in most cases, "directing" the investigation, at least as far as the legal aspects are concerned. As the text of this workbook will make clear, an internal investigation can be a veritable hornet's nest of legal questions. Should the company report the results of the investigation, and to whom? How can the company preserve the confidentiality of the investigation? How should the investigation be conducted so as to avoid lawsuits? What areas can the company search and what information can be gathered without violating an employee's rights? When and how can an employee be fired for wrongful conduct? These are just some of the issues that investigators will be faced with. The investigation team must have legal counsel on hand to sort out these questions; otherwise, the company risks exposing itself to greater danger than the threat it is investigating. In addition, by having an attorney directing the investigation, the company might be able to protect the confidentiality of its investigation under the attorney-client privilege and the work-product doctrine.

Video	
▶	In the video titled "Chapter I: Working with Counsel," fraud investigation expert Meric Bloch, J.D., CFE, explains some of the complicated dynamics of working with legal counsel during a fraud investigation. (Go to www.acfe.com/internalinvestigations to view the video.)

Internal Auditors

Internal auditors are often used to review internal documentary evidence, evaluate tips or complaints, schedule losses, and provide assistance in technical areas of the company's operations. As was pointed out earlier, auditors are frequently the people who detect financial anomalies that lead to fraud investigations. They are expected to be able to identify fraud indicators and notify management if an investigation is required. They are also charged with assessing the probable level of complicity within the organization and helping design procedural methods to identify the perpetrators, as well as the extent of the fraud.

Security Personnel

Security department investigators are often assigned the "field work" stage of the investigation, including interviewing outside witnesses and obtaining public records and other documents from third parties. It is crucial that their work be integrated with the financial side of the investigation so that the team does not devolve into two de facto investigations—one for "financials" and one for "field work." The process works best when all aspects of the investigation are coordinated and focused on the same goal.

Human Resources Personnel
The human resources department should be consulted to ensure that the laws governing the rights of employees in the workplace are not violated. Such involvement will lessen the possibility of a wrongful discharge suit or other civil action by the employee. Advice from a human resources specialist might also be needed. Normally, this person would not directly participate in the investigation.

Management Representative
A representative of management, or in significant cases, the audit committee of the board of directors, should be kept informed of the progress of the investigation and be available to lend necessary assistance. A sensitive employee investigation has virtually no hope of success without strong management support.

Outside Consultants
In some cases, particularly when the suspect employee is very powerful or popular, it might be useful to employ outside specialists who are relatively immune from company politics or threats of reprisals. Such experts might also have greater experience and investigative contacts than insiders.

Investigative Strategy: Fraud Examination Methodology
An investigation of suspected fraud should follow the fraud examination methodology, which requires that all fraud examinations be handled in a uniform, legal fashion and be resolved on a timely basis. Assuming there is sufficient reason (i.e., predication) to conduct a fraud examination, specific examination steps are usually employed in an orderly manner. The fraud examination moves from the general to the specific, gradually zeroing in on the perpetrator through a process of careful acquisition and analysis of evidence. At each step of the examination, the evidence that has been obtained is assessed and compared to the overriding investigative theory. Where necessary, that theory is refined to direct the investigation at the most logical source of the fraud. The investigation team must be careful throughout the investigation to observe the rights of all individuals affected by the investigation.

Predication
An internal fraud investigation consists of a multitude of steps, all of which might be necessary to resolve allegations of fraud: interviewing witnesses, assembling evidence, writing reports, and dealing with prosecutors and the courts. Because the investigation of fraud deals with the individual rights of others, an investigation must be conducted only with adequate cause or predication.

Predication is the totality of circumstances that would lead a reasonable, professionally trained, and prudent individual to believe a fraud has occurred, is occurring, or will occur. Predication is the basis upon which an examination is commenced. Internal fraud investigations should not be conducted without proper predication.

Video	
▶	In the video titled "Chapter I: Predication," fraud investigation expert Meric Bloch, J.D., CFE, further explains the concept of predication. (Go to www.acfe.com/internalinvestigations to view the video.)

Fraud Theory Approach

To solve a fraud without complete evidence, the examiner must make certain assumptions. This is not unlike the scientist who postulates a theory based on observation and then tests it. In the case of complex fraud, fraud theory is almost indispensable.

Fraud theory begins with an assumption, based on the known facts, of what might have occurred. Then that assumption is tested to determine whether it is provable. As new evidence is gathered, the hypothesis is continuously refined and modified to conform to known facts.

ANALYZING AVAILABLE DATA

Prior to the commencement of any interview or other overt investigation, the investigation team analyzes the available data to determine what facts are known. If the data requires an audit, it should be performed at this time.

CREATING A HYPOTHESIS

The hypothesis is invariably a "worst case" scenario; that is, after analyzing all the data, the investigator would determine the fraud(s) involved. For example, the hypothesis could refer to a possible bribery, embezzlement, ghost employee scheme, and so on.

TESTING THE HYPOTHESIS

Testing the hypothesis involves creating a "what if" scenario. For example, if, as part of the hypothesis, bribery of a purchasing agent were suspected, the fraud examiner would likely find some or all of the following facts:
- A personal relationship between the buyer and vendor
- Ability of the purchasing agent to steer business toward a favored vendor
- Higher prices or lower quality for the product or service being purchased
- Excessive spending by the purchasing agent.

This is not to imply that investigators should set out to "pin" a fraud on a particular employee. The idea is that the company must approach the problem from the standpoint that there is something wrong. Investigators should seek to eliminate the most likely causes first.

REFINING AND AMENDING THE HYPOTHESIS

In testing the hypothesis, the fraud examiner might find that all of the facts do not fit a particular scenario. If such is the case, the hypothesis should be revised and retested. (If the known facts are tested with negative results, it could be that a fraud is not present, or it could indicate that the fraud cannot be proven.)

The following is a flow chart setting forth how the fraud examination process is used to resolve allegations.

Preparing for an Investigation

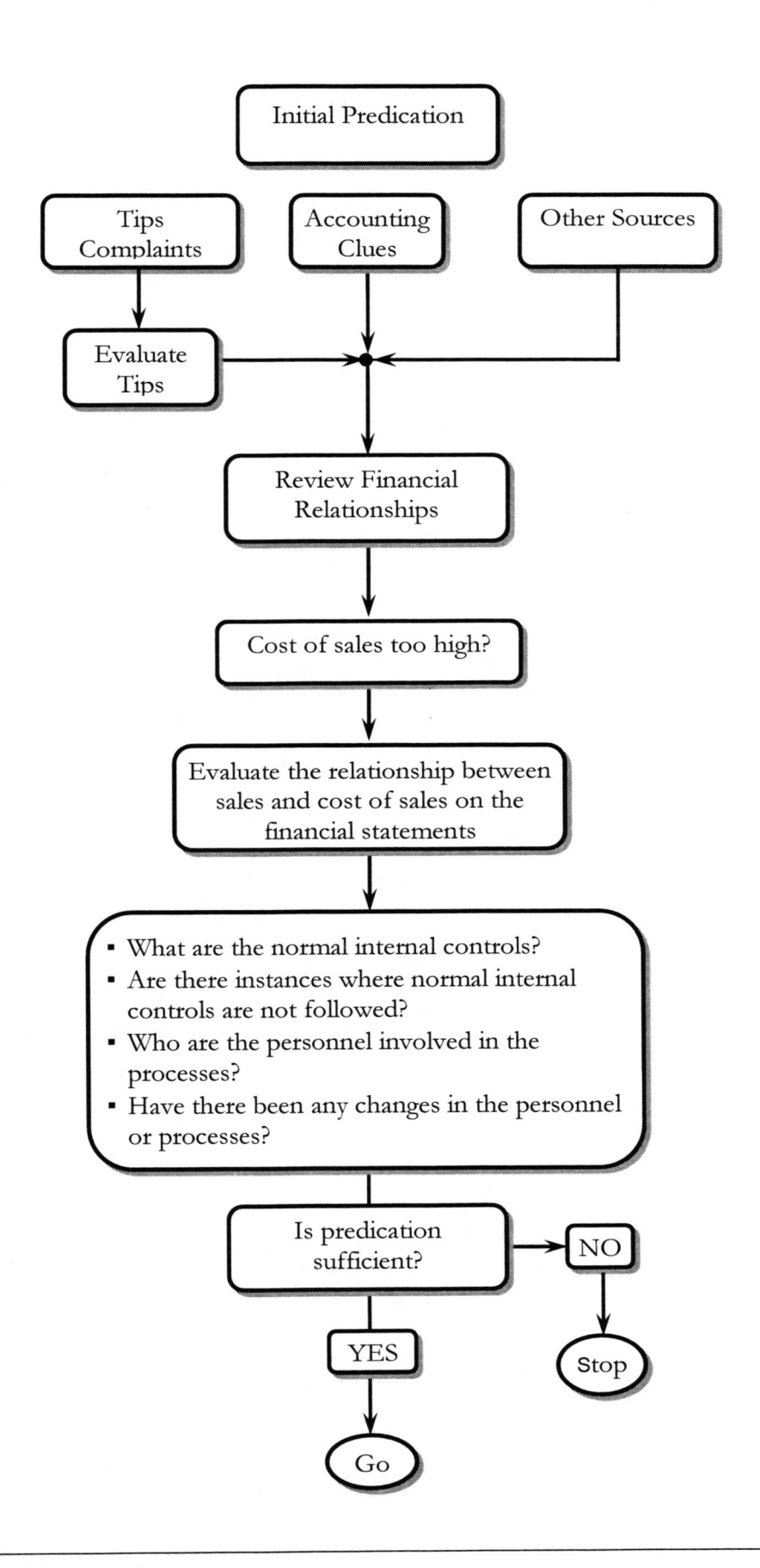

```
                    ┌─────────────────┐
                    │ Initial Predication │
                    └─────────────────┘

    ┌──────────┐      ┌──────────┐      ┌──────────────┐
    │   Tips   │      │ Accounting │      │ Other Sources │
    │ Complaints │      │   Clues   │      └──────────────┘
    └──────────┘      └──────────┘
          │
    ┌──────────┐
    │ Evaluate │
    │   Tips   │
    └──────────┘
                         ●
                         ↓
                ┌──────────────────┐
                │ Review Financial │
                │  Relationships   │
                └──────────────────┘
                         ↓
                ┌──────────────────┐
                │ Cost of sales too high? │
                └──────────────────┘
                         ↓
         ┌────────────────────────────────┐
         │ Evaluate the relationship between │
         │ sales and cost of sales on the    │
         │      financial statements         │
         └────────────────────────────────┘
                         ↓
    ┌──────────────────────────────────────────────┐
    │ ▪ What are the normal internal controls?     │
    │ ▪ Are there instances where normal internal  │
    │   controls are not followed?                 │
    │ ▪ Who are the personnel involved in the      │
    │   processes?                                 │
    │ ▪ Have there been any changes in the personnel│
    │   or processes?                              │
    └──────────────────────────────────────────────┘
                         ↓
                ┌──────────────────┐         ┌────┐
                │  Is predication  │ ──────→ │ NO │
                │    sufficient?   │         └────┘
                └──────────────────┘            ↓
                         ↓                   ┌──────┐
                       ┌─────┐               │ Stop │
                       │ YES │               └──────┘
                       └─────┘
                         ↓
                       ┌────┐
                       │ Go │
                       └────┘
```

Conducting Internal Investigations

Develop fraud theory:
- Who might be involved?
- What might have happened?
- Why might the allegation be true?
- Where are the possible concealment places or methods?
- When did this take place (past, present, or future)?
- How is the fraud being perpetrated?

Determine where the evidence is likely to be:
- On-book vs. off-book
- Direct or circumstantial evidence
- Identify potential witnesses

What evidence is necessary to prove intent?
- Number of occurrences
- Other areas of impropriety
- Witnesses

Revise fraud theory

Prepare chart—linking people and evidence

Determine defenses to allegations

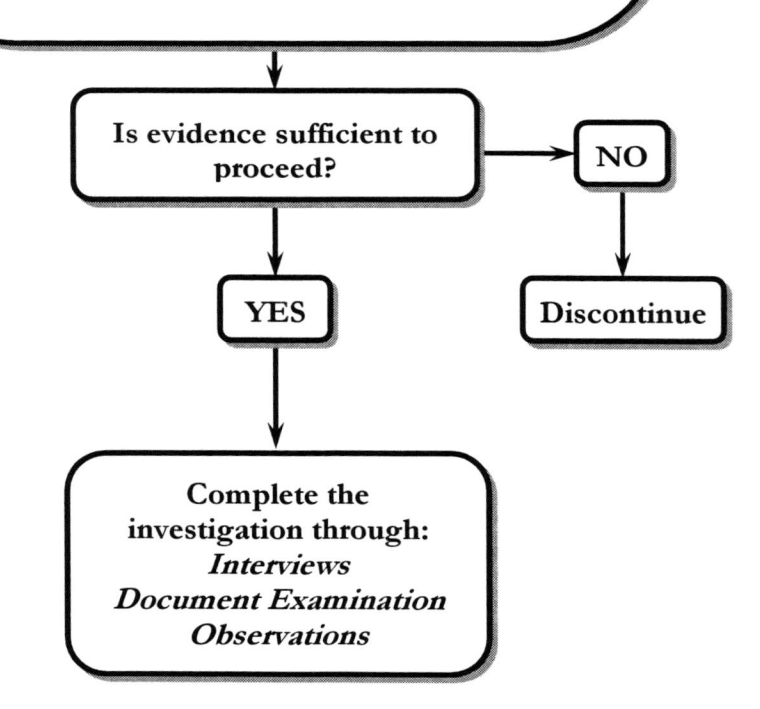

Is evidence sufficient to proceed?

→ NO → Discontinue

↓ YES

Complete the investigation through:
Interviews
Document Examination
Observations

Steps in the Fraud Examination

Fraud examination methodology is constructed so that all cases are handled in a uniform fashion. The methodology involves working from the general to the specific, commencing with the examination of documents.

DOCUMENT EXAMINATION

As a general rule, documents should be examined before interviews commence. This is to gain an understanding of the potential evidentiary value of the case, as well as to protect the security of documents.

NEUTRAL THIRD-PARTY WITNESSES

After conducting sufficient document examination, witnesses should be interviewed in a logical fashion starting from the least likely to the most likely to be involved. Neutral third-party witnesses should usually be interviewed first.

CORROBORATIVE WITNESSES

Interviews of witnesses to corroborate facts should be conducted after the neutral third-party witness interviews. These witnesses might be cooperative or uncooperative.

> **Video**
>
> In the video titled "Chapter I: Corroborative Witnesses," fraud investigation expert Jonathan Turner, CFE, further explains the role of corroborative witnesses in an investigation. Mr. Turner, Managing Director at Turner and Wilson Incorporated, specializes in the prevention and detection of financial fraud and has been featured on CNN and ABC News. (Go to www.acfe.com/internalinvestigations to view the video.)

CO-CONSPIRATORS

Those suspected of complicity should be interviewed next, from the least culpable to the most culpable. If appropriate, law enforcement and prosecutors can frequently promise leniency in return for cooperation. Investigators outside of prosecution and law enforcement must not make promises of leniency; such decisions are left to the respective enforcement agencies.

> **Video**
>
> In the video titled "Chapter I: Co-Conspirators," fraud investigation expert Jonathan Turner, CFE, further explains the process of interviewing co-conspirators. (Go to www.acfe.com/internalinvestigations to view the video.)

ACCUSED

In general, the accused is examined last. Even if it is felt that the accused will not offer a confession, an interview is usually scheduled; in many instances, it can later be used for impeachment—the process in which the accused's testimony in a trial or administrative proceeding is contradicted by his previous statements.

Review Questions

1. A company can be held liable for the illegal conduct of an employee if the employee was acting within the course and scope of his employment. Which of the following statements regarding course and scope is true?
   I. Any act an employee commits while on duty is considered to be within the course and scope of his employment.
   II. In order to be considered within the course and scope, the employee's acts must be of the kind the employee was authorized by the company to perform.
   III. Unless a company expressly authorizes illegal conduct by its employees, an illegal act will never be considered to be in the course and scope.
   IV. In order to be considered within the course and scope, the employee's acts must be intended to benefit the company.

   A. II and III
   B. I
   C. II, III, and IV
   D. II and IV

2. _____ covers the internal auditor's responsibilities to deter, detect, investigate, and report fraud.
   A. SIAS 1220
   B. AU 315
   C. SIAS 1210
   D. AU 200

3. Fraud examination methodology is constructed so that all cases are handled in a uniform fashion. In general, what is the order in which an investigator should interview witnesses and suspects (from first to last)?
   I. The accused
   II. Neutral third-party witnesses
   III. Suspected co-conspirators
   IV. Corroborative witnesses

   A. I, II, III, IV
   B. II, IV, III, I
   C. IV, II, III, I
   D. IV, III, I, II

4. Which of the following is NOT one of the three conditions of a fraud risk factor identified by AU 240?
   A. Incentives or pressures to commit fraud
   B. Opportunities to carry out fraud
   C. Attitudes or rationalizations to justify fraudulent conduct
   D. Fraudulent mindset of employee

5. According to the text, internal auditors are often used to do which of the following?
   A. Provide assistance in technical areas of the company's operations
   B. Review internal documentary evidence
   C. Evaluate tips or complaints
   D. All of the above

6. The totality of circumstances that would lead a reasonable, professionally trained, and prudent individual to believe a fraud has occurred, is occurring, or will occur is known as:
   A. Declaration
   B. Fraud theory approach
   C. Predication
   D. None of the above

7. Public disclosure of internal fraud can subject a company to:
   A. Loss of collateral business or trading partners
   B. Loss of government licenses necessary for certain regulated activities
   C. A decline in the value of publicly traded equities
   D. All of the above

8. Senior management and corporate counsel who fail to investigate certain instances of alleged misconduct and fail to establish appropriate procedures for limiting the prohibited conduct might be held liable for violating which of the following?
   A. Foreign Corrupt Practices Act
   B. Generally accepted accounting principles
   C. Private Securities Litigation Act
   D. None of the above

9. While conducting a fraud investigation, it is NOT recommended that internal auditors:
   A. Assess the probable level and extent of complicity within the organization
   B. Design procedural methodology to identify the perpetrators, the extent of the fraud, the techniques used, and the cause of the fraud
   C. Call law enforcement in at the beginning of the investigation
   D. Be aware of the rights of the alleged perpetrators and personnel within the scope of the investigation and the reputation of the organization itself

10. When choosing an investigation team, it is critical to identify those who can legitimately assist in the investigation and those who have a legitimate interest in the outcome of the investigation. Why should these people be included on the investigation team and all other personnel be segregated?
    A. The more people involved in the investigation, the greater the chance that one of them might leak confidential information about the investigation
    B. The individuals involved in the investigation team might have to testify in legal proceedings
    C. Limiting the size of the team decreases the risk of tort claims
    D. All of the above

II. COLLECTING DOCUMENTARY EVIDENCE

Introduction

In most internal fraud investigations, there will be a great deal of documentary evidence to obtain. It is critical that investigators understand the relevance of this evidence and how it should be preserved and presented. Always keep in mind that documents can either help or hurt a case, depending on the information they contain and how they are presented. The goal is to make certain that all relevant documents are included and all irrelevant documents are eliminated.

There can be a tendency for investigators to pay too much attention to documentary evidence. It is easy to get bogged down in detail when examining records and to lose sight of a simple fact: documents do not make cases—witnesses make cases. Documents make or break the witness. They provide the foundation of the case on which the investigator will build the structure of the investigation. They provide the facts that an investigator can use to corroborate or contradict what a witness says. Documentary evidence is not an end in and of itself; so-called paper cases often confuse and bore a jury. Nevertheless, it is important to gather as much valuable documentary evidence as possible at an early stage in the investigation because this evidence will enable the investigator to "flesh out" the case in the interview stage.

The investigator must always be aware of the potential for litigation in any internal investigation. Any documents that are gathered during an investigation must be handled properly so that they will later be accepted by a court. There are basic procedures that any court will require before evidence can be admitted. Proof must be provided that the evidence is relevant and material. Evidence submitted must be properly identified, and it must be established that the proper chain of custody was maintained.

A document's relevance cannot be easily determined early in a case. For that reason, all possibly relevant documents should be obtained. If they are not needed, they can always be returned. Here are a few general rules regarding the collection of documents:

- Obtain original documents when feasible. Make working copies for review, and keep the originals segregated.
- Do not touch originals any more than necessary; they might later have to undergo forensic analysis.
- Maintain a good filing system for the documents. This is especially critical in cases where large numbers of documents are obtained. Losing a key document can mortally damage the case. Documents can be stamped sequentially for easy reference.

The proper handling of documents should be a concern of any investigator, but equally important is the proper acquisition of documents. If an investigator acting as an agent for the government violates an employee's constitutional rights in obtaining documentary evidence, that evidence can be excluded from a criminal prosecution. Furthermore, the company or the investigator can face a lawsuit from the employee whose rights were violated. There are also a host of common law and statutory provisions that limit the way in which an investigator can gather evidence or monitor employee activity. Again, violation of any of these laws can result in liability for the investigator or his company. The following sections provide an overview of the more common legal issues that can arise in any search of employee workspaces or surveillance of employee communications. However, this is only a general overview; laws vary among jurisdictions, and investigators are cautioned to consult legal counsel before engaging in any activity that could conceivably violate an employee's rights.

Laws Governing Public Record Information

There is a surprising amount of information about both individuals and businesses that can be accessed without a subpoena. In fact, the government is bound by law to facilitate the public's access to government information and to encourage a diversity of sources to acquire and use the information. There are three tenets supporting the public's right to access government records:

- The public has a broad right of access to government information.
- The government may not discriminate in the dissemination of public information.
- Restrictions on the use of public information are contrary to governmental policy in general.

Freedom of Information Act

The Freedom of Information Act (FOIA) is the primary statute that governs the availability of governmental records to the general public. The Act sets very specific guidelines regarding what governmental records are open to the public. The records that are available are known as *public records*, which consist of documents that a governmental agency is required by law to keep, or are documents necessary to discharge the duties imposed by law. Conversely, records not available to the public are known as *non-public records*.

The various sources of public records are maintained at one of the three governmental levels: federal, state, or county and local. Although the FOIA is a federal Act, most states have adopted very similar versions of the FOIA to cover the state and local jurisdictions. While these versions are similar to the original FOIA, the individually passed state acts may differ slightly in specific legal areas from state to state.

The FOIA and its individual state counterparts regulate:

- The type of records that a governmental agency may maintain about a person
- The conditions under which such information may be disclosed to another governmental agency
- The circumstances and methods under which an individual may obtain copies of agency records that pertain to him

Generally speaking, governmental records about an individual are prohibited from release. The disclosure of these records constitutes an invasion of privacy. A person may obtain copies of his own records by requesting them in writing from the agency that maintains them. Such requests often are denied, in whole or in part, because of numerous exceptions to the disclosure requirements. Some of these exceptions include the pendency of an ongoing investigation or concerns about national security. A person denied access to records may appeal through that agency or through the courts.

Most records are maintained at the county or local level. This is a fact that can seriously hamper any fraud investigation; it can be very difficult for the fraud examiner to catch up with a fraudster who understands the county filing procedures and chooses to operate in different counties. However, the following records are available at different levels of government.

The FOIA provides for public access to the following information:
- Tax rolls
- Voter registration
- Assumed names
- Real property records
- Divorce or probate suits

Information NOT deemed to be public under the FOIA includes:
- Banking records
- Trust records
- Telephone records
- Passenger lists
- Stock ownership

Despite the public's broad right of access, there are numerous laws that limit access to certain types of information, and a number of risks to privacy are raised by the collection of information. Therefore, fraud examiners must be certain that information obtained is done so legally.

Fair Credit Reporting Act
One of the primary statutes limiting access to information is the federal Fair Credit Reporting Act (FCRA). This statute regulates the dissemination of consumer information to third parties by consumer reporting agencies. Historically, the FCRA only applied to consumer credit reports, but due to amendments in 1997, the FCRA now applies to the gathering of many other types of information about an individual through third parties (e.g., consumer report agencies).

Collecting Documentary Evidence

The FCRA applies in the employment context when an employer contracts with a consumer reporting agency (CRA) to collect consumer reports on employees or potential employees. A *CRA* is defined as anyone who sells information about people (e.g., a private investigator or an online public records service). A *consumer report* is defined as any written, oral, or other communication by a consumer reporting agency bearing on a customer's credit worthiness, credit standing, character, general reputation, personal characteristics, or mode of living.

However, the FCRA does not apply if the person or organization seeking the information gathers it directly from the source.

If the FCRA does apply, it generally means that an examiner cannot use a third party to obtain certain information about a person unless that person has received certain notices and has signed a consent form. The failure to do so can mean civil penalties.

Complying with the FCRA

Before an employer can obtain consumer information about a current or prospective employee from a third party, it must comply with all of the following requirements:
- Provide the individual with a "clear and conspicuous" separate written disclosure that the employer might obtain a report
- Obtain the individual's written authorization
- Inform the third party that the employer has complied with the FCRA's notice requirements
- Inform the third party that the employer will not use the information to violate any equal employment law

The disclosure and the authorization can be contained in the same document, as long as the document contains nothing else.

If the employer relies on a consumer report for an adverse action (e.g., denying a job application, terminating an employee, or denying a promotion), then it must provide the individual with a pre-adverse action disclosure before taking the adverse action. This disclosure must include a copy of the individual's consumer report and a copy of "A Summary of Your Rights Under the Fair Credit Reporting Act," which is available from the FTC.

After adverse action is taken, the employer must notify the individual via an adverse action notice. That notice must include the following information:
- The name, address, and phone number of the consumer reporting agency (CRA) that supplied the report
- A statement that the CRA did not make the adverse action decision and cannot explain why the adverse action was taken
- A notice of the individual's right to dispute the accuracy or completeness of the information furnished, and their right to an additional free consumer report from the agency upon request within 60 days

Workplace Investigations of Fraud and Misconduct

The Fair and Accurate Credit Transactions Act of 2003 amended the FCRA to exempt certain reports involving employee misconduct investigations.

As a result of these amendments, an employer who uses a third party to conduct a workplace investigation no longer has to obtain the prior consent of an employee if the investigation involves suspected:
- Misconduct
- Violation of laws or regulations
- Violation of any pre-existing policy of the employer

To qualify for this exception, the report from the third party must not be communicated to anyone other than the employer, an agent of the employer, or the government. However, if adverse action is taken against the employee based on the results of the investigation, the FCRA still requires the employer to provide the employee with a summary of the report. The summary must "contain the nature and substance of the communication upon which the adverse action is based." It does not, however, have to identify the individuals interviewed or the sources of the information.

Investigative Consumer Report

Under the FCRA, as amended, an *investigative consumer report* is a report containing information about an individual's character, general reputation, personal characteristics, or mode of living that is obtained through personal interviews with neighbors, friends, or associates. If such a report is made, then other notices and consents might need to be obtained from the individual. For example, a separate disclosure must be used to inform the employee that an investigative consumer report is being obtained. The form must also state what sort of information will be collected.

Also, the company must disclose to the individual the nature and scope of the investigation (if requested). If any adverse action is to be taken against the person, he can ask to receive a copy of the report before such action occurs. Further, the report given to the individual must not be redacted, meaning that if the report contains names of the people providing the information and what they reported, such information cannot be deleted from the report. The person must also be given an opportunity to dispute the report's findings.

Contact Your Attorney

Unfortunately for fraud examiners, the FCRA has created several more hoops that examiners must jump through before they can obtain certain types of information. The FCRA is not clearly written, but the FTC has published several letters giving its interpretation of the statute. These letters and the text of the FCRA can be obtained through its website at www.ftc.gov.

The most important thing for the fraud examiner to remember is to consult his in-house or outside counsel. Your attorney will help you determine what procedures you need to institute in order to comply with the FCRA.

Gramm-Leach-Bliley Act

The Gramm-Leach-Bliley Act (GLB) was passed in 1999, and rules implementing the Act became final in 2001. GLB was originally enacted to allow banks and other companies to offer previously forbidden services, such as insurance and securities brokerage services. Congress was worried that these "super banks" would share customers' financial data with affiliates and other companies to hawk their products. Therefore, Congress added a provision requiring financial intuitions to tell customers about their privacy policies, to notify customers of private information they intend to share, and to give customers the chance to block such information sharing.

To implement the law, Congress ordered regulators to define *financial institution* in the broadest possible terms. Thus, financial institutions include not just banks, but also insurance companies, accountants, tax preparation and real estate settlement services, and investment advisors. The text of the rule can be found at 16 C.F.R. Part 313. Additional information about the rule can be found at the FTC's website at www.ftc.gov.

GLB is important for fraud examiners because the privacy rules implemented as part of the Act have been interpreted to prevent the selling of credit header information, and under the FTC's interpretation of the rule, credit header information cannot be sold except for the very limited purposes allowed under the Fair Credit Reporting Act. The agency reached this decision by concluding that such basic personal information, such as names and addresses, is financial information, and, therefore, must be protected under the GLB Act. Therefore, the GLB prevents credit bureaus from selling credit header information (including names, addresses, phone numbers, and Social Security numbers) to private investigators, direct marketers, or other information brokers.

As a general rule, financial information can be obtained only by subpoena.

GLB also made it a criminal offense to engage in *pretexting* (i.e., gaining access through the use of false statements). Some individuals used pretexting as a means to gather financial information about a subject. Pretexters would contact a financial institution and pretend to be the customer or someone else authorized to obtain financial information and basically trick the financial institution into providing information about the subject.

15 U.S.C. § 6821 (added by GLB) makes it an offense to:
- Use false, fictitious, or fraudulent statements or documents to get customer information from a financial institution or directly from a customer of a financial institution.
- Use forged, counterfeit, lost, or stolen documents to get customer information from a financial institution or directly from a customer of a financial institution.
- Ask another person to get someone else's customer information using false, fictitious, or fraudulent statements or documents, or using forged, counterfeit, lost, or stolen documents.

Violators can, under certain circumstances, be fined and/or imprisoned up to ten years.

Telephone Records and Privacy Protection Act of 2006

The Telephone Records and Privacy Protection Act of 2006 (TRPPA), which was enacted in response to the Hewlett-Packard (HP) pretexting scandal that surfaced in 2006, also criminalizes pretexting. The HP pretexting scandal provides an excellent example of what can happen when an internal investigation is not properly conducted.

The HP scandal began in 2005, when officials at HP initiated a secret internal investigation to discover the source of boardroom leaks. To uncover the source, HP's chairman hired a team of investigators to procure the private phone records of HP's board members through pretexting.

Through such efforts, the investigation uncovered the source, and at a board meeting in May of 2006, HP's chairman informed the board of the investigation scheme and identified the source of the leaks. After the board asked the leaker to resign, a fellow HP director resigned in protest of the methods used during the leak investigation.

Although HP's chairman was confident that pretexting was permissible, she could not foresee the disastrous fallout from the investigation. By November of 2006, HP was facing investigations by the California attorney general's office, the U.S. attorney in San Francisco, the FBI, the Federal

Collecting Documentary Evidence

Communications Commission, and the Securities and Exchange Commission. Ultimately, HP paid $14.5 million to the state of California, and the chairman was removed from her position.

In January of 2007, President Bush signed the TRPPA into law. Specifically, the TRPPA criminalizes the practice of obtaining and attempting to obtain, sell, or buy confidential phone records through the use of false statements, unless otherwise permitted by law. Violations of the Act are criminal, and if convicted, a violator faces up to ten years in prison and up to $100,000 in fines. These fines and prison terms may be increased in cases of violations compounded with other activities, or some other egregious crimes.

Therefore, before engaging in any type of pretexting activity, investigators should consult with an attorney to determine whether the information sought is protected by state or federal law, as well as whether the planned impersonation method is legally acceptable.

Right to Financial Privacy Act

The Right to Financial Privacy Act prohibits financial institutions from disclosing financial information about individual customers to government agencies without any of the following:
- The customer's consent
- A court order
- A subpoena
- A search warrant
- Other formal demand, with limited exceptions

Although the statute applies only to demands by government agencies, most banks and other financial institutions will also not release such information to private parties absent legal process, such as a subpoena issued in a civil lawsuit.

Driver's Privacy Protection Act

In 1999, Congress made significant changes to the Driver's Privacy Protection Act (DPPA) of 1994 (18 U.S.C. § 2721). The law bars states from releasing drivers' Social Security numbers, photographs, or certain other information unless they obtain "the express consent" of each person in advance. Before the 1999 amendments, drivers could "opt out" and ask that their information not be released. Under the law, drivers are under an "opt in" system that requires their express authorization of the release of information. Although the law was challenged, the U.S. Supreme Court, in January 2000, upheld the constitutionality of the amendments.

These amendments make it extremely difficult to obtain almost any up-to-date information from state motor vehicle departments. Such information can only be obtained if the driver has expressly consented to its release. Therefore, companies may wish to consider having employees sign a consent form as early as the employment application stage. For example, the Driver's Privacy Protection Act does not prohibit the use of motor vehicle records (MVR) for pre-employment screening, but the state can only release the records with the driver's consent.

The National Highway Traffic Safety Administration is in the process of implementing a requirement that event data recorders, or *black boxes*, be installed in all new cars sold in the United States. The devices record detailed information about the driver and his actions for use by insurance companies, law enforcement officials, and others. At this time, it is unclear how the Driver's Privacy Protection Act will affect the release of information obtained by the data recorders and with whom it may be shared.

Health Insurance Portability and Accountability Act
The Health Insurance Portability and Accountability Act (HIPAA) instituted several additional privacy rules concerning personal health information. While most of the rules do not directly affect fraud investigations, fraud examiners should be aware of the rules because they might have an impact on the type of information that can be legally gathered on employees.

The HIPAA privacy rules place restrictions on the availability and use of "protected health information." The definition of this term is extremely broad and covers any information relating to an individual's past, present, or future physical or mental health, payment for services, or health care operations.

If information about the health of an individual or payments for services becomes an issue during an investigation, fraud examiners should immediately contact the human resources (HR) department. The HR department should have information about whether the entity is subject to HIPAA rules and can assist in compliance with those rules.

The most important thing to note is that if HIPAA rules do apply, you are restricted as to the type of health information you can access without specific written authorization. You should never contact the health care provider, the health-plan administrator, or a medical-billing service for copies of an employee's records without first consulting the employer's legal counsel or the HR department.

Sources of Information

In any internal investigation, a large proportion of the documentary evidence that is gathered will come from inside the company. The specific documents that need to be assembled will depend on the facts of the case; contracts, journals and registers, invoices, time cards, balance sheets, income statements, personnel files, and a host of other internal documentation may be relevant, depending on the circumstances. These documents belong to the company, and in most cases, they can be assembled without any significant legal ramifications. Where they are held in the possession of a particular employee, there might be privacy issues involved in gathering them. These concerns will be addressed later in this chapter.

For the most part, the business's internal documents will be readily obtainable by investigators. But some internal investigations, particularly those involving suspected fraud among a company's executives, are bound to meet resistance in the acquisition of evidence. The politics of getting around this information barrier will vary from case to case, as each organization has a unique state of affairs. Litigation may help to compel the production of certain documents, but some investigations may not get to that stage or simply are not to that point yet.

Therefore, it should be remembered that external sources of information will also play a large role in most internal investigations. External sources can be particularly crucial in helping investigators locate missing assets; locate witnesses and suspects; determine ownership in vendors, competitors, and other related parties; research the assets and financial condition of suspects; and document lifestyle and background information on suspects. All of this information will help an investigator build a case and will provide the basis for conducting interviews and obtaining confessions later in the investigation.

Generally, it will require more effort on the part of investigators to assemble external information. These documents will be in the possession of outside parties in varying locations. Some of this information is open to the public, while other information might be privately held. Investigators may need to file formal requests, present notice to suspects, or even obtain subpoenas to gather particular documents. There are a variety of commercial databases and research reference services that can compile this information for the investigator, but their cost and effectiveness must be weighed.

Public Sources of Information

A significant amount of information regarding an individual's personal and business history is a matter of public record. The investigator must determine those points of identity that separate that person from others with the same name or set of circumstances. Many types of public records will contain similar information about individuals or entities. Yet each agency or governmental unit that houses public records is responsible for quite different functions that might require them to maintain very unique information. Investigators should be prepared to consult a variety of public records in order to gather the necessary information.

Public source information can be useful for a number of reasons. It can supply invaluable background information on employees, suspects, and witnesses. It can be used to corroborate or refute witness statements, can help investigators track the flow of stolen cash or other assets, and can be extremely important in a company's efforts to recover losses.

Video

In the video titled "Chapter II: Public Records," fraud investigation expert Jonathan Turner, CFE, explains why public records should be used in every fraud investigation. (Go to www.acfe.com/internalinvestigations to view the video.)

The following sections describe several public record sources that can be accessed by investigators at the city, county, state, and federal levels of government.

City Government Records

The following items are basic types of public records that can be accessed at the city level of government:
- Building inspector records
- Health and fire department records
- City personnel department records
- Public school records
- Regulatory agency records
- City tax assessor or collector records
- Utility company records

Building Inspector Records

The following information is generally available through a city building inspector's office:
- Building permits showing the name of the applicant, address of construction, estimated cost, and the name of the builder or contractor
- Blueprints and plans showing construction details that often are submitted with applications for building permits
- Building inspectors' reports containing information regarding compliance with construction specifications

Health and Fire Department Records

Most local health or fire departments conduct routine inspections of businesses for health and safety code or fire code violations. These inspectors might have valuable information about the business, its operations, the employees, and the owners.

Collecting Documentary Evidence

Death certificates usually can be found at city, county, or state health departments. A death certificate provides the name of the deceased, the address, sex, age, race, birthplace, birth date, death place, date and time of death, Social Security number, medical certificate, and coroner's certificate for the deceased. Additionally, a death certificate generally provides information about the deceased's parents and their occupations.

City Personnel Department Records
The city personnel department maintains personal-history statements from city employees and political leaders, as well as employment records, efficiency reports, and records of salary liens on city employees.

Public School Records
City school systems maintain teachers' biographies with their personal background, education, and former employment; and student records, consisting of biographies (in some school districts), grades, and disciplinary actions. The Family Educational Rights and Privacy Act (FERPA) of 1974 prohibits the disclosure of student records, other than to educational institutions, without the consent of the student. Directory information such as name, address, and dates attended may be disclosed; however, students may opt out of the release of directory information.

Regulatory Agency Records
Applications for business licenses, contained in the files of city regulatory agencies, often have valuable information on certain types of enterprises. In many cities, the following businesses would have to apply for licenses to operate:
- Professionals, including certified public accountants, dentists, doctors, plumbers, electricians, and optometrists
- Restaurants, bars, and night clubs (which are frequently inspected by health and fire departments)
- Businesses operating under names other than the owners' names (such businesses must register under assumed names and are included in the city's DBA [doing business as] files)

City Tax Assessor or Collector Records
A city's tax assessor's office maintains maps of real property in the city, including a property's dimensions, address, owner, taxable value, and improvements. A tax collector's office maintains the following information:
- Names and addresses of payers of property taxes, even if the taxes were paid by individuals other than the apparent owners
- Legal descriptions of property
- Amounts of taxes paid on real and personal property
- Delinquency status of taxes
- Names of former property owners

Utility Company Records

Many utility companies are non-profit corporations or municipalities. Although the recent trend has been to restrict access to utility company records, check with the utility companies in the subject's area to see what, if any, information is available. Utility records might contain the phone number of the customer, even if that number is unlisted. In addition, be sure to check the names of friends or relatives.

County Government Records

The following items are basic types of public records that can be accessed at the county level of government:
- County court records
- County coroner's register
- County personnel department records
- Building permit records
- Public school records
- Voter registration records
- County recorder's office records
- Sheriff or county prosecutor records
- County fire marshal records
- Regulatory agency records
- Welfare commission records

County Court Clerk

The majority of an individual's civil records can be found at the county courthouse in the jurisdiction where the subject does business or resides. A great deal of litigation occurs each year, and many people might be subject to judicial action, voluntarily or not. Researching civil and criminal suits can provide invaluable information assisting in:
- Locating individuals
- Identifying pending actions
- Uncovering closed cases
- Insight into marital status (family)
- Tracing sources of funds (probate)
- Identifying financial conditions (bankruptcy)
- Litigation history
- Outstanding judgments

Although a wealth of information is available in court files, civil or criminal actions might not be readily known and the researcher must be able to identify the jurisdiction, county, or court involved.

Collecting Documentary Evidence

The investigator will typically have access to microfiche listings of cases or parties within the individual court system through the clerk's office. Some courts are set up to provide computerized access to this information. Normally, one must be able to provide a case number in order to access the actual court file. The Party Name Index will provide the case number.

Court clerks maintain files on all active and closed lawsuits in their jurisdictions. Information regarding these suits is public record and can be searched by scanning the indexes for the subject's name as a plaintiff or defendant.

Subject data fields will contain:
- The complaint for or against the subject (direct and reverse indexes)
- The subject's last known address (either through the lawsuit's pleadings or the court officer's citation and subpoena returns)
- Other personal information on the subject, depending on the type of suit

Court levels vary by jurisdiction, as do the names of the levels. Different case types are filed at different levels and in different courts.

Different levels of courts are assigned jurisdiction over any given case, based on court issues and the nature of the claim. To determine the full extent of the litigation history against a company or individual, the examiner must search each of the various types of local court records.

CIVIL COURT RECORDS

The key to locating civil court records is knowing the correct spelling of your subject's name, where the person currently lives, and where he lived in the past.

Depending on the type of suit, civil court records will provide potentially valuable information.

PERSONAL INJURY SUIT RECORDS

Records for a personal injury suit, for example, will often contain an accident report, injury history, statements of the involved parties, and the financial settlement of the case.

FINANCIAL SUIT RECORDS

Financial suit records will disclose an individual's debtors and creditors, and they will present an outside view of a business's history or ability to perform.

DIVORCE RECORDS

Divorce record searches will return marriage partner names, addresses, location of marriage, divorce filing date, and file number. In addition, divorce records frequently contain the subject's financial inventory, which is submitted at the time of the divorce or separation, and should also include the partition of assets to each party in the settlement.

CRIMINAL COURT RECORDS

When conducting a criminal records search, certain types of information are critical. Like civil courts, criminal courts across the country are divided into jurisdictions that generally encompass a single county in a single state.

Although most states have their criminal courts divided by county, some states offer indexes with criminal convictions for the entire state.

Criminal convictions should not be confused with criminal filings. When you search for criminal records at the county level, you will find all cases filed by the district attorney, even if the person was not found guilty of a crime. When searching a statewide convictions database, you will find only cases that resulted in conviction.

The county criminal court clerk maintains criminal court files that might contain information describing a subject's offenses and the counts. These files might also contain the complainant's signature (exemplar); a transcript of the preliminary hearing; the names of the prosecuting and defense attorneys; the probation officer's report, with a background investigation of the defendant; and the subpoenas issued in the case.

PROBATE COURT RECORDS

Probate court records are documents filed to show the dispersal of assets after a subject's death. The probate court conducts an investigation to verify any debts owed by an individual estate and sees to the dispersal of assets according to the deceased's will (or in case there is no will, by state law) after all debts are paid.

The debts left in an individual's estate may show:
- Names of individuals having an interest in the deceased's estate
- The subject's financial position at the time of death

The dispersal of assets may reveal:
- The names and addresses of heirs to the deceased
- Some indication of the value of the property willed to them

Collecting Documentary Evidence

County Coroner
A county coroner's register generally contains the name or a description of the deceased; date of inquest, if any; property found on the deceased and its disposition; and the cause of death.

Personnel Department Records
A county personnel department maintains information similar to that maintained by a city personnel department.

Building Permit Records
If a business or individual constructs a new building or makes improvements to an existing building, there should be a building permit on file with the local building authority. In addition, before most businesses can open their doors, the city or county may require that they possess certain permits. The local fire department may require permits ensuring that the business complies with the fire code. The city health department will require permits for restaurants or other businesses that serve food. Planning and zoning departments enforce regulations regarding the types of businesses and their locations.

Public School Records
County public school systems maintain information similar to that found in city public school systems. Access to these records is limited and is regulated by the Family Educational Rights and Privacy Act.

Voter Registration Records
To be eligible to vote, U.S. citizens must be registered in their respective precincts. To register, citizens must fill out a registration application. The information required to process the application includes: name, address, date of birth, signature, and Social Security number.

Voter registration records are routinely verified by the county and old addresses are deleted as new ones appear.

County Recorder's Office Records
A county recorder is a government office responsible for maintaining public records and documents, especially records relating to real estate ownership. A county recorder's office maintains the following information:
- Documents pertaining to real estate transactions—including deeds, grants, transfers and mortgages of real estate, releases of mortgages, powers of attorney, and leases that have been acknowledged or approved
- Mortgages on personal property
- Marriage license records and applications including information on previous marriages, maiden names, addresses, and dates of birth

Collecting Documentary Evidence

- Wills admitted to probate
- Official bonds
- Notices of mechanic's liens
- Transcripts of judgments that are made for liens on real estate
- Notices of attachment on real estate
- Papers in connection with bankruptcy
- Certified copies of decrees and judgments of courts of record
- Other documents permitted by law to be recorded, such as the Department of Defense's DOD 214 forms that are recorded by some veterans as evidence of veteran status, particularly in those states where veterans are granted reduced property tax rates

Real estate transaction records are extremely important. They are relatively easy to access and contain a vast amount of information. Real estate records are usually found in the county in which the land is located. When an individual purchases real estate, he becomes a taxpayer and a registrant in the following county records: real property records, property tax records, and tax assessor records.

Each real estate transaction will list a deed verifying the transfer of the property. If an individual either buys or sells real property or it becomes subject to a state or federal lien, the transaction will be reflected in the county real property indexes. If improvements are made to the property, such as the addition of a new room or the installation of a pool, then a mechanic's lien or other notice may be on file in the county property records.

Real property records generally will include the following:
- Residency and addresses of the buyer and seller (referred to respectively as grantor and grantee)
- Price of the property (see tax stamps if listed)
- Mortgage company and amount originally financed
- Real estate ownership
- Who financed the transaction, if applicable
- Title companies involved
- Improvements to the property and the names and addresses of the contractors

In addition to the property records themselves, counties charge new landowners property taxes for upkeep of their schools, courthouses, police, and other public buildings. These records can provide:
- An idea of the estimated value, for tax purposes, of the property listed
- The identity of the owner of a vacant piece of land or a piece of property, if ownership is unknown
- The name of the last person to pay taxes on the property

Collecting Documentary Evidence

Video

In the video titled "Chapter II: Real Property Records," fraud investigation expert Jonathan Turner, CFE, further explains the usefulness of real estate records. (Go to www.acfe.com/internalinvestigations to view the video.)

Sheriff or County Prosecutor Records

The county sheriff or the county prosecutor may maintain general incident files related to the businesses within the county. Incident files can provide leads on managers or owners of the business or third parties who have made complaints against the business.

County Fire Marshal Records

The county fire marshal should have a record of any fires that have occurred at specific properties. These records may contain information about a property's insurer, as well as information about any previously conducted investigations.

Regulatory Agency Records

County regulatory agencies maintain information similar to that held by city regulatory agencies. County tax assessor's and collector's offices maintain information similar to that held by city tax assessor's offices.

Welfare Commission Records

Files of a county welfare commission are based on information gathered by social workers, psychologists, and physicians. Frequently, the recipient of benefits provides the information, which is generally not verified. Files contain such information as the recipient's address, previous employment, how much the recipient earned, property the recipient or the recipient's relatives might own, the state of the family's health, and criminal records.

State Government Records

The following items are basic types of public records that can be accessed at the state level of government:
- Business flings
- State court records
- Uniform Commercial Code filings
- Employee and labor department records
- State tax filings
- Professional associations and licensing boards
- State attorneys general records

- Workers' compensation records
- Department of motor vehicles records
- Bureau of vital statistics
- Other state regulatory agencies

Business Filings

To conduct business in a name other than one's own, the law requires the filing of documents of the ownership of that name. These documents can include:

- Articles of incorporation
- Foreign corporation registration
- DBA or fictitious name registration
- Tax-related filings

ARTICLES OF INCORPORATION

Corporations are formed by filing articles of incorporation with the secretary of state (or state corporation bureau or corporate registry office) in the state in which the company does business. These corporate records are public record and will include:

- Corporate name
- Ownership information
- Stock value
- Initial shareholders
- Names of the directors and officers
- Registered agent
- Location of the principal office
- Date of incorporation
- Standing or status

This information will permit the investigator to review a corporate structure, identify the registered agent, and trace incorporation dates. The records will often include limited partnership information as well. This might be particularly valuable in trying to trace the disposition of funds in a billing scheme.

FOREIGN CORPORATION REGISTRATION RECORDS

Some states require foreign corporations (i.e., corporations which were incorporated in another state) to register with the state corporation office if the foreign corporation transacts business in that state. For example, if a corporation that was chartered in Delaware wishes to transact business in Texas, it must file an Application for Certificate of Authority. The application is filed with the secretary of state and must include the date of incorporation, the principal office, the address of the registered agent, and the names of the officers and directors.

FICTITIOUS BUSINESS NAMES AND DOING BUSINESS AS INFORMATION

Doing business as (DBA) information for sole proprietorships (individuals) or partnerships is typically filed at the county level, although some states require filing at the state level as well. Most states also require limited partnerships, trusts, and joint ventures to file DBA information at the state or county level. DBA filings will provide insight into the true business venture behind the name. DBA information is very similar to corporate filings with the secretary of state, and these records will allow for the identification of the type of business entity, the date the business was started, and the owners or principals of the business.

State Court Records

STATE CIVIL COURT RECORDS

State civil court records searches are conducted by court, by county, and are divided between upper and lower courts (generally a monetary division) where applicable. Searches of state civil court records may return the identities of the plaintiff and defendant, case number, filing date, cause of action, and disposition or current status. Depending on the court, divorces, domestic, family law, child support, name changes, or probate matters may also be included.

STATE CRIMINAL COURT RECORDS

State criminal court records searches are conducted by court or by county for felonies, misdemeanors, or a combination of both. Searches of state civil court records may return the identity of the defendant, a physical description of the conduct, the arrest date, arresting agency, case number, filing date, charges, and disposition or current status. An index search is available for some states and counties, and most states have some type of release requirement for obtaining this information.

Uniform Commercial Code (UCC) Filings

A search of Uniform Commercial Code (UCC) filings can help you identify personal property than an individual or business has financed. This is because a lender must file UCC statements with the secretary of state or with the county-level unit.

Banks, finance companies, and other lenders will generate records or recorded filings of financial transactions conducted with individuals and businesses, such as:

- Household furniture
- Appliances
- Boats and yachts
- Automobiles
- Aircraft
- Business equipment

These filings, produced as the result of the transactions, will identify the:
- Name of the debtor or joint debtors
- Current address of the debtors
- Name of the financial lender
- Type of collateral pledged as security
- Date of filing and continuations

UCC filings can also disclose when and where a person obtains personal loans, the type of property pledged to secure the loan, and the current address of the debtor. And an itemized list of personal property held by the debtor.

These documents can be readily retrieved from the secretary of state's office, through service companies, or through online services.

Employee and Labor Department Records
Some states, under their labor departments, require the filing of periodic lists of employees—revealing their names, Social Security numbers, and salaries. In addition, by examining previous filings, an investigator can locate former employees.

State Tax Filings
Some state revenue departments require certain businesses to obtain licenses or permits, such as a sales tax permit. These licenses and applications are generally public record. If a business is delinquent in the payment of its taxes, the local or state tax investigator or collector might be able to provide inside information concerning the business.

Law enforcement officials might be able to gain access to corporate, business, and personal state tax information. These records might unwittingly reveal hidden assets or investments. Loans to or from officers, stockholders, or related entities should be examined closely. Also, mortgages, notes, and bonds shown as liabilities on a corporate return should be investigated. Tax returns might also disclose the identity of the accountant or attorney preparing the return.

Professional Associations and Licensing Boards
Many state and local agencies maintain records identifying individuals holding special licenses or memberships. These can include:
- Medical practitioners such as doctors, dentists, nurses
- Social workers
- Attorneys
- Certified Public Accountants

Collecting Documentary Evidence

- Real estate licensees
- Notaries
- Law enforcement personnel
- Firefighters
- Security guards
- Stockbrokers
- Teachers
- Insurance agents
- Private investigators
- Bail bond agents
- Travel agents
- Barbers, cosmetologists
- Contractors, engineers, electricians, architects

The licenses and applications granted by the state may be public record. Although some applications contain no more than a name and address, other applications contain lengthy personal information, such as previous residential addresses, previous employers, education and training, and financial statements. Some agencies are required to conduct a background investigation before issuance of a license.

Also, the state regulatory or licensing agency might have the authority to suspend or revoke the licenses necessary for the business to operate.

Many professional organizations maintain their own listings of members or licensees. They might be reluctant to provide information beyond the person's name and current standing in the association.

State Attorneys General Records
State attorneys general are good sources of information on whether a particular entity or individual was the subject of an enforcement action by a particular state. For links to the attorney general's website for any of the 50 states, consult the National Association of Attorneys General at www.naag.org.

Worker's Compensation Records
Records of worker's compensation claims are available in most states; however, the breadth of coverage will vary from state to state. Some states require some type of authorization from the target of the search. Worker's compensation searches may return the subject's name, Social Security number, date of birth, employer's name, date and type of accident, and nature and extent of inquiry.

The Americans with Disability Act, however, purports to prevent prospective employers from using workers' compensation records to deny employment to otherwise qualified job applicants.

Department of Motor Vehicles Records

The Department of Motor Vehicles (DMV) maintains information on drivers' licenses, vehicle registrations, titling, car dealers, car salespeople, wrecking yards, tow companies, smog inspection facilities, and (in some states) auto repair businesses.

DMV records were once thought to be good locator tools, but recent restrictions on the use of such data has reduced the effectiveness of such searches. Moreover, the update quality of individual state records supplied by state authorities may not be adequate to locating people in a transient, fast-paced society. Still, searches such as Driver Identification can be useful on a spot basis.

Vehicle ownership information will identify vehicles registered to a specific person or business. These records include trailers, motor homes, or motor vessels. Information on disability placards may also be available. Current ownership of a particular vehicle can be obtained through the use of a plate number or a vehicle identification number (VIN). Information returned will include plate number, VIN, expiration date, make, model, model year, registered owner's name and address, and legal owner's name and address.

However, federal law bars states from releasing drivers' Social Security numbers, photographs, or certain other information unless they obtain "the express consent" of each person in advance.

Bureau of Vital Statistics

A state's bureau of vital statistics, where birth certificates are generally filed, is an excellent source of information. Birth certificates can provide a child's name, sex, date of birth, and place of birth; the names of the attending physician, midwife, or other assistants; the parents' names, ages, addresses, races, places of birth, and occupations; the mother's maiden name; and the number of siblings. (In some states, birth certificates might be found at the city or county level.)

Other State Regulatory Agencies

At the state level, the following additional records can be found:
- Auto licenses, auto transfers, and sales of vehicles
- Civil service applications
- Driver's licenses
- Health department records
- Inheritance and gift tax returns
- Name changes
- Occupancy and business licenses
- Parole officers' and probation departments' files
- Personal property tax returns

Collecting Documentary Evidence

- School and voter registrations
- State income tax returns
- Welfare agency records

The following state departments and agencies might also maintain information valuable to fraud examiners:

- Bureau of Professional and Vocational Standards or the Department of Licensing (especially professional associations, partnerships, and corporations)
- Controller or treasurer
- Department of Agriculture
- Department of Industrial Relations
- Department of Natural Resources
- Horse-Racing Board and Gambling Commission
- Secretary of State (corporations division)
- State Board of Equalization
- State Police or Highway Patrol
- State Securities Commission
- State Utility Commission

Federal Government Records

A huge amount of information is available to the public through the various federal agencies. Information about these agencies can be obtained through the following reference guides:

- *Congressional Staff Directory and Federal Staff Directory*, prepared annually by Congressional Staff Directory, Ltd., Mount Vernon, Virginia
- *Congressional Directory*, prepared by the U.S. Government Printing Office
- *The United States Government Manual*, prepared by the National Archives

The following records are of particular note.

Federal Court Records
CIVIL AND CRIMINAL COURT RECORDS
Federal civil and criminal court records can provide valuable information, including the plaintiff and defendant's name, the case number, the filing date, the cause of action, and the case disposition of current status.

BANKRUPTCY COURT RECORDS
Bankruptcy proceedings are conducted in federal bankruptcy courts. In these courts, all documents filed with the court are public record and can be examined by anyone without charge. These on-site federal

court records may include the case number, debtor's name(s), Social Security number, address, filing date, chapter designation, and closure date. The search is available for all federal jurisdictions, usually covering a seven-year span that starts from the present and moves backward.

Bankruptcy documents are usually located in the federal bankruptcy court for the district where the debtor resided or had his principal place of business. When checking bankruptcy court records, the examiner should remember to check not only the individual or business filing for bankruptcy, but also any related businesses, principals, employees, or relatives.

A bankruptcy is initiated by the filing of a bankruptcy petition. The petition can be either voluntary or involuntary. Three or more creditors who have outstanding claims that have not been paid can file an involuntary petition.

The bankruptcy petition contains valuable information, such as the type of bankruptcy (voluntary or involuntary, Chapter 7, Chapter 11, etc.); Social Security number or tax ID number; street address and primary place of business; location of principal assets of business; type of business; name of attorney; estimated amount of assets; estimated number of creditors, liabilities, and employees; financial data; and a list of shareholders.

Inspectors General

Inspectors general can provide valuable information, especially to official law enforcement personnel, about businesses they have investigated or audited. They are also good guides to other information sources in their departments or agencies.

U.S. Postal Service

The Postal Service, which is responsible for providing postal service in the United States, maintains valuable information, including the names and addresses of post office box holders. Check with the local post office to learn the identity of the inspector who can furnish the information. Requests for copies of postal money orders are made through the local U.S. Postal Inspection Service office, usually by subpoena.

Social Security Administration

The Social Security Administration retains original applications for Social Security numbers. Applications list an applicant's name (maiden and married names for women), date of birth, place of birth, sex, race, parents' names, and address at time of application.

Collecting Documentary Evidence

Department of Housing and Urban Development

The Department of Housing and Urban Development's (HUD) Compliance Division conducts investigations of alleged HUD violations. This division handles investigations of false statements on credit applications for Federal Housing Administration (FHA) loans, mortgagers' certification of no outstanding obligations, cost certificates, and other areas of fraud. HUD maintains central index files in Washington, D.C., containing information regarding HUD programs and participants, including such individuals and businesses as mortgage companies, developers, and borrowers.

Department of Defense

The Department of Defense (DOD) maintains information concerning military pay, dependents, allotments, deposits, and other financial information is maintained by the following:

Army
Defense Finance and Accounting Service
Indianapolis Center
8899 East 56th Street
Indianapolis, IN 46249-0001
(888) 332-7411 (Select option #2)
Email: dfas.bean.jfl.mbx.ampo-inquiries@DFAS.MIL

Air Force
Defense Finance and Accounting Service
Indianapolis Center
8899 East 56th Street
Indianapolis, IN 46249-0875
(888) 332-7411 (Select option #2)
Email: dfas.bean.jfl.mbx.ampo-inquiries@DFAS.MIL

Navy
Defense Finance and Accounting Service
Cleveland Center
1240 East Ninth Street
Cleveland, OH 44199-2055
(888) 332-7411 (Select option #2)
Email: CCL-CATCH-62@DFAS.MIL

Marine Corps
Defense Finance and Accounting Service
Cleveland Center
1240 East 9th Street
Cleveland, OH 44199-2005
(888) 332-7411 (Select option #2)
Email: CCL-MC-CATCH62@DFAS.MIL

Department of Justice

The Department of Justice's U.S. National Central Bureau of the International Criminal Police Organization (USNCB-INTERPOL) has direct contact with law enforcement authorities in more than 187 INTERPOL member countries and access to Interpol's various databases containing information on wanted persons, terrorists, missing persons, stolen and lost passports and travel documents, stolen vehicles, and other law enforcement information. The USNCB, therefore, can request information regarding ownership, previous investigations, and any other material which is legally releasable. The information available is determined by the laws of the countries from which the material is requested.

The Bureau of Alcohol, Tobacco, Firearms, and Explosives (ATF) is a principal law enforcement agency within the U.S. Department of Justice that is dedicated to preventing terrorism, reducing violent crime, and protecting the United States. The ATF retains:

- Data on distilleries; wineries; breweries; manufacturers of tobacco products; wholesale and retail dealers of alcoholic beverages; and certain other manufacturers, dealers, and users of alcohol
- Investigative reports of alleged violations under its jurisdiction
- A list of federally licensed firearms manufacturers, importers, and dealers
- A complete list of all federally licensed explosive manufacturers, importers, and dealers
- Data on firearms licenses given; also conducts firearms licensee qualification and compliance inspections

Federal Bureau of Investigation

An agency within the Department of Justice, the Federal Bureau of Investigation (FBI), provides information on criminal records and fingerprints, as well as non-restricted information pertaining to criminal offenses and subversive activities. It also provides information about wanted, missing, and unidentified people and foreign fugitives. The FBI currently investigates cases involving counterterrorism, counterintelligence, cybercrime, public corruption, civil rights, white-collar crime, organized crime, major thefts, and violent crime.

The Integrated Automated Fingerprint Identification System, more commonly known as IAFIS, is a national fingerprint and criminal history system maintained by the FBI, Criminal Justice Information

Services (CJIS) Division. The IAFIS provides automated fingerprint search capabilities, latent searching capabilities, electronic image storage, and electronic exchange of fingerprints and responses, 24 hours a day, 365 days a year. As a result of submitting fingerprints electronically, agencies receive electronic responses to criminal ten-print fingerprint submissions within two hours and within 24 hours for civil fingerprint submissions.

The IAFIS maintains the largest biometric database in the world, containing the fingerprints and corresponding criminal history information for more than 55 million subjects in the Criminal Master File. The fingerprints and corresponding criminal history information are submitted voluntarily by state, local, and federal law enforcement agencies.

The FBI maintains the Index to State Criminal History Records and Criminal History Records of Federal Offenders.

Department of Labor

The Department of Labor (DOL) has information about the Federal Employees Compensation Act, the Job Partnership Training Act, the Occupational Safety Health Act, and the Mine Safety Health Act. The department retains substantial data on businesses that have special work programs affiliated with it.

Under the Employment Standards Administration of the DOL, the Office of Labor-Management Standards (OLMS) administers and enforces most of the provisions of the Labor-Management Reporting and Disclosure Act of 1959 (LMRDA). The LMRDA has reporting requirements for certain labor organizations, union officers and employees, employers, labor relations consultants, and surety companies. The LMRDA requires covered labor organizations to annually file reports with the OLMS. The information required includes names and titles of officers; rates of dues and fees; loans receivable; other investments; other assets; other liabilities; fixed assets; loans payable; sales of investments and fixed assets; disbursement to officers; disbursement to employees; purchase of investments and fixed assets; benefits; and contributions, gifts, and grants.

In addition, surety companies that issue bonds required by LMRDA or the Employee Retirement Income Security Act of 1974 (ERISA) are required to report premiums received and claims paid.

Department of the Treasury

The Department of the Treasury includes statutory inspector general law enforcement agencies.

Within the Internal Revenue Service (IRS), the Criminal Investigation (CI) Division conducts investigations of tax fraud relating to income tax, excise tax, occupational tax, and violations of currency-transaction reports. Enforcement efforts include tax violation, money laundering, currency crimes, and asset forfeiture. The release of taxpayer information to other than IRS personnel requires special procedures. The IRS Inspection Service maintains information on subjects of investigation and their relationships to IRS employees (e.g., threats made against, collusion with, and bribery of IRS employees).

The Financial Crimes Enforcement Network (FinCEN) safeguards the financial system from the abuses of financial crime, including terrorist financing, money laundering, and other illicit activities. FinCEN works to maximize information sharing among law enforcement agencies and its other partners in the regulatory and financial communities. Through cooperation and partnerships, FinCEN's network approach encourages cost-effective and efficient measures to combat money laundering domestically and internationally. The PATRIOT Act Section 314(b) permits financial institutions, upon providing notice to the United States Department of the Treasury, to share information with one another in order to identify and report to the federal governmental activities that may involve money laundering or terrorist activity. However, access to these records by outside parties is extremely limited.

Department of Homeland Security

Under the Border and Transportation Directorate of the Department of Homeland Security, the U.S. Customs and Border Protection Service retains data on businesses that are involved in imports and exports, including lists and records of importers, exporters, custom house brokers, and truckers. The Office of Investigations looks into alleged violations of import and export practices. The Customs and Border Protection Service is also involved in the National Narcotics Border Interdiction System, and special agents from the Office of Investigations have been participating in the Organized Crime Drug Enforcement Task Force. Customs might provide information relative to businesses that violate the statutes it enforces.

The U.S. Secret Service maintains records on forgers, counterfeiters, and businesses that have contacted the Service concerning forged or counterfeit obligations of the United States, such as Treasury notes. In addition, the Treasurer of the United States can provide copies of canceled checks paid by the U.S. Treasury. The Secret Service also investigates counterfeiting and other financial crimes, including financial institution fraud; identity theft; computer fraud; and computer-based attacks on our nation's financial, banking, and telecommunications infrastructure.

Department of Veterans Affairs

The Department of Veterans Affairs (VA) maintains records of loans, tuition payments, and insurance payments. Nonrestrictive medical data related to disability pensions is maintained at VA regional offices located in several metropolitan areas throughout the country.

Collecting Documentary Evidence

Drug Enforcement Administration
The Drug Enforcement Administration (DEA) maintains information on licensed handlers of narcotics and the criminal records of users, pushers, and suppliers of narcotics.

Federal Aviation Administration
The Federal Aviation Administration (FAA) maintains records reflecting the chain of ownership of all civil aircraft in the United States. These records include documents about the manufacture, sale, transfer, inspection, and modification of an aircraft, including the bill of sale, sales contract, mortgage, and liens.

The FAA also maintains records on pilots, aircraft mechanics, flight engineers, and other individuals whom it certifies for flight safety positions. These records include information on certificates held and medical and law enforcement history.

Federal Energy Regulatory Commission
Electric utility and natural gas companies are required to file annual reports with the Federal Energy Regulatory Commission. The reports provide excellent financial pictures of the companies and provide information about officers, directors, and stockholders who own more than ten percent of the company.

Federal Maritime Commission
The Federal Maritime Commission investigates applicants for licenses to engage in oceangoing freight-forwarding activities. Applicants provide information to the Commission covering most aspects of their history, including name, residence, date and place of birth, and citizenship of all corporate officers and directors; names of partnership members of individual proprietors; and names of direct holders of five percent or more of company stock.

General Services Administration
The General Services Administration (GSA) has considerable information on architects, engineers, personal property auctioneers, real estate appraisers, construction contractors, sales brokers, and businesses that contract with the GSA. The agency also maintains the "GSA Consolidated List," a computerized roster of suspended and debarred bidders.

Securities and Exchange Commission
The Securities and Exchange Commission (SEC) maintains public records of corporations with stocks and securities sold to the public. These records include the following information:
- Financial statements
- Identification of officers and directors
- Identification of owners of more than ten percent of a business's stock
- A description of the registrant's properties and businesses

- A description of the significant provisions of the security to be offered for sale and its relationship to the registrant's other capital securities
- Identification of events of interest to investors
- Identification of accountants and attorneys
- A history of the business

The SEC also maintains files on individuals and firms reported to it for violating federal or state securities laws. The information in these files pertains to official actions taken against such people and firms, including denials, refusals, suspensions, and revocations of registrations; injunctions, fraud orders, stop orders, and cease-and-desist orders; and arrests, indictments, convictions, sentences, and other official actions.

The SEC created EDGAR, the Electronic Data Gathering, Analysis, and Retrieval system, to perform automated collection, validation, indexing, acceptance, and forwarding of submissions by companies and others who are required by law to file forms with the SEC. Its primary purpose is to increase the efficiency and fairness of the securities market for the benefit of investors, corporations, and the economy by accelerating the receipt, acceptance, dissemination and analysis of time-sensitive corporate information filed with the agency.

All publicly traded companies, foreign and domestic, are required to file registration statements, periodic reports, and other forms electronically through EDGAR. Anyone can access and download this information for free through the SEC website at www.sec.gov/edgar.shtml.

Corporate filings include the following:
- Annual Report of Publicly Traded Company (Form 10-K): excerpts or complete report available via LexisNexis or Dialog databases(e.g., Disclosure)
- Quarterly Report of Publicly Traded Company (Form 10-Q): same as 10-K, but filed quarterly instead of annually
- Special Events in Publicly Traded Company (Form 8-K): transactions resulting in change of controlling interest
- Registration of Security (Form 8-A): prospectus and data relative to the issuer
- Registration of Security by Successor (Form 8-B): name of issuer, relationship to primary registrant or issuer
- Special Events in Foreign Security (Form 6-K): information similar to 10-K and 8-K, except the security is registered under another U.S. law
- *Report of Acquisition of Beneficial Ownership of Five percent or More of Capital Stock of Public Company* (Form 13-D): identity of each person or firm acquiring beneficial ownership of five percent or more of capital stock, or identity of each person or firm constituting a group that acquires such beneficial

ownership; description of security; agreements or other undertakings by reporting entity; if acquisition results in change of control, background on each person reporting; and sources of funds for acquisition, purpose of acquisition, and relationship of parties

U.S. Small Business Administration

The U.S. Small Business Administration (SBA) is a federal agency that provides support to small businesses. The SBA guarantees loans made by private lenders and makes direct loans for business construction, expansion, or conversion; for purchase of machinery, equipment, facilities, supplies, or materials; and for working capital. A loan applicant (sole owner, partnership, corporation, or other) must complete SBA forms, providing information about the business and its principals (owners, officers, and directors).

Additionally, the SBA arranges contracts and guarantees loans for qualified, small, minority-owned businesses. For some of these businesses, the SBA might be the only source for financial and other information about the businesses, their principals, their assets, and other data. Because their stock is not publicly held, these businesses are not subject to public disclosure laws.

The SBA also connects small firms owned by socially and economically disadvantaged Americans with contracts set aside by other federal agencies for the purposes of increasing opportunities for small businesses generally.

U.S. Citizenship and Immigration Services

Formerly the Immigration and Naturalization Service, the U.S. Citizenship and Immigration Services (USCIS) is a bureau of the Department of Homeland Security. The USCIS is charged with overseeing lawful immigration in the United States, and it retains a number of records, including alien registration records issued after August 27, 1940 (from July 1, 1920, to August 27, 1940, each immigrant was given an Immigrant's Identification Card); lists of passengers and crews on vessels from foreign ports; passenger manifests and declarations (ship, date, and point of entry); naturalization records (names of witnesses to naturalization proceedings and acquaintances of the individual); deportation proceedings; and financial statements of aliens and people sponsoring an immigrant entry.

Bureau of Public Debt

The Bureau of Public Debt maintains information on purchased and redeemed U.S. saving bonds (registered bonds), marketable securities, and special securities. Information maintained includes the series of bonds involved and the surname, given name, middle name or initial, and address of each person in whose name bonds were purchased.

Collecting Documentary Evidence

Using Databases to Find Information

Access to an online database service is accomplished in either one of two ways. Some services allow users to log in through an Internet site. Others provide access to their database through a software program and a modem. Each user has a user ID and password to gain access.

The following is a description of how online searches can be used to conduct background checks and locate people, assets, and legal records.

Locating People Using Online Records

The first step to maximize search results is to discover a past address of the suspect; search activities should begin from that point. Second, the user should know the most powerful and useful types of searches, which are identified below. Third, it is important to keep in mind the cost effectiveness of the search activity and avoid ordering online searches that yield unnecessary or impractical information.

The search methodology used by most online services is known as "text-string matching," which means that all information entered in the data inquiry field will seek an exact match in the database. Typically, truncation techniques (partial or abbreviated entries, such as the first initial of the first name) may be used only with first names and business names.

Some common types of searches used to locate people using online records are discussed below.

Types of Searches

- *Credit header* searches are among the most powerful people locator tools. These searches return information from credit reports on individuals. They are a valuable source because almost all people have been involved in some credit activity either under their true names or assumed (or known as) names. It is appropriate to keep in mind that for common names, it may be necessary to use the Social Security number or date of birth to differentiate the subject from other people with the same name. The credit bureau headers offer two search mechanisms. First, the examiner can discover a current address, an address history, and Social Security number(s) associated with the target by using a past address up to seven years old. Second, once the Social Security number is in hand, the headers can be searched for matches, because the Social Security number is a national identity number. Although Social Security numbers are protected from disclosure by the Privacy Act, it has become practically impossible for individuals to avoid disclosing them on public records.
- *A current occupant or new address* search may be used to identify the occupant of an address, to confirm occupancy, to uncover a forwarding address, or to develop a list of neighbors who might know the suspect's current whereabouts.
- *Last name* searches can be used if the past address is unknown. This search produces better results if the name is not common; however, if the last name is common, differentiating information should

Collecting Documentary Evidence

be included in the search. It should also be noted that some searches will return the identities of neighbors, who can be contacted for additional information about the suspect.

- *Bankruptcy filings, tax liens, and court judgments* have emerged in recent years as locator tools because such records contain valid Social Security numbers. The dramatic increase in individual bankruptcy claims has also prompted an increased use of these search tools.
- *Department of Motor Vehicles (DMV)* records used to be good locator tools, but recent restrictions on them have reduced the effectiveness of such searches. Moreover, individual states may not update their records frequently enough to provide the examiner with useful information. Searches such as *Driver Identification* can be useful on a spot basis, however.
- *Voter registration* records are available in a few states, but as with DMV records, they may not be updated frequently. However, to the extent that date of birth information is available, such records can augment other searches. Also note any legal restrictions attached to the use of voter information.
- *Fictitious business name and doing business as* filings include owner name(s), business name(s), file date, and file number. Some counties provide business address information, and the examiner can also conduct searches using the business address.
- *Federal Tax ID Searches* involve using the IRS website (www.irs.gov) to enter both the name and Federal Tax ID of a vendor or other business to confirm that the two match.

Obtaining Financial Information and Locating Assets

Discovering whether assets exist, where they exist, and whether they are recoverable can be accomplished with a search of federal, state, local, and proprietary records. These records can be further divided into those identifying "hard" assets and those regarding the potential for assets, credit capacity, or credit worthiness.

Searches for Hard Assets

- The ownership of real property may be discoverable through the use of *property* searches, to the extent that they are available at the local or county level within individual states.
- The ownership of vehicles can be inferred through the use of the *DMV Vehicle Name Index*, to the extent that the records within the controlling state agency reflect vehicles registered to a specific person or organization at a particular address. Conversely, the ownership of a particular vehicle might be inferred from the *DMV vehicle registration* searches.
- An assumed business name search might be helpful in identifying a sole proprietorship business in which attachable assets are available.
- The *Uniform Commercial Code (UCC)* is extraordinary in that it can be useful in a wide variety of business situations. A search of UCC filings can help identify personal property that an individual or business has financed. UCC filings can also disclose when and where a debtor obtained personal loans, the type of property that he pledged to the lender to secure the loan, and the debtor's current address.

- The ownership of an aircraft can be determined by searching the *Aircraft Ownership Database* by business name, person name, or wing number.

Searches for Asset Potential
- The question of whether it is realistically possible to recover known assets may be partially answered by searching bankruptcy filings, tax liens, and tax judgments.
- Again, the versatility of a UCC filings search is seen through the identification of assets that may have been pledged, in whole or in part, to secure a loan.
- Consumer credit report and business credit report searches may develop a clearer picture of the target's potential for asset recovery in terms of credit capacity and creditworthiness. Unlike consumer credit reports, business credit reports are not governed by the FCRA.

Finding Legal Records
The searches available to find these records can be grouped in three broad categories: on-site court searches, index or broad coverage searches, and public filings.

On-Site Court Searches
On-site court records searches are performed by individuals who travel to county and municipal courthouses to search for records that match the search criteria that have been provided to them.

These searches are directed by court, by county, or, as is the case with federal records, by the district court for the particular area. Accordingly, the examiner must carefully consider the potential location of court records. Such considerations should take into account the locations of the suspect's current and past residences and his current and past businesses or employers. The results will include any litigation in which the individual was involved, including civil actions, criminal actions, divorces, and judgments. However, it will not return information concerning litigation that has been sealed by the court or information concerning juvenile offenders.

The coverage for these searches varies according to the service used. Additionally, each court has varying rules regarding how the search is conducted, the times when searches may be conducted, the repository location, and search methods. If the subscriber is interested in a particular type of record, such as a divorce record, it might be necessary to call the company's customer-support unit to adjust the search query. Types of records available include:
- Federal civil court records, including bankruptcy records, are available for all types of civil litigation conducted in federal court.
- Federal criminal court records are available for felony charges.
- State civil court records are available based on a division of upper and lower court records. The division is a function of the differences within each state concerning the amounts in controversy.

- State criminal court records can be obtained on a ten- or seven-year search basis for felonies, misdemeanors, or a combination of both.

Index and Broad Coverage Searches

These searches are useful when an examiner needs a search strategy broader than the by court/by county method used with on-site court record searches or that makes use of an index of basic information in court records.
- Searches of defendant suits are available in all states but provide coverage limited to specific counties and courts. When searching a specific state's database, the examiner should review the help menu to determine the scope of the search abilities.
- Searches of statewide criminal convictions are available in some jurisdictions. Review the help menu for special release requirements, the number of years available, if the record is for convictions only, and if the search encompasses both felonies and misdemeanors.
- Searches of marriage and divorce indexes are available in some states.

Conducting Background Checks

This type of search activity generally involves two broad areas: discovering what the public records reveal with respect to individuals and businesses with whom the subscriber may wish to do business and discovering information about prospective employees. In general, online public records databases are generally the best sources of background information.

But before conducting any background checks, consult with legal counsel, as certain regulations (such as the FCRA) may apply to the use of third-party data collectors.

Due Diligence

As business organizations seek to identify vendors, clients, or strategic partners, or seek to loan or collect money, they frequently conduct public record inquiries focused on other businesses or individuals who are principals of business organizations. This type of public record inquiry involves such issues as verification of application information, debt burden, adverse financial information, credit capacity or worthiness, business relationships (the so-called family tree), litigation history, and criminal background. Useful searches include the following:
- Corporate or limited partnership searches are available in all states to verify information, identify principals, and develop other business relationships.
- Bankruptcy filings, tax liens, and judgments searches respond to issues of adverse financial information and credit capacity and worthiness.
- UCC filings answer questions of debt burden. This search will be helpful to identify hidden ownership or partnership interests, and it will be helpful to locate address information on debtors.

- State and federal civil court records provide answers to questions concerning litigation history, past business relationships, and the potential for debt burden either as a function of an adverse judgment or as a function of financing expensive litigation.
- State and federal criminal court records identify the possibility of a criminal background.
- The use of consumer credit reports and business credit reports helps resolve questions concerning credit capacity and creditworthiness. In addition, the business report is useful in verifying information, understanding business relationships, and developing basic financial information about an organization.
- Occupational Safety and Health Administration *(OSHA)* searches may be useful in developing adverse information or verifying information given by a prospective vendor, client, or strategic partner.
- Aircraft mechanics, airmen, medical licenses, DEA controlled substances, and other licenses may serve to verify that basic professional and occupational standards are met by a prospective vendor, client, or strategic partner.

Employment Background

Online record inquiries regarding employment history have increased significantly over the past few years. Corporate downsizing has disaffected an increasing number of workers to the point that it is easier for them to rationalize employee defalcation, fraud, or embezzlement. The same economic phenomenon of downsizing, combined with business pressure to increase productivity and the friction of modern life, have apparently produced an increase in workplace violence. Liabilities for employers and businesses have expanded through negligence standards and the *respondeat superior* doctrine for such tortious conduct as vehicle operation, assault, battery, false imprisonment, sexual harassment, and discrimination. Finally, the potential to be held liable for negative references has deterred past employers from responding to prospective employers' inquiries about an employee. Therefore, prospective employers must increasingly rely on public information.

Some of the searches useful in developing background information (where permitted by law) are listed below:
- Credit header searches are useful in confirming address and Social Security number information.
- State and federal criminal court records and statewide criminal convictions may be used to uncover past criminal problems presaging similar difficulties. Indeed, criminal background checks may be mandated by law. For example, the Violent Crime Control and Law Enforcement Act of 1994 makes it a felony for insurance companies, as well as people employing anyone to conduct the business of insurance, to hire any individual convicted of a felony involving dishonesty or a breach of trust.
- Aircraft mechanics, airmen, medical licenses, and other licenses are available to ensure that basic job requirements are met in the appropriate circumstance.

Collecting Documentary Evidence

- Consumer credit reports may be obtained for purposes of employee selection, retention, and promotion.
- Public filings such as bankruptcy filings, tax liens, and judgments may be obtained to identify adverse financial matters that can serve as potential motivators for fraud, defamation, and embezzlement.
- Where a prospective or current employee drives a personally owned vehicle or an employer-owned vehicle in furthering the interests of the employer, such activity may expose the employer to liability for damages; therefore, *DMV* driving records must be checked.
- Basic information concerning job qualification can be verified through education verification and employment verification searches. Note: These are verification tools only; they are not definitional in terms of discovering past or current employment.
- Although workers' compensation searches may return the subject's name, Social Security number, date of birth, employer's name, date and type of accident, and nature and extent of inquiry, the Americans with Disabilities Act may limit usage of the search results. The Act purports to prevent prospective employers from using workers' compensation records in denying employment to otherwise qualified applicants.

Public Record Database Vendors

Listed below is information about some of the larger records service companies. You can shop various services to find the one that meets your needs in the most cost-effective manner and the one that fits your current case. In some instances, it might be necessary to use more than one service to get an accurate and complete profile. These companies get their information from various sources and on various update schedules, so a search in any one database might return different results than a search done elsewhere.

Primary Online Information Vendors

The following list contains the names and websites of some of the companies that offer wide access to public records, credit reports, and newspapers and periodicals.

KNOWX

KnowX is a product of the LexisNexis Risk and Information Analytics Group, and it claims to be the most comprehensive source of public information on the Web. It offers public records searches in various categories, including asset searches, adverse filings, property valuation, and people- and business-locator tools. One can also verify licenses, conduct background checks, and look up a company's history. Users can run KnowX's business background check to uncover bankruptcies, judgments, lawsuits, liens, and UCC filings against a business. In addition, KnowX's asset locator service enables users to locate assets such as real estate, aircraft, and watercraft. KnowX can be found at www.knowx.com.

ACCURINT

Accurint is a LexisNexus service and one of the most widely used public records databases on the Internet. Subscribers gain access to Accurint's claimed 34 billion public records including names, aliases, phone numbers, property ownership, bankruptcy, and historic personal information. Accurint is also useful as a relational tool to find a search target's associates, neighbors and relatives. Accurint can be found at www.accurint.com.

INFOUSA

infoUSA compiles business and consumer data, and it offers a wide range of data processing services. infoUSA users have access to information on 14 million U.S. businesses, 13 million executives and professionals, and 210 million U.S. consumers. Searches of infoUSA's database can produce results for a broad range of information, including sales volume, corporate linkage, contact names and titles, company history, credit ratings, and any headlines involving the business. Furthermore, searches can be performed according to business size, location, length of time in operation, gender or race of owners, and industry. infoUSA is located at www.infousa.com.

CSC

CSC (Corporation Service Company) is a Web-based due diligence service. CSC can produce a business's financial statements, records pertaining to corporate status, business credit, and licensing information. UCC filings, bankruptcy, judgments, and corporate good-standing searches are also available through this service. CSC is located at www.cscfinancialonline.com.

PROQUEST DIALOG

ProQuest Dialog offers users access to more than 1,200 databases. It contains nearly 2 billion records, including references and abstracts of published literature; statistical tables; the full text of selected articles; and directory, business, and financial data. Proquest Dialog can be accessed at www.proquest.com.

DUN & BRADSTREET

Dun & Bradstreet (D&B) is a business information service provider. It is probably one of the most comprehensive and diverse sources available, with facts on more than 130 million companies in more than 190 countries. D&B products include the *Business Information Report* and *Industry Norms and Key Business Ratios*. D&B can be accessed at www.dnb.com.

HOOVER'S

Hoover's, a D&B company, provides comprehensive, up-to-date business information on U.S. and global companies, industries, and professionals. Hoover's database consists of 65 million companies, with in-depth coverage of 40,000 public and non-public U.S. and international companies. Subscribers

Collecting Documentary Evidence

also have access to information on more than 15 million small, private businesses across the United States. Hoover's is located at www.hoovers.com.

EXPERIAN

Experian is one of the major providers of consumer credit information, and it provides a variety of other public information. Experian provides services on consumer and business credit, direct marketing, and real estate information services. Experian maintains credit information on more than 210 million U.S. consumers and more than 18 million U.S. businesses. Experian can be found at www.experian.com.

DCS INFORMATION SYSTEMS

DCS is a provider of online investigative solutions for business and government. DCS provides information comprising public records and publicly available information through its AmeriFind service, which they claim covers 95 percent of the adult population. DCS can be found at www.dcsinfosys.com.

G.A. PUBLIC RECORDS SERVICES

G.A. Public Records Services provides on-site county-level criminal record information. The company claims the ability to provide reports within 24-72 hours from any of more than 3,100 counties. G.A. Public Records Services provides search services for employment screening, corporate due diligence, fraud investigations, private investigations, and tenant screening. G.A. Public Record Services can be found at gaprs.thomsonreuters.com.

TRANSUNION

TransUnion is one of the big three credit report companies, and it offers credit information and services for consumers and businesses. More specifically, TransUnion is a global provider of business intelligence services including credit-decision and fraud-prevention tools, advanced target-marketing products, risk and profitability models, and portfolio management. TransUnion can be found at www.transunion.com.

Newspaper and Media Databases

Newspapers, periodicals, and journals can be excellent sources of information in a fraud investigation, particularly when searching for background information on an individual or a business. Searchable databases containing information from literally hundreds of sources can usually be accessed for free at most libraries. There are also a number of online databases that deal specifically with news and media resources. These databases compile a number of different media resources and allow the user to search for a specific topic, returning articles or transcripts that pertain to the requested subject. Most publications allow users to at least search their archives for free; the full text article is available, usually for a fee.

Newspaper and media databases have a clear advantage over the individual websites of daily newspapers on the Internet (which will be discussed in the next section) because these services allow the user to search thousands of sources at the same time. For instance, when searching for information on Dell, a media resource database will almost certainly return articles from around the world. The speed at which an investigator can conduct such searches with the aid of one of these databases makes them a valuable resource. Listed below are some of the largest databases of newspaper and magazine articles.

FACTIVA

Factiva, from Dow Jones, is tailored for business and financial news searches, maintaining a catalog of more than 28,000 of the world's leading news and business sources from 159 countries, 350 geographic regions, and in 23 languages. Factiva allows users to pay only for the articles downloaded and does not require an annual subscription. For more information, visit www.factiva.com.

LEXISNEXIS

LexisNexis is a legal and business information database that provides its subscribers with daily newspapers for either a flat fee or a per-use fee. LexisNexis maintains a cavernous database of U.S. and international media sources, including daily newspapers, magazines, and television transcripts. In addition, LexisNexis offers a service in which the user can request immediate information on difficult-to-find topics. LexisNexis will research the topic and give the user the information as quickly as possible. For more information, visit www.lexisnexis.com.

HIGHBEAM RESEARCH

HighBeam has an extensive archive containing millions of documents from leading publications that are updated daily and go back as far as 20 years. Searchable sources include newspapers, magazines, journals, transcripts, books, dictionaries, and almanacs. For more information, visit www.highbeam.com.

PROQUEST

ProQuest is a data service that offers access to thousands of online journals and magazines covering a wide array of subjects. ProQuest's vast content pools are available to researchers through libraries of all types and include the world's largest digital newspaper archive; periodical databases comprising the output of thousands of titles and spanning more than 500 years, with many in full-text, full-image format; an extensive dissertation collection; and various other scholarly collections. For more information, visit www.proquest.com.

OTHER NEWS DATABASE SERVICES

- Newspapers on the Net (www.onlinenewspapers.com)
- Newswise (www.newswise.com)

Investigating with the Internet

A great deal of information can be accessed through the Internet for little or no cost. This section explains how the Internet can assist in obtaining information about people, businesses, and fraud.

Pitfalls of the Internet

Upon listening to various national media reports or the promises of Internet service providers, it is very easy to believe that by logging on to the Internet, a user can simply type the subject of interest into the computer and be instantly provided with pertinent information.

In practice, the Internet is not as all-knowing as the advertisements would lead one to believe. While there is certainly a wealth of information to be found on the Internet, not everything can be located there. The information available on any given subject (health care fraud, for example) is solely dependent on an individual or company making that information available on the Web.

Even when the information is out there, it can still be difficult to find. Persistence is a quality that an investigator must possess when surfing the Net. When using a search engine to seek out a topic, one should understand that just because one search engine does not return any solid websites, it does not mean that a website isn't out there somewhere. When researching, the fraud examiner should use at least three different search engines every time if the search is to be considered thorough.

Finally, one must make certain that the information that is found is from a credible source. One truly unique aspect of the Internet is that it offers any person the opportunity to express an opinion or disseminate information. The fact that the Internet is a truly democratic forum is a virtue; it is also, unfortunately, one of its greatest weaknesses. Any conspiracy theorist can create a website that makes all sorts of outlandish claims with little fear of reprimand. The Internet is not a newspaper and it certainly is not a library. Information gathered on the Internet is only as credible as the source from which it came.

Search Engines

The most basic way to find information is to execute Internet searches using search engines and website directories. Search engines are website tools that allow you to type in keywords describing the subject in which you are interested. The search engine will then scour the pages of the Internet and attempt to locate pages that may have pertinent information. For instance, in a search for the keyword *fraud*, the search engine will likely bring back a number of pages that have some relevant link to fraud (such as the Association of Certified Fraud Examiners' website, located at www.acfe.com). There are several prominent search engines on the Internet, and each functions in a different way. An extensive list of search engines is provided at the end of the chapter; however, a few of the more popular sites are described below.

Collecting Documentary Evidence

Google
Google is the most popular and well-known search engine. In addition to Web searches, Google offers several other services that can be useful during an investigation, such as Google Street View or Google Blog Search. Individual Web pages are ranked by the engine's software according to how often the page is linked to by others, determining the page's "importance" by the number of links and the identity of the linking page. Google can be found at www.google.com.

Bing
Bing is currently the second ranked Web search engine and is owned by Microsoft. Like Google, Bing offers several services that investigators might find useful. Bing automatically groups search results in different categories, depending on the type of searches users are conducting. Bing also provides the ability to save and share search histories via Windows Live SkyDrive, Facebook, and email. Bing can be found at www.bing.com.

Yahoo!
Yahoo! is a multifaceted website containing a first-rate directory and equipped with an excellent search engine. Yahoo!'s filters will return far fewer pages than some other search engines, concentrating on ten to twenty pages that will likely be of interest. Investigators should not use Yahoo! to find minute, hard-to-discover information, but it is a good source for locating information they're sure is out there. Yahoo! can be found at www.yahoo.com.

Ask.com
Formerly known as AskJeeves, Ask.com is a good site for beginners and for general queries. The engine leads users through questions to help narrow the search, and also searches six other search sites. (For similar services, see the upcoming section on metasearch engines.) Ask.com's ability to interpret natural language makes it easy to use, though constructing precise queries can be difficult for the same reason. Ask.com can be found at www.ask.com.

A Guide to Successful Searching
Running Searches
Search engines all have their limitations, but the most serious impediment to locating good information is the user's lack of search skills.

Most searches use keywords. For instance, hunting for the latest statistics on check fraud, the logical keywords are *check* and *fraud*. But if you typed in those words, the search engine would return numerous sites that have nothing to do with check fraud. By placing both words inside quotation marks ("check fraud") you will get better results. Still, the list of hits will be in the thousands, so you might want to narrow the search using the techniques below.

Boolean Operators

The best way to use a search engine is to use two, or possibly three, keywords that best describe the topic. If the words succeed one another, as in the case of "check fraud," then it may be beneficial to use *Boolean operators* to aid one's search. Boolean operators are symbols that help the search engine to better understand exactly what it is searching for. Putting the "+" symbol in "check+fraud," for example, will indicate to the search engine that it is to search only for pages that have the word *fraud* immediately following *check*. If you insert the word *and*, so that the search reads "check and fraud," the search engine will understand to search for websites and pages that contain both the words "check" and "fraud," but not necessarily right next to each other.

Some of the more common Boolean operator symbols, or connectors, are shown below.

Boolean Operators

+	Designates words that must appear right next to each other.
−	Designates words that should not appear on a Web page.
" "	Designates a list of words that must appear together in an exact order, such as "holy cow."
and	Designates two or more words that must both appear on a page, but not necessarily next to each other.
or	Designates two connected words, one of which must appear on a page.
not	Designates words that should not appear on the page, much like the minus sign.
near	Designates words that should appear within a certain number of words of each other.
( )	Designates a group of advanced search keywords together.

Directories

The road to mining information on the Internet does not always go through search engines. Some of the best investigative tools an examiner has online are directories. As the name suggests, *directories* are specialized websites that collect the names of numerous other related websites, allowing the user to browse through a complete listing of possible sites to visit. Directories contain direct links to pages that have a common interest. Some all-inclusive directories that cover a plethora of different topics, and there are others that are more focused on particular subjects or disciplines. These include several accounting and auditing directories that fraud examiners might find very useful.

Collecting Documentary Evidence

The upside to using directories is that you can logically navigate a search, easing through the different categories until you find what you are looking for. However, directories contain only a portion of the sites and pages available on the Internet, so fraud examiners should use directories in concert with a search engine and not instead of one.

Yahoo! Directory

In addition to its search engine, Yahoo! has an intricate directory, possibly the most comprehensive and all-inclusive on the Internet. The directory is built and maintained by Yahoo! employees, with input from users. Yahoo! functions much like a pyramid, beginning with several large pools of categories, such as entertainment and government, and allowing the user to select more specific options from each. For instance, an examiner could select *education,* then *universities,* then *university libraries,* until he encounters a direct link to the main library catalog for the University of Texas. By paring down your selections to increasingly narrow topics, you can usually find several useful websites. Yahoo! Directory can be found at dir.yahoo.com.

WWW Virtual Library

The Virtual Library (VL) is the oldest catalog of the Web, started by Tim Berners-Lee, the creator of HTML. Unlike commercial catalogs, it is run by a loose confederation of volunteers who compile pages of key links for particular areas in which they are experts. While not the biggest index available, the VL pages are widely praised as guides to particular sections of the Internet. The URL is vlib.org.

Internet Public Library

Run by librarians, this service indexes Web pages by topic. The Internet Public Library also contains an array of guides, such as online magazines and newspapers, associations, and tips for conducting research. The Internet Public Library can be found at www.ipl.org.

Internet Archive

The Internet Archive is a nonprofit organization seeking to archive vast swaths of Internet data for posterity. Most applicable for investigative research is the Wayback Machine, which has archived more than 435 billion Web pages since 1996. This is useful for when searching for older online information that has been deleted or changed. The Internet Archive can be found at archive.org.

Meta-search Engines

Meta-search engines send user requests to several other search engines and display the results. Some of the more common meta-search engines are described below.

Metacrawler

Metacrawler uses meta-search technology to search the Internet's top search engines, including Google, Yahoo! Search, Bing, Ask.com, and more. It searches the best results from the combined pool of the world's leading search engines, instead of results from only one search engine. Metacrawler can be found at www.metacrawler.com.

Dogpile

Owned by Infospace, this engine sends a query to a customizable list of search engines, directories, and specialty search sites (e.g., Google, Yahoo! Search, Bing, Ask) and then displays the results from each search engine individually. Once the results are retrieved, the innovative meta-search technology used by Dogpile goes to work removing duplicates and analyzing the results to help ensure that the best results top the list. The Comparison View feature lets users compare results from the leading engines. Dogpile can be found at www.dogpile.com.

Mamma

Mamma is a "smart" meta-search engine; every time users type in a query, Mamma searches a variety of engines, directories, and content sites; properly formats the words and syntax for each; compiles their results in a virtual database; eliminates duplicates; and displays them in a uniform manner according to relevance. Mamma can be found at www.mamma.com.

Useful Websites

The following is a link to a list of websites grouped by topic that should prove useful to fraud examiners and other anti-fraud professionals:

www.acfe.com/uploadedFiles/ACFE_Website/Content/documents/sample-documents/Useful-Websites-2014.pdf

Review Questions

1. The Freedom of Information Act (FOIA) provides for public access to which type of information?
   A. Trust records
   B. Divorce or probate suits
   C. Telephone records
   D. None of the above

2. Most states require a doing business as (DBA) filing for which of the following business types?
   A. Limited partnerships
   B. Trust
   C. Joint ventures
   D. All of the above

3. All of the following information can be obtained through a UCC filings search EXCEPT:
   A. Name of the debtor or joint debtors
   B. Name of the financial lender
   C. Amount of debt incurred by the debtor
   D. Type of collateral pledged as security

4. Each of the following is an online public records database EXCEPT:
   A. Factiva
   B. KnowX
   C. Accurint
   D. Hoover's

5. One of the most powerful people locator tools is the:
   A. Department of Motor Vehicles
   B. Credit bureau header
   C. Last name search
   D. Bankruptcy filings

6. The question of whether it is realistically possible to recover known assets may be partially answered by searching:
   A. Bankruptcy filings
   B. Tax liens
   C. Judgments
   D. All of the above

Collecting Documentary Evidence

7. The Boolean operator symbol that designates a list of words that must appear together in an exact order is:
   A. +
   B. " "
   C. Near
   D. None of the above

8. Specialized websites that collect the names of numerous other related websites, allowing the user to browse through a complete listing of possible sites to visit are known as:
   A. Search engines
   B. Directories
   C. Public records databases
   D. None of the above

III. WORKPLACE SEARCHES

Introduction

There are a host of potential problems that can arise when an organization chooses to perform a workplace search as part of an internal investigation. If not conducted properly, workplace searches can subject the employing organization to liability for violations of its employees' constitutional rights, common law invasions of privacy, and a host of statutory violations. This does not mean that workplace searches should be absolutely avoided. On the contrary, searches, when done right, are a key weapon in the arsenal of any fraud investigator. But before engaging in a workplace search, the investigator must understand the ramifications of his actions. This requires an understanding of employees' legal rights and how they limit or affect the ways in which a search may be conducted.

Although employees have a duty to cooperate during an internal investigation as long as what is requested from them is reasonable, they also have certain other rights that further define the scope of that duty. Employee rights vary from case to case, generally depending on the employee's contractual rights, applicable statutes, and constitutional protections. Therefore, fraud examiners conducting internal investigations must be flexible enough to adapt quickly to the unique situations they encounter.

Constitutional Privacy Rights: The Fourth Amendment

The Fourth Amendment of the U.S. Constitution is the principal constitutional limitation on investigative searches and surveillances by law enforcement, public employers, and other government representatives. It states:

> *The right of the people to be secure in their persons, houses, papers, and effects, against unreasonable searches and seizures, shall not be violated, and no warrants shall issue, but upon probable cause, supported by oath or affirmation, and particularly describing the place to be searched, and the persons or things to be seized.*

In general, the Fourth Amendment prohibits a government employer from making unreasonable searches in areas that a reasonable employee would expect to be free from the employer's intrusion; it does not limit the powers of private employers in conducting a corporate investigation. The Fourth Amendment's inapplicability to private employers, however, is subject to several limitations, and, although a private employer usually cannot be sued for a violation of the Fourth Amendment, these provisions still have important implications for the fraud investigator.

Public Employers Versus Private Employers

For an employee to sue an employer for violating some constitutional right, there must be some form of state action involved. In other words, there must be some sort of governmental involvement in the conduct that caused the violation.

In some circumstances, a private employer's conduct may be considered to involve state action. When this is the case, the employees of that company enjoy constitutional protections, and they would be able to sue their employer for violating their constitutional rights.

Unfortunately, it is not always clear when a private company's investigation takes on an aspect of state action. In general, it happens when the private company is acting as an agent of the government, or when its actions are sufficiently intertwined with the interests of the government that the private company is essentially acting on the government's behalf.

The following actions conducted by private companies or individuals could be considered to involve state action:

- Investigations conducted by a private company at the suggestion of state or federal authorities.
- Investigations begun by a private company, but later taken over by or expanded by state or federal authorities.
- Joint investigations with or aided by state or federal authorities.
- Investigations that are required by state or federal law.
- A private company hires outside investigators who are off-duty state, local, or federal authorities to conduct searches or interrogations.

As these examples show, it may not always be clear during an investigation whether a private company's conduct constitutes or will eventually constitute some form of state action. Therefore, regardless of whether the investigation is being conducted by a private or public entity, it is best to tread lightly where an employee's privacy interests are concerned.

In addition to constitutional privacy rights, employees also enjoy common law privacy protections. These common law rights apply to private as well as government employers; no state action is required to trigger their protections.

Finally, a private employer's investigation may be limited by statutes that regulate or proscribe specific search or surveillance techniques. The upshot is that in any internal investigation, regardless of whether the employer is public or private, due consideration must be given to the privacy interests of all employees.

Employee Privacy Rights Under the Fourth Amendment

The Fourth Amendment protects against unreasonable searches by government employers in areas where a reasonable employee would expect to be free from the employer's intrusion. These are areas in which the employee is said to have a *reasonable expectation of privacy*. In short, the law prohibits public employers from unreasonably invading their employees' privacy to conduct a workplace search. It also prohibits unreasonable surveillance of employees (e.g., videotaping, wiretapping, etc.) where they would reasonably expect privacy.

There is essentially a two-part test to determine whether a search of an employee's workspace is proper. The first question is "Does the employee have a reasonable expectation of privacy in the area to be searched?" If so, the second question is "Was the search conducted in a reasonable manner?"

If an employee has a reasonable privacy expectation in a particular area or communication, this does not mean that the area cannot be searched. What it means is that any search of that area must be conducted reasonably and according to the standards of protection set forth by the Fourth Amendment.

Reasonable Expectations of Privacy

The Fourth Amendment will only apply to a workplace search if an employee has a reasonable expectation of privacy. Thus, to determine if a workplace search will violate an employee's Fourth Amendment rights, an employer must first determine if the employee has a reasonable expectation of privacy in the area to be searched. There is no bright-line rule for determining whether an employee has a reasonable privacy expectation in a particular area. Such a privacy interest can exist for a desk drawer, a file cabinet, a locker, or even an entire office, depending on the circumstances. The issue is whether a reasonable person would expect the area to be free from intrusion. The employee does not have to have an ownership interest in the area to have a reasonable expectation of privacy in the area. Thus, even though a public employer may own the office where an employee works, that employee can still have a privacy interest in the office that prohibits the employer from conducting a search.

The key factor to consider is whether the employee has *exclusive control* over the area in question. If so, this tends to show that the employee has a reasonable expectation of privacy in that area. For instance, assume that an employee has a file cabinet in his office, that he is the only person who uses that file cabinet, that the cabinet has a lock on it, that the employee is the only person with a key, and that the cabinet remains locked when the employee is not using it. These facts indicate that the employee has exclusive control over the contents of the file cabinet, and thus has a reasonable expectation of privacy in its contents. In other words, based on the circumstances, the employee would be justified in believing that others cannot and will not enter the file cabinet without his consent. The employee in this scenario has a constitutionally protected privacy interest in the contents of the file cabinet. A search of this file cabinet by the public employer would have to comport with the reasonableness standard as discussed above.

But if the file cabinet does not have a lock, if several employees store and retrieve files from that cabinet, and if it is generally understood that they can do so without the employee's consent, then the employee cannot reasonably expect that the contents of the file cabinet will be private. Under these facts, the employee would not have a reasonable expectation of privacy in the file cabinet; therefore a search of that file cabinet would not violate the employee's Fourth Amendment rights.

Reasonable privacy expectations can also attach to communications. Employees might reasonably expect personal phone conversations or email messages to be private and free from monitoring. In terms of surveillance, employees are likely to have reasonable privacy expectations in bathrooms, changing rooms, and other personal areas within the workplace.

Obviously, there are a lot of factors that go into determining whether an employee has a reasonable expectation of privacy. Before conducting a search or surveillance, employers should consult legal counsel to make sure they are not intruding upon an employee's privacy interests.

EXAMPLE

Adams is an employee at a government-owned waste treatment plant. Like other employees, Adams has been assigned a locker where he is permitted to store his personal effects during work hours. Each employee is assigned one and only one locker. A number of employees, including Adams, keep combination locks on their lockers to prevent others from opening them. In fact, the manager of the plant encouraged employees to obtain locks after a recent spate of miscellaneous thefts occurred. Adams purchased his lock from a local hardware store and is the only person at the plant who knows the combination. Adams keeps the locker locked at all times while he is at work.

The security director at the plant has reason to suspect that Adams is selling drugs to other employees at the plant, which is not only illegal, but directly violates the facility's substance abuse policy. The security director wants to conduct a search of Adams' locker to see if he is storing the narcotics there.

Given these facts, Adams probably has a constitutionally protected privacy interest in the contents of his locker. First, the plant is government-owned, meaning that Adams is a public employee and therefore has access to Fourth Amendment protection. Second, these facts indicate that Adams has a reasonable expectation of privacy in the contents of his locker. He clearly has exclusive control over the locker, as he keeps it locked while he is at work and no one else has the combination. It would be reasonable for Adams to expect that no one else could enter the locker. This does not mean that the locker cannot be searched, but it does require that any search must be reasonably tailored so that it does not violate Adams's constitutional rights.

On the other hand, there are a number of factors that could diminish Adams's expectation of privacy in the contents of his locker. For instance, if he had to share the locker with other employees, if he were not permitted to place a lock on the locker, or if the facility issued locks to employees and clearly explained that management kept the combinations and reserved the right to search employee lockers—such factors as these would tend to show that Adams did not have exclusive control over the contents of the locker, and therefore, that he did not have a reasonable expectation of privacy in its contents.

Workplace Searches by Government Employers

If a public employee has a reasonable expectation of privacy in an area, then a search of that area may only be conducted if it is done in such a way that it does not violate the suspect's Fourth Amendment rights. The general rule for criminal investigations by law enforcement authorities is that a search must be carried out pursuant to a search warrant issued upon a showing of probable cause. However, in *O'Connor v. Ortega*,[3] the Supreme Court held that requiring warrants for all forms of public workplace searches would be unworkable and would impose intolerable burdens on public employers. Therefore, the Court ruled that workplace searches should be held to a lower standard.

The Court also found that while public employees have some legitimate privacy interests in the workplace, these interests are less than in other places, such as their homes. Government offices are provided to public employees for the purpose of doing government work, and employees can avoid exposing truly personal belongings at work by simply leaving them at home. Thus, by balancing the strong government interest in maintaining an efficient workplace against the diminished privacy interests of government employees, the court justified the use of a lower standard for workplace searches by government employers. Instead of a warrant requirement based on probable cause, government employers are generally held to a standard of "reasonableness under all the circumstances."

THE REASONABLENESS STANDARD

Workplace searches by government employers are subject to the reasonableness standard in two circumstances:
- For non-investigatory, work-related purposes, which are wholly unrelated to illegal conduct (such as retrieving a file from someone's desk)
- For investigations of work-related misconduct

---

[3] 480 U.S. 709 (1987).

When a public employer conducts an investigation of work-related misconduct, and when that investigation necessitates a search of the suspect's workspace, the employer is not generally required to obtain a warrant to perform the search, nor is the employer required to make a showing of probable cause that the suspect has committed a crime. This does not mean, however, that there are no restrictions on the employer's ability to conduct the search; it still must meet the test for "reasonableness under all the circumstances."

There is a two-part test to determine if a workplace search is reasonable:
- The search must be justified at its inception.
- The search must be conducted in a way that is reasonably related in scope to the circumstances which justified the interference in the first place.

A search is justified at its inception if there are reasonable grounds for suspecting that the search will turn up evidence that the employee is involved in work-related misconduct, or if the search is necessary for a non-investigatory purpose, such as to retrieve a file. A search is not justified at its inception simply because an employer thinks that the suspect might be engaged in workplace misconduct. The employer must be able to demonstrate a reasonable, clear suspicion based on factual information that the area to be searched contains evidence of misconduct.

The second part of the test requires that the search be reasonable in scope. The fact that a search is justified at its inception does not give the employer unrestricted authority to intrude upon the suspect's privacy in all areas. The search must be no broader than is necessary to serve the organization's legitimate, work-related purposes.

Criminal Investigations by Law Enforcement Authorities

As was stated above, law enforcement authorities in a criminal investigation are held to a higher standard for conducting searches where an individual has a reasonable expectation of privacy. The police must normally obtain a warrant based on probable cause to search and conduct surveillance or eavesdrop on an individual anywhere that a reasonable privacy expectation exists—unless an exception to the warrant requirement applies. (See discussion below of exceptions to the warrant requirement.)

The Fourth Amendment states that "no Warrants shall issue but on probable cause …." A neutral and detached magistrate or judge must make the determination that probable cause exists in issuing a search warrant. *Probable cause* has been defined as those facts and circumstances sufficient to cause a person of reasonable caution to believe that a crime has been committed and that the accused committed it. It requires more than mere suspicion or a hunch, but less than virtual certainty.

In addition to the probable cause requirement, the Fourth Amendment also prohibits searches that are overly broad, either in the area to be searched or the things to be seized. The purpose is to prevent general searches, a form of abuse that was particularly offensive to the constitutional draftsmen. There must be reasonable grounds to believe that a search will uncover the evidence that is sought. Thus, the police cannot obtain a warrant in a white-collar investigation to seize all the suspect's books and records, whether or not they are relevant to the investigation. This would be too broad in scope; it would allow too great an intrusion into the private financial affairs of the suspect.

EXCEPTIONS TO THE FOURTH AMENDMENT WARRANT REQUIREMENT

Despite the general rule that law enforcement authorities must obtain warrants before conducting a search, courts have held that there are some circumstances in which warrantless searches are allowable. These exceptions to the warrant requirement arise in situations where, on balance, the privacy intrusion on the suspect is minimal or there is a particularly compelling need for the intrusion (i.e., the search). Keep in mind, though, that these are only exceptions to the general rule. In most circumstances, the police must obtain a warrant to conduct a search of an area in which an employee has a legitimate expectation of privacy.

The following are among the major exceptions to the warrant requirement:
- Searches incident to arrest
- Searches of motor vehicles
- When the search is conducted pursuant to a valid, voluntary consent
- When the evidence is in plain view
- Border, customs, and prison searches
- Exigent or emergency circumstances, to prevent the destruction of evidence, or while in hot pursuit of a suspect

<u>SEARCHES INCIDENT TO ARREST</u>
Police officers may, without a warrant, conduct a limited search incident to a lawful arrest. The search, however, must be limited to the arrestee's body and the area within his immediate control. This exception is designed to protect officers and to prevent the destruction of evidence. For the search to be valid, the arrest must be valid (i.e., based on probable cause and not merely a pretext to justify a search). If the arrest is unlawful when made, it cannot be justified by the fruits of the subsequent search, and all evidence obtained must be suppressed.

<u>SEARCHES OF MOTOR VEHICLES</u>
An automobile, airplane, or vessel may be searched without a warrant if there is probable cause to believe it contains contraband or other evidence of a crime. This is because of the mobility of vehicles (hence the risk that evidence may be lost or destroyed while a warrant is being obtained) and the lower

expectation of privacy associated with vehicles. If there is probable cause to believe that a vehicle contains contraband, the police are also permitted to remove the vehicle from the scene to a stationhouse to conduct a search without obtaining a warrant. Furthermore, the police may also conduct warrantless "inventory" searches of impounded vehicles to secure and protect the owner's personal property, and they may seize contraband or other evidence discovered as a result.

It may also be permissible for law enforcement to make warrantless searches of containers and luggage found within a vehicle. This applies if the police have probable cause to believe there is contraband in the containers or in the car, or that contraband could be hidden in the containers.

The search incident to arrest exception also applies in the motor vehicle context. However, the boundaries of this search have changed with time. Most recently, on April 21, 2009, the Supreme Court imposed new restrictions on the exception in *Arizona v. Gant*, 556 U.S. ___ (2009). For many years, the rule had been that the police may search the entire passenger compartment of a vehicle incident to the custodial arrest of an occupant of the car. In *Gant*, however, the Supreme Court added a new limitation: Vehicle searches following an occupant's arrest are legal "only when the arrestee is unsecured and within reaching distance of the passenger compartment at the time of the search" or when the officer has reason to believe the vehicle has evidence of the crime that forms the basis for the arrest.

The motor vehicle exception to the warrant requirement does not extend to passengers in the car. However, once a passenger has been arrested, the police are permitted to make a warrantless search of the suspect and the area within their control pursuant to the exception for searches incident to arrest, as discussed above.

CONSENT SEARCHES

Individuals are always free to waive their Fourth Amendment rights. If a suspect consents to a search by police, this eliminates the need for a warrant. However, the courts will closely scrutinize any such "consent" to make sure it was truly voluntary, particularly when it leads to the seizure of incriminating evidence. Consents obtained by deceit, bribery, or misrepresentations are generally held to be involuntary and invalid. (However, when an undercover police officer conceals his identity and, as a result, an individual allows the officer to enter an area, this amounts to consent even though the person did not know they were granting permission to a police officer.) Consent might not be voluntary if it requires a choice between exercising constitutional rights and continued employment. There is also no requirement that the suspect be informed of his right to refuse consent.

Consent may be implied in circumstances where the individual can choose between entering an area and submitting to a search or not entering, as when one enters a secured courthouse, boards an airplane, or crosses an international border. Consent may be given by third parties to searches of property over which the third parties have authority, such as a co-tenant in a leased apartment.

EVIDENCE IN PLAIN VIEW

Evidence in plain view of an officer who has a right to be in a position to observe it can also be seized without a warrant. This situation typically occurs when contraband or evidence of another crime is inadvertently discovered during a lawful search or arrest for another offense, or when the officer has been invited onto the premises for a lawful purpose. The police must still have probable cause to believe the items in plain view are evidence of a crime before they can seize them. The police also must truly have a right to be in a position to view the items in order for the exception to apply. If an officer has already entered in violation of the Fourth Amendment, the fact that evidence is in plain view will not justify the intrusion; this evidence will be suppressed.

EXAMPLE

Officer Grant was voluntarily admitted to Jones's office to talk with Jones about the recent misappropriation of funds of Jones's employer. While in the office, Grant noticed Jones's personal bank account statement sitting face-up on Jones's desk. Grant could read lines on the statement that showed some large deposits to the account around the same time as the misappropriations. Since Grant was properly in Jones's office and the evidence was in plain view, no warrant was required to obtain that evidence for use in Jones's subsequent trial. Moreover, Grant could cite that evidence in a later affidavit in an effort to show probable cause for a warrant to search other parts of Jones's office and for a court order to the bank for Jones's other account records.

BORDER, CUSTOMS, AND PRISON SEARCHES

Border and customs searches are a long-standing exception to the Fourth Amendment and may be conducted without probable cause or a warrant. Searches of prison cells and the monitoring of inmates' telephone conversations can also be conducted without a warrant or probable cause because of security concerns and the absence of a realistic expectation of privacy in prison. These exceptions are unlikely to be an issue in an internal investigation and are included in this discussion only for the sake of completeness.

SEARCHES IN HOT PURSUIT, TO PREVENT DESTRUCTION OF EVIDENCE, OR IN EMERGENCY SITUATIONS

Police officers are permitted to make warrantless searches and seizures of fleeing felons. They are also permitted to seize evidence without a warrant if that evidence is likely to disappear before a warrant can be obtained. Finally, certain emergencies, such as burning fires, may justify the police entering an area or otherwise conducting a search without first obtaining a warrant.

Determining Which Search Standard Applies

The Court in *O'Connor v. Ortega* made it clear that public employer workplace searches for investigations of work-related misconduct are to be judged by a reasonableness standard. In criminal investigations, however, the more stringent probable cause standard applies. Suppose a situation arises in which an employer suspects one of its employees of stealing inventory. If the employer conducts an internal investigation, this would be for work-related misconduct, and thus one could argue that the reasonableness standard should apply—meaning the employer would not be required to obtain a warrant to conduct a search of an employee's private workspace. On the other hand, this investigation clearly involves criminal conduct and one could also argue that this is a criminal investigation subject to the probable cause standard, particularly where the results are likely to be referred to the police or a prosecutor. If this were the case, the employer would need a warrant to conduct a workplace search.

How does one tell which standard to apply? The court in *Lowe v. City of Macon* provided some guidance on this issue. In *Lowe*, the court held that "the purpose of the search is controlling as to which standard ... will be applied,"[4] meaning that the appropriate standard will depend on the circumstances of the case and the purpose of the search, whether it be for work-related purposes or for criminal investigation. This case, however, involved a workplace search in a police station that was conducted by police officers. Does the standard change if no police are involved, or if the search is conducted entirely by administrative personnel?

One case seems to indicate that searches by administrative personnel will usually, if not always, fall under the reasonableness standard. In *Gossmeyer v. McDonald*[5] the Seventh Circuit Court of Appeals applied the reasonableness standard to a search by personnel from the Office of the Inspector General of the Department of Children and Family Services (OIG). Even though the search involved an employee who was allegedly in possession of pornographic pictures of children (thus clearly involving criminal conduct), and even though several law enforcement officers were present when the search was conducted, the court found that the reasonableness standard should apply instead of the probable cause standard. Hence, no warrant was required. The court relied heavily on the fact that the individuals who conducted the search worked for an investigative agency charged with investigating employee misconduct and that the actual search was performed by an OIG investigator, not the police. The result might have been different if the police had participated in the search.

State Constitutions

Most states have enacted constitutional provisions similar to the Fourth Amendment, and many of the same issues that arise under the federal Constitution also arise under state constitutions. In most states,

---

[4] 720 F.Supp. 994, 998 (M.D. Ga. 1989).
[5] 128 F.3d 481 (7th Cir. 1997).

standards similar to those under the federal Constitution apply. However, some state constitutions might grant employees more protection than what is afforded by the federal Constitution. Before conducting a workplace search, check the law in your jurisdiction.

Effect of a Violation of an Employee's Constitutional Rights

Illegally seized evidence will be excluded in criminal proceedings. A public employer cannot use illegally seized evidence to discipline an employee. There is no Fourth Amendment prohibition against a private employer using illegally seized evidence to discipline an employee; however, the employer might be exposing itself to litigation for invasion of privacy, trespass, or other common law causes of action described below.

The Exclusionary Rule

Under the *exclusionary rule*, which is in effect in all federal and state courts, evidence seized in violation of the Fourth Amendment will be suppressed—that is, it becomes inadmissible in any prosecution against the suspect except under a few limited exceptions. In addition, all evidence that is obtained as a result of the illegally obtained evidence will also be excluded. An unlawful search and seizure does not mean the suspect cannot be prosecuted, and it does not invalidate a conviction based on other evidence. It does, however, prevent the wrongfully obtained evidence and all evidence derived from it from being presented at trial. Recall that, for the Fourth Amendment to apply, there must be state action.

Evidence that has been suppressed under the exclusionary rule might still be admissible in a civil trial or an administrative proceeding, such as an employee disciplinary hearing. The primary goal of the exclusionary rule is to deter police misconduct. If the deterrent effect of excluding the evidence from a civil or administrative proceeding is outweighed by the costs that would result from excluding the evidence, and if the party whose rights were violated has other forms of redress for the violation, then evidence that was suppressed in a criminal trial may be admissible in a non-criminal proceeding. However, there are some circumstances where wrongfully-obtained evidence will be excluded from civil proceedings, so public employers should not feel free to disregard their employees' constitutional rights under the assumption that any illegally obtained evidence can still be used against an employee in a non-criminal matter.

Civil Liability for Damages (42 U.S.C. § 1983)

42 U.S.C. § 1983 provides a remedy for individuals whose federally protected rights are violated where state action is involved. There are certain immunities for those who are subject to the law; they are complicated and fact-specific, so consult your legal counsel.

Generally, private employers whose investigations are private and lack any indicia of government participation do not involve state action and are not liable under this statute. However, the use of the courts to compel testimony or evidence, if not otherwise privileged, may be a sufficient act to bring a private employer to court under this law.

Moreover, some states may have their own civil rights statutes that offer remedies (damages or injunctive relief) for deprivation of civil rights by private individuals or employers, even when no state action is involved.

Common Law Invasion of Privacy: Intrusion Upon Seclusion

In addition to constitutionally created rights, employees also have common law privacy interests that limit an employer's right to search. These common law protections, which are similar in nature and scope to the Fourth Amendment protections discussed above, cover both public and private employees. As long as an employee does not have a reasonable expectation of privacy in an area, the employer can search that area without violating an employee's common law right to privacy.

The tort of invasion of privacy actually consists of four separate causes of action: intrusion upon seclusion, public disclosure of private facts, false light invasion of privacy, and appropriation of likeness. Intrusion upon seclusion is the cause of action that is most frequently raised with regard to workplace searches.

In order to state a claim for intrusion upon seclusion, an employee must be able to prove that the employer (1) made an intentional intrusion, (2) into an area where an employee had a reasonable expectation of privacy, and (3) the intrusion would be highly offensive or objectionable to a reasonable person. As with constitutional actions, an intrusion upon seclusion claim can be based not only on physical intrusions, but also on wiretapping, eavesdropping, and other forms of surveillance.

This cause of action is very similar in nature and scope to the Fourth Amendment claims discussed above. As long as an employee does not have a reasonable expectation of privacy in an area, the employer can search that area without committing a common law invasion of privacy. As with Fourth Amendment considerations, the existence of a reasonable expectation of privacy is usually determined by the amount of control an employee exercises over the area to be searched. An employee probably cannot claim a privacy expectation in a work area that is open to the public and shared with other employees. On the other hand, purses, briefcases, and other personal effects tend to be regarded as personal items that an employee would reasonably expect to be private. If the employee has a reasonable privacy expectation in an area or a communication, then the employer's search must be done in such a way that it would not be offensive to a reasonable person.

EXAMPLE

Horton has a higher expectation of privacy in his office, which is space assigned to him for his exclusive use and to which he can control access, than in the public corridors or group meeting spaces of his employer's place of business, where other employees can observe or overhear him in the normal course of business. Accordingly, any surveillance or monitoring of Horton in his office will pose a higher degree of intrusion than surveillance or monitoring in the halls or other group areas.

Similarly, a search of space over which Horton has exclusive, or near exclusive, control such as a locked filing cabinet or desk or his personal briefcase, is a greater intrusion on his privacy than an area that is open to other employees, such as his desktop or the trash can in the copy machine room.

If an employee succeeds in a claim for intrusion upon seclusion, he may be able to recover for both physical suffering and any mental anguish that resulted from the privacy invasion.

Reducing Employees' Expectation of Privacy

Employers can reduce their potential liability for invasion of privacy claims by lowering employees' expectation of privacy in the workplace. If an employer puts employees on notice that their offices, desks, files, voice mail, etc. are not private, then logically, employees cannot assert that they have a reasonable privacy expectation in those areas.

Employers should adopt a written policy which provides that, to maintain the security of its operations, the company retains the right to access and search all work areas and personal belongings, including desks, file drawers, lockers, briefcases, handbags, pockets, and personal effects. Include in the policy that workplace areas are subject to surveillance and that business phone calls might be monitored. The policy should also state that the employer can monitor all electronic communications, such as email, as well as monitor what sites are visited over the Internet. Restricting use of computers and communications equipment to business purposes only will also reduce the perception that they are within the employee's personal sphere.

Take appropriate steps to ensure that all employees are aware of and understand these policies. For instance, give a copy of the policies to each employee at the time of hiring and have them sign an acknowledgment that the policies were read and understood. Provide all employees with copies of any changes or updates. Post the policies in a prominent place in the workplace.

In addition to the above, employers should also consider the following steps to reduce their potential liability for invasion of privacy claims:
- Retain a key to all desks, lockers, etc. so that the employee cannot assume that any space is secured exclusively for him.

Workplace Searches

- Require employees to provide keys to all personal locks.
- Obtain the employee's consent to search.

Balancing the Need to Search or Conduct Surveillance and the Employee's Privacy Rights

As with Fourth Amendment issues, an employee's common law privacy rights are not absolute, and the reasonableness of his expectation of privacy—and of any investigative intrusion thereon—depends on a balancing of the privacy interest, the purpose and objectives of the search, the degree and scope of the proposed intrusion, and whether the purpose and objectives of the search can be attained with a lesser intrusion. A low expectation of privacy or a minimal intrusion—coupled with a compelling need for the proposed intrusion—can support a reasonable search or surveillance. However, the determination is very fact-specific in each case and can differ between jurisdictions. You should consult with an attorney if the question is at all close or troublesome.

In any event, the intrusion must be as limited in scope and duration as is minimally necessary to achieve the legitimate purposes of the search. Even if an employee has a low expectation of privacy in an area, a search of that area can still be found unreasonable if it is conducted in an unnecessarily broad or invasive manner. You must ask yourself if there is another way to achieve the objective that is less intrusive.

Other Tort Liabilities in Connection with Searches and Surveillance

Other possible common law violations that can occur as a result of a workplace investigation will be discussed in Chapter 6 in connection with interviews. Each of the violations—improper disclosure of private information, false light, defamation, intentional infliction of emotional distress, wrongful termination, breach of the implied covenant of good faith and fair dealing, and false imprisonment—can occur as a result of an imprudently conducted workplace search or surveillance. In addition, an improper search or surveillance can result in a claim for *trespass*, which is the unauthorized, intentional entry upon another's land or interference with another's personal property. For instance, a claim of trespass might arise from an unreasonable search of an employee's locker, or from unreasonable surveillance at an employee's home.

Other Prohibitions Regarding Searches

Searching an Employee's Mail

An employer may not conduct searches of an employee's mail before it has been delivered. Under federal law, any person who takes a letter, postcard, or package from the mail before it has been delivered to the person to whom it was directed, with design to obstruct the correspondence, faces up to five years imprisonment, a fine, or both. See Title 18 U.S.C., Section 1702. Once the mail has been delivered, however, the ordinary rules regarding searches apply.

Federal and State Nondiscrimination Statutes

Nondiscrimination statutes, such as the federal Civil Rights Acts of 1866 and 1871, Title VII of the Civil Rights Act of 1964, and the Age Discrimination in Employment Act of 1970, as well as similar state statutes, protect employees from being singled out for searches based on such characteristics as race, national origin, sex, religion, and age. These laws also protect employees against disparate discipline assessed as a result of a search.

Monitoring Employee Phone Calls

The Wiretap Act provisions of the Electronic Communications Privacy Act of 1986 (ECPA)[6] limit an employer's ability to monitor employee phone calls. In addition to the ECPA, a company's right to monitor employee phone calls is also limited by an employee's constitutional and common law privacy rights, as discussed previously.

Although interception is generally forbidden under the Wiretap Act, employers may monitor phone calls if they fall under one of the statutory exceptions, including the ordinary course of business exception and the consent exception.

Ordinary Course of Business Exception

Under the ordinary course of business exception, employers are permitted to monitor their employees' wire or electronic communications, including phone calls, if done for a legitimate business purpose.

This exception could apply in various scenarios. For example, it would apply where the employer routinely monitors phone communications for purposes of quality control (e.g., monitoring the phone calls of operators, telemarketers, or customer service personnel). It may also apply where there is a legitimate business purpose for the monitoring, such as preventing business losses or employee misconduct. Keep in mind, however, that there must be a specific, legitimate business purpose for the interception. Blanket monitoring probably will be found to violate the Act. For example, in *Sanders v. Robert Bosch*,[7] an employer who used a *voice logger*—a device or program used to record audio information from telephones and other sources for storage on a computer—to record all telephone conversations on certain company lines did not fall within the ordinary course of business exception because the employer was unable to state a legitimate business purpose for the interceptions.

---

[6] Title 18, U.S.C., Section 2510, *et. seq.*
[7] 38 F.3d 736 (4th Cir. 1994).

Even if a company has a legitimate business purpose for monitoring a phone call, the method used to intercept and monitor the call must be no more intrusive than necessary to achieve the purpose. In *Deal v. Spears*, an employer who tape-recorded and listened to all calls, including personal calls, was found to have violated the statute even though the employer had legitimate suspicions of theft.[8] Once it becomes apparent that a communication is personal and not otherwise unauthorized, the employer must immediately stop listening to the call. Overly broad efforts to monitor employee calls may give rise to a claim for invasion of privacy.

Consent Exception

The ECPA allows an entity to intercept an electronic communication if that entity is a party to the communication, or if one of the parties to the communication has given prior consent to the interception.

For an employer to monitor an employee under this exception, the employee must expressly consent to the monitoring. Generally, employers must obtain written consent(e.g., an employer provides its employees with a written policy explaining that phone calls may be monitored, and the employees sign the policy). It is important to note that providing a notification that employees might be monitored (as opposed to being notified that the phone calls or email will be monitored) may not satisfy the consent exception. At least one court has held that a notification to an employee that her phone calls might be monitored was not enough to establish that the employee consented to the recording of her phone calls. See *Deal v. Spears*.[9] Even when an employee consents to monitoring, this does not give the employer unlimited access to the employee's communications. Monitoring should still be conducted for only legitimate business purposes and should be no more broad than necessary.

Pen Registers

In addition to governing the interception of electronic communications, the ECPA also regulates the use of pen registers. *Pen registers* are devices that can detect the telephone number from which an incoming call has been made. Federal law generally prohibits the installation of pen registers without a court order.[10] However, there are a number of exceptions under which employers can use pen registers to track their employees' phone activity. Those exceptions include:

- Phone service providers can use pen registers to protect users (employers) from abuse of service or unlawful use of service.

---

[8] 980 nF.2d 1153 (8th Cir. 1992).
[9] Ibid.
[10] Title 18, U.S.C., Section 3121.

- Phone service providers can use a pen register to record the fact that a phone call was initiated or completed to protect users of the service (employers) from fraudulent, unlawful, or abusive use of the service.
- Phone service providers can use a pen register where consent of the user of the service has been obtained.

Monitoring Employees' Email

Whether an employer is permitted to monitor an employee's email depends on whether a message is transmitted over an internal email system or an external, web-based email system.

If a message is sent over an employer's purely internal email system, the growing trend is that an employer is entitled to monitor the message in the ordinary course of business. The principal argument to support this theory is that employees have no reasonable expectation of privacy regarding communications sent over a company's internal email system because that system was set up solely to provide business communications. If there is no privacy expectation in these messages, there would be no constitutional or common law restriction on monitoring them.

An employee's personal, web-based email (e.g., Yahoo!, Hotmail, or Gmail) is more protected than a purely internal email system. Employees are likely to have a greater expectation of privacy in external messages—particularly those of a personal nature—than they would in messages sent over an internal system. Although the Stored Communications Act (Title II of the ECPA) generally prohibits third parties from accessing stored communications, there are two key exceptions:
- The provider exception
- The consent exception

The Provider Exception

The provider exception exempts providers of electronic communications services from the restrictions of the SCA. In other words, if a message is stored on an email or voice mail system that the company provides, then the employer can access those messages as it sees fit without violating the ECPA. Note, however, that this exception does not allow the employer to access messages stored with an outside provider such as Yahoo!, Google, or Hotmail.

The Consent Exception

The consent exception permits access of stored messages if such access is authorized by the intended recipient of the communication. This means that employers will be free to access employee email and voice mail (including messages stored with outside providers) as long as the employees have given their consent. This exception provides the safest haven for employers who want to monitor their employees' stored messages. To make sure the consent exception will apply, companies should obtain express written consent from all employees for such monitoring as a condition of employment.

As with phone conversations, employers generally need to obtain express written consent to monitor their employees' email. The best way to accomplish this is to disseminate a written policy that clearly informs employees that they cannot expect privacy in their Internet and email use over company facilities. The written policy should specifically provide that any electronic communication sent over the company system, whether sent to an internal source or someone outside the company, is subject to monitoring. Employees should be required to sign the policy, thereby acknowledging their consent. A sample email and Internet policy is included later in this chapter.

Monitoring Employees' Internet Activity

As with monitoring employees' email, employers should be aware of federal protections against monitoring employees' Internet use, including an employee's instant messages and website postings. This is true even though federal law provides employees little protection from an employer's electronic monitoring. For example, although the ECPA prohibits the intentional interception of electronic communications when employees have a reasonable expectation of privacy, an employer may monitor Internet use when there is employee consent, when there are legitimate business purposes, or when an employer has reason to believe that the company's interests are at risk. In addition, the common law right to privacy also extends to employees in the workplace; however, the public nature of the workplace has led many courts to reject most invasion claims on the basis that there was no reasonable expectation of privacy.

Monitoring Social Media

In recent years, the rise of social media and the pervasiveness of its use in everyday society has spurred some employers to demand social media account passwords from current and prospective employees. These demands have elicited threats of legislation from several members of the U.S. Congress but, thus far, federal action has not been taken. As of early 2015, legislation limiting or prohibiting employer demands for social media credentials had been enacted in 19 states and was pending in 30 other states.

The National Labor Relations Board (NLRB) issued memoranda expressing the right of employees to use social media to engage in "protected concerted activity" as protected by the National Labor Relations Act.[11] Discussions on social media related to the terms and conditions of employment are protected, however, the memoranda have not implied protection for non-work-related social media activity.

---

[11] National Labor Relations Board, "Acting General Counsel releases report on employer social media policies," 2012. Retrieved from www.nlrb.gov/news/acting-general-counsel-releases-report-employer-social-media-policies

Video Surveillance of Employees

In some scenarios, investigators may consider the use of video surveillance equipment as part of an internal investigation. In general, video surveillance is not permissible in areas where employees have a legitimate expectation of privacy. For instance, an employer is not allowed to install video cameras in a restroom or dressing room unless there are special circumstances to justify this intrusion on employees' privacy. However, an employer is much more likely to be allowed to use video surveillance in open areas such as around cash registers or in public hallways. These areas are open to the public and an employee could not reasonably expect privacy there. It is advisable to provide written notice to employees, in advance of any surveillance, informing them that their activities are subject to monitoring. Again, the scope of the surveillance should be no greater than necessary to fulfill the employer's legitimate business purposes.

If video surveillance is accompanied by audio recording, then this type of surveillance would be covered by the Wiretap Act, which prohibits the interception of wire, electronic, or oral communications except in limited circumstances. (See "Monitoring Employee Phone Calls" section.) However, the ECPA does not cover silent video surveillance. The question in this type of surveillance is whether the surveillance violates the employee's constitutional or common law privacy rights.

Searching Employees' Trash

All federal courts and most state courts now hold that there is no reasonable expectation of privacy in what a person throws in the trash can, especially when it is put out in an area where trash is normally collected. Once a person leaves their trash out for the janitor to gather, that person can no longer reasonably expect that the contents of the trash will be kept private. The person in this case has ceded exclusive control over the contents of the trash; indeed, the whole purpose of placing the trash in an area for collection is that it will be gathered up by other people (trash collectors) and commingled with other people's trash.

A more problematic case, even under federal law, is the trash can in a private office. Office trash cans are frequently kept in an area of the office where their contents are not normally exposed to others. Thus, an employee may have a better argument that they have a reasonable expectation of privacy in the contents of their office trash can. On the other hand, assuming a janitor regularly empties the private office trash can, and assuming the janitor can properly view the contents of that trash can in the course of his job, then that janitor could share the contents with others. Hence, even in that situation the employee probably has a fairly low expectation of privacy. Be aware, however, that a small minority of states (such as California) hold under their own constitutions or privacy laws that one has a reasonable expectation of privacy in one's trash until it is actually picked up and commingled with the trash of others. Always consult the laws of your jurisdiction before conducting any kind of workplace search.

Special Privacy Rights Under Collective Bargaining Agreements

A union contract or collective bargaining agreement might contain restrictions on a company's investigative procedures. These generally concern employee interviews, where a company might be required to notify the union before interviewing an employee, or where an employee might have the right to have a union representative present at an interview. However, a collective bargaining agreement can also limit the employer's capacity to conduct searches or can define the areas in which employees have a privacy interest. Employers should consult applicable union contracts before engaging in searches or surveillance of employee workspaces or communications.

State Statutes

Most states have enacted laws governing an employee's right to privacy in the workplace. Many states have enacted statutes that restrict surveillance, including wiretapping or electronic surveillance, cameras, pen registers, two-way mirrors, or surveillance in particular areas, such as locker rooms, lounges, and rest areas.

Sample Workplace Policy for Workplace Searches

As noted above, a workplace policy that puts an employee on notice that the workplace is not private can help negate later contentions that the employee had a reasonable expectation of privacy. In wording such a policy, however, care should be taken to balance the company's needs with some sensitivity to the effect on morale that such a policy can have. The company's objective of overcoming employee privacy interests should not be attained at the price of unhappy or paranoid employees.

The following is a sample policy that might be considered for inclusion in the company's employee manual or for separate distribution. It should be adapted as necessary to reflect the actual needs and culture of a particular organization.

> *All employees are advised that the company's office premises and all equipment and furnishings therein, including but not limited to desks, filing cabinets, and closets, are the property of the company to which the company's managing and supervising employees have full and complete access. Except as otherwise specifically provided elsewhere in this employee manual, the company does not provide any private areas for the storage of an employee's private property or papers, including areas that are used exclusively by one employee. Any employee who keeps personal property or papers does so at his or her own risk, and the company assumes no responsibility for any loss, damage, or other disposition of an employee's personal property or papers while in the company's office. The company may open and search any desk, filing cabinet, trash can, or other area of the office if there is any reasonable cause to believe that evidence of an offense by, or in conjunction with, a company director, officer, or employee may be found there. An offense*

means any act or omission in violation of any law, government regulation, or company policy that has caused, or is likely to cause, a loss or liability to the company.

Any common areas of the office, other than the bathrooms, are subject to periodic and random surveillance.

Computers, networks, servers, storage media, email accounts, phone, cable or DSL lines, Internet accounts, messaging devices, and other communications devices furnished by the company are the property of the company and are furnished for the sole purpose of facilitating and enabling the employee to do the company's work to which the employee has been assigned. Employees are expected to keep personal telephone calls to a minimum, and may not use any of the foregoing electronic equipment or media (other than telephones) for personal business or reasons. Employees also may not connect to or access company computers, computerized files, networks, servers, company storage media, messaging devices, or other company communication devices from computers or communications devices outside of the company for any personal business or other reasons. All of the foregoing electronic equipment and media are subject to periodic and random monitoring for quality assurance purposes and to ensure compliance with the foregoing policy. In addition, these electronic equipment and media are subject to search in the event of an offense, or suspected offense, as defined above.

The company should require each employee to sign a statement indicating that they have read and understand the policy.

Obtaining Evidence by Subpoena

In a purely internal investigation, you probably will not be using compulsory legal processes—subpoenas and other court orders—to obtain books, records, documents, and other forms of tangible evidence. Compulsory legal process is typically available only to parties in litigation, so until a lawsuit is filed, you will not have access to subpoenas as a means to gather documentary evidence. (Pre-litigation depositions to preserve testimony are available under limited circumstances in many states.) However, because it is possible for litigation to parallel or follow an internal investigation, the investigator should understand the process and related legal concerns and issues. It is also possible that an outside party could subpoena your company's books, records, or other tangible evidence in connection with a parallel government investigation or litigation to which the company is not a party.

Subpoenas are used to compel the attendance of a person or entity on a specified date and time at a legal proceeding for the purpose of giving testimony or producing tangible evidence. A subpoena that compels the production of tangible evidence is called a *subpoena duces tecum*. This type of subpoena must include a particularized description of the books, records, or other documents or tangible evidence that is to be produced. Disobedience of a subpoena is punishable as contempt of court.

If a company is the subject of the subpoena, it generally will be ordered to designate one or more knowledgeable employees to testify on its behalf in response to the subpoena. A subpoena duces tecum typically is directed to the custodian of records who maintains the evidence to be produced. Typically, the custodian is only required to identify the evidence as being authentic; he is not required to testify as to the substance of the documents. Under Rule 45(c) of the Federal Rules of Civil Procedure and similar state rules, the custodian need not appear in person, but he can produce the tangible evidence by mail or messenger with an affidavit attesting to the identity and authenticity of the evidence. If the party or his attorney wants to ask substantive questions about the tangible evidence after it has been produced, he will generally also subpoena and question other individuals who are believed to have the knowledge or information that he seeks.

The procedures for issuing subpoenas may vary from jurisdiction to jurisdiction. Typically, subpoenas are issued and signed by the clerk of the court upon request by a party or his attorney, but Rule 45(a) of the Federal Rules of Civil Procedure and the rules of many states also permit an attorney to issue and sign a subpoena on his own for (1) a court to which he is admitted to practice, or (2) "a court for a district in which a deposition or production is compelled by the subpoena, if the deposition or production pertains to an action pending in a court in which the attorney is authorized to practice." In some states, an affidavit of good cause must be submitted by the party or his attorney to support issuance of a *subpoena duces tecum* for at least some kinds of tangible evidence, especially where privacy issues are likely to be in issue, such as medical and financial records. Generally, a person who is subpoenaed must respond within a reasonable time; most statutes authorizing the issuance of subpoenas do not set a specific number of days for compliance.

In addition to service of the subpoena on the person or business to which it is directed, many states require notice of the subpoena to a person whose consumer records are the subject of the subpoena. For instance, if the subpoena orders a bank to produce a customer's bank records, or a hospital to produce a patient's medical records, then the customer or patient must receive notice within a statutorily-designated period of time before the production date on the subpoena.

The recipient of the subpoena (or an interested party such as a bank customer whose records have been subpoenaed from the bank) may object to the subpoena within a statutorily prescribed time. Federal Rule of Civil Procedure 45(c) requires an objection to be raised within 14 days after service or "before the time specified for compliance if such time is less than 14 days after service … ." An objection is raised by filing a timely *motion to quash the subpoena*. If the court finds the objections are well-founded, it may quash (annul) the subpoena, modify it, or impose conditions in order to protect the legitimate interests of the objecting person.

> EXAMPLE
>
> *Clarke moved to quash a subpoena to the telephone company for all of his telephone service records for the last two years. The court agreed that records for certain spans of time during that two-year period were not relevant to the legal issues in the proceeding for which the subpoena was issued. However, rather than quash the entire subpoena, the court modified it so that only records for relevant periods of time had to be produced.*

Workplace Searches

Review Questions

1. The _____ is the principal constitutional limitation on investigative searches and surveillances by law enforcement, public employers, and other government representatives.
   A. Fourth Amendment
   B. Fifth Amendment
   C. Sixth Amendment
   D. Seventh Amendment

2. When a government employer searches an employee's workspace, the search must satisfy which two of the following conditions in order to be constitutionally valid?
   I. The search must be based on probable cause.
   II. The search must be reasonable in scope.
   III. The employer must obtain a warrant.
   IV. The search must be justified at its inception.

   A. I and II
   B. I and III
   C. I and IV
   D. II and IV

3. ABC Corp., a private company, intentionally searched the purse of one of its employees. Assume that the employee had a reasonable expectation of privacy in the purse, and that the search was conducted in such a manner as to be highly offensive to a reasonable person. Also assume that there was no state action involved in the search. Which of the following statements is true?
   A. The employee can sue ABC for violating her Fourth Amendment rights
   B. The employee can sue ABC for common law invasion of privacy
   C. Both A and B are correct
   D. The employee has no grounds to sue ABC; only public employers can be sued for invasion of privacy

4. Which of the following is NOT true of reasonable expectations of privacy?
   A. The Fourth Amendment only applies to workplace searches if the employee has a reasonable expectation of privacy
   B. The employee has to have an ownership interest in the area to have a reasonable expectation of privacy
   C. If an employee has exclusive control over the area, that tends to show the employee had a reasonable expectation of privacy
   D. None of the above

5. Public employer workplace searches for investigations of work-related misconduct are to be judged on a:
   A. Reasonableness standard
   B. Probable cause standard
   C. Plain view standard
   D. All of the above

6. Which of the following are recommended methods by which employers can reduce their liability for invasion of privacy claims?
   A. Lowering employees' expectations of privacy in the workplace
   B. Conducting a workplace search only with the government's involvement
   C. Adopting a written policy providing that, in order to maintain the security of its operations, the company retains the right to access and search all work areas and personal belongings
   D. Both A and C are correct

7. The Electronic Communications Privacy Act (ECPA) does NOT cover:
   A. Audio-video surveillance
   B. Silent video surveillance
   C. Any video surveillance
   D. None of the above

8. Which of the following exceptions to the Electronic Communications Privacy Act (ECPA) allows suppliers of wire or electronic communications services to intercept electronic communications in the normal course of business?
   A. The ordinary course of business exception
   B. The consent exception
   C. The provider exception
   D. None of the above

IV. ANALYZING AND ORGANIZING EVIDENCE

Forensic Examination of Documents

In an internal investigation of fraudulent transactions, forged, altered, fabricated, and other suspicious documents are regularly encountered in fraud cases. Most business, legal issues, or financial transactions will produce a substantial amount of paper, including contracts, agreements, wills, order forms, invoices, and statements. These documents can be evidence in establishing that a fraud was committed, in determining the nature and scope of the fraud, and in identifying the parties responsible.

The fraud examiner is not expected to be a document expert. He should, however, be aware of ways to spot phony documents and have knowledge of the capabilities and limitations of forensic examinations. In addition, if the fraud examiner suspects that significant documents are phony, he should consider consulting with an expert. Expert forensic examinations conducted as a part of a fraud investigation can contribute to its success in several ways:

- Expert examination results can assist in developing and proving the fraud theory: who did what and when they did it.
- Expert examination results can corroborate or refute statements by witnesses or fraud suspects.
- Having the results of expert examinations before interviews can provide significant leverage for the examiner during his interviews with fraud suspects, even resulting in admissions of guilt from suspects who are confronted with the factual evidence.
- Forensic handwriting examinations and comparisons can result in the positive identification of the writer or signer of a document. Since writing is a conscious act, the identification might serve to prove that a particular act is intentional or willful. Proof of intent is usually necessary to prosecute a wrongdoer successfully.

Fraud examiners should consider consulting with experts early in their investigation or inquiry if they suspect that significant documents are phony or have been forged, altered, or otherwise manipulated. Many times the scope of an investigation can be narrowed or directed by eliminating multiple suspects through handwriting examinations. The expert's findings might solidify the fraud examiner's theories of how the fraud was committed, or they can prevent wasted effort by proving theories incorrect at an earlier stage.

Sources for Expert Document Examinations
Law Enforcement Laboratories
In cases where criminal prosecutions are likely, there are excellent forensic laboratories available through law enforcement agencies at the local, state, and national levels of the criminal justice system.

Analyzing and Organizing Evidence

Forensic Document Experts in Private Practice

When an expert's services are needed, a fraud examiner can identify and locate fully qualified, court-certified, expert forensic document examiners available in a particular geographical area by contacting the following organizations:

American Board of Forensic Document Examiners
7887 San Felipe, Suite 122
Houston, TX 77063
(713) 784-9537
www.abfde.org

American Academy of Forensic Sciences Questioned Document Section
410 North 21st Street
Colorado Springs, CO 80904
(719) 636-1100
www.aafs.org

Types of Forensic Document Examinations

There are many different types of forensic document examinations. However, most examinations (more than 95 percent of all FBI laboratory document examinations) concern signatures, handwriting, hand printing, or documents created by a typewriter or word processor. Additionally, issues concerning photocopies and determining when a document was prepared frequently arise. Investigators should be aware that many different types of forensic examinations are possible, but that the following forensic examinations could be of particular value when a fraud involves documents:

- Detection of forged signatures
- Identification of the writers of signatures, handwriting, and hand-printing
- Detection of altered documents
- Detection and restoration of erasures and eradications
- Determination of when a document was or was not prepared
- Detection of counterfeited documents and examination of printed documents
- Detection and restoration of faint indented writings
- Comparisons of paper and inks
- Determination of whether two sheets of paper came from the same tablet or pad of paper
- Examinations of paper folds and sequence of folds
- Comparisons of torn or cut paper edges
- Restoration of charred and partially burned documents
- Identification of the machine that made a photocopy and determination of whether two copies were made on the same machine

Analyzing and Organizing Evidence

- Examinations of facsimile (fax) copies
- Identification of the source of, or alterations to, notary seals, wax seals, and cachets
- Detection of the opening and resealing of sealed documents and examination of adhesives
- Detection of inserted text in typewritten, printed, or handwritten documents
- Determination of the sequence of handwritten text, signatures, and typewriting
- Identification of rubber stamp impressions
- Identification of mechanical check-writer and numbering device impressions

Handling Documents as Physical Evidence

A document can be a piece of physical evidence and not just a source of information. As a piece of evidence, it should be handled carefully and stored properly in a sealed, initialed, and dated paper folder or envelope to avoid damage or contamination. If necessary, make a working copy and preserve the original document for submission to a forensic document examiner. Most forensic examinations will require the original document, not a copy of it, since most photocopies do not reproduce original writings, typewriting, or other features with sufficient clarity or detail to allow adequate examination.

When initialing a document for future identification, do it in a non-critical area and use a different type of writing instrument than was used for the questioned writings on the document. The examiner should never write or make markings on the original document other than his unobtrusive initials for identification. Do not add new folds, staple it, place paper clips on it, crumple it, or do anything else that would affect or change its original condition. If stored in an envelope, be careful not to write on the envelope and cause indentations on the original document inside. Photocopies and laser-printed documents should always be stored in paper folders or envelopes, not transparent plastic envelopes, which can result in the copies sticking to the plastic and destroying some features of the document.

Authentication and Chain of Custody

Under the rules of evidence, tangible evidence must be properly authenticated; it cannot be admitted in a legal proceeding unless a competent witness first testifies as to its identity. Essentially, *authentication* consists of testimony from a person with first-hand knowledge that the evidence is what it purports to be. Thus, in addition to obtaining the evidence itself, an investigator must identify or locate witnesses and other evidence necessary to authenticate the document or other tangible evidence.

EXAMPLE

Larson, who has been subpoenaed to appear and produce Acme, Inc.'s expense ledger, testifies that he is the head of Acme's accounting department and that he is familiar with the company's books and records and its bookkeeping procedures. As a result, he is aware that Acme maintained expense ledgers during the period requested in the subpoena. He further testifies that, pursuant to the request in the subpoena, he caused a search to be made for the expense ledger for the time period specified in the subpoena, and

Analyzing and Organizing Evidence

that the bound volumes which he has brought with him and which he has produced are the ledgers that are responsive to the subpoena. This authenticates the records as the expense ledgers sought by the subpoena.

If evidence is subject to change over time, or is susceptible to alteration, the offering party may need to establish that the evidence has not been altered or changed from the time it was collected through its production in court. This is done by establishing a chain of custody. The *chain of custody* is both a process and a document that memorializes (1) who has had possession of an object, and (2) what they have done with it; it is simply a means of establishing that there has not been a material change or alteration to a piece of evidence.

Chain of custody consists of establishing each person who had control or custody of the evidence; how and when it was received; how it was maintained or stored while in each person's possession; what changes, if any, it underwent in that person's custody; and how it left that person's custody. The end result is a chain of testimony that accounts for all the time between when the evidence was obtained and when it is proffered at trial. The goal is to show that access to the evidence was limited to those who testified in the chain of custody and thereby demonstrate that the evidence has not been materially altered.

Generally, to be admissible as evidence, digital evidence must meet the same authentication standards as hard copy documents (i.e., a party offering digital evidence must show that the item is what the proponent claims); however, courts have recognized that the authentication of digital evidence may require greater scrutiny because it can easily be altered after creation. In addition, different forms of digital evidence may require different authentication approaches. Moreover, because digital evidence can be easily altered or destroyed, a chain of custody must be maintained for all digital evidence gathered and analyzed in an investigation. Therefore, it is good practice to consult with an attorney to help ensure authentication.

At a minimum, the following chain of custody procedures should be followed:
- Identify each item that contains relevant information.
- Document each item, whom it was received from, who authorized its removal, the location of the item, and the date and time the item was received.
- Maintain a continuous record of the item's custody as it changes hands.

Maintaining Confidentiality

It is important that investigators treat any tangible evidence they collect as confidential. Documents should be stored securely and logged under a reliable classification and retrieval system to demonstrate accountability for the evidence. Access to the evidence should be limited to the company's lawyer and to others on the investigative team and in the company's control group.

Similarly, it is a good idea to restrict any memoranda or reports that summarize and evaluate the documentary evidence that has been gathered. These summaries and evaluations are likely to be regarded as opinion work product and should be privileged from discovery by outside parties. (See the section on Preserving the Confidentiality of the Investigation in Chapter 6, "Legal Considerations in Interviews.") If the contents of the documentary evidence are indiscriminately published, however, the work product privilege may be waived and the confidentiality of those reports, along with the underlying evidence, will be lost.

Preserving for Fingerprint Examinations

If fingerprint examinations are anticipated, use gloves to handle the documents (be careful if tweezers are used because they can leave indentations that might obscure faint indented writings or the identifiable indentations that are sometimes left by photocopy and fax machines). If you or other known people have inadvertently handled the documents with bare hands, your names should be provided to the fingerprint specialist. It might be necessary to provide the expert with sets of inked fingerprints of these people for elimination purposes.

Recognizing Phony Documents

Forensic document examiners apply scientific methods and use a variety of technical instruments in conducting examinations and comparisons of documents. Individual minute characteristics in handwriting and typewriting are examined and compared with genuine comparison standards. Detailed analyses are made of document features for proof of changes or modifications. Some of the more recent innovations in the field include the use of video spectral comparison, the electrostatic document examination technique, and the application of computer image enhancement. Almost all government crime laboratories staffed with forensic document examiners are equipped to provide support in video spectral comparison and electrostatic imaging. As these techniques are often complex and require precision and expertise, it is best to consult with forensic document examination specialists if such methods are required.

If possible, questioned documents should be examined by an expert. However, there are a few tricks that fraud examiners can use to help identify certain document features that could be suspicious.
- *Signature forgeries* might be recognized by irregularities noticeable in the written letters or by their differences in size from a genuine signature. A side-by-side comparison with a genuine signature might reveal the differences. However, remember that advanced age, poor health, temporary injury, and the use of drugs and alcohol can result in similar characteristics and might mislead the

investigator. Genuine comparison samples should be obtained, and a forensic document examiner should be consulted to make an expert determination.
- *Substituted pages* in multiple-page documents, such as contracts and wills, can often be spotted by holding each page in front of a bright light. Differences in the whiteness, density, thickness, opacity, and paper-fiber patterns of the substituted sheets might be apparent.
- Some *ink differences, alterations, erasures,* and *obliterations* are also revealed by holding the paper in front of a bright light or holding a light over the writings at different angles and observing differences in the color and reflectivity of the inks or disturbances to the paper surface.
- *Counterfeited printed documents,* such as checks, stock and bond certificates, business forms and stationery, birth certificates, driver's licenses, and other identification documents, are sometimes readily disclosed by side-by-side comparisons with corresponding genuine documents. Be alert for the use of incorrect or different versions or form revisions of the documents. For forensic examinations, it will be necessary to obtain and furnish genuine comparison samples of the printed documents to the document examiner.
- *Suspicious indentations from writings* might be revealed by reducing the light in the room and holding a bright beam of light (a narrow-beam flashlight or small high-intensity lamp will do the job) low and parallel to the page surface.

Photocopies

Increasingly, photocopies are retained as original records of documents (particularly in outgoing correspondence files) and can become the only evidence of a document because the original document cannot be located or, in some cases, cannot be released, such as in the case of official public records.

When at all possible, the fraud examiner should obtain the original document for the document examiner and should not submit a copy. Photocopies do not permit the forensic expert to uncover clues such as indentations and erasures. As a result, the document examiner may not be able to determine features and reach conclusions that could have been made from the original document.

Organizing Documentary Evidence

Keeping track of the amount of paper generated is one of the biggest problems in fraud examinations. It is essential that the documents obtained be properly organized early on in an investigation, and that they continuously be reorganized as the case progresses. It is usually difficult to ascertain the relevance of the evidence early in the case, so re-evaluation is critical. Good organization in complex cases includes the following:
- Segregating documents by either witness or transaction. In the first method, the examiner takes the list of names, whether employee, associate, or witness, and begins assembling collected documents by witness. Alternatively, the fraud examiner might find it easier to organize the information by

Analyzing and Organizing Evidence

grouping evidence of the same or similar transactions together. Chronological organization (i.e., organizing the documents by date), however, is the least preferred method.

- Make a *key document file*—a separate file that contains copies of certain important pieces of information for quick access—for easy access to the most relevant documents. The examiner should periodically review the key documents, move the less important documents to backup files, and keep only the most relevant documents in the main file.
- Establish a database early if there is a large amount of information to process. This database can be manual or computerized, and can be accessed by keywords or Bates Stamp numbering. The database should include, at a minimum, the date of the document, the individual from whom the document was obtained, the date obtained, a brief description, and the subject to whom the document pertains.

Chronologies

A chronology of events should be commenced early in the case. The purpose of maintaining a chronology is to establish the chain of events leading to the proof. The chronology might or might not be made a part of the formal report; at a minimum, it can be placed in a working paper binder and used for analysis of the case. Keep the chronology brief and include only information necessary to prove the case. By making the chronology too detailed, you defeat its purpose. The chronology should be revised as necessary, adding new information and deleting that which is irrelevant.

To-Do Lists

Another indispensable aid is the to-do list. The list, which must be updated frequently, should be kept in a stenographer's pad or other permanent ring binder to allow a cumulative record. In a very complex case, the list can be broken into long- and short-term objectives: that which must be done eventually (e.g., prove elements of a particular count), and that which should be done tomorrow (e.g., conduct an interview or draft a subpoena). However organized, some sort of list must be kept; otherwise important points will be forgotten in the lengthy case.

Using Computer Software to Organize Documents and Other Data

Computers are one of the most valuable tools for fraud examiners. In complex fraud cases, the amount of information to be examined can be enormous. Performed manually, an investigation of a complicated fraud scheme could become overwhelming, requiring so much time and effort that it might cease to be cost-effective. With a computer, however, investigators can establish a database to store pertinent information about the case and the documents that have been assembled. Once a database is established, special software can be used to sort, chart, and graph the information in the database, making it easier to analyze relationships and identify anomalies.

Digital Evidence

The proper handling of digital evidence is critical and requires special consideration by the fraud examiner, as electronic documentation is easily altered or destroyed if handled improperly. The destruction of digital evidence through improper handling can result in a finding of spoliation of evidence by a judge or can raise questions about the alteration of exculpatory evidence by the defense. If a judge determines that the authenticity of the evidence cannot be satisfactorily made, then they may rule that the evidence is inadmissible. Because of digital evidence's sensitivity to alteration, fraud examiners should consult with computer forensic experts if an investigation involves more than cursory analysis of electronic evidence.

Understanding Digital Evidence

Many people think of digital evidence as just evidence that is extracted from a computer's hard drive. The term *digital evidence,* however, is not limited to files contained on magnetic storage media. While much digital evidence comprises data recovered from a computer, forensic investigations often go far beyond searching hard drives. Therefore, fraud examiners should be knowledgeable about all forms of digital evidence that might be encountered.

Hardware

It is important for the examiner to understand and be able to recognize various pieces of computer hardware so that he can decide whether he should seize a particular computer component. The examiner should be familiar with the various forms that digital evidence can take. Items used for digital storage have become so compact that it is now possible to store vast amounts of data on items that can fit in a pocket or attach to a keychain. Many of these devices are smaller than a matchbook and are capable of storing any type of information.

Examiners might only have one opportunity (especially in a legal proceeding, such as a search-warrant execution) to determine the items they need to seize. Because of this, examiners must be able to assess the hardware at the scene to determine its relevance to the investigation. Items that are as small as a matchbook can be hidden almost anywhere.

As mentioned previously, digital evidence can take many forms. Not all devices, however, are made so that an examiner can interface with the device to conduct an analysis. It is for this reason that it is important for the examiner to be familiar with the current technology in computer forensics. For example, an entire subset of computer forensics has been developed specifically for mobile phones, smartphones, and MP3 players.

Printers

Examiners must also be aware of the latest advances in printer technologies. Many computer networks have installed printers with large hard drives that eliminate the need for a large print server. The printers themselves might now be the repository of additional evidence that at one time resided on a local machine or on a print server.

Mobile Phones

Mobile phones are frequently used to facilitate crimes. While a small subset of people continue to use relatively basic mobile phones, the vast majority have switched to powerful smartphones that include high-quality video and photo capabilities, audio recording, full Internet access, and the ability to store and view documents in various formats. While these smartphones can be a rich source of information relative to an investigation, gaining access to that information can be very complicated.

Tablets

Tablets have become increasingly common in recent years. As the lines dividing computer, phone, and media player have blurred, the convenience of the all-in-one tablet has proven irresistible to consumers. Most tablets, such as the iPad, Google Nexus, and Kindle Fire, are equipped with high-definition video capabilities and relatively large amounts of storage space. These devices are able to view, store, edit, and transmit documents and other media using the same software as a personal computer or laptop.

Digital Cameras

As digital camera use increases, more criminal cases will require the forensic analysis of this type of data. Deleted pictures can be recovered from digital cameras and must be handled properly. The same holds true for digital video recorders, pen cams, and Web cams. They contain content as well as metadata about the origin and ownership of the content itself.

Credit Card Readers

Credit card readers are used for fraud and identity theft. It is very common to receive many different types of credit card readers as computer evidence. Some readers store the data inside, and it must be retrieved. Others connect to a computer and send the data to the computer either wirelessly or over a cable.

MP3 Player Devices

Digital MP3 players are ubiquitous and have the ability to store large amounts of media. When used as storage mediums, these devices can contain artifacts relating to the fraud.

Analyzing and Organizing Evidence

Watches

Some watches allow for the storage of contact information, notes, and telephone numbers within their memory. Several companies have launched smartwatches that include advanced features such as body sensors and Internet connectivity. The market for wearable technology will continue to expand in the near future.

GPS Navigation Systems

GPS navigation systems are configured with a snail trail feature, as well as integrated Bluetooth access, enabling Internet connectivity through a mobile phone connection. These devices can contain the whereabouts of a car or portable receiver, and can add yet another angle to the investigation.

Considerations When Seizing Digital Evidence

Surveying the Systems Involved

To provide the digital forensics expert with what he needs, as well as to prepare for reporting and litigation concerns, the fraud examiner should attempt to obtain as much information about the subject's electronic equipment as possible. The expert does not need exact hardware specifications or the exact versions of software installed, just a high-level description of the environment.

Be certain to document the scene with photographs or a diagram, depending on the complexity of the setup, remembering that it may be a year or longer before testimony about what the office looked like on the day of the seizure will be asked for in a legal proceeding. Additionally, it is important to document what is on the screen if the system is on, as well as what processes are currently running. Many people have a habit of writing down or recording their passwords near their computer, so examiners should look around for notes that may appear to be passwords. This practice may aid in the discovery of passwords needed to access encrypted data in the event the subject of the investigation is being uncooperative.

Take thorough notes regarding the time and date that the system was seized and the personnel involved in the seizure. The status of the system should also be noted. Was it on, off, or on standby? Was there anything unusual attached to the system? Was there any obvious damage? Did any files have to be saved? Also, if the computer was active, record any open applications. Make sure to start a chain of custody document and note each person and storage location through which each piece of evidence passes.

System Components

USER SYSTEMS

- *Computer towers*. Traditional computer system used at the office. Not designed to be portable.

- *Laptop*: Usually assigned to key individuals and personnel who travel routinely or regularly work from home. If a laptop is involved, ask about remote access capability while the user is on travel.
- *Flash drives*: These devices are now capable of storing up to 1 terabyte of information, and their capacities are continuing to increase. The forensic specialist will be able to determine, by conducting a link file analysis, what files were accessed while a flash drive was inserted. He can also determine if a seized flash drive was ever inserted into a computer.
- *CD/DVD*: Optical storage is rated to last five years before the optical surface begins to decay. CD/DVD use in the workplace is not as common as at home. The specialist will be able to determine if any CD/DVD burning activity was performed, and what files were placed onto the media.

SERVER SYSTEMS
- *Email*: If an email system is involved, the fraud examiner will likely need to work with the company's IT personnel to gain access to backups, or have them archive an active email store to an archival personal email folder—called a PST file—for the forensic expert's analysis.
- *File server*: A standard server where individuals and groups are assigned access to files and folders based upon membership in a group.
- *Domain server*: The central authentication server in a domain, which provides access and authentication to a network. This is where users are created and assigned rights, group membership, and other security settings.
- *Proxy*: Large corporations will implement proxy servers in an effort to manage Internet access and route all Internet traffic through a single computer. This minimizes the amount of traffic traversing the network, as common pages are cached on the proxy server. All incoming and outgoing requests are handled by the proxy server and are logged by user request. Fraud examiners should ensure these logs are preserved at the start of an investigation.

PERIMETER DEVICES
- *Routers*: Hardware devices that route network traffic between routable domains. They can be configured to log certain types of traffic, as well as caching Address Resolution Protocol (ARP) information.
- *Switches*: Multiple computers are plugged into these hardware devices, and the traffic is switched between computers and the connected network. May be configured to trunk connections into Virtual Local Area Networks (VLANs).
- *Firewalls*: Devices designed to permit or deny access between networks or hosts based upon predefined rules. Incoming requests are inspected prior to granting access. These will also contain log information that may be useful during the investigation, depending on the type of case.

Analyzing and Organizing Evidence

REMOTE ACCESS METHODS
- *VPN client*: A Virtual Private Network (VPN) is a means to connect to a network as though the user were sitting in their office. The VPN concentrator negotiates authentication and proxies the encrypted traffic between a public network and the protected private network. VPN servers contain access logs and can be used to match activity back to a specific machine as the Media Access Control (MAC) address is logged.
- *OWA*: Outlook Web Access (OWA) can be set up by the company to allow a Web user to access his email from a machine outside the network. Access is likely to be logged on the Web server.
- *PCAnywhere or GoToMyPC*: These remote-control applications allow access to a user's work station from a machine outside the network. They require that the machine be publicly addressable from the outside and that the user connects to it as though he were sitting at his system.

Securing the Computer System

Fraud examiners should be aware that computer files can be altered simply through the normal startup process. Most of the Microsoft operating systems, such as Windows 7, change the time and date stamps on a number of files during startup and delete a number of temporary files during the shutdown process. These pieces of information could be critical to the investigation. Therefore, it is essential that the system be properly secured to prevent unintentional changes to the data.

When securing a computer system, follow the two golden rules. First, if the computer is off, don't turn it on. Also, if a computer is on, an investigator will not want it to go through its normal shutdown routines because Windows is very good about cleaning up after itself. A number of temporary files will be deleted and possibly overwritten during a normal shutdown, and some of these files may be important to the investigation. In most cases, the investigator should simply unplug a running computer. Once the investigator takes possession of the computer, he should not allow anyone access it, with the exception of a trained forensic examiner.

Further, once the computer is seized, it is necessary to secure it in such a way that will allow the investigator to testify, if need be, that no unauthorized access to the suspect system occurred. By preserving the state of the system at the time of seizure, the examiner can help to defeat an argument by opposing counsel that exculpatory information was somehow tainted or erased due to mishandling of the system. If one bit is changed on the system's data, the data will have a completely different hash value; that is to say, it will be different from the original, even though the average person may not be able to recognize any difference at all.

The second golden rule when securing a computer is: Don't peek through the files. This also applies to disks. If a system is running, the examiner might be tempted to click on the My Computer icon to look for evidence or copy files to a flash or optical storage device. This should never be done, because each file the investigator touches will have its original time stamps changed; once this occurs, the original time stamps cannot be recovered. It will be obvious to the forensic examiner that this has happened.

Laptop Computers

Laptop computers present additional considerations. When seizing a laptop, it is important to remove the battery first and then pull the plug. It is essential when seizing a laptop to recover all of the components that belong to the laptop, such as zip drives, CD- and DVD-ROMs, and power supply cords. Often, laptop computers must be imaged with their drives installed, and because of the proprietary nature of the laptops themselves, they will only function with their own components. Many times these components can be located in the laptop carrying case.

Privacy Issues

Personal digital devices are becoming more common in the workplace. Employees often carry smartphones, tablets, flash drives, or MP3 players into the office. Each of these devices is capable of storing large amounts of data and can easily be used to steal a company's intellectual property. Because these devices are often purchased by the employee for personal use, a search warrant may be needed to seize or search these devices since employees may have a "reasonable expectation of privacy" in these types of personal devices. Therefore, it is extremely important to include such devices in the company's search policy. The policy should clearly state that any personal electronic devices, including laptops, mobile phones, tablets, flash drives, MP3 players, and so forth, are (just like handbags and briefcases) subject to search if brought onto the company's premises.

Defining the Parameters of the Expert's Search

Once the components housing the digital evidence have been seized, the fraud examiner must consider the parameters of the computer forensics expert's search. Narrowing the search for digital evidence to a realistic set of parameters ensures speed and focus of the investigation. "Dig up as much dirt as possible on this person" is an unrealistic request, and one that will lead to wasted time and money. Automated software exists to make the process of data extraction more efficient, but it requires a bit of front-end customization to tighten up the search criteria. Once the parameters for the search are defined, the forensic examiner can create the subject and let the process run overnight, oftentimes yielding results the next business day. The more specificity the fraud examiner can provide to the search request, the better and faster the results will be.

It is also wise for the examiner to ask questions and converse with the expert about the best methods to achieve the desired result. This open dialogue provides the opportunity for both parties to understand the requirements and discuss methods to achieve the objectives of the investigation. Ask the forensics expert to explain back the request as he heard it. Something as simple as, "I want all deleted files back," can have many different meanings, with many different methods to get there. For instance, did the fraud

Analyzing and Organizing Evidence

examiner mean "I'd like you to recover any user-deleted documents that are recoverable" or "I'd like you to search through unallocated space and file slack for any remnants of deleted files"? Each describes the process to search for deleted files, but one can be achieved in a few hours while the other might take a few days and yield fragments of files whose creator is often difficult to prove.

Reviewing the Evidence

As with all types of investigations, computer forensic examinations seek to establish the details of the case—the who, when, what, where, how, and why—only using a slightly different approach and meaning:

- Who? (Ownership) Attempt to determine ownership or responsibility for a given action or artifact.
- When? (Time line) Establish a time line of activity leading up to and after an event.
- What? (File characteristics) Determine the type of file or programs involved in the event and what they were used for in relation to the action.
- Where? (Physical disk geometry) Analyze the presence, by location on the hard disk, where proof of an event resides.
- How? (Created, accessed, copied, printed, etc.) Attempt to determine how the action was carried out, with an eye on science and the ability to replicate behavior to reach the same conclusion.
- Why? (Deleted, copied, or manipulated) Using the digital evidence, attempt to determine the intent of the accused. Whether they were seeking to destroy data or copy it for their own gain often can be proven via computer forensics.

Review Questions

1. Which of the following is the LEAST preferred method of organizing documentary evidence?
   A. By witness
   B. By date received
   C. By transaction
   D. None of the above are preferred methods of organizing documentary evidence

2. _____ is a means of establishing that there has not been a material change to a piece of evidence.
   A. Evidence restoration
   B. Authentication
   C. Chain of custody
   D. None of the above

3. According to the text, which of the following is NOT true when seizing digital evidence?
   A. The fraud examiner should document the scene using photographs, diagrams, or video.
   B. If the computer is on, the fraud examiner should turn it off using the standard shutdown procedure.
   C. The fraud examiner should search near the computer's location for notes that appear to be passwords.
   D. When seizing a laptop computer, the fraud examiner should also recover all power supply cords and related components.

4. Which of the following is NOT a source of digital evidence?
   A. A printer
   B. A GPS navigation system
   C. A watch
   D. All of the above are sources of digital evidence

5. According to the text, many counterfeited printed documents can be detected by:
   A. Shining a light across the paper surface at a low oblique angle or parallel to the surface
   B. Developing inconsistencies in the paper by shading or scratching on the surface with a pencil
   C. Making a side-by-side comparison with a corresponding genuine document
   D. None of the above

Analyzing and Organizing Evidence

6. When organizing documentary evidence, the least preferred method is:
    A. By witness
    B. By evaluation
    C. Chronologically
    D. All of the above

7. Whenever possible, which of the following should be submitted to the forensic expert for examination?
    A. Original document
    B. Photocopy of document
    C. Carbon copy of document
    D. None of the above

8. The chain of custody is a process that memorializes which of the following?
    A. Who has had possession of an object
    B. What a person has done with an object
    C. Whether an object has been materially altered
    D. All of the above

V. INTERVIEWING WITNESSES

Interview Mechanics

As with all other phases of an internal investigation, an interview will be most successful if the investigator is thoroughly prepared. By the time an interview is conducted, the investigator will have gathered as much relevant documentation as possible, and will have spoken to as many other witnesses as necessary to optimize his ability to elicit information from the subject at hand. Going into the interview, the effective interviewer will have a clear idea of what information the subject should be able to provide, and will have a game plan of how to uncover that information. This means that the interviewer will be attuned to every aspect of the interview process. He will have chosen an appropriate location for the interview, he will have a good idea of what questions he wishes to ask and what information he hopes to elicit, and he will have planned how to record the subject's responses. In order to properly address all of these issues, the interviewer must understand interview mechanics.

> **Video**
>
> In the video titled "Chapter V: Before the Interview," fraud investigation expert Jonathan Turner, CFE, provides insight on how to effectively prepare to conduct an interview. (Go to www.acfe.com/internalinvestigations to view the video.)

Choosing a Venue for the Interview

The term *venue* refers to the physical location at which the interview takes place. When possible, the interview should be held in a location where the subject will feel comfortable and secure. The interview room should be quiet and free from distractions, comfortably lit, and well-ventilated. There should be no locks on the doors or any physical barriers placed between the subject and the exit. If the interview location causes the subject to feel that his freedom is restricted, this can inhibit communication and may subject the interviewer or his company to liability for false imprisonment. (The legal elements of false imprisonment are discussed in the next chapter, "Legal Considerations in Interviews.")

The interviewer should consider whether the location of the interview makes a statement to the subject, the subject's associates, or the subject's coworkers. The interviewer should be aware that tightening or loosening the level of privacy for an interview might signal to others that there is something unique about a particular interview, and might therefore create an implication about the subject's involvement in the conduct that is under investigation. This should be avoided. The level of confidentiality should remain constant for all interviews, from the most tangential witness to the prime suspect. It is preferable to maintain a single location for all interviews; however, when this is not possible, alternate locations should be comparable in terms of security and atmosphere.

Interviewing Witnesses

If there is no way to achieve a desired level of privacy on-site, the interviewer should consider conducting interviews at an off-site location. Again, once this decision is made, all interviews should be conducted off-site. If employees A, B, and C are interviewed in an on-site office, but employee D is asked to go off-site for his interview, this might create a perception—perhaps inaccurately—that employee D has a greater degree of culpability than the others who were interviewed.

Establishing Proxemic Control over the Interview

Proxemics is a term used to describe the use of interpersonal space to convey meaning. It is important for the interviewer to establish proxemic control over the interview. This requires paying attention to the relative positions of the interviewer and the subject within the interview room, and to the arrangement of furniture and other objects that might create barriers between the interviewer and the subject.

The interviewer should position himself approximately four to six feet from the subject. The interviewer and the subject should be seated in such a manner that the interviewer can face the subject and, at the same time, create an open atmosphere that is conducive to communication. It is best not to have any barriers such as chairs, tables, and desks between the interviewer and the subject. Where no physical object separates the interviewer from the subject, the interviewer is in a better position to observe the subject's nonverbal communication. If the interviewer plans to take notes, he should attempt to place the desk or table next to his writing hand.

It is never advisable to interview a subject in his office or at his desk. A desk can be a physical as well as a psychological barrier, creating a symbol of authority for the person seated behind it. The interviewer does not want to confer a sense of authority upon the subject.

> **Video**
>
> In the video titled "Chapter V: Proxemics," fraud investigation expert Jonathan Turner, CFE, explains the importance of considering proxemics when preparing to conduct an interview. (Go to www.acfe.com/internalinvestigations to view the video.)

Taking Notes

It is critically important to document the results of an interview. In most cases, this is accomplished by taking notes. Interviews without notes are significantly limited in their value because they leave the results of the interview open to interpretation or outright dispute.

At the beginning of the interview, the interviewer should ask the subject if he objects to the interviewer taking notes. This is the polite and professional thing to do, and it serves two purposes:

- It is part of the process by which the subject is encouraged to be a participant.
- If the subject tells the interviewer that he does mind, this can open a line of questioning to determine the reason for the subject's objections.

The subject should be advised that note-taking is critical to the integrity of the process and that notes ensure that what the subject says is documented properly. It may be helpful to inform the subject that the interviewer will review his notes with him at the end of the session to confirm that they are accurate.

In a professional setting, most subjects will understand the critical value of notes. Very few people will refuse to allow the interviewer to take notes, regardless of how they feel about it. If a subject is absolutely opposed to notes being taken, the interviewer should attempt to find out why and see if he can alleviate the subject's concerns. With a hostile subject who opposes note-taking, the interviewer can ask if it is alright for him to make selected notes regarding dates or things the interviewer might not remember later. The interviewer should explain that it is important that he understand the subject's position correctly. If the subject is adamant about the interviewer not taking notes, it should be documented in the interviewer's report. In these cases, the interviewer should refrain from note-taking and reduce the interview to notes as quickly as possible after the interview.

As the interviewer develops his skill sets, he should concentrate on taking verbatim notes. Some practitioners recommend that the interviewer not attempt to write everything down. The argument is that in doing so, the interviewer will not have an opportunity to observe the subject's nonverbal communications. For purposes of this discussion, however, it is recommended that the interviewer take down verbatim as much of what the subject says as is possible. This includes repeated words and parenthetical comments. This practice allows the interviewer to later review what the subject said as opposed to what the interviewer thought the subject said.

When taking notes, the interviewer should specifically concentrate on recording specific nouns, pronouns, verbs, and qualifiers that the subject uses. The interviewer should take note of any indicators of responsibility, innocence, or guilt by the subject. He should also note (in an objective manner) any unusual change in body language or tone, and document these changes in conjunction with notes of what the subject or interviewer said at the time the body language or tone changed.

The interviewer should not, however, document his own opinions and conclusions of the respondent's guilt. Such notes can hurt the interviewer's credibility if they are later produced in court.

Interviewing Witnesses

Maintain Eye Contact
The interviewer should maintain eye contact with the respondent as much as possible during note taking. Just as eye contact personalizes all human communication, it creates a more comfortable environment and facilitates the flow of information during the interview process.

Remain Calm and Professional
Also, the interviewer should remain calm and professional during the interview; do not become hurried or scramble to jot down a particular fact or statement, as this may convey the interviewer's opinion about the significance of the information that is being conveyed.

Review and Document
At the conclusion of the interview, the interviewer should review the notes with the subject in an effort to confirm what the subject has said. The notes should be reduced to a typewritten report as quickly as possible following the interview.

Do Not Interview More Than One Person
One of the basic rules for conducting interviews is to question only one person at a time. The testimony of one respondent will invariably influence the testimony of another. There are few hard and fast rules, but this is one of them.

Do Not Promise Confidentiality
Some subjects may be hesitant to speak to the interviewer for fear that the information will not be confidential. The subject may request a promise of confidentiality for any statements he makes. When this happens, the interviewer should inform the subject that all of the information that is gathered will be provided to individuals who have a need to know.

The interviewer should not make any promises to the subject that the matters discussed will be confidential. Any information gathered in an interview belongs to the client or employer, not the interviewer. The interviewer does not have the right to limit the use of the information or to decide how the information will be used. Examiners employed by government agencies may even have an absolute duty not to hold sources and informants in confidence. Therefore, to promise the subject that the information will be kept confidential is misleading to the subject and may taint subsequent use of the information.

Handle Negotiation Attempts
In some situations, a subject may attempt to negotiate with the interviewer, offering information in exchange for something from the company or the client. If this happens, the interviewer should keep the discussion open and listen to what the subject might want. However, unless otherwise authorized to

do so, the interviewer should not represent to the subject that there is a *quid pro quo* with respect to his cooperation. The interviewer should tell the subject that any information he provides will be conveyed to the appropriate individual and will be taken into account. To negotiate with a subject is to lose control of the interview and investigation.

Do Not Discuss the Source of Allegations

In the event the interviewer is following-up on a complaint or allegation, he should not discuss either the fact that there is an allegation or where the information originated. It is not the role of the interviewer to provide information. If a subject asks where the complaint or information originated, the interviewer may advise the subject that, as a matter of policy, the basis for any inquiry is not discussed.

Common Problems Arising During the Interview

There are a number of situations that might arise during the interview requiring that the examiner proceed cautiously. This section discusses the more common scenarios.

Resistance

There is always the possibility that the individual will refuse a request for an interview. In general, an individual is less reluctant to be interviewed when contacted in person. When the respondent and the interviewer have no connection, studies show that as many as 65 percent of the respondents will refuse an interview if contacted first by telephone. In contrast, one study concluded that only one-third of respondents will be reluctant to be interviewed when contacted in person. Furthermore, the more unpleasant the topic, the more likely the respondent is to refuse.

With inexperienced interviewers, there is a danger that the interviewer will perceive resistance when there is none. As a result, the interviewer might become defensive. It is incumbent upon the interviewer to overcome such feelings to complete the interview. The following paragraphs discuss some common types of resistance and ways to overcome them.

"I'M TOO BUSY"

When the interviewer contacts the respondent without a previous appointment, there is a possibility that the respondent will be too busy at the moment to cooperate. I'm too busy also is used as an excuse for the real source of the person's resistance, which might be lethargy, ego threat, or dislike of talking to strangers. These situations can be diffused by the interviewer stressing that:
- The interview will be short
- The interviewer is already there
- The project is important
- The interview will not be difficult
- The interviewer needs help

"I DON'T KNOW ANYTHING ABOUT IT"

The interviewer will sometimes get this response immediately after stating the purpose of the interview. This resistance is typically diffused by accepting the statement, and then returning with a question. For example, if a witness says "I don't know anything," a typical response by the interviewer would be: "I see. What do your duties involve, then?"

"I DON'T REMEMBER"

Usually, this is not an expression of resistance. Instead, it is an expression of modesty, tentativeness, or caution. One of the best ways to respond is to simply remain silent while the person is deliberating. He is saying, in effect, "Give me a moment to think." If this is not successful, the best way to counter is to pose an alternate, narrower question. As with other symptoms of resistance, the resistance should be accepted and diffused. Then, the examiner should pose an alternate question.

"WHAT DO YOU MEAN BY THAT?"

When the respondent asks this question, it might represent a symptom of mild resistance with which the respondent is attempting to shift the attention from himself to the interviewer. It also might be a way for the respondent to stall for time while deliberating. Or it could be that the respondent is not sure what the interviewer's question means. The interviewer should typically react to such a question by treating it as a mere request for clarification. The interviewer should not become defensive; to do so generally will escalate the resistance.

Difficult People

The interviewer invariably will encounter a few difficult people. There are five common-sense steps to take with such people.

DON'T REACT

Sometimes a respondent will insist on giving the interviewer a "hard time" for no apparent reason. Though, in reality, there can be a multitude of reasons why the person refuses to cooperate. There are three natural reactions for the interviewer verbally assailed by the respondent: to strike back, to give in, or to terminate the interview. None of these tactics is satisfactory, as none leads to a productive interview. Instead, the interviewer should consciously ensure that he does not react to anger with hostility.

DISARM THE PERSON

A common mistake is to try to reason with an unreceptive person. The interviewer must disarm the hostile person. The best tactic is surprise. If the person is stonewalling, he expects the interviewer to apply pressure; if attacking, the person expects the interviewer to resist. To disarm the person, the interviewer should listen, acknowledge the point, and agree wherever possible.

CHANGE TACTICS

In some situations, changing tactics to reduce hostility might be the only viable option. This means casting what the respondent says in a form that directs attention back to the problem and to the interests of both sides. This normally means asking the respondent what he would do to solve the problem.

MAKE IT EASY TO SAY "YES"

In trying to negotiate with difficult people, the usual tactic is for the interviewer to make a statement and attempt to get the respondent to agree with it. A better choice is to agree with one of the respondent's statements and go from there. It is better to break statements into smaller ones that would be difficult to disagree with. This helps the difficult person save face.

MAKE IT HARD TO SAY "NO"

One way of making it difficult to say "no" is by asking reality-based (what-if) questions. These types of questions are used to get the respondent to think of the consequences of not agreeing.

EXAMPLE

Interviewer:
"What do you think will happen if we don't agree?"

"What do you think I will have to do from here?"

"What will you do?"

Volatile Interviews

A *volatile interview* is one that has the potential to bring about strong emotional reactions in the respondent. A typical scenario for a volatile interview occurs when the investigator interviews close friends or relatives of a suspect. Some individuals, by nature, are resentful of authority figures, such as fraud examiners and law enforcement officers. It is important for the investigator to know how to approach a volatile interview.

There are various methods the investigator can use to help control volatile interviews. One method is to have two interviewers involved in potentially volatile situations. This procedure provides psychological strength for the interviewers. Additionally, the second person can serve as a witness in the event that the subject later makes allegations of improper conduct.

Potentially volatile interviews should be conducted on a surprise basis, meaning that the subject should be given little or no advance notice of the interview. If the interview is not conducted by surprise, the interviewer runs the risk of the respondent not showing up, showing up with a witness, or being present with counsel.

In addition, the order of questions should be out of sequence in a potentially volatile interview. This is to keep the volatile respondent from knowing the exact nature of the inquiry and where it is leading. Although the interviewer will endeavor to obtain information regarding who, what, when, where, why, and how, the order of the questioning will vary from that of other interviews. This is especially important in situations where the respondent might be attempting to protect himself.

Furthermore, *hypothetical questions* (i.e., fictional situations, analogous to the act in question, that clarify and highlight particular aspects of a question at issue) are generally considered to be less threatening and are, therefore, ideally suited for the potentially volatile interview. For example, in an interview of Smith regarding Jones, rather than saying "*Did Ms. Jones do it?,*" the interviewer should ask "*Is there any reason why Ms. Jones would have done it?*"

Types of Questions

When conducting an interview, there are five general types of questions an interviewer can ask:
- Introductory questions
- Informational questions
- Closing questions
- Assessment questions
- Admission-seeking questions

Because fraud examinations move in a linear order, starting with the general and working to the specific, the first interviews should be with those that are least likely to be involved, working toward those that are more likely to be involved. The first interviews are conducted for the purpose of gathering information, and therefore they should be non-confrontational, non-threatening, and should encourage open communication. In these routine interview situations, only three of the five types of questions will normally be asked: introductory, informational, and closing questions. If the interviewer has reasonable cause to believe the respondent is not being truthful, assessment questions can be asked. Finally, if the interviewer decides with reasonable cause that the respondent is responsible for misdeeds, admission-seeking questions can be posed.

> **Video**
>
> ▶ In the video titled "Chapter V: Asking Questions," fraud investigation expert Jonathan Turner, CFE, explains why he doesn't recommend preparing specific questions in advance of conducting an interview. (Go to www.acfe.com/internalinvestigations to view the video.)

Introductory Questions

One of the most difficult aspects of an interview is getting started. The interviewer and the respondent, in many instances, have not met before. The interviewer has a tall order: meet the person, state a reason for the interview, establish necessary rapport, and get the information. The introduction is accomplished through questions, as opposed to statements, that allow the interviewer to assess feedback from the respondent. If the respondent is reluctant to be interviewed, that fact will come out through the introductory questions.

Four Objectives

Introductory questions are designed to serve the following four objectives: to provide an introduction, to establish a rapport between the interviewer and the subject, to establish the theme of the interview, and to observe the suspect's reactions.

PROVIDING THE INTRODUCTION

The interviewer should indicate his name and company, but avoid using titles. As a general proposition, the more informal the interview, the more relaxed the respondent will be. This leads to better communication.

Making physical contact helps break down psychological barriers to communication; therefore, the interviewer should also shake hands with the subject. The interviewer is cautioned from invading the respondent's personal space, however, as this might make the person uncomfortable. The interviewer generally should remain at a distance of four to six feet.

One of the goals of the introduction is to create a comfortable climate for the subject—one that will encourage open communication. Once the subject is seated, it is a good idea to ask the subject if he would like something to drink, if he needs to take off his coat or jacket, etc. It is best to take care of these matters before beginning the interview so that delays and interruptions can be avoided.

ESTABLISHING RAPPORT

It is important to establish *rapport*—a relationship of common understanding or trust and acquiescence between people—during the introductory phase of an interview. In other words, there must be some common ground established before questioning begins. This is usually accomplished by engaging in small talk with the subject for a few minutes. This should not be overdone, but should be used as a means to break the ice and establish a flow of communication between the interviewer and the subject.

> **Video**
>
> In the video titled "Chapter V: Establishing Rapport," fraud investigation expert Jonathan Turner, CFE, explains the process of establishing rapport with an interview subject. (Go to www.acfe.com/internalinvestigations to view the video.)

ESTABLISHING THE INTERVIEW THEME

The interviewer must state the purpose of the interview in some way before asking serious questions. The interview theme might be related only indirectly to the actual purpose of the interview. The goal of the theme is to get the respondent to "buy in" to assisting in the interview. The theme for the interview should be one that is logical for the respondent to accept and easy for the interviewer to explain. At this stage of the interview, less specific, open-ended inquiries are generally more effective than narrow, closed questions. One of the most effective interview themes is that the interviewer is seeking the subject's help. Nearly all human beings get satisfaction from helping others. Throughout the interview, it is important to include the subject as part of the process, as opposed to making him feel like a target or less than a full participant in the process. During this phase of the interview, the respondent must not feel threatened in any way.

OBSERVING REACTIONS

The interviewer must be skilled in interpreting the respondent's reactions to questions. The majority of communication between individuals is non-spoken; the subject will provide clues about what he knows—consciously or subconsciously—with his body language, tone of voice, and attitude. The interviewer must, therefore, systematically observe the various responses the subject gives during the course of the conversation.

This is done by first posing non-sensitive questions while establishing rapport. By observing the subject's reactions to the non-sensitive questions, the interviewer can establish a baseline for the subject's verbal and nonverbal behavior. Later, when more sensitive questions are asked, the interviewer will observe the respondent's reactions. If the respondent's verbal and nonverbal behavior significantly changes as particular questions are posed, the interviewer must attempt to determine why. (For more detailed discussion, see the upcoming section on Physiology of Deception.)

General Rules for the Introductory Phase of the Interview

ASK NON-SENSITIVE QUESTIONS

Sensitive questions should be scrupulously avoided until well into the interview. Even then, such questions should be asked only after careful deliberation and planning. Likewise, interviewers are encouraged to formulate their questions in a way that will not bring about a strong emotional reaction from the respondent, and emotive words of all types should be avoided during the introductory phase. Such words normally put people on the defensive, making them more reluctant to answer and to cooperate.

EXAMPLE

Instead of:	*Use:*
Investigation	*Inquiry*
Audit	*Review*
Interview	*Ask a few questions*
Embezzle, steal, theft	*Shortage or paperwork problems*

GET A COMMITMENT FOR ASSISTANCE

It is critical for the interviewer to obtain a commitment for assistance from the subject. The commitment must consist of some positive action on the part of the subject; remaining silent or simply nodding the head is not sufficient. The interviewer should ask for the commitment before the interview commences, and should encourage the respondent to voice that "yes" aloud. If the interviewer encounters silence the first time, the question should be repeated in a slightly different way until the respondent verbalizes commitment.

MAKE A TRANSITIONAL STATEMENT

Once the interviewer has a commitment for assistance, he must describe the purpose of the interview in more detail. This is done with a *transitional statement*, which sets forth a legitimate basis for the inquiry and explains to the subjects how they fit into the inquiry. After making the transitional statement, the interviewer should seek a second commitment for assistance, as in the following example.

EXAMPLE

Interviewer:

"It's pretty routine, really. I'm gathering some information about the purchasing function and how it is supposed to work. It would be helpful to me if I could start by asking you to tell me about your job. Okay?"

SEEK CONTINUOUS AGREEMENT

Throughout the interview process—from the introduction to the close—the interviewer should attempt to phrase questions so that they can be answered "yes." It is easier for people to reply in the affirmative than the negative.

Informational Questions

Once the proper format for the interview has been set, the interviewer should turn to the fact-gathering portion. Informational questions should be non-confrontational and non-threatening, and should be asked for the purpose of gathering unbiased factual information. The great majority of the interviewer's questions will fall into this category.

Three Types of Questions

There are essentially three types of questions: open, closed, and leading. These question types are discussed in more detail below. Each type of question is used in a logical sequence to maximize the development of information. If the interviewer has reason to believe that the respondent is being untruthful, then assessment questions can be posed. Otherwise, the interview is brought to a logical close at the end of the informational phase.

OPEN QUESTIONS

Open questions are those questions worded in a way that makes it difficult to answer "yes" or "no." The typical open question calls for a monologue response, and it can be answered in several different ways. During the informational phase of the interview, the interviewer should endeavor to ask primarily open questions. This is to stimulate conversation and allow the subject to convey as much information as possible.

An open question does not restrict the subject's response. So instead of asking "You are in charge of posting expenses, aren't you?," which directs the subject's response to one particular area, the investigator might ask "Would you tell me about your job?" The latter example allows a broad response in which more information will be conveyed. Later, the interviewer can go back and draw out more information about a particular topic.

CLOSED QUESTIONS

Closed questions are those which limit the possible responses by requiring a precise answer, usually "yes" or "no." Closed questions are used to deal with specifics, such as amounts, dates, and times. Generally, closed questions should be avoided in the informational part of the interview. They are used extensively in the closing phase.

EXAMPLE

Interviewer:

"Did you make this entry?"

*"What day of the week **did it happen?**"*

> **Video**
>
> In the video titled "Chapter V: Open and Closed," fraud investigation expert Jonathan Turner, CFE, explains the appropriate uses of open and closed questions during an interview. (Go to www.acfe.com/internalinvestigations to view the video.)

LEADING QUESTIONS

Leading questions contain the answer as a part of the question. They are usually used to confirm facts that are already known. An example of a leading question is: "There have been no changes in the operation since last year, have there?" This type of question gives the subject much less room to maneuver than an open or closed question.

Notice how the leading question directs the subject to answer in a particular way—that there have not been any changes. It implies that the interviewer already knows the answer, and asks the subject to confirm what is already known. The open question allows more latitude, allowing the subject to make any comments he wants about changes in the operation. The closed question narrows the subject's options a bit, but it still allows the subject to confirm or deny that changes have been made. Leading questions can be particularly effective in obtaining confessions or getting subjects to make unpleasant admissions.

Question Sequences

As stated above, questioning should generally proceed from the general to the specific; that is, it is best to gather general information before seeking details. A variation is to "reach backward" with the questions, by beginning with known information and working toward unknown areas. An efficient method of doing this is to recount the known information and then frame the next question as a logical continuation of the facts previously related.

> **Video**
>
> In the video titled "Chapter V: Question Sequence," fraud investigation expert Jonathan Turner, CFE, provides insight on determining the sequence of questions when conducting an interview. (Go to www.acfe.com/internalinvestigations to view the video.)

Interviewing Witnesses

Informational Question Techniques

Below are suggestions to improve the quality of the interview during the information-gathering phase.

- Begin by asking questions that are not likely to cause the respondent to become defensive or hostile.
- Ask the questions in a manner that will develop the facts in the order of their occurrence, or in some other systematic order.
- Ask only one question at a time, and frame the question so that only one answer is required.
- Ask straightforward and frank questions; generally avoid shrewd approaches.
- Keep interruptions to a minimum, and do not stop the subject's narrative without good reason.
- Give the respondent ample time to answer; do not rush.
- Try to help the respondent remember, but do not suggest answers; be careful not to imply any particular answer through facial expressions, gestures, methods of asking questions, or types of questions asked.
- Repeat or rephrase questions, if necessary, to get the desired facts.
- Be sure you understand the answers, and if they are not perfectly clear, have the respondent interpret them at the time instead of asking for more explanation later.
- Give the subject an opportunity to qualify his answers.
- Separate facts from inferences.
- Have the subject give comparisons by percentages, fractions, estimates of time and distance, and other such methods to ensure accuracy.
- After the respondent has given a narrative account, ask follow-up questions about every key issue that has been discussed.
- Upon conclusion of the direct questioning, ask the respondent to summarize the information given. Then summarize the facts as you understand them, and have the respondent verify that these conclusions are correct.

Methodology of Informational Questions

To begin the informational phase of the interview, the investigator must first make a transition out of the introductory phase. The transition is a signal that the interviewer and subject are going to begin discussing the substantive issues that are the purpose of the interview. The transition is usually accomplished by asking the subject a non-threatening question about himself or his duties. It often begins with a re-statement of the purpose of the interview—"As I said, I am gathering information about the company's operations. Can you tell me about what you do on a day-to-day basis?"

BEGIN WITH BACKGROUND QUESTIONS

Assuming the subject does not have a problem answering the transitional question, the interviewer should proceed with a series of easy, open questions designed to follow-up on the subject's answer and get him to expand on the information he has already provided. Questions like "How long have you been working here?," "What do you like best about your job?," or "What do your responsibilities involve?"

are good examples of background questions that will help the interviewer get a better understanding of what the subject does and what information he might possess.

OBSERVE VERBAL AND NONVERBAL BEHAVIOR

During the period when the respondent is talking about himself, the interviewer should discreetly observe his verbal and nonverbal behavior. This will help the interviewer calibrate the subject's mannerisms. Later, when more sensitive questions are posed, the interviewer can look for deviations in the subject's behavior that might indicate discomfort or deception.

ASK NONLEADING (OPEN) QUESTIONS

The interviewer should use open questioning techniques almost exclusively during the informational phase of the interview. The questions must be inquisitive and not accusatory. Once the respondent has answered open questions, the interviewer can go back and review the facts in greater detail. If the subject's answers are inconsistent, the interviewer should try to clarify them. But the interviewer should not challenge the honesty or integrity of the respondent at this stage of the interview. This can cause the subject to become defensive and make him reluctant to provide information.

APPROACH SENSITIVE QUESTIONS CAREFULLY

Words such as "routine questions" can be used to play down the significance of the inquiry. It is important for information-gathering purposes that the interviewer does not react excessively to the respondent's statements. The interviewer should not express shock, disgust, or similar emotions during the interview. Every answer the subject gives should be treated evenly.

Closing Questions

In routine, informational interviews, closing the interview on a positive note is a must. Beyond maintaining good will, closing questions serve the following purposes: to reconfirm facts, to gather additional facts, and to conclude the interview.

Reconfirm Facts

It is not unusual for the interviewer to have misunderstood or misinterpreted the respondent's statements. Therefore, to ensure that the interviewer understood the information that the witness provided, he should review the key facts during the closing phase of the interview.

The interviewer should not attempt to revisit all the information that the subject has provided. This is wasteful, unnecessary, and may engender frustration or resentment by the subject. Instead, the interviewer needs to identify the most relevant facts and go over each of them in summary form.

Interviewing Witnesses

It is a good technique to pose leading questions at this phase of the interview. This allows the interviewer to state what he understood the subject to have said, and it gives the subject a chance to confirm or deny the interviewer's interpretation. For example, the interviewer might ask "You knew Ms. Jones had some financial problems, is that right?"

Gather Additional Facts

The closing phase also seeks previously unknown facts. It provides the subject further opportunity to say whatever he wants about the matter at hand. The interviewer should make it a point to ask the subject if he knows of any other documents or witnesses that would be helpful to the investigation. This information is not always volunteered, and the interviewers should not promise confidentiality. The theme of the closing phase should be to provide the subject with an opportunity to furnish any relevant facts or opinions that might have been overlooked.

Conclude the Interview

Concluding the interview is important because it helps maintain goodwill and ensure future cooperation. Ask the subject if there is anything else he would like to say. This gives the correct impression that the interviewer is interested in all relevant information, regardless of which side it favors. It can be helpful to involve the respondent in solving the case (e.g., "*If you were trying to resolve this issue, what would you do?*"). In addition, asking the witness if there is anything else he would like to say gives the respondent an opportunity to assist the interviewer, and it makes the respondent feel like a vital part of the interview. It also opens the door for him to provide additional information that was not specifically asked for. Similarly, asking the subject if he knows of someone else whom the interviewer might talk to can be helpful and lead to other potential sources of information.

When concluding the interview, it is also a good idea to ask the subject if he believes he has been treated fairly. This is particularly important at the conclusion of an admission-seeking interview or when the subject has been uncooperative. The interviewer should generally ask the question as if it were perfunctory (e.g., "*Mr. Martin, this is just a standard question. Do you feel that I have treated you fairly in this interview?*").

Moreover, it is a good idea to give the subject a business card or a telephone number and invite him to call if he remembers anything else that might be relevant.

Finally, the interviewer should shake hands with the subject, thanking him for his time and information.

Assessment Questions

If the interviewer has reason to believe that the respondent is being deceptive, he should begin asking assessment questions. These are questions specifically designed to establish the respondent's credibility.

When assessing credibility, the interviewer must observe the subject's verbal and nonverbal responses. By making such observations, the interviewer can assess the respondent's credibility with some degree of accuracy. That assessment will form the basis of the interviewer's decision about whether to pose admission-seeking questions to obtain a legal admission of wrongdoing.

If the subject has answered all of the informational questions about the event and the interviewer has reason to believe the subject is being deceptive, a theme must be established to justify additional questions. This theme can ordinarily be put forth by saying "I have a few additional questions." The interviewer should not indicate in any way that these questions are for a different purpose than seeking information.

Norming or Calibrating

Norming or *calibrating* is the process of observing behavior before critical questions are asked, as opposed to doing so during questioning. Norming should be a routine part of all interviews. People with truthful attitudes will answer questions one way; those with untruthful attitudes will generally answer them differently. Assessment questions ask the subject to agree with matters that go against the principles of most honest people. In other words, dishonest people are likely to agree with many of the statements, while honest people will not. Assessment questions are designed primarily to get a verbal or nonverbal reaction from the respondent. The interviewer will then carefully assess that reaction.

Physiology of Deception

It is said that everyone lies and does so for one of two reasons: to receive rewards or to avoid punishment. In most people, lying produces stress. The human body will attempt to relieve this stress (even in practiced liars) through verbal and nonverbal clues. A practiced interviewer will be able to draw inferences from a subject's behavior about the honesty of their statements.

Conclusions concerning behavior must be tempered by a number of factors. The physical environment in which the interview is conducted can affect behavior. If the respondent is comfortable, fewer behavior quirks might be exhibited. The more intelligent the respondent, the more reliable verbal and nonverbal clues will be. If the respondent is biased toward the interviewer, or vice versa, this will affect behavior.

People who are mentally unstable or are under the influence of drugs will be unsuitable to interview. Behavioral symptoms of juveniles are generally unreliable. Ethnic and economic factors should be carefully noted. Some cultures, for example, discourage looking directly at someone. Other cultures use certain body language that might be misinterpreted. Because pathological liars are often familiar with advanced interview techniques, they are less likely to furnish observable behavioral clues. The interviewer must take all of the relevant factors into account before drawing any conclusions about the meaning of the verbal and nonverbal signals that a subject demonstrates.

When evaluating signs of deception, it is easy to draw the wrong conclusions. It must be understood that no one sign is an indicator of deception. Therefore, no single behavior should be isolated and no conclusion should be drawn from it; behaviors must be considered together.

> **Video**
>
> In the video titled "Chapter V: Signs of Deception," fraud investigation expert Jonathan Turner, CFE, describes how to detect signs that an interview subject is being deceptive. (Go to www.acfe.com/internalinvestigations to view the video.)

VERBAL CLUES TO DECEPTION

Verbal clues are those behaviors relating to wordings, expressions, and responses to specific questions. Verbal responses include spoken words and gestures that serve as word substitutes, including nodding or shaking the head to indicate "yes" and "no." The following are some examples of verbal clues.

CHANGES IN SPEECH PATTERNS

Deceptive people often speed up or slow down their speech, or speak louder. There might be a change in the voice pitch; as a person becomes tense, the vocal chords constrict. Deceptive people also have a tendency to cough or clear their throats during times of deception.

REPETITION OF THE QUESTION

Repeating the question is a means for a deceptive respondent to gain more time to think of what to say. The respondent may repeat the question verbatim, or he may frame the answer with a request to repeat the question (e.g., "What was that again?" or similar language). Conversely, a truthful subject usually does not have to contemplate his answer.

COMMENTS REGARDING INTERVIEW

Deceptive people will often comment on the physical environment of the interview room, complaining that it is too hot, too cold, etc. As they come under increasing stress, they may frequently ask how much longer the interview will take.

SELECTIVE MEMORY

In some cases, a deceptive person will have a fine memory for insignificant events, but will claim to be unable to remember important facts.

MAKING EXCUSES

Dishonest people frequently make excuses about things that look bad for them, such as "I'm always nervous; don't pay any attention to that."

EMPHASIS ON CERTAIN WORDS

On frequent occasions, dishonest people will add what they believe to be credibility to their lies by use of emphasis.

OATHS

Dishonest individuals frequently use expressions such as *I swear to God, honestly, frankly,* or *to tell the truth* to add credibility to their lies.

CHARACTER TESTIMONY

A dishonest person will often request that the interviewer "Check with my wife" or "Talk to my minister." This tactic is often used to add credibility to a false statement.

ANSWERING WITH A QUESTION

Rather than deny allegations outright, a deceptive person frequently answers a question with a question, such as "Why would I do something like that?" As a variation, the deceptive person sometimes will question the interview procedure by asking "Why are you picking on me?"

OVERUSE OF RESPECT

Some deceptive people go out of their way to be respectful and friendly. When accused of wrongdoing, it is unnatural for a person to react in a friendly and respectful manner (e.g., "I'm sorry, sir, I know you're just doing your job. But I didn't do it.").

INCREASINGLY WEAKER DENIALS

When an honest person is accused of something he did not do, that person is likely to become angry or forceful in making denials. The more the innocent person is accused, the more forceful the denial becomes. The dishonest person, on the other hand, is likely to make a weak denial. Upon repeated accusations, the dishonest person's denials become weaker, to the point that the person becomes silent.

FAILURE TO DENY

Honest people are more likely than dishonest people to deny an event directly. An honest person might offer a simple and clear "no," while the dishonest person will qualify the denial: "No, I did not steal $43,500 from the company on June 27." Other qualified denial phrases include *to the best of my memory,* and *as far as I recall,* or similar language.

Interviewing Witnesses

AVOIDANCE OF EMOTIVE WORDS

A deceptive person will often avoid emotionally provocative terms such as *steal*, *lie*, and *crime*. Instead, the dishonest person frequently prefers "soft" words such as *borrow* and *it* (referring to the deed in question).

REFUSAL TO IMPLICATE OTHER SUSPECTS

Both the honest respondent and the dishonest respondent will have a natural reluctance to name others involved in misdeeds. The dishonest respondent, however, will frequently refuse to implicate possible suspects—no matter how much pressure is applied by the interviewer. This is because the culpable person does not want the circle of suspicion to be narrowed.

TOLERANT ATTITUDES

Dishonest people typically have tolerant attitudes toward criminal conduct. The interviewer in an internal theft case might ask "What should happen to this person when he is caught?" The honest person will usually say "He should be fired and prosecuted." The dishonest individual is much more likely to reply "How should I know?" or "Maybe he is a good employee who got into a bad situation. Perhaps he should be given a second chance."

RELUCTANCE TO TERMINATE INTERVIEW

Dishonest people will generally be more reluctant than honest ones to terminate the interview. The dishonest individual wants to convince the interviewer that he is not responsible so that the investigation will not continue. The honest person generally has no such reluctance.

FEIGNED UNCONCERN

The dishonest person will often try to appear casual and unconcerned, will frequently adopt an unnatural slouching posture, and might react to questions with nervous or false laughter or feeble attempts at humor. The honest person, conversely, will typically be very concerned about being suspected of wrongdoing, and will treat the interviewer's questions seriously.

NONVERBAL CLUES

Nonverbal clues to deception include various body movements and postures accompanying the verbal reply. Some of these are discussed below.

FULL-BODY MOTIONS

When asked sensitive or emotive questions, the dishonest person will typically change his posture completely—as if moving away from the interviewer. The honest person will frequently lean forward—toward the interviewer—when questions are serious.

ANATOMICAL PHYSICAL RESPONSES

Anatomical physical responses are those involuntary reactions by the body to fright, such as increased heart rate, shallow or labored breathing, or excessive perspiration. These reactions are typical of dishonest people accused of wrongdoing.

ILLUSTRATORS

Illustrators are the motions made primarily with the hands to demonstrate points when talking. During non-threatening questions, the illustrators will be used at one rate. During threatening questions, the use of illustrators might increase or decrease.

HANDS OVER THE MOUTH

Frequently, dishonest people will cover their mouth with the hand or fingers during deception. This reaction goes back to childhood, when many children cover their mouths when telling a lie. It is done subconsciously to conceal the statement.

MANIPULATORS

Manipulators are habitual motions like picking lint from clothing, playing with objects such as pencils, or holding one's hands while talking. Manipulators are displacement activities that reduce nervousness.

FLEEING POSITIONS

During the interview, dishonest people will often posture themselves in a "fleeing position." While the head and trunk might be facing the interviewer, the feet and lower portion of the body might be pointing toward the door in an unconscious effort to flee from the interviewer.

CROSSING THE ARMS

Crossing one's arms over the middle zones of the body is a classic defensive reaction to difficult or uncomfortable questions. A variation is crossing the feet under the chair and locking them. These crossing motions occur mostly when a person is being deceptive.

REACTION TO EVIDENCE

While trying to be outwardly unconcerned, the guilty person will have a keen interest in implicating evidence. The dishonest person will often look at documents presented by the interviewer, attempt to be casual about observing them, and then shove them away, as though wanting nothing to do with the evidence.

FAKE SMILES

Genuine smiles usually involve the whole mouth; false ones are confined to the upper half. People involved in deception tend to smirk rather than to smile.

Interviewing Witnesses

TYPICAL ATTITUDES DISPLAYED BY RESPONDENTS	
Truthful	**Untruthful**
Calm	Impatient
Relaxed	Tense
Cooperative	Defensive
Concerned	Outwardly unconcerned
Sincere	Overly friendly, polite
Inflexible	Defeated
Cordial	Surly

Methodology of Assessment Questions

Assessment questions should proceed logically from the least to the most sensitive. In most examples, the basis for the question should be explained before the question is asked. The following questions illustrate the pattern that an interviewer might take in questioning a witness when he has some reason to believe the respondent, a company employee, has knowledge of a suspected fraud.

EXAMPLE

Interviewer:

"The company is particularly concerned about fraud and abuse. There are some new laws in effect that will cost the company millions if abuses go on and we don't try to find them. Do you know which law I am talking about?"

EXPLANATION

Most individuals will not know about the laws concerning corporate sentencing guidelines, and will therefore answer "no." The purpose of this question is to get the respondent to understand the serious nature of fraud and abuse.

EXAMPLE

Interviewer:

"Congress recently passed a law last year that can levy fines of more than $200 million against companies that don't try to clean their own houses. $200 million is a lot of money, so you can understand why the company is concerned, can't you?"

EXPLANATION

The majority of people will say "yes" to this question. In the event of a "no" answer, the interviewer should explain the issue fully and thereafter attempt to get the respondent's agreement. If that agreement is not forthcoming, the interviewer should assess why this is so.

EXAMPLE

Interviewer:

"*Of course, they are not talking about a loyal employee who gets in a bind; they're talking more about senior management. Have you ever read in the newspapers about what kind of people engage in company misdeeds?*"

EXPLANATION

Most people read the news and are at least generally familiar with the problem of fraud and abuse. Agreement by the respondent is expected to this question.

EXAMPLE

Interviewer:

"*Most of them aren't criminals at all. A lot of times, they're just trying to save their jobs or just trying to get by because the company is so cheap that it won't pay people what they are worth. Do you know what I mean?*"

EXPLANATION

Although the honest person and the dishonest person will both probably answer "yes" to this question, the honest individual is less likely to accept the premise that these people are not wrongdoers. Many honest people will reply to the effect that, while they might understand the motivation, that does not justify stealing.

EXAMPLE

Interviewer:

"*Why do you think someone around here might be justified in taking company property?*"

EXPLANATION

Because fraud perpetrators frequently justify their acts, the dishonest individual is more likely than the honest person to attempt a justification, such as "Everyone does it" or "The company should treat people better if they don't want them to steal." The honest person, on the other hand, is much less likely to offer a justification for theft.

EXAMPLE

Interviewer:

"How do you think we should deal with someone who got in a bind and did something wrong in the company's eyes?"

EXPLANATION

Similar to other questions in this series, the honest person tends to want to punish the criminal, while the culpable individual will typically avoid suggesting a strong punishment. For example, "How should I know? It's not up to me" or "If he was a good employee, maybe we should give him another chance."

EXAMPLE

Interviewer:

"Do you think someone in your department might have taken something from the company because he thought he was justified?"

EXPLANATION

Most people—honest or dishonest—will answer "no" to this question. However, when the interviewer gets a "yes," the culpable person is more likely to do so without responding. If the honest person answers "yes," he will most likely provide details.

EXAMPLE

Interviewer:

"Have you ever felt yourself—even though you didn't go through with it—justified in taking advantage of your position?"

EXPLANATION

Again, both honest and dishonest people will usually answer "no" to this question. However, the dishonest person is more likely to acknowledge having at least "thought" of doing it.

EXAMPLE

Interviewer:

"Who in your department do you feel would think himself justified in doing something against the company?"

EXPLANATION

The dishonest person will not likely furnish an answer to this question, frequently saying something to the effect that anyone could have a justification. Dishonest individuals will be reluctant to provide any answer that narrows the list of possible suspects. The honest individual, on the other hand, is more likely to name names—albeit reluctantly.

EXAMPLE

Interviewer:

"Do you believe that most people will tell their manager if they believed a colleague was doing something wrong, like committing fraud against the company?"

EXPLANATION

The honest person is much more likely to report a misdeed himself, and is more likely to respond "yes" to this question. The dishonest person is more likely to say "no." When pressed for an explanation, he might qualify the "no" by adding that his report would be ignored or that it would not be believed.

EXAMPLE

Interviewer:

"Is there any reason why someone who works with you would say he thought you might feel justified in doing something wrong?"

EXPLANATION

This is a hypothetical question designed to place the thought in the mind of a wrongdoer that someone has named him as a suspect. The honest person will typically say "no." The dishonest person is more likely to try to explain by saying something like "I know there are people around here who don't like me."

EXAMPLE

Interviewer:

"What would concern you most if you did something wrong and it was found out?"

EXPLANATION

The dishonest person is less likely to accept the proposition of having done something wrong and to focus on possible repercussions—for example, "I wouldn't want to go to jail." The honest person, however, is more likely to reject the notion of having committed a crime. If the honest person does address his concerns about being caught in an illegal act, his concerns will usually be along the lines of disappointing friends or family; the dishonest person is more likely to discuss punitive measures.

Admission-Seeking Questions

The choice of when to conduct an admission-seeking interview of a suspect is critical. Admission-seeking interviews are reserved specifically for individuals whose culpability is reasonably certain, all other reasonable investigative steps have been completed, as much information as possible has been developed from other sources, and the interviewer can reasonably control the place, time, and subject matter of the interview.

The interviewer must be careful during this phase not to violate the rights and privileges of the person being interviewed. These rights are discussed in detail in the next chapter.

Admission-seeking questions serve at least three purposes. The first purpose is to distinguish the innocent from the culpable. A culpable individual will frequently confess during the admission-seeking phase of an interview, while an innocent person will not do so unless threats or coercion are used. In some instances, the only way to differentiate the culpable from the innocent is to seek an admission of guilt.

The second purpose is to obtain a valid confession. Confessions, under the law, must be voluntarily obtained. The importance of a valid and binding confession to wrongdoing cannot be overstated.

The third purpose of admission-seeking questions is to convince the confessor to sign a written statement acknowledging the facts. Although oral confessions are as legally binding as written ones, the written statement has greater credibility. It also discourages a person from later attempting to recant.

Video

In the video titled "Chapter V: Admission Seeking Interview," fraud investigation expert Jonathan Turner, CFE, provides strategies for conducting admission seeking interviews. (Go to www.acfe.com/internalinvestigations to view the video.)

Preparation

The interview should be scheduled when the interviewer can control the situation. It normally should not be conducted on the accused's turf and is best conducted by surprise.

Note-Taking

When conducting an admission-seeking interview, note-taking should be kept to a minimum. In some cases, taking notes should be avoided altogether. Because the ultimate goal of the admission-seeking interview is to obtain a signed statement in which the suspect admits guilt, it is not necessary to take extensive notes, which can be distracting to the suspect and can reveal what points the examiner believes to be important. Notes, if taken during the interview, should be done in a way that does not reveal their significance.

Presence of Outsiders

When an admission-seeking interview is conducted by a private employer, it is usually not necessary to inform the subject that he is entitled to have an attorney or other representative present. However, there are cases in which an employee may have the right to have a union representative or even a coworker present. (These instances are discussed in more detail in the next chapter.) Of course, even if the person has a right to have an attorney or other representative present, the interviewer should make it clear that the representative will be an observer only; representatives (even attorneys) should not ask questions or object.

Other than the subject and two investigators, no other observers should be permitted in the admission-seeking interview if at all possible. Having others in the room (even representatives) might present legal problems by making the allegation known to a third party. Also, it is very difficult to obtain a confession with witnesses present. In situations where third parties in the room cannot be avoided, the interviewer should therefore consider whether the case can be proven without the admission-seeking interview.

Miranda *Warnings*

As a general rule, private employers conducting an internal investigation are not required to give *Miranda* warnings; however, there are exceptions to the rule. (See the discussion on *Miranda* warnings in the next chapter, "Legal Considerations in Interviews.")

Theme Development

People will confess when they perceive that the benefits of confession outweigh the penalties. Through the application of sophisticated techniques, a good interviewer will be able to convince the respondent that a confession is in his best interest.

People generally will not confess if they believe that there is doubt in the mind of the accuser regarding their guilt; therefore, the interviewer must convey absolute confidence in the premise of the admission he seeks from the subject—even if he is not fully convinced of the subject's guilt. The interviewer should make his accusation in the form of a statement of fact; the subject's guilt should already be assumed in the form of the question. Instead of asking "Did you do it," the interviewer asks "Why did you do it?"

> **Video**
>
> In the video titled "Chapter V: Saying Too Much," convicted fraudster Tom Hughes explains how saying too much during an interview and letting the subject know that you're guessing can destroy your chances of eliciting a confession. (Go to www.acfe.com/internalinvestigations to view the video.)

Remember that the first purpose of an admission-seeking question is to distinguish an innocent person from a culpable one. An innocent person will generally not accept the premise that he is responsible. The guilty person, on the other hand, knows he has committed the act, so he is not shocked by the premise of his guilt. His objection, if he offers one, is more likely to focus on excuses for the conduct rather than outright denial.

The interviewer must offer a morally acceptable reason for the confessor's behavior. The interviewer should not imply that the subject is a bad person, and he should never express disgust, outrage, or moral condemnation about the confessor's actions. Culpable people will almost never confess under these conditions. To obtain a confession, the interviewer must be firm, but he must project compassion, understanding, and sympathy. The goal is to maximize sympathy and minimize the perception of moral wrongdoing.

The threat of a lawsuit is always present when allegations of wrongdoing are made against certain employees. Obviously, there is a danger during this phase that the interviewer will accuse an innocent person of a crime. It is generally legal to accuse innocent people of misdeeds they did not commit as long as:
- The accuser has reasonable suspicion or predication to believe the accused has committed an offense.
- The accusation is made under conditions of privacy.
- The accuser does not take any action likely to make an innocent person confess.
- The accusation is conducted under reasonable conditions.

More information on the dangers of making false accusations is included in the next chapter, "Legal Considerations in Interviews."

Steps in the Admission-Seeking Interview
MAKE A DIRECT ACCUSATION
During the admission-seeking interview, the interviewer must accuse the subject of wrongdoing. The accusation should not be made in the form of a question, but rather as a statement. Emotive words such as *steal, fraud,* and *crime* should be avoided during the accusatory process. The accusation should be phrased as though the accused's guilt has already been established so that the accused is psychologically trapped with no way out.

EXAMPLE

Instead of:	Say:
"We have reason to believe that you …"	*"Our investigation has clearly established that you …"*
"We think you might have …"	*"We have been conducting an investigation into _____, and you are the only person we have not been able to eliminate as being responsible."*

OBSERVE THE REACTION
When accused of wrongdoing, the typical culpable person will react with silence. If the accused does deny culpability, those denials will usually be weak. In some cases, the accused will almost mumble the denial. It is common for the culpable individual to avoid outright denials. Instead, that person will give reasons why he could not have committed the act in question. The innocent person sometimes will react with genuine shock at being accused. It is not at all unusual for an innocent person, wrongfully accused, to react with anger. As opposed to the culpable person, the innocent person will usually strongly deny carrying out the act or acts in question.

REPEAT ACCUSATION
If the accused does not strenuously object after the accusation is made, the interviewer should repeat the accusation with the same degree of conviction and strength.

INTERRUPT DENIALS
Both the truthful and untruthful person will normally object to and deny the accusations. However, when compared to an innocent person, a culpable person is more likely to stop short of an outright denial ("I didn't do it.") and is more apt to furnish the interviewer with explanations as to why he is not the responsible party. It is very important in instances where the examiner is convinced of the

individual's guilt that the denial be interrupted. An innocent person is unlikely to allow the interviewer to prevail in stopping the denial.

Both the innocent and the guilty person will make an outright denial if forced to do so. Accordingly, the interviewer should not solicit a denial at this stage of the admission-seeking interview. Instead of asking "Did you do this?," which gives the subject a chance to say "no," the interviewer should phrase the accusation as though the subject's wrongdoing has already been determined: "Why did you do this?"

The interviewer must prevent the subject from making an outright denial because it becomes extremely difficult for the accused to change a denial once it has been uttered. If the subject denies the accusation and later admits it, he is admitting to lying, and this is very hard to do. Therefore, the interviewer's job is to prevent the subject from making an outright denial, thereby making it easier for the subject to confess to the act.

DELAYS

One of the most effective techniques for stopping or interrupting a denial is through the use of a delaying tactic. The interviewer should not argue with the accused, but rather attempt to delay the outright denial.

EXAMPLE

Interviewer:
"I hear what you are saying, but let me finish first. Then you can talk."

The innocent person usually will not allow the interviewer to continue to develop the theme.

REPEAT INTERRUPTIONS

Occasionally, it might be necessary to repeatedly interrupt the accused's attempted denial. Because this stage is crucial, the interviewer should be prepared to increase the tone of the interruptions to the point where he is prepared to say: "If you keep interrupting, I am going to have to terminate this conversation." The culpable individual will find this threatening because he wants to know the extent of incriminating evidence in the interviewer's possession.

REASONING

If the above techniques are unsuccessful, the interviewer might attempt to reason with the accused and employ some of the tactics normally used for diffusing alibis (see below). In this technique, the accused is presented with evidence implicating him in the crime. The interviewer, however, should not disclose all the facts of the case, but rather small portions here and there.

EXAMPLE

Interviewer:

"I know what you are saying but that doesn't square with these invoices here in front of me. Look at the invoice for $102,136. The facts clearly show you are responsible." (Do not ask the accused to explain the evidence at this point.)

ESTABLISH RATIONALIZATION

Assuming the subject does not confess to the misconduct when faced with direct accusations, the interviewer should proceed to establishing a morally acceptable rationalization that will allow the accused to square the misdeed with his conscience. It is not necessary that the rationalization be related to the underlying causes of the misconduct. It is acceptable for the accused to explain away the moral consequences of the action by seizing on any plausible explanation other than being a "bad person."

If the accused does not seem to relate to one theme, the interviewer should go on to another and another until one seems to fit. Thereafter, that theme should be developed fully. Note that the rationalization explains away the moral—but not the legal—consequences of the misdeed. The interviewer is cautioned not to make any statements that would lead the accused to believe he will be excused from legal liability by cooperating.

Rather than being confrontational, the interviewer should constantly seek agreement from the accused. The goal is to remain in control of the interview while still appearing compassionate and understanding. Again, no matter what conduct the accused has supposedly committed, the interviewer should not express shock, outrage, or condemnation.

<u>UNFAIR TREATMENT</u>

Probably the most common explanation for criminal activity, particularly internal fraud, is unfair treatment and the accused's attempt to achieve equity. Studies have shown that counter-productive employee behavior—including stealing—is motivated primarily by job dissatisfaction. Employees and others feel that "striking back" is important to their self-esteem. The sensitive interviewer can capitalize on these feelings by suggesting to the accused that he is a victim.

EXAMPLE

Interviewer:

"If you had been fairly treated, this wouldn't have happened, would it?"

<u>INADEQUATE RECOGNITION</u>

Some employees might feel that their efforts have gone completely without notice by the company. As with similar themes, the interviewer should be empathetic.

EXAMPLE

Interviewer:

It looks to me that you have given a lot more to this company than management has recognized. Isn't that right?"

FINANCIAL PROBLEMS

Internal criminals, especially executives and upper management, frequently engage in fraud to conceal a problematic financial condition—either personal or business-related. The interviewer can exploit this theme by expressing sympathy and understanding for the subject's financial problems, as well as understanding for the misconduct.

EXAMPLE

Interviewer:

"I know a lot of your investments have taken a beating. I don't know how you managed to keep everything afloat as well as you did. You just did this to stay alive financially, didn't you?"

ABERRATION OF CONDUCT

Many fraudsters believe their conduct constitutes an aberration in their lives and that it is not representative of their true character. The interviewer might establish this theme by agreeing that the misconduct was an aberration.

EXAMPLE

Interviewer:

"I know this is totally out of character for you, and this would never have happened if something wasn't going on in your life. Isn't that right?"

FAMILY PROBLEMS

Some people commit fraud because of family problems—financial woes caused by divorce, an unfaithful spouse, or demanding children. Men especially—who have been socially conditioned to tie their masculinity to earning power—might hold the notion that wealth connotes family respect. For their part, women have been found to commit white-collar crime in the name of their responsibility to the needs of their husbands and children. The skillful interviewer can convert this motive to his advantage.

EXAMPLE

Interviewer:

"I know you have had some family problems. I know your divorce has been difficult for you. And I know how it is when these problems occur. You would have never done this if it hadn't been for family problems, isn't that right?"

ACCUSER'S ACTIONS

The interviewer should not disclose the accuser's identity if it is not already known. But in cases where the accuser's identity is known to the accused, it can be helpful to blame the accuser for the problem. Alternatively, the problem can be blamed on the company.

EXAMPLE

Interviewer:

"I really blame a large part of this on the company. If some of the things that went on around this company were known, it would make what you've done seem pretty small in comparison, wouldn't it?"

STRESS, DRUGS, ALCOHOL

Employees sometimes will turn to drugs or alcohol to reduce stress. In some instances, the stress itself will lead to aberrant behavior in a few individuals. A rationalization established by the interviewer could be similar to the following.

EXAMPLE

Interviewer:

"You're one of the most respected people in this company. I know you have been under tremendous pressure to succeed. Too much pressure, really. That's behind what has happened here, isn't it?"

REVENGE

Similar to other themes, revenge can be effectively developed as a justification for the subject's misconduct. In this technique, the interviewer attempts to blame the offense on the accused's feeling that he needed to "get back" at someone or something.

EXAMPLE

Interviewer:

"Linda, what has happened is out of character for you. I think you were trying to get back at your supervisor because he passed you over for a raise. I would probably feel the same way. That's what happened, isn't it?"

DEPERSONALIZING THE VICTIM

In cases involving employee theft, an effective technique is to depersonalize the victim. The accused is better able to cope with the moral dilemma of his actions if the victim is a faceless corporation or agency.

EXAMPLE

Interviewer:

"It's not like what you've done has really hurt one person. Maybe you thought of it this way: 'At most, I've cost each shareholder a few cents.' Is that the way it was?"

MINOR MORAL INFRACTION

The interviewer in many cases can reduce the accused's perception of the moral seriousness of the matter. This is not to be confused with the legal seriousness. Fraud examiners and interviewers should be careful to avoid making statements that could be construed as relieving legal responsibility. Instead, the interviewer should play down the moral seriousness of the misconduct. One effective way is through comparisons, such as the illustration below.

EXAMPLE

Interviewer:

"This problem we have doesn't mean you're 'Jack the Ripper.' When you compare what you've done to things other people do, this situation seems pretty insignificant, doesn't it?"

ALTRUISM

In many cases, the moral seriousness of the matter can be reduced by claiming the subject acted for the benefit of others. This especially is true if the accused views himself as a caring person.

EXAMPLE

Interviewer:

"I know you didn't do this for yourself. I have looked into this matter carefully, and I think you did this to help your husband, didn't you?"

GENUINE NEED

In some cases, employee fraud is predicated by genuine financial need. For example, the accused might be paying for the medical care of sick parents or a child. In those cases, the following techniques might be effective.

EXAMPLE

Interviewer:

"You're like everyone else—you have to put food on the table. But in your position, it is very difficult to ask for help. You genuinely needed to do this to survive, didn't you?"

DIFFUSE ALIBIS

Even if the accused is presented with an appropriate rationalization, it is likely that he will continue to deny culpability. When the interviewer is successful in stopping denials, the accused will frequently present one or more reasons why he could not have committed the act in question. The interviewer must quickly and decisively diffuse these alibis by convincing the accused of the weight of the evidence against him. Alibis can generally be diffused using one of the methods listed below.

DISPLAY PHYSICAL EVIDENCE

It is common for culpable people to overestimate the amount of physical evidence that the interviewer possesses. The interviewer should try to reinforce this notion in the way the evidence is presented to the accused. The physical evidence—usually documents in fraud matters—should generally be displayed one piece at a time, in reverse order of importance. In this way, the full extent of the evidence is not immediately known by the accused. When the accused no longer denies culpability, the interviewer should stop displaying the evidence.

Each time a document or piece of evidence is displayed, its significance should be noted by the interviewer. During this phase, the accused is still trying to come to grips with being caught. The interviewer should, therefore, expect that the accused will attempt to lie his way out of the situation. Like denials, the interviewer should stop the alibis and other falsehoods before they are fully articulated. Once the alibis are diffused, the interviewer should return to the theme being developed.

DISCUSS WITNESSES

Another technique for diffusing alibis is to discuss the testimony of witnesses. The objective is to give enough information about what other people would say without providing too much. Ideally, the interviewer's statement will create the impression in the accused's mind that many people are in a position to contradict his story.

The interviewer is again cautioned about furnishing enough information to the accused for him to identify the witnesses. This might place the witness in a difficult position, and the accused could contact the witness in an effort to influence testimony. The accused could also take reprisals against potential witnesses, though this is rare.

DISCUSS DECEPTIONS

The final technique is to discuss the accused's deceptions. The purpose is to appeal to the accused's logic, not to scold or degrade. This technique is sometimes the only one available if physical evidence is lacking. As with other interview situations, the word *lying* should be avoided.

PRESENT AN ALTERNATIVE QUESTION

After the accused's alibi has been diffused, he normally will become quiet and withdrawn. Some people in this situation might cry. (If so, be comforting. Do not discourage the accused from showing emotion.) In this stage, the accused is deciding whether to confess. The interviewer at this point should present an alternative question to the accused. The alternative question forces the accused to make one of two choices. One alternative allows the accused a morally acceptable reason for the misdeed; the other paints the accused in a negative light. Regardless of which answer the accused chooses, he is acknowledging guilt.

EXAMPLE

Interviewer:

"Did you plan this deliberately, or did it just happen?"

"Did you just want extra money, or did you do this because you had financial problems?"

OBTAIN A BENCHMARK ADMISSION

Either way that the accused answers the alternative question—either "yes" or "no"—he has made a culpable statement, or a *benchmark admission*. Once the benchmark admission is made, the subject has made a subconscious decision to confess.

The questions for the benchmark admission should be constructed as leading questions so they can be answered "yes" or "no"; they should not be constructed so that the answer requires some type of explanation. That will come later. The accused might also answer in the negative—"I didn't do it deliberately."

In the cases where the accused answers the alternative question in the negative, the interviewer should press further for a positive admission.

EXAMPLE

Interviewer:

"Then you did it to take care of your financial problems?"

Should the accused still not respond to the alternative question with a benchmark admission, the interviewer should repeat the questions or variations thereof until the benchmark admission is made. It is important for the interviewer to get a response that is tantamount to a commitment to confess.

REINFORCE RATIONALIZATION

Once the benchmark admission has been made, the interviewer should reinforce the confessor's decision by returning to the theme for his rationalization. This will help the confessor feel comfortable and will let him know that the interviewer does not look down on him. After reinforcing the subject's rationalization, the interviewer should make the transition into the verbal confession, where the details of the offense will be obtained.

> **Video**
>
> In the video titled "Chapter V: Rationalization," convicted fraudster Diann Cattani explains how she rationalized embezzling hundreds of thousands of dollars from her former employer. (Go to www.acfe.com/internalinvestigations to view the video.)

Verbal Confession

The transition to the verbal confession is made when the accused furnishes the first detailed information about the offense. Thereafter, it is the interviewer's job to probe gently for additional details—preferably those that would only be known to the perpetrator. As with any interview, there are three general approaches to obtaining the verbal confession: chronologically, by transaction, or by event. The approach to be taken should be governed by the circumstances of the case.

During the admission-seeking interview, it is best to first confirm the general details of the offense. For example, the interviewer will want the accused's estimates of the amounts involved, other parties to the offense, and the location of physical evidence. After these basic facts are confirmed, the interviewer can then return to the specifics, in chronological order. It is imperative that the interviewer obtain an early admission that the accused knew the conduct in question was wrong. This confirms the essential element of intent.

Because of the psychology of confessions, most confessors will lie about one or more aspects of the offense, even though confirming overall guilt. When this happens during the verbal confession, the interviewer should make a mental note of the discrepancy and proceed as if the falsehood had been accepted as truthful.

Such discrepancies should be saved until all other relevant facts have been provided by the accused. If the discrepancies are material to the offense, then the interviewer should either resolve them at the end of the verbal confession or wait and correct them in the written confession. If not material, the information can be omitted altogether from the written confession.

Interviewing Witnesses

The interviewer should focus on obtaining the following items of information during the verbal confession:
- That the accused knew the conduct was wrong
- Facts known only to the perpetrator
- A motive for the offense
- When the misconduct began
- When or if the misconduct was terminated
- Others involved
- Physical evidence
- Disposition of proceeds
- Location of assets
- Specifics of each offense

THE ACCUSED KNEW THE CONDUCT WAS WRONG

Intent (i.e., the state of mind with which something is done) is an essential element in all criminal and civil actions involving fraud. The confessor must not only have committed the act, but also must have known the conduct was wrong and intended to commit it.

EXAMPLE

Interviewer:

"*As I understand it, you did this, and you knew it was wrong, but you didn't really mean to hurt the company. Is that right?*" (Note that the question is phrased so that the confessor acknowledges intent, but "didn't mean to hurt" anyone. Make sure the question is not phrased so that the confessor falsely says that he "didn't mean to do it.")

FACTS KNOWN ONLY TO THE PERPETRATOR

Once the intent question has been answered, the questioning turns to those facts known only to the person who committed the crime. These facts include—at a minimum—the accused's estimates of the number of instances of wrongful conduct, as well as the total amount of money involved. It is best to use open questions here to force the subject to provide as much information about the offense as possible.

MOTIVE FOR THE OFFENSE

Motive is the moving power that prompts a person to act. Motive, however, should not be confused with *intent,* which refers to the state of mind of the accused when performing the act. Motive, unlike intent, is not an essential element, and criminal law generally treats a person's motive as irrelevant. Even so, motive is relevant for other purposes: It will often guide the interviewer to the proper rationalization, it further incriminates the accused, and it is important for a successful prosecution. Therefore, it is best that the interviewer elicits the suspect's motive when obtaining a verbal confession.

The motive might be the same as the theme the interviewer developed earlier—or it might not be. The most common response when a subject is asked about his motive is "I don't know." The interviewer should probe for additional information, but if it is not forthcoming, then attribute the motive to the theme developed earlier. The motive should be established along the lines below.

WHEN THE OFFENSE WAS COMMENCED

The interviewer will need to determine the approximate date and time that the offense started. To do this, the interviewer might say: "I am sure you remember the first time this happened." Once the subject has admitted to remembering the first instance (which will usually play into the motive), the interviewer should simply ask him to "Tell me about it." This is phrased as an open question to get the subject to provide as much information as possible.

WHEN OR IF THE OFFENSE WAS TERMINATED

In fraud matters, especially internal fraud, the offenses are usually ongoing. That is, the fraudster seldom stops before he is discovered. If appropriate, the interviewer should seek the date the offense was terminated.

OTHERS INVOLVED

Most frauds are solo ventures—committed without the aid of an accomplice. However, the interviewer should still seek to determine if other parties were involved. It is best to use soft language, such as "Who else knew about this besides you?"

By asking who else "knew," the interviewer is in effect not only asking for the names of possible conspirators, but also about others who might have known what was going on and failed to report it. This question should not be worded as "Did someone else know?", but rather "Who else knew?"

OBTAIN PHYSICAL EVIDENCE

Physical evidence—regardless of how limited it might be—should be obtained from the confessor. In many instances, illicit income from fraud is deposited directly into the bank accounts of the perpetrator. The interviewer should ask the confessor to surrender his banking records voluntarily for review. It is recommended that the interviewer obtain a separate written authorization for this release, or that language be added to the confession noting the voluntary surrender of banking information. The first method is generally preferable. If there are other relevant records that can only be obtained with the confessor's consent, permission to review those records should also be sought during the oral confession.

DISPOSITION OF PROCEEDS

If it has not come out earlier, the interviewer should find out what generally happened to any illicit income derived from the misdeeds. It is typical for the money to have been used for frivolous or ostentatious purposes. It is important, however, that the confessor casts his actions in a more positive light; the interviewer should avoid comments or questions relating to a lavish lifestyle.

LOCATION OF ASSETS

In appropriate situations, the interviewer will want to find out if there are residual assets that the confessor can use to reduce losses. Rather than ask the accused "Is there anything left?," the question should be phrased as "What's left?"

SPECIFICS OF EACH OFFENSE

Once the major hurdles have been overcome, the interviewer should return to the specifics of each offense. Generally, it is best to start with the first instance and work forward chronologically.

Because this portion of the interview is information-seeking in nature, the interviewer should use open questions. It is best to seek the independent recollections of the confessor before displaying physical evidence. If the confessor cannot independently recall something, documents can be used to refresh his recollection. It is generally best to resolve all issues relating to a particular offense before proceeding to the next one.

Taking a Signed Statement

At the conclusion of the admission-seeking interview, it is best for the interviewer to obtain a written confession from the subject, if possible. As was discussed earlier, a written statement has greater credibility than an oral confession, and it discourages a culpable person from later attempting to recant. The information to be included in the signed statement is essentially the same as that which the interviewer should obtain in an oral confession. There are, however, a few extra inclusions that should be made in a written confession.

VOLUNTARINESS OF THE CONFESSION

The general law of confessions requires that they be completely voluntary. The statement should contain language expressly stating that the confession is being made voluntarily.

INTENT

Most crimes require, as part of the elements of proof, the fact that the confessor knew the conduct was wrong and intended to commit the act. This can best be accomplished by using precise language in the statement that clearly describes the act (e.g., "I wrongfully took assets from the company that weren't mine" versus "I borrowed money from the company without telling anyone").

As a general rule, strong emotive words such as *lie* and *steal*, should be avoided, as the confessor might balk at signing the statement. Still, the wording must be precise. The following are suggested wordings:

EXAMPLE

Instead of:	**Use:**
Lie	*I knew the statement or action was untrue.*
Steal	*Wrongfully took the property of _____ for my own benefit.*
Embezzle	*Wrongfully took _____'s property, which had been entrusted to me, and used it for my own benefit.*
Fraud	*I knowingly told _____ an untrue statement and he/she/they relied on it.*

APPROXIMATE DATES OF OFFENSE

Unless the exact dates of the offense are known, the word *approximately* must precede any dates of the offense. If the confessor is unsure about the dates, language to that effect should be included.

APPROXIMATE AMOUNTS OF LOSSES

Include the approximate losses, making sure they are labeled as such. It is satisfactory to state a range ("probably not less than $_____ or more than $_____").

APPROXIMATE NUMBER OF INSTANCES

Ranges are also satisfactory for the number of instances. The number is important because it helps establish intent by showing a repeated pattern of activity.

WILLINGNESS TO COOPERATE

It makes it easier for the confessor to cooperate and sign the statement when he perceives that the statement includes language portraying him in a more favorable light. The confessor can convert that natural tendency by emphasizing cooperation and willingness to make amends (e.g., "I am willing to cooperate in helping undo what I have done. I promise that I will try to repay any damages caused by my actions.").

Interviewing Witnesses

EXCUSE CLAUSE

The confessor's moral excuse should be mentioned. The interviewer should make sure that the confessor's excuse does not diminish his legal responsibility for his actions. Instead of using language like "I didn't mean to do this," which implies lack of intent, the interviewer should focus on an excuse that provides only a moral explanation for the misconduct (e.g., "I wouldn't have done this if it had not been for pressing financial problems. I didn't mean to hurt anyone.").

HAVE THE CONFESSOR READ THE STATEMENT

The confessor must acknowledge that he read the statement and should initial all of the statement's pages. It might be advisable to insert intentional errors into the statement so that the confessor will notice them. In such a case, cross out the errors, insert the correct information, and then ask the confessor to initial the changes. Whether this step is advisable depends on the likelihood that the confessor will attempt to retract the statement or claim that it was not read.

TRUTHFULNESS OF STATEMENT

The written statement should state specifically that it is true. However, the language should also allow for mistakes. Typical language reads: "This statement is true and complete to the best of my current recollection."

Preparing a Signed Statement

There is no legal requirement that a statement must be in the handwriting or wording of the declarant. In fact, it is generally not a good idea to let a confessor draft the statement. Instead, the investigator should prepare the statement for the confessor to sign.

The confessor should read and sign the statement without undue delay. Instead of asking the confessor to sign the statement; the interviewer should say "Please sign here." Although there is no legal requirement, it is a good idea to have two people witness the signing of a statement.

When preparing a written statement, there should not be more than one written statement for each offense. If facts are inadvertently omitted, they can later be added to the original statement as an addendum. For legal purposes, the investigator should prepare separate statements for unrelated offenses. This rule applies because the target might be tried separately for each offense.

The interviewer should preserve all notes taken during an interview, especially those concerning a confession. Having access to pertinent notes can aid in a cross-examination regarding the validity of a signed statement. Stenographic notes, if any, also should be preserved. Once a confession has been obtained, the interviewer should substantiate it through additional investigation, if necessary.

> **Video**
>
> In the video titled "Chapter V: Ask for the Signature," fraud investigation expert Jonathan Turner, CFE, explains his simple strategy for convincing an interview subject to sign a confession. (Go to www.acfe.com/internalinvestigations to view the video.)

Review Questions

1. Which of the following is NOT one of the purposes of an admission-seeking interview?
   A. Notify the suspect of his right to an attorney
   B. Distinguish the innocent from the culpable
   C. Obtain a valid confession
   D. Obtain a written statement acknowledging the facts

2. If the interviewer has reasonable cause to believe that a respondent is not being truthful, _____ questions can be asked.
   A. Informational
   B. Admission-seeking
   C. Closed
   D. Assessment

3. Which of the following would be an appropriate excuse clause to include in a signed confession?
   A. "I didn't mean to do it."
   B. "I didn't mean to hurt anyone."
   C. "I didn't do it."
   D. None of the above—a confession should never contain an excuse by the confessor.

4. *Proxemics* is a term used to describe:
   A. The environment of an interview
   B. The use of interpersonal space to convey meaning
   C. The subject's attitude
   D. None of the above

5. While taking notes during an interview, the interviewer should NOT:
   A. Take down verbatim as much of what the subject is saying as possible
   B. Concentrate on recording specific nouns, pronouns, verbs, and qualifiers that the subject uses
   C. Document his own opinions and conclusions about the respondent's guilt
   D. Maintain eye contact with the respondent as much as possible during note-taking

6. In routine interview situations where the object is to gather information from neutral or corroborative witnesses, which of the following types of questions will generally NOT be used?
   A. Assessment
   B. Introductory
   C. Informal
   D. Closing

7. _____ questions are usually used to confirm facts that are already known.
   A. Closed
   B. Leading
   C. Complex
   D. Open

8. A volatile interview is one that has the potential to bring about strong emotional reactions in the respondent. Which of the following is a method an investigator can used to control volatile interviews?
   A. Have two interviewers involved in the interview
   B. Conduct volatile interviews on a surprise basis
   C. Ask the order of questions out of sequence
   D. All of the above

9. In most people, lying produces stress. The human body will attempt to relieve this stress through verbal and nonverbal clues. A practiced interviewer will be able to draw information about the honesty of a subject's statements from his behavior. Which of the following is NOT considered a clue to deception?
   A. Increasingly weaker denials
   B. Character testimony
   C. Comments regarding the interview
   D. A strong apparent concern regarding the accusations

10. Probably the most common explanation for criminal activity, particularly internal fraud, is:
    A. Unfair treatment
    B. Inadequate recognition
    C. Financial problems
    D. Family problems

11. According to the text, which of the following is true of benchmark admissions?
    A. Questions are structured so that the positive alternative is presented first, followed by the negative alternative
    B. Questions should be constructed so that the answer requires some type of explanation
    C. Questions should be constructed so that they can be answered "yes" or "no"
    D. All of the above

12. When preparing a written statement, how many unrelated offenses should be included?
    A. Only one offense should be included per written statement.
    B. At least two unrelated offenses should be included per written statement.
    C. A maximum of five unrelated offenses should be included per written statement.
    D. All offenses should be included in the same written statement.

VI. LEGAL CONSIDERATIONS IN INTERVIEWS

Employees' Duty to Cooperate

Employees have a duty to cooperate during an internal investigation as long as what is requested from them is reasonable. This duty exists in every employer-employee relationship. Some states have statutes defining the scope of the employee's duty. For instance, Section 2856 of the California Labor Code states that an employee "shall substantially comply with all directions of his employer concerning the service on which he is engaged" unless compliance is impossible, unlawful, or would impose unreasonable burdens on the employee. An interview should be considered reasonable if the interview addresses matters within the scope of the employee's actions or duties.

The real question, of course, is what a company can do when it is confronted with an employee who refuses to cooperate in the investigation. Employers are generally permitted to discipline or terminate an employee who refuses to cooperate with a reasonable request to provide information. If, however, the employee has an employment contract or is employed under a collective bargaining agreement that requires the employer to have good cause to terminate employment, then the question will be whether the refusal to cooperate amounted to good cause for termination. This, in turn, depends on the nature and reasonableness of the request for information, the reasons for the refusal, and the overall impact that the refusal has on the investigation. A good cause requirement can also arise if the company's policies and practices create an implied employment contract.

Employees who do not have an employment contract for a specified term—so-called at-will employees—can be fired without any specific cause, so the employer will generally not have to justify firing an employee who refuses to cooperate. The employer, however, does not have a right to fire any employee—including an at-will employee—if the firing contravenes a fundamental public policy (for instance, firing an employee who refuses to commit an illegal act) or if it violates the company's established or customary disciplinary practices and procedures. (See Chapter 8, "Discharging Employees," for more information about these topics.)

EXAMPLE

In an internal investigation of suspected embezzlement by employee Jones, she was asked about how well she and her husband were getting along. She also was asked about her gambling debts. She refused to answer both questions. She probably could not be terminated for non-cooperation based on her refusal to answer the first question. Unless her relationship with her husband is somehow related to her motive for the suspected embezzlement, this is not a reasonable request for information. Her relationship with her husband is not reasonably related to the investigation; it is none of the company's business.

The inquiry about gambling debts is more obviously related to motive and is reasonable in light of the investigation; Jones probably has a duty to answer this question. Whether she could be fired for refusing to answer the second question depends on a number of factors. If Jones is an at-will employee, she can probably be fired for non-cooperation, unless the company's disciplinary procedures or practices call for a different punishment. If Jones is employed under an express or implied contract, then the company must have good cause for dismissing her. Whether her refusal to answer the second question amounts to good cause would depend on how important the information is to the investigation and how the refusal to answer impacts the investigation.

In the same investigation, a records clerk, Smith, was asked who has access to certain financial records in the ordinary course of business, whether Jones was authorized to access those records, and if she did in fact access those records. He declined to answer because he did not want to "rat" on Jones or get her in trouble. These questions are clearly reasonable requests for information and Smith has a duty to answer them. He may be subject to discipline for refusing to cooperate with the investigation, although what that discipline may be—and whether it may include termination—depends on the employer's disciplinary policies and procedures.

Employees' Rights During the Investigation

While the employee has a duty to cooperate with an investigation, the employee also has certain rights that define and limit the scope of that duty. However, employee rights vary from case to case, generally depending on the employee's contractual rights, applicable federal and state statutes, and constitutional protections. Thus, before beginning any fraud examination, it is important for the fraud examiner to determine the employee's rights.

Employees' Constitutional Rights
In General
The United States Constitution— the Bill of Rights in particular—protects individuals from intrusive state action. The Fourth Amendment, for instance, prohibits unreasonable searches and seizures; the Fifth Amendment provides that a person cannot be compelled to give information which might incriminate him; and the Sixth Amendment assures the right to an attorney and to confront the witnesses against the individual. (All of these federal rights have been imposed on state governments as well by the Fourteenth Amendment's Due Process clause.) Additionally, while the Constitution contains no express guarantee of privacy, courts have found that individual privacy rights are implied from many of the express protections in the Bill of Rights. Specific constitutional protections are discussed below in the different investigative contexts in which they might arise.

Constitutional protections are important to an investigation both because they limit the scope of the government's investigative and prosecutorial powers and because they might be the basis for a damages lawsuit to be brought by an employee for deprivation of constitutional rights. 42 U.S.C. § 1983 permits recovery of damages against both state and federal officers for deprivation of constitutional rights under *color of law* (i.e., the party is acting on behalf of the government or at the government's direction).

The materials that follow principally address federal constitutional protections, but the investigator should also be aware of and familiar with the particular provisions of any applicable state constitution, and he should seek legal advice where needed.

These protections are also important because many of the federal constitutional protections are mirrored in state constitutions, but some state guarantees and protections may be even broader than the federal Constitution. For instance, some state constitutions include an express guarantee of privacy that is not found in the federal Constitution. Also, some states statutorily protect employees from discipline or discharge due to exercising their constitutional rights.

Private Action Versus State Action

The Constitution protects individuals from intrusive state action. *State action* is involved during any investigation by a governmental entity, including investigations of its own employees. However, the Constitution generally does not limit the powers of private employers in conducting an internal investigation. A private employer is usually not acting under color of law when conducting its own internal investigation; therefore, in general, private employers are not liable under civil rights statutes for deprivation of their employees' constitutional rights.

However, an otherwise private investigation can involve state action. This occurs when the private employer's actions are directed by the government or are so intertwined with the government's interests that the private company is essentially acting as an agent of the government. (See the discussion of public versus private employers in Chapter 3, "Workplace Searches.") When this is the case, the private employer is acting under color of law, and constitutional limitations will apply to its investigation. It is important for the fraud investigator to recognize when an investigation by a private employer may implicate state action.

EXAMPLE

The U.S. Supreme Court found that a private railroad acted as an agent for the government when it complied with the provisions of the Federal Railroad Administration Act in administering drug tests to its employees. Under the regulation at issue, the railroad was required by law to conduct the test, and the Federal Railroad Administration was authorized to receive the test results. Accordingly, the railroad was acting under color of law, and Fourth Amendment limitations on drug testing applied to the railroad's actions. See Skinner v. Railway Labor Executives Association, 489 U.S. 602, 109 S.Ct. 1402, 103 L.Ed.2d 639 (1989).

As was discussed in Chapter 1, an employer may be compelled to investigate a matter internally to comply with federal laws such as the Securities Exchange Act of 1934 or the Foreign Corrupt Practices Act of 1977. While this does not rise to the level of the expressed obligation for drug testing in *Skinner*, employers should be aware of the possible implications of state action under the *Skinner* rationale. It is possible that a company conducting an internal investigation under these circumstances could be found to be acting under color of law, in which case its employees would enjoy constitutional protections. In general, it is advisable for a company to be cautious any time constitutional issues are or may be implicated in an investigation.

Also, investigators must be aware that courts have applied some state constitutional rights, such as express guarantees of privacy, to private employers even where there is no state action. For instance, state courts have held, among other things, that private employers may not use unreasonably invasive drug and alcohol tests; network news personnel may not intrude into an individual's apartment without consent; financial institutions may not disclose confidential financial information; and psychotherapists may not reveal confidential communications.

Employee's Right Against Self-Incrimination: The Fifth Amendment

The Fifth Amendment to the U.S. Constitution provides in relevant part:

> *[N]or shall [any person] be compelled in any criminal case to be a witness against himself, nor be deprived of life, liberty, or property, without due process of law … .*

The Fifth Amendment's right against self-incrimination contains two basic protections: It protects the employee from being coerced or compelled to provide information that could be used to convict him of a criminal offense, and it prevents the state from punishing him for his silence or otherwise using his exercise of that right against him.

The right against self-incrimination is a personal right. It extends to any individual, whether acting as an individual, sole proprietor, employee, manager, director, or officer. However, corporations, partnerships, unincorporated associations, and other legally recognized collective entities have no right against self-incrimination.

The Fifth Amendment applies only to *testimonial statements* (i.e., any testimony or communicative evidence that might tend to incriminate the individual, either directly or indirectly, by leading the government to incriminating evidence). However, it does not extend to incriminating real or physical evidence, such as the person's physical image (e.g., line-ups, show-ups, or photos), blood samples, handwriting exemplars, or voice samples. These are not regarded as testimony.

> EXAMPLE
>
> *Federal agents are interrogating Parker, the CEO, about a suspected provider fraud involving his corporation. In addition to questions about his personal conduct and about claims submitted by his company, he is asked to provide handwriting samples for comparison to documentary evidence in the case. Parker may refuse on Fifth Amendment grounds to answer questions whose answers would incriminate him or lead to other incriminating evidence against him, but he may not refuse to give answers that incriminate only the corporation without reflecting on him personally. He also cannot refuse on Fifth Amendment grounds to provide the requested handwriting samples, which are real evidence, not testimony.*

Keep in mind that the Fifth Amendment only protects against self-incrimination. The privilege applies in criminal investigations or trials, and it applies any time the threat of criminal liability exists. It does not, however, apply where there is no possibility of criminal punishment.

This does not mean that an employee has to answer questions in an internal investigation. Individuals are always entitled to assert their rights against self-incrimination during an investigation, regardless of whether the investigation is conducted by a public or private entity, and regardless of whether the investigation is criminal or civil. The key is that the Fifth Amendment's protections only apply in criminal investigations. If a suspect refuses to answer questions in a criminal investigation, the refusal cannot be held against him. A suspect may also refuse to answer questions in a civil matter, but his refusal *can* be held against him.

Therefore, assuming that there is no state action in a private employer's investigation, the private employer may discipline an employee for refusing to answer questions. (Remember, the Fifth Amendment only applies to state action. Therefore, public entities cannot force employees to choose between their Fifth Amendment right to silence and their jobs. The same is not true for private entities.) Discipline by non-public entities may include suspension or termination, depending on what is reasonable under the circumstances.[12] There is also authority that a plaintiff in a civil suit can comment on the employee's refusal to answer questions, and that a jury can draw adverse inferences from his refusal. (None of this is permitted in a criminal trial.) This puts the employee in a difficult position, for if

---

[12] Some have argued that firing an employee for exercising his constitutional rights violates fundamental public policy and is wrongful. (See discussion of Wrongful Termination below and in Chapter 8, "Discharging Employees.") Courts have not generally accepted this reasoning yet, and the weight of legal authority is that the employer may discharge the employee who asserts his self-incrimination rights and fails to cooperate in the investigation.

he does testify or answer questions in an investigation to avoid disciplinary action, he may waive his self-incrimination rights in any subsequent criminal proceeding. Moreover, he has no way to prevent the government from using his earlier answers or testimony in a criminal proceeding.

EXAMPLE

An employee declines on self-incrimination grounds to answer questions by ABC Corp. investigators about a suspected computer fraud at its offices. She subsequently is indicted and tried. At trial, the prosecutor may not introduce evidence of, or comment on, her refusal to answer the investigator's questions. ABC Corp. also sues the employee for civil damages. At that trial, ABC's attorney is permitted to comment on her refusal to answer questions, because the privilege only protects the employee from criminal liability. As a private employer, ABC can also suspend or terminate her employment for refusing to answer questions (although provisions in her employment contract or in a collective bargaining agreement might prevent such action). But if ABC Corp. was a public employer or government agency, it could not suspend or fire her for invoking her Fifth Amendment privilege against self-incrimination, because in this case state action would be involved.

APPLICATION OF THE RIGHT TO PRODUCTION OF BOOKS, RECORDS, AND OTHER TANGIBLE EVIDENCE

In general, the Fifth Amendment does not protect the records and documents of a collective entity, such as a corporation, partnership, labor union, or other organization. A corporate officer or employee may be required to produce these records, even if they are personally incriminating to that individual. The Fifth Amendment is not designed to protect people from having to turn over incriminating evidence; it only protects them from having to give testimony against themselves. In most cases, courts do not consider the act of producing such documents as testimonial. (However, this issue is fact-specific, and some courts have found production of records as testimonial in very limited circumstances.) Thus, an employee usually may not object to the production of a company's books and records—by him or by another—on the grounds that the documents would incriminate him.

EXAMPLE

Citing his Fifth Amendment right against self-incrimination, Parker moves to quash two subpoenas: one for copies of bank statements concerning his personal bank accounts and the other for his company's financial books and records which he holds as its custodian of records.

Held: The production of Parker's bank statements is not testimonial in nature; therefore, the statements are not protected by the Fifth Amendment, and he probably will have to produce them. The same reasoning applies to the subpoena for his company records, and in any event, the Fifth Amendment privilege does not apply to collective entities, only individuals. The company has no privilege against self-incrimination.

There is one very limited exception whereby the right against self-incrimination may protect individuals from having to produce their own personal records or documents when the act of producing those personal records is itself testimonial. If the production of one's personal records would explicitly or implicitly require the individual to describe or confirm the nature, location, or existence of those records, then the production amounts to testimony. In these circumstances, the individual may refuse under the Fifth Amendment to produce them. There is also authority that an attorney may refuse to produce a client's documents under subpoena if they otherwise would be protected under the Fifth Amendment.

EXAMPLE

In a criminal trial against an employee for tax evasion, a key issue is whether the employee was the owner of a shell company, a fictitious business that had made false billings and failed to pay taxes on these illegal profits. The government subpoenas tax records for the shell company. The employee moves to quash the subpoena, asserting his Fifth Amendment right against self-incrimination. The judge may uphold the motion and quash the subpoena, because by turning over the tax records for the shell company, the employee would be required to implicitly admit his control over that business. This sort of production is testimonial in nature and would perhaps violate the employee's Fifth Amendment rights.

In addition, the Fifth Amendment does not protect against production of any records or documents that an individual or business is legally required to make or keep pursuant to a legitimate administrative purpose of government, such as tax returns or (for a car dealer) vehicle mileage records. However, a person can decline on Fifth Amendment grounds to answer specific incriminating questions that appear in a required form or record.

MIRANDA WARNINGS

Pre-interrogation *Miranda* warnings were mandated by the Supreme Court to protect a suspect's Fifth Amendment right against self-incrimination. These warnings advise suspects that they have the right not to answer questions and the right to legal counsel during interrogations. (The right to legal counsel is discussed below.) *Miranda* warnings are required only if a person is being interrogated by public authorities in a custodial setting (meaning law enforcement officers have deprived the subject of his freedom in a significant way). As a result, private employers do not have to give *Miranda* warnings, and both private and public employers may interview employees in non-custodial settings without giving *Miranda* warnings.

EXAMPLE

ABC's internal investigator is ready to confront and interrogate the principal suspect in a computer fraud investigation that is entirely in-house. The interrogation takes place in the investigator's office behind a closed door with only the investigator, his assistant, and the suspect present. The investigator is not obligated to give Miranda warnings to the suspect, even if the circumstances could be construed as custodial. However, if the police had participated in the investigation, if the police requested the investigator to interrogate the suspect, or if there was some other indicia of state action, then Miranda warnings should be given.

Employee's Right to Counsel: The Sixth Amendment

TEXT OF THE SIXTH AMENDMENT

The Sixth Amendment provides in relevant part:

> *In all criminal prosecutions, the accused shall enjoy the right ... to be confronted with witnesses against him; to have compulsory process for obtaining witnesses in his favor; and to have the assistance of counsel for his defense.*

The Sixth Amendment right to counsel applies at what the courts call crucial stages in the criminal proceeding. Investigative questioning is not generally considered such a crucial stage. However, courts have held that the right to counsel applies to police questioning at any time that the subject is in custody or has been charged.

APPLICABILITY

If no state action is involved, a private employer can interview an employee without the presence of his attorney. The employee always has the right to consult an attorney, but there is typically no legal obligation to consult the employee's lawyer prior to the interview or to allow the employee's lawyer to sit in during an interview.

Investigators should avoid giving advice to the employee as to whether or not he needs an attorney; that is the employee's choice and the investigator should not risk misleading the employee about either his rights or his needs. (While a private employee has no constitutional right to have an attorney present during an investigative interview, he may have a statutory right to have a representative attend the interview; see the forthcoming discussion of the National Labor Relations Act.)

PRESENCE OF CORPORATE COUNSEL

The company's attorney may conduct or be present during an interview of a corporate employee, director, or officer. The company attorney serves as the legal representative of the corporation—not the suspect—and his exclusive purpose is to represent the company's interests and to advise the company. Accordingly, his presence does not fulfill any right that the witness may have to counsel during the interview.

The Employee's Right to Leave an Interview or Interrogation: The Fourth Amendment
TEXT OF THE FOURTH AMENDMENT

The right of the people to be secure in their persons, houses, papers, and effects, against unreasonable searches and seizures, shall not be violated, and no warrants shall issue, but upon probable cause, supported by oath or affirmation, and particularly describing the place to be searched and the persons or things to be seized.

APPLICATION

The Fourth Amendment's prohibition against unreasonable seizures limits the right of government officers and representatives to arrest or otherwise restrain an individual's freedom of movement. This includes law enforcement's right to detain a person for interview or interrogation if the person is not under arrest. Therefore, under the Fourth Amendment, a suspect has a right to leave a non-custodial interview or interrogation (e.g., at the suspect's home or on the street, without arrest-like restraints) by law enforcement officers.

This provision does not apply to purely private action, although the right of a private employer or its representatives to retain an employee or other individual for questioning, or for any other reason, may be limited by other common law and statutes. (See the forthcoming discussion of False Imprisonment.)

Employee's Right to Due Process: The Fifth and Fourteenth Amendments
TEXT OF CONSTITUTIONAL CLAUSES

Fifth Amendment (in relevant part):

[N]or shall [any person] ... be deprived of life, liberty, or property, without due process of law ....

Fourteenth Amendment:

All persons born or naturalized in the United States, and subject to the jurisdiction thereof, are citizens of the United States and of the state wherein they reside. No state shall make or enforce any law which shall abridge the privileges and immunities of citizens of the United States; nor shall any state deprive any person of life, liberty, or property without due process of law; nor deny to any person within its jurisdiction the equal protection of the laws.

APPLICATION

In the context of a fraud investigation, the constitutional right to due process usually refers to procedural rights that must be observed before the employee suffers any adverse consequence. Again, this right is not applicable to employees of private companies, absent some state involvement or action.

Legal Considerations in Interviews

State or federal employers might be required to provide the employee suspected of wrongdoing with the following:

- Written notice of the charges upon which any disciplinary action may be based
- Adequate opportunity to rebut any charges brought prior to any disciplinary action being taken, which might include the right to call witnesses and the right to be represented by an attorney

Even in the absence of constitutional due process protections, similar procedures to ensure fundamental fairness may be required even of private employers because of contractual provisions, collective bargaining agreements, established company policies, or applicable labor or employment statutes.

Employees' Contractual Rights

An employee may have contractual rights that limit the ability of the employer to compel full cooperation in a fraud examination. If the employee is a member of a union, the union contract or collective bargaining agreement might contain certain restrictions on the company's investigative procedures. For instance, the company might be required to notify the union before the interview, and the employee might have the right to have a union representative present. (See also the discussion below regarding the National Labor Relations Act.)

The terms and conditions of an employment contract define the scope of employment and will therefore help determine whether employee questioning or other investigation is reasonable. This is a key issue in determining whether the employee's common law privacy rights have been violated. Questions or investigative steps that are reasonably related to employment generally do not violate an employee's privacy rights. (See later discussion of Common Law Rights.)

Finally, the contract's terms and conditions of employment—including any that concern the scope of work, disciplinary actions, and grounds for firing—will be relevant to whether a wrongful termination has occurred if the employee is fired.

Employees' Statutory Rights
In General
A number of state and federal statutes specifically regulate the employer-employee relationship; regulate or limit the use of certain investigative tools and techniques (e.g., wiretapping, other kinds of eavesdropping, and surveillance); and regulate or limit access to financial and other confidential records. The following sections present an overview of some of the more significant statutorily created employee rights.

National Labor Relations Act

The National Labor Relations Act prohibits any form of interrogation by employers that interferes with the rights of the employee to organize, bargain, or otherwise engage in concerted activities for the purpose of bargaining or other mutual aid or protection. An employer may not question an employee about any of these protected activities, either his own or that of other employees.

RULES REGARDING NON-UNION REPRESENTATION DURING INTERVIEWS

In June 2004, the National Labor Relations Board (NLRB) overruled a controversial decision regarding the rights of non-union employees to have a "representative" present during interviews, and reinstated the former 1975 ruling that non-union employees are not entitled to representation during investigatory interviews (*IBM Corp.*, 341 NLRB No. 148 (2004)). The NLRB reasoned that allowing coworkers to sit in as representatives during investigatory interviews would compromise the requisite confidentiality, sensitivity, and thoroughness of the interview. Accordingly, non-union employers no longer have a legal obligation to accept an employee's request for such representation.

<u>UNION EMPLOYEES</u>

Since 1975 and the U.S. Supreme Court decision of *NLRB v. Weingarten*, 420 U.S. 251 (1975), union employees have had the right to union representation during an investigatory interview, provided that the employee "reasonably believes" the interview "might result in disciplinary action." This right derived from the National Labor Relations Act, which provides that employees have the right "to act in concert for mutual aid and protection." In the years since *Weingarten*, this right has only been applied in cases where the employee under investigation was covered by a collective bargaining agreement.

<u>NON-UNION EMPLOYEES</u>

For non-union employees, a representative may be present where the employer allows for such.

No longer must an employer allow a representative to be present when a non-union employee specifically requests representation. However, an employer is not precluded from allowing the employee to have representation upon request.

Employers can always decide not to conduct an interview, but refusing to do so may cause problems of its own. If the company administers disciplinary action without first hearing the employee's side of the story, then the company might be handing the employee a lawsuit for wrongful discharge or a discrimination claim. As a general rule, it is difficult to defend a termination action if the employer did not at least listen to the employee's version of events prior to taking action.

Where the employer allows for employee representation, the employer need not "bargain with" the employee's representative.

Presumably, the ruling in *Weingarten* will continue to control this issue. In *Weingarten,* the Supreme Court stated that the representative's role is to assist the employee, and he "may do so by attempting to clarify facts or suggest other employees who may have knowledge of them." The Court made it clear that the employer may insist on hearing the subject's version of events, and the representative is not allowed to direct the subject not to answer a question or to tell the subject to answer questions only once. Therefore, the employer is allowed to conduct the interview without interference by the representative.

Employees do not have a right to be represented by a private attorney at an interview.

Under *Epilepsy,* where an employer failed to comply with the rules requiring representation upon employee request, it could have been subjected to an administrative cease-and-desist order and/or reinstatement of the employee with back-pay. Due to the overturning of *Epilepsy* and reinstatement of *Weingarten*, however, these penalties will probably not apply unless the non-union employer agrees to allow employee representation.

If an employee requests any type of representation at an interview, you should immediately consult your legal counsel. You should also consult counsel to review your existing policies and procedures to ensure that you are aware of the legal duties, ramifications, and remedies surrounding employee representation.

Nondiscrimination Statutes
The Civil Rights Acts of 1866 and 1871, Title VII of the Civil Rights Act of 1964, and the Age Discrimination in Employment Act of 1970 prohibit, among other things, singling out employees for interviews based on their race, national origin, religion, sex, or age.

Whistleblowers
Federal law and many state laws provide protection to employees who report improper or illegal acts to government authorities. Designed to encourage individuals to bring complaints of wrongdoing, most of these laws protect the employee from any adverse or retaliatory employment action by the employer.

Fair Labor Standards Act
The Fair Labor Standards Act requires an employer to pay an employee for time spent in an interview.

Employee Polygraph Protection Act of 1988
The Employee Polygraph Protection Act prohibits the use of polygraphs by most private employers, and it permits polygraph testing by a private employer only where the following criteria are satisfied:
- It is part of an ongoing investigation.
- It is in connection with incidents involving economic loss or injury to the employer.
- The loss is the result of intentional wrongdoing.

- The employee to be polygraphed must have had access to the missing material.
- There must be articulable facts giving rise to *reasonable suspicion* of the employee to be polygraphed.
- The employer must draft a statement containing the foregoing items.
- The polygrapher must follow a strict set of rules.

Private employers cannot use polygraphs to screen applicants for employment or discharge an employee for refusing to take an exam. This Act does not protect government employees.

Other federal statutes do not address the use of polygraphs directly, but nonetheless might give rise to liability if a polygraph test is administered in a discriminatory fashion (e.g., based on race, sex, or some other prohibited factor) or used to ferret out union sympathies in connection with a union organizing campaign.

Several states have enacted laws addressing the use of polygraph examinations, and some are more restrictive than the federal statute. Courts have recognized claims arising from unlawful administration of polygraph exams, such as wrongful discharge for refusal to take an exam after having been accused of fraud.

Common Law Employee Rights and Protections
In General
All employers and investigators, private and public, are subject to laws that protect an individual's reasonable expectations of privacy and which are enforceable through a civil lawsuit for damages or equitable remedies (e.g., an injunction to restrain the offending conduct.) These various rights are discussed in more detail in the specific investigative contexts below, but in general they include the following rights:
- The right to be left alone
- Freedom from undue or unwarranted inquiry about one's life
- Freedom from unreasonable surveillance and eavesdropping
- Freedom from unwarranted or objectionable publicity
- The right to be secure in one's home and possessions
- Freedom from improper injury to one's good name and reputation
- Freedom of movement
- Freedom from improperly motivated or groundless loss of employment
- Freedom from another's outrageous and intentionally harmful behavior

Legal Considerations in Interviews

Invasion of Privacy

While modern tort law includes four categories of invasion of privacy, this discussion only addresses the three most common forms of invasion of privacy applicable to the workplace: intrusion upon seclusion, public disclosure of private facts, and false light.

INTRUSION UPON SECLUSION

The common law cause of action of intrusion into seclusion occurs when an employer makes an intentional intrusion into an area where an employee has a reasonable expectation of privacy, and the intrusion would be highly offensive or objectionable to a reasonable person.

This tort claim most frequently arises in the context of workplace searches— for instance, when an employer searches an employee's personal belongings for evidence of suspected wrongdoing. An intrusion into seclusion claim can also arise when an employer questions an employee—or seeks information from third parties—about activities not reasonably related to the employee's job performance or to the subject matter of the investigation. More information about this cause of action is contained in Chapter 3, "Workplace Searches."

PUBLIC DISCLOSURE OF PRIVATE FACTS

The tort of public disclosure of private facts occurs when an employer (1) makes public statements about an employee's private life, when (2) the information is not of public concern, and when (3) the disclosure of the information would be highly offensive to a reasonable person.

This cause of action can arise even if the statements are true. The key is that the information is private in nature and is not a matter of public interest. For instance, if an employee is terminated for misconduct, it is certainly reasonable to inform that employee's supervisors of the reasons for the termination. Depending on the circumstances, it may be appropriate to tell the employee's coworkers why he was terminated, perhaps to discourage future misconduct or in the process of explaining how to handle inquiries about the reasons for the employee's departure. It would probably not be reasonable, however, to contact friends or acquaintances of the employee to tell them that he was fired for misconduct. This information, although true, would be highly objectionable to a reasonable person in the terminated employee's position, and there is probably not a legitimate reason for disclosing this information to these people.

FALSE LIGHT

A false light invasion of privacy claim arises when the public disclosure of information places an employee in a false light in the public eye. This typically occurs when an employee is wrongfully accused of misconduct on the job. Unlike public disclosure of private facts, a claim for false light invasion of privacy can only succeed if the information that is disclosed about an employee is false. This tort is committed when an individual receives "unreasonable and highly objectionable publicity that attributes to him characteristics, conduct, or beliefs that are false, and so is placed before the public in a false position." *Restatement 2d., Torts*, Section 625E, Comment b.

This cause of action is similar to defamation (see next page) in that the employer must publicize false information about the employee, the information must be highly objectionable, and the employer must have made the disclosure intentionally (i.e., with knowledge that it was false or with a reckless disregard for the truth). Whereas a defamation claim requires damage to the employee's reputation, this is not a requirement under false light cause of action. It is enough that the false statement attributes to the plaintiff views that he does not hold or actions that he did not take.

EXAMPLE

Abel has spent half of his professional adult life advocating a particular theory about the origins of the universe. A newspaper publishes an article about Abel that falsely associates him with a religious sect that holds a completely different theory about the universe's beginnings. Abel may sue on the grounds that, even if not defamatory, the article put him in a false light and damaged him in the community, especially the professional community where he had toiled so long on behalf of the first theory.

This cause of action is not recognized in all jurisdictions. In the context of internal investigations, defamation claims are much more likely to arise.

Defamation (Slander and Libel)

Defamation is an unprivileged publication of a falsehood about a person that tends to harm the reputation of that person. The law of defamation actually consists of two torts: libel and slander. *Libel* is basically defamation that appears in written form, while *slander* involves defamatory remarks that are only spoken. Aside from the method of publication, the elements of these two causes of action are essentially the same.

In general, the elements of a defamation claim are (1) a false and defamatory statement is made about the plaintiff, (2) this statement is communicated (i.e., published) to a third party, (3) the statement was made on an unprivileged occasion, and (4) the plaintiff suffers harm to his reputation or good name as a result.

In any internal investigation, it is likely that there will be unflattering allegations made against certain individuals at some point. It is therefore important that investigators understand exactly what constitutes defamation so that they can avoid this potential liability.

Legal Considerations in Interviews

Statements of pure opinion are not defamatory because, according to the first element of the cause of action, a statement must be false to support a defamation suit. An opinion cannot really be proven true or false. Therefore, only statements of fact can give rise to a defamation claim. This does not mean that an investigator can shield himself from liability by phrasing all accusations as statements of opinion—"In my opinion, Jones took the money." Although the preceding statement purports to be an opinion, it implies a fact—that Jones took money. Therefore, this statement could be found to be defamatory. Conversely, a statement that a particular employee is "difficult" or that he "seemed uncomfortable" are more likely to be found to be statements of opinion, and thus not actionable.

The second element of the cause of action requires that the statement be *published* (i.e., communicated to a third party or parties). The crux of defamation law is that the plaintiff's reputation is harmed by a false statement. If no one else hears the statement, the plaintiff's reputation cannot be harmed. This is why publication is a required element of the cause of action. Although the term *publication* is used, this does not mean that the statement has to be published in the traditional sense; it is enough that the statement is communicated to a third person, either in writing (libel) or through spoken word (slander). In some cases, even hand signals have been found to amount to a publication. If a statement is never communicated to a third person, it cannot be defamatory. Thus, if during an interview an investigator accuses the subject of having stolen money, this will not amount to defamation as long as no one else hears the comment. Conversely, if during an interview of Smith, the interviewer states that "It appears Jones took the money," this could amount to defamation, since the accusation against Jones has now been published to Smith.

This is one reason why the risk of defamation is particularly high in internal investigations, particularly during interviews. Interviewers frequently confront a witness or suspect with facts or evidence in order to refresh memory, obtain confirmation, or otherwise prod the witness. Interrogation of a suspect is especially likely to include confrontations and accusations in order to lead the suspect into a confession. However, especially in the early stages of an investigation, there may be questions about the accuracy of such facts and evidence, as well as about any accusations or inferences drawn from them. Defamation can result any time the interviewer confronts a third-party witness—or a suspect in the presence of unprivileged third parties—with information about the suspect that turns out to be false, or with resulting accusations or statements about the suspect's conduct that ultimately cannot be proven true.

Thus, the investigator needs to balance the usefulness of the confrontation technique with attention to the risks of defamation. Consider the following as possible ways to reduce the risk of defamation in an interview:

- Be sure of the accuracy of any facts or evidence stated to the witness or suspect.
- Avoid characterization of preliminary information or suspicions as factual.
- Do not make any statements about the plaintiff except to individuals within an applicable privilege (see discussion of the privilege defense below).

This means, among other things, limiting participants in the interview to the witness and members of the investigative team, including necessary support staff (e.g., a secretary or stenographer to take notes).

There are a number of defenses to a claim of defamation, including truth, the common interest privilege, and the judicial privilege.

TRUTH AS A DEFENSE

Recall that the first element in a defamation claim is that the employer made a false and defamatory statement. If the employer can show that the statement was in fact true, then a claim for defamation cannot succeed.

THE COMMON-INTEREST PRIVILEGE

Aside from truth, the most important defense to a defamation action for internal investigators is the common-interest privilege. The *common-interest privilege*, sometimes called the qualified business privilege, applies to communications made between parties that share a common interest in the information. Under this privilege, a statement is exempt from a defamation claim if it is made (1) in good faith, (2) regarding a subject in which the person making the statement has a legitimate interest or duty, and (3) to another person with a corresponding interest or duty. The statement will be privileged even if it is false, even if it injures the reputation of the employee, and even if it is published to a third person.

The common interest privilege extends to communications about the internal investigation among individuals with a legitimate interest in the investigation. Interested individuals include the investigative team, members of the company's management who requested the investigation, those who have an interest in the results of the investigation, and those who have authority to implement the recommendations or otherwise make decisions based on the results of the investigation. Some courts have also concluded that a government agency that receives a required or mandated report from the company has a common interest in the report. The law recognizes that these people have a legitimate need to communicate about the investigation, and that the nature of such an investigation necessarily involves the discussion about actual or suspected wrongdoing of employees. If every allegation were subject to a defamation suit, this would have a chilling effect on the ability of companies to investigate internal misconduct. Therefore, statements made in good faith among these interested individuals are privileged from defamation suits.

Keep in mind that the common interest privilege is *qualified*, which means that it can be lost. To be privileged, the communication must have been made in good faith. If the person who made the communication knew that it was false or had a reckless disregard for whether it was true, then this statement is not privileged and the speaker can be successfully sued for libel. Furthermore, the communication is only privileged among those with a need to know. If a statement is disseminated outside the group of interested people, it loses its privilege. Therefore, it is extremely important to limit the distribution of any internal reports to those discussed in the preceding paragraph.

JUDICIAL PRIVILEGE

While the common interest privilege is subject to being taken away, statements made in connection with judicial proceedings are *absolutely* privileged. This means that the statements cannot be the subject of a defamation suit, regardless of the speaker's motives. The judicial privilege attaches to all statements made by judges, jurors, attorneys, witnesses, and other parties to a judicial proceeding. It applies to all aspects of the proceedings, including pre-trial depositions and hearings, as well as all papers or pleadings filed in the case. The idea is that we do not want to hinder the court's ability to get at the truth, so all those who testify in a judicial proceeding are absolutely privileged from defamation claims. Keep in mind that intentional falsehoods can still be punished in these settings under perjury laws.

Intentional Infliction of Emotional Distress

Most jurisdictions recognize a right to recover civil damages for intentional infliction of emotional distress. This tort has three basic elements:

- The defendant's conduct must have been extreme and outrageous.
- The defendant must have acted with the intent of causing severe emotional distress, or with reckless disregard of whether his actions would cause severe emotional distress.
- The plaintiff must have actually suffered severe distress.

Mere insults, threats, petty oppression, or annoyances are not grounds for suit. However, racial slurs and false accusations of poor job performance for the purpose of securing an employee's termination have been held actionable. Privileged conduct is not actionable. So as long as the employer has a privilege to investigate the matter—and as long as the employer does not exceed the bounds of a reasonable investigation (e.g., by ethnic or racial slurs or improperly motivated false accusations)—questioning alone, even coupled with accusations and raised voices, probably will not give rise to such a claim.

Wrongful Termination

Wrongful termination is a cause of action that arises when an employee is fired in violation of a right to which he is entitled. The action may be styled as a breach of contract or a tort, depending on the jurisdiction. For a company, the risk of wrongful termination liability arises in the interview context when an employee is fired for refusing to be interviewed or otherwise not cooperating with the internal investigation. Obviously, it also can arise when an employee is fired because of misconduct that he admitted to in an interview, or that has been established by evidence gathered in the investigation, including interviews.

A wrongful termination suit can arise when an employee is fired in violation of the company's standard employee disciplinary procedures. These policies may specify the range of discipline that is permitted for a particular kind of offense, or they may state the procedural steps that must be followed before certain types of disciplinary action, including firing, can be instituted. If the company fails to follow its own internal procedures for firing employees, it can be subject to a wrongful termination suit, even if the employee who was terminated otherwise worked in an at-will capacity. Moreover, firing an employee (regardless of whether he is term or at-will) in violation of a fundamental, overriding public policy interest (e.g., avoidance of racial, ethnic, or religious discrimination) may give the employee the right to sue for wrongful termination. (See Chapter 8, "Discharging Employees," for more information.)

EXAMPLE

A plaintiff employee was fired for refusing to submit to an unannounced urinalysis drug test. Held: The test violated the employee's privacy rights under the circumstances, and therefore her firing was a wrongful termination for which she was entitled to recover damages.

As noted above, some private employees have argued that their ability to exercise their constitutional right against self-incrimination and other constitutional rights is a fundamental right and that public policy should preclude terminating an employee for that exercise. That position, however, is without substantial legal support at this time.

Good Faith and Fair Dealing

Several states recognize a duty on the part of employers to deal with their employees fairly and in good faith. This duty is implied in most contracts, including contracts of employment. The scope of this duty might also be shaped from specific obligations found in the provisions of an employee handbook or from company personnel policies or practices. For instance, a breach of a provision in the employee handbook which states that interviews will be conducted in a professional manner, and only concerning job-related matters, might expose the employer to liability for breach of the implied covenant of good faith and fair dealing. Furthermore, terminating an employee for refusing to answer questions when company policies or past practices have been to apply a lesser level of discipline could support a bad faith suit (as well as a claim of wrongful termination) from the employee.

False Imprisonment

False imprisonment is the restraint by one person of the physical liberty of another without consent or legal justification. A claim of false imprisonment arises if an employee is detained against his will for any

Legal Considerations in Interviews

appreciable time, however short, in any way. Actual force is not required; threats or other words, gestures, or acts that create an apprehension of force may suffice.

Potential liability for false imprisonment arises any time an employee is involuntarily detained for an interview or interrogation, or to conduct a search. (Law enforcement officers may lawfully detain people incident to a lawful search under certain circumstances.) A search of an employee's person would be especially problematic, as it presumes a detention of the person. Generally, an employer may question an employee at work about a violation of company policy without incurring liability as long as the employee submits to the questioning voluntarily—that is, not as a result of threats or force.

There are no precise rules as to when a false imprisonment occurs. However, factors used to determine if an individual has been falsely imprisoned include:

- Length, nature, and manner of the interview
- Size and nature of the room where the interview takes place (e.g., small, windowless, not easily accessible)
- Lighting in the room (e.g., soft versus severe)
- Requiring the employee's presence or continued presence by any amount of force, including holding the employee's arm to escort him
- Violent behavior of any kind during the interview, including yelling, pounding on the desk, or kicking furniture or walls
- Refusing to allow the employee to leave the room, such as by pushing the employee into a chair or locking the door
- The number of people involved in the interview

Polygraph Examinations

In addition to the statutory restrictions discussed above, some courts have found the use of polygraphs actionable on common law grounds under certain circumstances. Most courts have not held that the giving of a polygraph exam in and of itself is sufficiently outrageous to constitute intentional infliction of emotional distress. However, in some states, courts have held that polygraph tests can be invasions of privacy. Questions directly related to job performance or the incident under investigation are generally held not to be invasions of privacy. Control questions might be an invasion of privacy, though circumstances might warrant the intrusion. (Check with legal counsel.)

Presence of Corporate Attorney During Witness Interviews

A company's attorney may conduct or be present during the interview of company employees, though it should be remembered that the company's lawyer represents only the interests of the company, and not those of the individual employees, directors, or officers. Indeed, the interests of these individuals may be in conflict with those of the company in any particular case. An employee who is being interviewed must not be permitted—or misled—to believe that the company's lawyer represents his interests during an interview.

If a corporate attorney is present during the interview, it is good policy to inform the employee of several things before the interview begins. The employee should be clearly told at the start of any interview that:

- The company's lawyer represents the company, not the employee.
- The purpose of the interview is to obtain information to provide legal advice to the company.
- The company initially will treat communications by the employee as confidential, but the company ultimately will determine whether to disclose the information to law enforcement agencies or other third parties.
- The employee is expected to answer the questions fully and truthfully.
- The employee should not discuss the interview with anyone (either inside or outside the company) except his attorney.

However, do not tell an employee to refuse to answer questions from government investigators about the same subject matter. Interfering with the government's right to question potential witnesses could result in obstruction of justice charges. Conversely, to protect the company's right to counsel, the company's lawyer can ask to be informed of any contacts by government or other investigators and can ask for the opportunity to be present before the employee answers questions.

Preserving the Confidentiality of the Investigation

It is important for the investigator to understand that an internal investigation can become a source of information for outside investigators, who can reach the investigative materials through subpoenas and other compulsory processes. This includes government agents conducting criminal or administrative proceedings, as well as other companies or individuals who may be suing the employer in a civil suit. These outside individuals can subpoena investigative files, including memoranda or tapes of interviews, and can even compel investigators to testify in a judicial or administrative proceeding about the substance of witness and suspect interviews. Obviously, disclosure of the results of the internal investigation can have a significant impact on the company.

Concerns about preserving the confidentiality of the investigation typically get attention only after government lawyers—or the company's adversaries in a lawsuit—try to obtain access to investigative reports and underlying investigative materials. By then, of course, it may be too late to preserve the confidentiality of the investigation. If confidentiality issues are not given attention from the outset of the

Legal Considerations in Interviews

investigation, the company may find itself without options by the time third parties try to access investigative materials. This is because certain evidentiary privileges and discovery rules—which offer the best basis for preserving confidentiality of at least some of the investigation—depend largely on how information was gathered and secured by the investigative team. Therefore, investigators need to be familiar with these privileges and discovery rules—the attorney-client privilege, the attorney's work product doctrine, and the self-evaluation privilege—and must understand how the conduct of the investigation can affect the discoverability of investigative materials.

The Attorney-Client Privilege
Nature and Elements of the Privilege
The *attorney-client privilege* is an evidentiary privilege that protects against involuntary disclosure of communications between a client and his attorney. A corporation or other legally-recognized collective entity can be a client and can invoke the privilege in the same manner as an individual. However, because a corporation can only act through individuals, the privilege effectively extends to communications between a company's attorney and certain persons within the corporation. This means that interviews with at least some company employees, officers, and directors in the course of an internal investigation may be protected under the attorney-client privilege (assuming all other conditions of the privilege have been met), but more than likely not all.

The precise formulation of the privilege can differ from the federal to state level, as well as from state to state. Therefore, the investigative team should consult with the company's lawyer about the applicable law of privilege in their state before undertaking any investigation. However, the privilege generally applies to any communications that satisfy the following four elements:
- Communications are between an attorney and their client
- Made for the purpose of seeking or obtaining legal services or advice from the attorney
- Intended to be kept confidential
- The privilege has not been waived

The attorney-client privilege is a valuable defense against third-party attempts to discover investigative materials. To safeguard the confidentiality of an internal investigation and protect the company's findings from outsiders, it may be advisable to involve the company's lawyer in the internal investigation. This can allow the company to invoke the privilege with respect to certain aspects of the investigation. Keep in mind, however, that if the attorney's work on the investigation goes beyond merely providing legal advice, he may be forced to turn over his work related to these duties. The attorney-client privilege only exists to the extent that the attorney is providing legal advice. If his work crosses over into purely investigative functions, the communications might not be protected.

BETWEEN LAWYER AND CLIENT

The general rule is that the attorney-client privilege only applies to communications between a client and his attorney. Lawyers, however, must often rely on assistants or agents to carry out their work, and in recognition of this fact, the courts have extended the privilege to include client communications with non-lawyers who are working under the direct supervision, direction, and control of the lawyer. This includes secretaries, paralegals, law clerks, and even investigators. However, the privilege is only present if the attorney is using the investigator or other individual to facilitate the rendering of legal advice, and the person is working directly under the lawyer's supervision.

The use of this privilege can be tricky when it comes to non-lawyers. Therefore, if you wish to attempt to rely on the privilege for interviews conducted by investigators, the investigator should tell the person being interviewed that he is conducting the interview on behalf of the lawyer and at his direction to provide information that the lawyer needs in order to advise the company. This will help strengthen later claims by the company that the interview is protected by the attorney-client privilege.

EXAMPLE

AmeriCo, Inc., hired Lee, an attorney, to investigate alleged embezzlement by Baker and to advise AmeriCo if it had legal grounds to fire Baker and seek damages from him. Lee interviewed AmeriCo's employees about Baker's activities and other events surrounding the embezzlement. The only other person present during these interviews was Lee's secretary, who took notes of the interviews and later transcribed them for the file. At the conclusion of the investigation, Baker was fired for embezzlement. He subsequently sued the company for wrongful termination.

During pre-trial discovery in Baker's lawsuit against AmeriCo, his attorney requested the notes from the interviews. AmeriCo objected that the interviews were protected under the attorney-client privilege. The court agreed that the interviews were communications from Lee's client that were provided so he could legally advise AmeriCo, and that the interviews were privileged. The secretary's presence did not destroy the confidentiality of the communication, since she worked for Lee and was present at his direction for a purpose consistent with the confidentiality of the meeting. Therefore, Baker and his lawyer could not compel production of the interview notes.

The privilege also applies to *consulting experts*, outsiders who are retained to assist lawyers in providing legal services or advice to their client, such as accountants. Employee communications with consulting experts should remain privileged if they are made at the direction of the lawyer for the purpose of enabling the expert to assist the lawyer in providing legal advice or analysis. The privilege does not, however, apply to testifying experts (i.e., witnesses who serve to aid the judge or jury on a matter in which the expert has special knowledge or experience).

Legal Considerations in Interviews

PURPOSE OF THE COMMUNICATION

Communications are not privileged unless they are for the purpose of obtaining legal services or advice from the lawyer. If the lawyer is providing business advice, or is acting in a capacity other than as a legal counselor, the communication falls outside of the privilege. For instance, if the lawyer is asked to provide only a factual report to the corporation's board of directors without any legal analysis or advice, then interviews and other client communications in the course of the investigation would not be privileged. For that reason, the company's instructions to its lawyer should expressly state that the purpose of the internal investigation is to enable the lawyer to evaluate the company's legal rights and obligations and to provide legal advice to the company.

CONFIDENTIAL COMMUNICATIONS

Finally, only confidential communications are privileged. If the communication is shared with or made in the presence of a third person who is not a client and is not working under the direction of the lawyer, then a court may conclude that the communication was not intended to be confidential and therefore is not privileged. Similarly, the privilege may be waived if the communication is later disclosed by the client, even if the disclosure is inadvertent. Some jurisdictions have "snap-back" provisions, which allow parties to have privileged communications returned if they were inadvertently disclosed to the other party during discovery.

Waiver of the Privilege

The attorney-client privilege belongs to the client, not the lawyer. It can only be waived by the client or his successor in interest. For a corporation, that typically means its managing officers and directors. The client may waive the privilege by voluntarily disclosing the privileged communications, in testimony or otherwise. There is authority that voluntary disclosure of an investigative report that relies on privileged communications waives the privilege as to those underlying communications.

Of more immediate concern to the investigator is that the client may also waive the privilege by inadvertent disclosure, especially where the disclosure comes about as a result of inadequate efforts to maintain the confidentiality of the privileged information. Thus, investigators must use reasonable diligence to protect privileged communications from unintended disclosure. For example, if investigators show privileged communications to interviewees or include privileged communications in reports that are distributed to individuals other than the company's managing officers or directors, then the privilege may be waived.

Once waived, the privilege is completely lost, at least to the extent of the disclosed communication and related communications. Courts are divided over the so-called *partial waiver doctrine* (i.e., whether disclosure in a government investigation or in the course of litigation preserves the privilege in other forums or as to communications about other undisclosed facts).

Special care must also be taken to avoid inadvertent disclosure from the use of electronic communications, including email, mobile phones, faxes, text messages, and instant messages. It is clear that the attorney-client privilege extends to electronic communications; however, it is also clear that a matter which is voluntarily communicated to a third party who is not an agent of legal counsel is not confidential and, therefore, not privileged. Even inadvertent disclosures may waive the privilege. Therefore, when an investigator chooses to use a form of electronic communication, which is vulnerable to interception and inadvertent disclosure, he runs the risk that his messages might be intercepted by, or disclosed to, an unintended third party.

To successfully meet later challenges and to avoid inadvertently waiving the attorney-client privilege, the investigator should explain to the employee or interviewee that his communications with the company's lawyer (through the investigator) are intended to be confidential and should not be disclosed to others.

Furthermore, as discussed elsewhere in these materials, the employee should also be told that the lawyer represents the company—not the employee—and that the decision to keep the information confidential belongs to the company, which may later decide to disclose what the employee says. This is to avoid misleading the employee into any mistaken belief that the privilege is between him and the company's lawyer, or that he can rely on the company's lawyer to protect his interests.

What Communications Are Privileged?

There is no single test for deciding whose communications with the corporation's lawyer will constitute privileged client communications. The two predominant tests have been the control group test and the subject matter test. The *control group test* effectively protects only communications between the company's lawyer and senior management; the *subject matter test* extends the privilege to other employees when the employee's communication is made at the direction of his superiors and when the subject matter of the communication concerns the employee's performance of his duties.

When given the opportunity to choose between these tests, the U.S. Supreme Court in *Upjohn Co. v. United States* (449 U.S. 383 [1981]) neither embraced nor rejected either approach. Instead, it directed a case-by-case analysis, applying the following factors to determine if communications by an employee of a corporation qualify for protection under the attorney-client privilege:

- The communications were made by a corporate employee to the corporation's lawyer for the corporation to obtain legal advice.
- The employee's corporate superiors directed the employee to cooperate with corporate counsel.
- The communications concerned matters within the scope of the employee's employment.
- The information to be obtained from the employee was not available from upper management.
- The communications were intended to be, and have remained, confidential.

The *Upjohn* decision represents federal common law of privilege; not all states have adopted the *Upjohn* decision or rationale. Some states still apply either the control group or the subject matter test. Also, opinions are divided about whether, and when, the privilege extends to former employees. Again, the investigator should consult with corporate counsel to determine whether the company can assert the privilege as to a particular employee's communications.

Limitations of the Privilege

The attorney-client privilege only protects communications, whether oral, written, or otherwise recorded. It does not protect against disclosure of the underlying facts or knowledge. So, while a client does not have to answer a question about what he said to his lawyer, he cannot rely on the privilege to refuse to answer questions about what he knows simply because he has related those facts to his lawyer. Similarly, placing books, records, or other tangible real evidence in the hands of the company's lawyer does not protect that evidence from disclosure to others.

A lawyer's mere presence at a meeting of the board of directors or of the investigative team does not mean that the records of those proceedings or of communications between the participants are privileged. These are protected only when the proceedings and communications are for the purpose of requesting or rendering legal advice and are intended to be confidential. Thus, to ensure that the privilege will apply, any record of such proceedings should make it clear that the discussions and communications recorded were conducted with the lawyer for the purpose of obtaining his legal services and advice.

In a minority of states, communications from the lawyer to the client are not privileged, unless disclosure of that communication would result in disclosure of the client's communications to the lawyer. In an internal investigation, this will most likely affect the confidentiality of the lawyer's report and advice to the company. In states where this much-criticized rule is still followed, the lawyer's communication to his client should clearly explain the relationship of his conclusions and advice to the privileged communications that he received during the course of the investigation.

The privilege does not apply to communications between the lawyer and client if those communications are in furtherance of the client's contemplated or ongoing criminal conduct. This is true even if the lawyer has no knowledge of the client's intentions to commit or further a crime. Of course, that does not mean that communications made during the client's criminal activity necessarily lose their privilege; the privilege is lost only if the communication was intended by the client to facilitate or aid in the crime. The investigative team must be sensitive to the possibility that an internal investigation will be used by the company's officers or directors to cover-up or perpetuate the criminal conduct under investigation.

> EXAMPLE
> *A company's CEO asked the company's lawyer to investigate alleged corrupt payments by middle management employees. Unbeknownst to the lawyer, the company intended to use this investigation to locate and destroy any evidence of those payments that might expose its evasion of statutorily mandated reporting requirements. None of the communications between the CEO and the lawyer concerning this investigation are privileged.*

Attorney Work Product Doctrine
Nature and Elements of the Doctrine

The *attorney work product doctrine* is a discovery rule that prevents compelled disclosure of documents and materials that have been prepared in anticipation of litigation. It is codified in Rule 26(b)(3) of the Federal Rules of Civil Procedure and in Rule 16 (b)(2) of the Federal Rules of Criminal Procedure, which govern pre-trial discovery in federal cases. State statutes codifying the rule may vary and should be consulted for cases in state court. The rule prevents disclosure of protected materials in both civil and criminal proceedings (including the grand jury).

The privilege extends not only to information and documents prepared by a party or the party's attorneys, but also to materials prepared by consultants and experts who were hired by the attorney. Accordingly, the rule may protect the *work product*—documents and tangible things prepared in anticipation of litigation—of a company's internal investigation, including the investigative report and working memoranda, notes, outlines, and other materials even when the investigators are not lawyers.

As was stated above, the work product privilege only protects materials that are prepared in *anticipation of litigation*. Documents and reports prepared in the course of an in-house investigation, even if at the direction of an attorney, will not be privileged if they were not prepared in anticipation of litigation. It is not enough that there is a possibility of future litigation; the prospect of a lawsuit must not be not speculative or imaginary. Litigation must actually be planned, and the work for which protection is sought must have been undertaken for the specific purpose of preparing for that litigation. It is not necessary, however, for a lawsuit to have actually been filed in order for the privilege to apply. When an internal investigation is conducted in response to known or suspected employee misconduct, this will generally qualify as work done in anticipation of litigation. If the investigator is merely auditing the company's procedures to ensure against the possibility of future losses, however, the work product of the audit probably will not be protected.

Whether a document is created in anticipation of litigation is often not clear. For instance, there is a split in federal authority as to whether a company's tax accrual work papers (documents that estimate the company's potential tax liabilities and disputes) are discoverable by the IRS.

Legal Considerations in Interviews

It is also important to note that the work-product doctrine actually protects two kinds of materials: factual and opinion work products.

Factual Work Product

Factual work product refers to exhibits, documentary and real evidence, witnesses' written or recorded statements, and other purely factual materials that were collected and organized in anticipation of litigation.

Factual work product only enjoys a conditional privilege. This means that, although the materials are generally protected, an opposing party can obtain them if that party is able to demonstrate:
- A substantial need for that product in preparing its own case
- The information cannot be obtained from another source without undue hardship[13]

> EXAMPLE
>
> *Adams, a CFE, conducted an internal investigation of employee Dudley. The investigation was performed for Acme's corporate counsel in order to determine if there were grounds to sue Dudley and recover his gain from certain illegal transactions. During the investigation, Adams obtained tape-recorded interviews from employees Baker and Cain, as well as copies of a parallel set of books that Baker kept as personal evidence of Dudley's illegal transactions. He also obtained Cain's day planner, which contained references to some of Dudley's activities. Acme subsequently settled the claim against Dudley, and none of the investigation's evidence was made public.*
>
> *In a later government investigation of Dudley, the government sought production of the investigative report, as well as copies of the interviews, Baker's books, and Cain's day planner. Baker still worked for Acme, but Cain had resigned and moved to England with his day planner.*
>
> *Assuming the investigative report contains Adams's mental impressions and conclusions about the case, the report would be opinion work product and would therefore be absolutely privileged from disclosure. (See below.) The court will deny the government's request for this report.*
>
> *The statements, books, and planner sought by the government are factual work product of Adams's internal investigation, and as such, they are only entitled to a conditional privilege. In order to obtain them, the government would have to show a substantial need for these items, and also that it would suffer an undue hardship in obtaining them from another source. Regarding Baker's interview and the parallel set of books that he kept, the government's request for these materials will probably be denied. The*

---

[13] One exception to this rule should be noted: statements by the defendant and by witnesses are absolutely excluded from discovery in a federal criminal case, even though they are factual work product.

government would not suffer an undue hardship in obtaining these materials from another source since it could subpoena Baker, question him, and obtain his books directly.

The question of Cain's interview and day-planner is more difficult because Cain now lives beyond the government's jurisdiction. To obtain these materials through a source other than Acme, the government would probably have to request Cain's voluntary cooperation or pursue diplomatic procedures, asking the English courts to compel his testimony and production of evidence. If the government could show that this would be an undue hardship, Acme would have to turn over these materials. If Cain died in the meantime, or if his planner could not be located, the government would have a more compelling case for obtaining Cain's statement and copy of the day planner from Adams or Acme. (Note that, in either case, the facts themselves—Baker's and Cain's knowledge and their tangible evidence—are not protected from discovery by the rule. See Limitations of the Rule on the next page.)

Opinion Work Product

Opinion work product refers to the thought processes, mental impressions, and legal theories of an attorney (or an attorney's representative). The work product privilege affords greater protection for opinion work product, which is generally considered absolutely privileged from disclosure. It not only includes memoranda and notes containing reflections on the case, but also notes and memoranda of a witness's oral statement—as these can reflect the attorney's mental processes and conclusions as well.

EXAMPLE

In the preceding example, instead of recorded statements, suppose Adams made notes of his oral interviews with Baker and Cain, including thoughts about their veracity, credibility, and witness potential. He also noted the relevance of certain facts to the company's legal theories, which had been outlined for him by corporate counsel. His final investigative report contained similar factual summaries of the evidence, including Baker's and Cain's interviews, Baker's books, and Cain's day planner, and a more comprehensive analysis of the evidence, the law, and his conclusions.

The court probably would decline to compel production of the interview notes or of the report. The notes contain Adams's mental impressions of the witnesses and of their impact on the case. As such, the notes constitute opinion work product *that is entitled to absolute protection. Similarly, the report's legal and evidentiary analysis and conclusions are protected* opinion work product. *If the factual materials are completely segregated in the report, a court might order production only of those purely factual excerpts. But, otherwise, the government's request for the report is likely to be declined.*

To increase the chances of protecting his work from involuntary disclosure, an investigator should expressly include his mental impressions, conclusions, and legal theories in his investigative notes, memoranda, and reports. This will help qualify them as opinion work product, entitling them to an absolute privilege. Also, where feasible, the investigator should make notes of oral interviews and statements, rather than take written or recorded statements, which are more likely to be considered factual work product. (Of course, sometimes the need for a verbatim statement outweighs the concerns about creating a factual work product that might be discoverable by another party. This is but one of many judgments that the investigator will have to make during an internal investigation.)

Duration of the Privilege
Unlike the attorney-client privilege, this rule may not bestow a permanent privilege on the protected materials. The majority of courts have held that the rule continues to protect work product prepared in anticipation of one lawsuit from disclosure in any other lawsuit. Some courts, however, have limited that protection to subsequent litigation that is related to the first lawsuit, and some have even held that work product is freely discoverable in any lawsuit other than the one for which it was prepared.

Limitations of the Rule
Like the attorney-client privilege, the work product rule protects materials from disclosure, not the underlying information to which the materials refer. Although reports, interview notes, and transcripts might not be discoverable under the privilege, the facts learned may have to be provided in response to properly phrased discovery requests. Similarly, the privilege does not prevent discovery of the identity of witnesses and the existence of interview notes, tapes, or transcripts. Thus, while the company may be able to prevent disclosure of the work product of its internal investigation, it cannot prevent the government or another party from compelling the same information from the same or other sources.

The rule only helps preserve the confidentiality of an internal investigation conducted in anticipation of litigation to which the company is, or will be, a party. There is authority that, in a criminal proceeding solely against the company's employees, the rule does not prevent compelled disclosure of the company's internal investigation. Of course, if it is likely that the company will be charged later, then the work product of its internal investigation should remain protected by the rule.

Like the attorney-client privilege, the work product rule does not protect disclosure of materials that are used in furtherance of an ongoing crime or fraud. Again, it may be impossible to protect the confidentiality of an investigation through reliance on the rule if the company's motive in conducting the investigation is to conceal or perpetuate criminal conduct.

The Self-Evaluation Privilege
The *self-evaluation privilege* (also referred to as the *self-critical privilege*) is a qualified privilege that some state courts have used to protect self-investigative materials where confidentiality is essential to the purpose of the investigation and where the public policy interests in facilitating the self-investigation outweigh the needs of a third party for disclosure. This privilege differs from the attorney-client privilege in that it

does not require the participation of a lawyer in the investigation and potentially protects more than just lawyer-client communications. It also differs from the work product doctrine in that it may apply even in the absence of anticipated litigation.

> EXAMPLE
> *In* Bredice v. Doctors Hospital, Inc., *50 F.R.D. 249 (D.D.C. 1970), a plaintiff's husband died in the care of the defendant hospital, and she sued for medical malpractice. During the suit, she sought production of the records concerning her husband from the hospital's "medical staff review," a regular evaluative review which the hospital undertook in compliance with its accreditation requirements in order to improve care and treatment. In denying the discovery request, the court agreed that the overriding public interest in maintaining and improving health care required that the review participants be able to express constructive professional criticism without worrying that their comments would later be disclosed and used against a colleague in a malpractice suit.*

Despite the seemingly broad application of this privilege to internal investigations, it actually is of limited usefulness. Court decisions seem to limit its application to "materials prepared for mandatory government reports."[14] Voluntary self-evaluative investigations undertaken in the ordinary course of business (e.g., internal audit reports or investigations that concern specific employee or management misconduct that is not subject to mandatory government reporting) are probably not protected by the privilege. In fact, there is some case authority that a self-evaluative process whose purpose is to address a specific problem rather than to review general policies does not fall under the confidentiality protection of this privilege. Finally, the bulk of authority says that the privilege only applies in private civil suits, not in suits or actions by a government agency to enforce laws for which it is responsible.

Like other privileges and rules discussed in this section, the self-evaluation privilege does not protect objective data or facts contained in the materials. Only the subjective evaluative portions of the investigative materials are protected. Furthermore, courts closely scrutinize confidentiality claims and frequently find that the third party's need for disclosure outweighs the company's need for confidentiality.

Even where applicable, the self-evaluation privilege—like the privileges and rules discussed above—can be waived if there is a voluntary disclosure of the investigation or a lack of a good faith effort to preserve its confidentiality. Thus, the investigator should be aware that this qualified privilege *may* exist, and that if the investigation meets its prerequisites, it can potentially be used to protect the investigation's confidentiality. However, he should also recognize that this privilege has a limited application and should not rely on it to any great extent. Additionally, many states, such as Texas, have

---

[14] *Hoffman v. United Telecomms.*, Inc., 117 F.R.D. 440, 442 (D. Kan. 1987).

expressly refused to recognize the self-evaluation privilege, so check with your attorney for its applicability in your jurisdiction.

Avoiding Liability for Obstruction of Justice and Witness Tampering

It is assumed that no investigator would knowingly or intentionally suborn perjury, conceal evidence, or otherwise attempt to undermine a government investigation or a judicial proceeding. However, it is important to understand the potential for liability for these offenses during an internal investigation.

It is standard technique during an interview to prompt and refresh the memory of witnesses with facts or documents known to the interviewer. The interviewer may want to share other information or statements in order to test their truthfulness. If the witness's statement is inconsistent with other information, the interviewer may challenge the witness to see if he will change his statement. A certain amount of persuasiveness on the part of the interviewer is not uncommon if he thinks the witness is being evasive, uncooperative, or untruthful. And if confidentiality is a concern, the witness may be advised not to discuss his statement with anyone else or to share certain documents with others.

Yet, the information with which the interviewer confronts the witness may be inaccurate or incomplete. Indeed, the investigator might not possess all of the relevant facts early in the investigation and might be unaware that the information or evidence he cites to a witness is inaccurate or misleading. When confronted with incomplete or possibly misleading information or evidence, the witness may be influenced—however unintentionally—to give an inaccurate statement that is consistent with the information provided by the interviewer. "Leaning" on the witness whom the investigator suspects of lying or withholding information may be perceived as harassment by the witness or by others. Requests for confidentiality might be understood by the witness as instructions not to speak with anyone else, including government investigators. In extreme cases, it might even be misunderstood as a suggestion to conceal or destroy tangible evidence. This could conceivably lead to charges against the investigator or his company for unlawfully interfering with a government investigation.

The investigator should be especially sensitive to the possible risks of liability if the witness is a disaffected employee or has been fired by the company. That person may be tempted to seek revenge against the company or the investigators through accusations of impropriety. Accordingly, investigators should keep accurate records of interviews with potentially problematic witnesses and should have a third witness—another member of the investigative team—present for such interviews.

To understand what conduct could lead to accusations of impropriety or criminal liability; investigators should be familiar with the following federal statutes. There may be additional state statutes that prohibit similar conduct in connection with state investigations or even state civil lawsuits. An attorney should be consulted for the law of a specific jurisdiction.

Confidentiality Requests

In 2012, the National Labor Relations Board (NLRB) ruled that blanket confidentiality requests regarding employee complaints and internal investigations violate Section 7 of the National Labor Relations Act. In the past it was common for employers to request confidentiality during an internal investigation; however, the NLRB has found that such requests must be accompanied by a compelling need for secrecy. Before requesting confidentiality, an employer must "determine whether in any given investigation witnesses needed protection, evidence was in danger of being destroyed, testimony was in danger of being fabricated, or there was a need to prevent a cover up." The guidance from the NLRB applies to both unionized and nonunionized employers.[15]

Witness Tampering

The Victim and Witness Protection Act (VWPA), 18 U.S.C. § 1512 et seq., makes it a felony to engage in "misleading conduct toward another person" with the intent to "influence, delay, or prevent" a witness's testimony or to "cause or induce any person" to "withhold" testimony or documents.

As defined in Section 1515(3), *misleading conduct* includes, among other things:
- Knowingly making a false statement
- Omitting or concealing information that renders a statement misleading
- Knowingly inviting reliance on a writing that is false, forged, altered, or otherwise lacking in authenticity with intent to mislead
- Knowingly inviting reliance on a materially misleading sample, specimen, map, photograph, or other object with intent to mislead
- Knowingly using a trick, scheme, or device with intent to mislead

Unlike obstruction of justice (see below), the VWPA can be violated without any corrupt purpose to obstruct justice, and it can be violated even if there is no grand jury or other judicial proceeding pending. Section 1512 only requires proof that the defendant acted with intent to "influence, delay, or prevent" testimony or the withholding of evidence. The VWPA may be violated as to a witness in a prospective or anticipated proceeding, as well as a pending one.

In light of the VWPA, a fraud examiner must take care how he instructs a witness with regard to the confidentiality of the investigation. Confidentiality is a legitimate concern, and the investigator needs to

---

[15] National Labor Relations Board, Case 28-CA-023438, Banner Estrella Medical Center, 2012.

Legal Considerations in Interviews

instruct a witness on how to preserve privileges and confidentiality. However, instructing a witness not to speak with government investigators or other parties to litigation—or giving instructions that could be misunderstood in that way—exposes the investigator and the company to potential witness tampering liability.

The VWPA also makes it a misdemeanor to harass another person and thereby hinder, delay, prevent, or dissuade any person from attending or testifying in an official proceeding, reporting a federal offense, causing an arrest for a federal offense, or causing a criminal prosecution.

Obstruction of Justice

Obstruction of justice statutes punish efforts to impede or obstruct the investigation or trial of other substantive offenses. There are several federal criminal statutes that prohibit obstruction of justice. These statutes are contained in Chapter 73 of the United States Code and prohibit impeding, influencing, or obstructing virtually any type of federal proceeding (including criminal investigations) through the destruction of documents, threats, bribes, or witness tampering. Many are specific to a particular setting or industry, or to a particular kind of proceeding, such as influencing a juror through a writing (18 U.S.C. § 1504); theft or alteration of a record or process (18 U.S.C. § 1506); obstruction relating to court orders (18 U.S.C. § 1509); tampering with a witness, victim, or an informant (18 U.S.C. § 1512); obstruction of a federal audit (18 U.S.C. § 1516); and obstructing the examination of a financial institution (18 U.S.C. § 1517).

18 U.S.C. § 1510 prohibits any endeavor to obstruct the communication of information to federal criminal investigators of a financial institution by bribery, intimidation, force, threats, or misrepresentation. This statute also prohibits an officer of a financial institution, with intent to obstruct a judicial proceeding, from telling a customer or other person named in a subpoena about the existence or contents of the subpoena for the institution's records.

18 U.S.C. § 1503 more generally prohibits any corrupt effort to influence, impede, or obstruct "the due administration of justice" by threats or otherwise. Section 1503 applies not just to a grand jury or other criminal proceeding, but to civil litigation as well. Section 1505 prohibits the same conduct specifically in connection with a proceeding "before any department or agency of the United States" or a congressional hearing.

The phrase *due administration of justice* in Section 1503 has been interpreted to mean that there must be a pending judicial proceeding of which the defendant was aware at the time of the offense. Similarly, the express terms of other obstruction statutes contemplate a pending proceeding.

These broad statutes are unlikely to be applied to typical interviewing techniques because they require proof of a corrupt intent, not merely an effort to influence a witness. As with the witness tampering statutes, however, investigators must be careful how a witness is instructed regarding the confidentiality of the interview or of the investigation.

Spoliation of Evidence

Spoliation of evidence is broadly defined as the act of destroying evidence or making it otherwise unavailable. The act of spoliation can surface in just about any type of case—criminal or civil—and by any party, plaintiff, or defendant. The theory behind spoliation of evidence presumes that the individual who makes evidence unavailable following the probable initiation of a lawsuit is aware of its detrimental effect upon a case.

Although few jurisdictions have a separate cause of action for spoliation of evidence, almost every jurisdiction allows for sanctions resulting from such acts. Some courts require the spoliation to be intentional, though others merely require negligence or reckless spoliation.

Intentional spoliation claims usually involve the following elements: (1) the existence of a potential lawsuit; (2) the defendant's knowledge of the potential lawsuit; (3) the destruction, mutilation, or significant alteration of potential evidence; (4) intent on the part of the defendant to disrupt or defeat the lawsuit; (5) a causal relationship between the act of spoliation and the inability to prove the lawsuit; and (6) damages.

Conversely, *negligent spoliation* claims generally occur when a party unintentionally loses evidence valuable to its claim, or a third party loses or destroys evidence in a suit. An example of the required elements for a negligent spoliation claim include: (1) existence of a potential civil action, (2) a legal or contractual duty to preserve evidence that is relevant to the potential civil action, (3) destruction of that evidence, (4) significant impairment in the ability to prove the lawsuit, (5) a causal relationship between the evidence destruction and the inability to prove the lawsuit, and (6) damages.

Companies must be especially aware of spoliation of digital evidence. When compared to spoliation of physical documents, digital spoliation carries additional risks because there is often a lack of knowledge concerning electronic data.

Perjury and Subornation of Perjury

Perjury is the willful giving of false material testimony under oath, and includes falsely claiming that one cannot remember a material fact. There are three general federal perjury laws. First, section 1621 of Title 18, U.S. Code, is the general federal perjury statute; it makes it a crime to present material false statements under oath in federal proceedings. Section 1621 applies "in any case in which a law of the United States authorizes an oath to be administered." All states have similar statutes.

Second, section 1623 of Title 18, U.S. Code, makes it a crime to present false testimony or produce other false information under oath before, or ancillary to, a federal court or grand jury.

Third, section 1622 of Title 18, U.S. Code, criminalizes subornation of perjury; it makes it a federal crime to induce or cause another to commit perjury. A person violates section 1622 if he induces another to commit perjury in violation of either section 1621 or section 1623. The most obvious example of subornation of perjury is telling a prospective witness to lie or to conceal the conduct that is the subject of the investigation. Similarly, subornation also has been found to exist where a person counseled a witness to give testimony, the truth of which he recklessly disregarded, even though he did not know for certain that the information was untrue. Subornation is only an offense when the perjury has in fact occurred—proof of subornation requires proof of the perjury.

Misprision of a Felony
Even though citizens have no general duty to report criminal activity, 18 U.S.C. § 4 recognizes misprision of felony as a criminal offense. In general terms, *misprision of felony* is a crime dealing with the failure to report a crime where there is a legal duty to do so.

Under the federal statute, the prosecution must prove the following four elements to obtain a misprision of felony conviction: (1) the principal committed and completed the felony alleged; (2) the defendant had knowledge of the fact; (3) the defendant failed to notify the authorities; and (4) the defendant took affirmative steps to conceal the crime of the principal.

A company investigator is likely to be the one who will uncover evidence of felony offenses—indeed, that is frequently the purpose of an internal investigation. Moreover, absent a mandatory reporting requirement or some incentive for voluntary disclosure, the company may be inclined to treat the investigation as confidential and will not report the felony. Accordingly, the potential for violating Section 4 must always be born in mind. Although silence alone will not violate the statute, any conduct that could be construed as an effort to conceal the crime could expose the investigator and the company to liability for this offense. Again, the investigator should be careful about instructions given to witnesses for the purpose of protecting the investigation's confidentiality. Apparent efforts to silence a witness may—together with silence on the part of the company—constitute misprision of a felony. Also, investigators should carefully retain and account for tangible evidence collected during the investigation. Lost or misplaced records that evidence a felony—or destruction of such records other than in accordance with standard retention policies—could be perceived as efforts to conceal the felony.

Recording the Results of an Interview

There are many different ways that an investigator can memorialize the results of interviews and interrogations. Verbatim records can be made electronically or by a stenographer. The interviewer can take notes and use them to summarize the interview in a memorandum to the file. After questioning the witness, his statement can be reduced to writing, and he can review and sign it. And there are other variations among these methods. Each may be appropriate in different circumstances. However, the purpose of this section is not to discuss the practical advantages and disadvantages of these different methods, but rather their legal implications—specifically for the investigation's confidentiality and for the company's potential liability.

Protect the Company's Interests in Confidentiality

The investigator must understand that how an interview or interrogation is memorialized—and how that record is handled—affects the availability of the privileges and non-disclosure rules that were discussed previously. The investigator should try to record an interview or interrogation in a way that preserves—and reflects on its face—the elements of the attorney-client privilege, the work product doctrine, or the self-evaluation privilege. Similarly, the investigator must handle those records consistently with these privileges in mind. Above all, this means preserving the intended confidentiality by not sharing them with individuals other than the controlling company management or directors and corporate counsel.

Factual Work Product Versus Opinion Work Product

As was discussed earlier, the restrictions on disclosure under the work product doctrine vary considerably depending on whether the work product is primarily factual or whether it reflects the mental thought processes, analysis, and conclusions of the party or its representative. Records of interviews and interrogations that are verbatim or substantially verbatim are more likely to be considered factual work product, and therefore will be discoverable if the party seeking discovery can show a substantial need for the factual materials and an undue hardship in obtaining them from another source. Verbatim records include tape-recorded statements, video-taped interviews or interrogations, written statements or confessions that are signed by the witness, and even substantially verbatim accounts prepared by the investigator.

Therefore, wherever practical, the investigator should use notes to memorialize the interview rather than taped recordings. Moreover, the investigator should intersperse his factual notes with observations, analyses, evaluations, and conclusions. Explicitly including the investigator's mental impressions within the body of the interview notes will make it likely that a court will protect the notes as opinion work product, thus entitling them to an absolute privilege from discovery. (Naturally, this can only be done within the investigator's notes; it is not practical to incorporate the interviewer's mental impressions within a recorded or signed statement or confession.)

Legal Considerations in Interviews

Of course, sometimes the need for a verbatim record outweighs the need to preserve the company's rights under the work product doctrine. There often are compelling reasons to take verbatim statements or confessions from adverse parties and witnesses, or from individuals whose availability for a later trial is in doubt.

If the subject will be unavailable for trial, his statement may still be introduced in evidence if it is in a form that is admissible under the applicable evidence code. This almost always means a verbatim account. Moreover, a verbatim account is more reliable and credible than someone relying on the interviewer's memory to paraphrase what the witness said.

If the witness is adverse, the investigator and the company's trial attorney will want a verbatim account of his testimony to know exactly what the witness will say, to prevent the witness from varying his account at trial, and to enable the company's attorney to impeach him at trial if he does vary from his earlier statement. In each of these circumstances, the investigator must weigh the competing considerations and decide how to proceed. It is advisable to consult with the attorney in charge of the investigation or pending litigation, as these decisions can affect the attorney's later handling of any litigation.

Identify the Record as Work Product

The record of the interview or interrogation should also indicate on its face that it is work product (i.e., it is work prepared by a party or its representative in anticipation of litigation). That does not mean just labeling the record as "work product," although that cannot hurt. Rather, the interviewer should expressly state that the record contains information obtained in order to enable the company's lawyer to prepare to prosecute or defend a claim.

> EXAMPLE
>
> *CFE Adams's interview memoranda were addressed to the company's attorney and contained the following initial paragraph: "On [date], CFE Thompson and I interviewed [employee], pursuant to your request to trace and report to you about payments between foreign officials and [suspect] in connection with contracts issued [date] so that you can evaluate the company's potential liability under the Foreign Corrupt Practices Act and can plan appropriate legal action to recover any corrupt payments received by [suspect]. In the course of that interview, [employee] provided the following information:" A substantially similar notation appeared on her rough notes of the interviews as well.*

Identify the Record as an Attorney-Client Communication

The attorney-client privilege may not apply to all interviews (see earlier discussion of Attorney-Client Privilege). However, where it does apply, it can protect against unwanted disclosures even better than the work product doctrine. For instance, even factual work product, such as verbatim recordings and written confessions, may be absolutely privileged if they qualify as an attorney-client communication. In that case, not even the most convincing demonstration of the requesting party's substantial need for the materials will overcome the privilege.

Accordingly, just as with work product, the record should state on its face those facts that show it is an attorney-client communication. The investigator should explicitly state that the information has been obtained at the request of the company's attorney for communication to him. Because the privilege only covers communications to the attorney in the course of his providing legal services—as opposed, for example, to business advice—the investigator must also indicate the legal purpose for which the information was provided.

The record should also identify the position of the witness and any other facts that would qualify the interview with that particular employee as an attorney-client communication.

EXAMPLE
After interviewing an upper-level management employee with policy-making authority over the foreign contracts area, CFE Adams's interview memorandum also explicitly noted the employee's position and authority in order to indicate that this was an interview with a "control group" employee. Similarly, memoranda of interviews with lower-level employees explicitly:

A. Stated that the employee was asked by [a named upper-level or senior management employee] to provide information to CFE Adams

B. Included a description of the witness's position and authority which demonstrated that the subject of the interview was within the scope of the witness's employment and knowledge

C. Stated that the witness was asked to provide the information because it was not readily available from other, higher-level employees

Each or all of these facts could be important to a later claim of attorney-client privilege.

Identify the Self-Evaluation Purpose of the Interview
Similarly, if the interview was conducted as part of an investigation that may qualify for the limited self-evaluation privilege, investigators should explicitly state the supporting facts on the face of the record. As in the examples above, identify the specific purpose of the interview and the use to which the company expects to put the information. Further, identify the policy interests involved and caution how the company's purpose would be blocked or frustrated by disclosure of the information beyond the approved distribution list.

Identify and Treat the Record as Confidential

Because confidentiality is the cornerstone of any claim of privilege, investigators must identify and treat any interview record as confidential. All pages of any contemporaneous notes and subsequent reports must be prominently marked as "confidential." The confidentiality of the document can be further underscored by writing on the cover page and the top margin of each following page that its distribution is limited to specific persons, and that any other distribution or disclosure is unauthorized and prohibited. The individuals to whom distribution is authorized should be strictly limited to the company's directors or managing officers who have a need to know the information and who have authority to direct an action by the company in response to the information. These are the people who are most likely to be regarded as the company's alter ego for purposes of the privilege.

No matter how the record is marked, however, it will lose its confidentiality if it is not handled as a confidential document. Those in the control group must ensure that the restricted distribution is observed. It is essential that the company limits the number of copies to those absolutely necessary, and that it safeguards and accounts for all copies. Privileged communications should not be left where they can be seen or read by passers-by. When not being used, they should be kept in a locked filing cabinet to which only the investigators, the company's attorney, and authorized recipients have access. A company can protect against inadvertent disclosure by transmitting copies in sealed envelopes that are addressed only to approved recipients and that are marked with similar warnings to those on the face of the documents. It is also helpful to add an express instruction that the envelope is to be opened by the addressee only.

Review Questions

1. Green is an at-will employee of ABC Corporation, a private company. During an investigation of internal fraud, Green is interviewed by internal investigators about missing funds. Which of the following statements are correct? (Assume that there is no state action by ABC Corporation.)
   A. Green is entitled to have an attorney present at the interview
   B. The investigators must give *Miranda* warnings to Green
   C. Both of the above
   D. None of the above

2. Under which cause of action can an investigator be held liable for a TRUE statement made about a suspect?
   A. Defamation
   B. Public disclosure of private facts
   C. Both of the above
   D. None of the above—investigators can never be held liable for true statements

3. As a result of a ruling by the National Labor Relations Board, an employer's request for confidentiality regarding an internal investigation must be accompanied by which of the following?
   A. *Miranda* warning
   B. Self-evaluation privilege
   C. Compelling need for secrecy
   D. All of the above

4. Employers are generally permitted to discipline or terminate an employee who refuses to cooperate with a reasonable request to provide information. However, employers are never permitted to terminate employees on these grounds if the employee:
   A. Has an employment contract
   B. Is employed under a collective bargaining agreement
   C. Both of the above
   D. None of the above

5. The Fifth Amendment's protections apply to:
   A. Civil offenses
   B. Criminal offenses
   C. Internal offenses
   D. All of the above

Legal Considerations in Interviews

6. A suspect's right to leave a non-custodial interview or interrogation by law enforcement is provided by the:
   A. Fourth Amendment
   B. Fifth Amendment
   C. Sixth Amendment
   D. None of the above

7. For an individual to recover civil damages for intentional infliction of emotional distress, it must be proven that:
   A. A defendant's conduct must have been extreme and outrageous
   B. The defendant acted with the intent of causing severe emotional distress or with reckless disregard of whether his actions would cause severe emotional distress
   C. The plaintiff suffered severe distress
   D. All of the above

8. The attorney-client privilege can be applied to all of the following EXCEPT:
   A. Consulting experts
   B. Testifying experts
   C. Investigators working under the attorney's supervision
   D. Paralegals working under the attorney's supervision

9. There is no single test for deciding whose communications with a corporation's lawyers will constitute privileged client communications. The two predominant tests that have been used for this end are the control group test and which of the following?
   A. The subject matter test
   B. The truthfulness test
   C. The polygraph test
   D. None of the above

10. According to the text, which of the following is true of the attorney work product doctrine?
    A. Only protects materials that are prepared in anticipation of litigation
    B. Only protects the confidentiality of documents that are prepared by an attorney
    C. Only protects exhibits, documentary evidence, and witnesses' statements
    D. None of the above

11. Which of the following is NOT true of the self-evaluation privilege?
    A. Does not require the participation of a lawyer in the investigation
    B. Potentially protects more than just lawyer-client communications
    C. Only preserves the confidentiality of an internal investigation conducted in anticipation of litigation
    D. Protects self-investigative materials where confidentiality is essential to the purpose of the investigation

12. Since confidentiality is the cornerstone of any claim of privilege, investigators must identify and treat any interview record as confidential. Which of the following is a step investigators can take to try to ensure a document's confidentiality?
    A. Mark all pages of any contemporaneous notes and subsequent reports as "confidential"
    B. Write on the cover page and the top margin of each following page that its distribution is limited to specific individuals and that any other distribution or disclosure is unauthorized and prohibited
    C. Ensure that restricted distribution is observed
    D. All of the above

VII. WRITING REPORTS

Introduction

Investigators must always keep in mind that an internal investigation report might be read by outside parties, including litigation opponents, government investigators, and perhaps even the general public. Under no circumstances should the investigator prepare a report with the idea that the information will not be disclosed to adverse third parties. It is important for the investigator to understand what should and should not be included in a report, and how to safeguard the confidentiality of the document.

An investigation report should stand on its own. It should adequately answer the classic questions of who, what, when, where, why, and how. If the report is prepared properly, the reader should not have to refer to any other documents to understand the issues.

Characteristics of a Good Report

Accuracy

Written reports must be accurate because an inaccurate report will affect the credibility of the report and the report's author. Each contact an investigator makes during the course of an internal investigation should be recorded on a timely basis in a *memorandum of interview* (i.e., a written record used to document all interviews conducted during the investigation). The investigator should include all facts of possible relevance. Investigators should reconfirm dates and supporting information with the respondent. It is important to reconfirm the facts before the report is written, not after. Attachments to the report, if any, should be completely described. Inaccuracies and careless errors are inexcusable and can render a report useless.

Clarity

Investigative reports on internal investigations should convey pertinent information in the clearest possible language. If necessary, quote the respondent directly (provided the quotation does not distort the context). Reports should only convey *objective facts* (i.e., unbiased evidence that is not influenced by personal feelings, interpretations, or prejudice); it is inappropriate to editorialize or give judgments. If complex or technical terms must be used, the investigator should make sure they are used in their proper contexts, and, where necessary, the meaning of complex terms should be explained. In general, professional jargon should be avoided since the report might be read by people who will not be familiar with esoteric or technical terminology.

Impartiality and Relevance

All facts should be reported without bias, and everything relevant should be included regardless of which side it favors or what it proves or disproves. At the outset of an internal fraud investigation, the examiner should carefully determine what information will be needed to prove the case and attempt to include only this information. A report should include only those matters that are relevant to the investigation. However, almost every investigation yields information of which the relevance is not immediately known. In such cases, it is best to opt for completeness.

Timeliness

Timeliness of reports is extremely important because it tends to enhance the accuracy of witness testimony. All interviews should be transcribed as soon as possible after the questioning to preserve the examiner's memory of the interview(s). Upon completing the investigation, the examiner should prepare a final or interim report (whichever is appropriate) as soon as possible.

> **Video**
>
> In the video titled "Chapter VII: Writing Reports," fraud investigation expert Jonathan Turner, CFE, explains his belief that brevity is the single most important quality of an effective report. (Go to www.acfe.com/internalinvestigations to view the video.)

Legal Considerations for Written Reports

The information a report contains and who sees it can have legal consequences for the company and possibly for the investigators. Privileges upon which the company depends in order to preserve confidentiality may be preserved or waived. Employee rights may be affected, with resulting injury to one or more employees and possible company liability for those injuries. In addition, revelations in the report could expose the company to civil or criminal liabilities for violations of government regulatory statutes and rules.

The following materials briefly review the major legal issues and concerns in the context of written reports. All of these have been discussed extensively in earlier chapters, and it is recommended that you go back and reread those chapters for more detailed information about them.

Libel

As previously discussed, *libel* is the written form of defamation. A person can sue for libel when (1) someone makes a false written statement about him, (2) the false statement is communicated to a third party, (3) the person suffers harm as a result of the false communication, and (4) the statement was made on an unprivileged occasion. By its nature, an internal investigation almost certainly contains allegations against one or more individuals (likely employees) that are harmful to them and their reputations. If the injurious allegations are published (communicated to third persons) and if they turn out to be false, the company and its investigators face potential liability for being libel.

Of course, truth is a defense to a libel action; therefore, if the investigation is sound and the report accurately depicts the facts, a libel action should be defensible. That said, it is very important that the report be tightly written. It is a serious mistake to include allegations or conclusions that are not well-supported by the facts. Loosely-based allegations or unsupported conclusions are most likely to be the meat of a libel action.

Aside from the truth, the most important defense to a libel action for internal investigators is the common interest privilege. A statement is exempt from a libel claim under the *common interest privilege* if the statement is made (1) in good faith, (2) regarding a subject in which the person making the statement has a legitimate interest or duty, and (3) is communicated to another person with a corresponding interest or duty. This privilege extends to communications (e.g., reports or oral statements) about internal investigations among persons with a legitimate interest in the investigation. Statements made in good faith among these interested individuals are privileged from libel suits. Keep in mind, however, that malice defeats the privilege. If the person who made the communication knew that it was false or had a reckless disregard for whether it was true, then this statement is not privileged—meaning that the speaker can be sued for libel.

Privacy

Any time a report on an internal investigation is written, there is a chance that the report will contain private information about the subject(s) of the investigation. The disclosure of that information to others could result in an invasion of privacy action against the company and the investigator. A privacy action can result even if the information that is disclosed is true. If public statements are made about an employee's private life, and if those statements would be highly offensive to a reasonable person, the employee may be able to sue under the tort of public disclosure of private facts. (See discussion of the Employee's Common Law Rights in Chapters 3 and 6.)

The principal issue in this type of privacy action is whether the disclosure was reasonable. This is similar to the common interest privilege. It should be considered reasonable for the internal report to be shared with the company's controlling management and with any government agencies to whom reporting or disclosure is mandated. On the other hand, disseminating private information about an employee to his coworkers who are not otherwise involved in the investigation is probably not reasonable and may subject the investigator to liability. Limiting distribution to those who have a legitimate interest in the investigation may be the best insurance against a privacy suit. Certainly, any broader distribution of the report and its private information is much more difficult to justify.

Writing Reports

Just as with a libel suit, the quality of the report may also influence how a court or jury responds to a privacy action. Distributing a report that is incomplete or unreliable, or that contains loosely drawn, unsupported allegations and conclusions, suggests unreasonable conduct by the company throughout the investigation and invites liability. Make every effort to make the internal report a well-written, credible, and supported document.

Privileges

As illustrated in the preceding discussion, many of the potential adverse legal consequences of a written report result from improper dissemination of the report. If an internal report is shared only with the company's lawyer and controlling managers or directors (i.e., those who have a legitimate need to see it), these consequences will probably be avoided. It is equally important to limit access to the report to protect its confidentiality under the attorney-client privilege, the work product doctrine, or the self-evaluation privilege.

Actually, we need to think in terms of two kinds of internal reports. The first, prepared by the investigators, is largely factual in nature. That report may go first to the company's lawyer, who uses it in his legal analysis, or it may go directly to the company's management. A second kind of report—what we actually think of when we refer to a final internal report—is prepared by the company's lawyer for the company's controlling management (i.e., his client). This report includes not just a summary of the facts established by the investigation, but also the attorney's legal analysis and conclusions based on those facts.

Attorney-Client Privilege

The *attorney-client privilege* protects confidential communications between an attorney and a client where the communication was made for the purpose of giving or receiving legal advice. A purely factual report from the investigators is probably not protected by the attorney-client privilege for two reasons. First, the attorney is not a party to the communication, and second, the document is a purely factual report (i.e., one that does not contain legal advice). However, to the extent that the investigator's report contains or recounts privileged communications, it should remain protected. (The attorney-client privilege was discussed in more detail in Chapter 6.)

Ordinarily, the attorney's internal report to controlling management will be protected by the attorney-client privilege. However, even this type of report might not be privileged if a court finds that the attorney acted as an investigator, and the report's purpose was therefore to analyze and advise the company about the factual circumstances or to provide business advice rather than legal advice. For the same reason, courts have held that the privilege does not apply where the company did not voluntarily commission the investigation (e.g., where the investigation was initiated as the result of a consent decree or to comply with a regulatory reporting requirement). In those cases, the courts have concluded that the attorney's role was largely that of an investigator, not a legal counselor. Thus, while the attorney's internal report necessarily must address the factual results of the investigation, it should focus on legal advice to the company in order to qualify for the privilege.

In some jurisdictions, communications from the lawyer to the client are not regarded as privileged unless they are based on privileged communications that came from the client. Attorneys who operate in these jurisdictions should explicitly incorporate the privileged communications on which their report is based in order to make sure that they are covered by the privilege.

In any case, the internal report should not be shared with anyone who is not a controlling person for the company. Any disclosure of the internal report—intentional or otherwise—to a non-client will waive the privilege.

Remember that the privilege protects neither the underlying facts themselves nor any documents or other evidence in the possession of the company's attorney from disclosure. Either may be discovered by another party through appropriate means, even if the internal report may not.

Work Product Doctrine

The greatest degree of protection for internal reports probably comes from the work product doctrine. To review, the *work product doctrine* is a discovery rule that prevents compelled disclosure of documents and materials that have been collected, arranged, or prepared in anticipation of litigation. Most efforts to discover a company's internal investigation will probably come from adverse parties in legal proceedings.

The work product doctrine protects reports that are prepared or collected in anticipation of litigation; therefore, it limits the ability of opposing parties to discover internal reports. To make sure that internal reports will be protected under the work-product doctrine, the reports should explicitly state that they are for use in prosecuting or defending pending or anticipated legal claims. This should not be a problem because the object of an internal investigation is likely to be something that has a realistic potential for causing legal liability or loss.

Recall that there are two kinds of work product—factual and opinion—and that opinion work product receives the higher degree of protection. The internal report from the company's lawyer, by its very nature, contains a large amount of analysis and conclusions—the kinds of mental impressions and opinions that receive virtually absolute protection as opinion work product. However, even a factual report from investigators can receive the higher protection as opinion work product if, instead of presenting the information and evidence in a verbatim fashion, the investigator presents the evidence through his analysis and mental impressions. (See discussion of the work product doctrine in Chapter 6.)

Again, it is important to maintain the confidentiality of the report by limiting the number of copies, as well as their distribution and use. Work product protection for reports can be waived if the contents of the report are improperly disclosed. Investigators should abide by the same rules governing disclosure of materials that exist under the attorney-client privilege that was discussed previously.

Some courts have suggested that disclosure to the government may not negate the benefits of the work product rule if the disclosure is pursuant to a confidentiality agreement or if the right to continue to rely on the rule is reserved at the time of submission. These cases are very fact-specific and narrow, however, and the better rule is to assume that any disclosure of the internal report probably waives the protection for the report and for the underlying work product.

Self-Evaluation Privilege

It is unlikely that this privilege will offer much protection against involuntary disclosure of an internal report. As a relatively new addition to the body of privilege law, the courts have been reluctant to recognize it or broaden its scope. Even where recognized, it is subject to strict limitations that tend to override its modest protections. Courts have held that it applies only to protect materials gathered and prepared for the purpose of complying with government-imposed reporting requirements. Some courts have held that it does not provide protection from compelled disclosure of the investigation to government agencies.

Disclosing the Report to Government Personnel or Other Third Parties

As noted earlier, a company may not always have a choice about disclosure of an internal report, or at least of the underlying facts. As mentioned in Chapter 1, there are many mandatory reporting and disclosure laws in state and federal statutes and regulations.

If an internal investigation was undertaken to comply with one of these statutes, the company still may be able to assert the self-evaluation privilege to protect from further involuntary disclosures, at least to non-governmental parties. There is also some authority that disclosure to the government under certain circumstances or agreements might not waive the work product doctrine's protections.

However, where given a choice, a company may realize significant benefits from the voluntary disclosure of its internal report to government investigators. The internal report may convince prosecutors or regulators that the company has no liability in the matter under investigation. Even if not, the company's voluntary disclosure of the internal report may show such a high degree of cooperation and good faith that prosecutors or regulators may be convinced to decline to prosecute or pursue enforcement actions against the company. Prosecutors or regulators may reach this decision as a result of the exercise of their inherent prosecutorial discretion or in the context of a formal voluntary disclosure program. Even if liability is not completely avoided, punishment or discipline might be mitigated as a result of a voluntary disclosure.

In any case, timing is important. The benefits of voluntary disclosure will be lost if the government is already aware of the offenses and the company is simply telling the government investigators something they already know.

Of course, the possible benefits of disclosure must be weighed against the disadvantages. Of paramount concern is that voluntary disclosure may waive the privileges and rules on which the company relies to protect the confidentiality of its internal investigation and report. Once these privileges and rules have been waived, the company may be forced to disclose the results of its internal investigation to other third parties. Some courts have suggested that voluntary disclosure to the government is a "limited waiver," and that the company could still claim the investigation to be confidential and privileged. Most courts reject this suggestion, however, and hold that voluntary disclosure is a total waiver. Moreover, voluntary disclosure of the internal report may waive the protections for the underlying documents and evidence as well.

Voluntary disclosure of the internal report to the government (or to other third parties) may also lead to defamation and breach of privacy causes of action. Indeed, under certain voluntary disclosure programs, the company is expected to "finger" the responsible parties in any disclosure of wrongdoing or offenses, and that certainly will involve injurious allegations and otherwise private information. If the internal report contains any falsehoods, or if it was unreasonable for the information to be shared with the government, the company may be inviting a defamation or invasion of privacy lawsuit. On the other hand, investigators may be able to defend such lawsuits by showing that the government agency was among those with a common interest in the information, or that it was reasonable to share the information with the government under the circumstances.

If the internal report identifies certain individuals as potentially responsible for the offenses in question, and if the government later prosecutes them unsuccessfully, the suspects may blame the company for inducing the government to prosecute them. That might lead to a civil damages action for malicious prosecution against the company or the investigators. Fortunately, the standard for malicious prosecution is high. First, the suspects will probably have difficulty showing that the internal report actually caused the government to prosecute (a decision that is at the government's discretion), especially if the government already had them in its sights before it received the report. Second, they will find it difficult to argue that there was no reasonable basis for the decision to prosecute if the report is factually accurate, well-reasoned, and reaches reliable conclusions.

Writing Reports

Review Questions

1. What information should be included in an investigation report?
   A. All relevant facts
   B. Only those facts that support the fraud theory
   C. Only those facts that show culpability
   D. Only those facts that are not confidential

2. Green, an internal investigator, has prepared a report for his supervisor. The report summarizes the results of an internal investigation Green conducted. The report contains several facts that are harmful to the reputation of Blue, an employee. Some of the facts turn out to be false. Blue sues the company for libel. In order to successfully defend itself, the company will have to prove the following:
   I. The report was made in good faith.
   II. Green had a legitimate interest in the subject of the report.
   III. Green was working under the direct supervision of an attorney.
   IV. The report was only communicated to individuals with legitimate interests in the subject of the report.

   A. I
   B. I and IV
   C. I and III
   D. I, II, and IV

3. A good written report should only convey:
   A. Subjective facts
   B. Objective facts
   C. Editorial judgments
   D. All of the above

4. According to the text, an attorney's internal report to controlling management may NOT be protected by the attorney-client privilege if the courts find that:
   A. The attorney acted as an investigator, and the report's purpose was therefore to analyze and advise the company about factual circumstances
   B. The report's purpose was to provide business advice
   C. The report's purpose was to provide legal advice
   D. Both A and B

5. A characteristic of a good report is:
   A. Accuracy
   B. Clarity
   C. Impartiality and relevance
   D. Timeliness
   E. All of the above

VIII. DISCHARGING EMPLOYEES

Introduction

When an internal investigation indicates possible wrongdoing by an employee, or when an employee refuses to cooperate in the investigation, an employer may feel compelled to fire that employee. Whether the employee can or should be discharged depends on the facts of the case and the law in the employer's state. In general, most employment relationships have traditionally been considered *at-will*, which means that either party—the employee or the employer—is free to terminate the relationship at any time, for any reason. Just as an employee has the right to leave his job whenever he wants, an employer also has a right to fire an employee for any reason or for no reason at all.

However, modern wrongful termination cases have eroded the old at-will employment doctrine, and statutes and contractual relationships may put additional restrictions on the employer's right to fire or otherwise discipline an employee.

Moreover, public employers are governed by even stricter standards under constitutional and statutory laws. For example, a public employee is entitled to insist on disciplinary procedures that meet constitutional due process standards, and a public employee cannot be terminated for exercising his Fifth Amendment right against self-incrimination. Thus, it is practically a modern necessity to conduct an internal investigation to establish that grounds exist to fire or otherwise discipline an employee. The following sections discuss some of the more common restrictions on an employer's ability to fire an employee.

The Public Policy Exception

Many states now recognize some form of public policy exception to the at-will doctrine. The theory behind this exception is that employers should not be allowed to fire employees if the firing would undermine a fundamental public policy. For instance, suppose an employee becomes aware that his employer is dumping toxic chemicals in a public waterway. The employee reports the conduct to law enforcement authorities, and is subsequently fired by his company. Obviously, there is a fundamental public policy in encouraging citizens to report illegal conduct such as the dumping of hazardous waste. If the employer were allowed to fire the whistleblower in this scenario, the result would be that other employees would be reluctant to report similarly illegal activities in the future. In other words, by firing the whistleblower, the company would be contravening a legitimate public policy. The public policy exception was carved out of the at-will doctrine to prevent this kind of conduct.

In addition to whistleblower cases, the public policy exception has been applied to cases where employees were fired for refusing to perform illegal activities, for refusing to perform unsafe activities, for filing workers' compensation claims, or for fulfilling a legal duty such as serving on a jury. Discharging an employee for refusal to take a polygraph exam is allowable in some states, but is considered wrongful discharge in violation of public policy in others.

EXAMPLE

An employee is fired because he supported a particular political candidate in the last election. His termination violates the general public policy that people have a right to vote for whomever they please. However, if the employee was conducting fund-raising activities on company time, the company would likely have good cause to terminate the employee and such termination would not be in retaliation of the employee's support of a particular candidate.

Before firing an employee, it is best to document in the employee's file the legitimate reasons for the discharge in order to avoid any suggestion of improper or unlawful motive.

Breach of Contract

Employers and employees may enter into contracts that govern the length and terms of employment and the grounds upon which an employee may be fired. Employees who work under a contract are said to be *term employees* because they have agreed under the provisions of the contract to work for a specified term. Term employees do not operate under the at-will doctrine; therefore, the employer does not have the right to terminate their employment at its discretion and without cause. The employer's right to fire an employee will be governed by the provisions of the employment contract. In most cases, this means that the employer can only fire the employee for good cause.

Although there is no exact definition of *good cause*, there are several questions that a company should ask itself before firing a term employee. These questions will help determine if a discharge will be found to be for good cause:

- Did the employee know that the conduct would be subject to discipline?
- Was the rule the employee violated reasonably related to the safe, efficient, or orderly operation of the business?
- Did the company investigate to discover whether the employee violated the rule?
- Did the company conduct a fair and objective investigation?
- Did the company obtain significant evidence of a violation?
- Was the decision nondiscriminatory?
- Was the discipline related to the seriousness of the offense and the prior record of the employee?

Discharging Employees

If the employer violates the contract (i.e., fires an employee without cause when the contract specifies that there must be good cause), then the employee can sue for breach of contract. In a suit for breach of contract based on the firing of a term employee, the company will probably have to demonstrate affirmative answers to some, if not all, of the questions previously stated. This highlights the importance of conducting a thorough and reliable internal investigation, and of documenting the grounds for dismissal. If a company feels that discharge of an employee is likely, it should make sure that the employee's actions and the company's actions are well-documented and placed in the employee's personnel file.

Types of Contracts

Employment contracts can be express or implied. Just because the company has not signed a written, formalized contract with an employee does not mean that there is no employment contract. Collective bargaining agreements, employee handbooks, and even oral promises can establish an employment contract and limit the company's ability to discipline or fire an employee. Before taking any disciplinary action against an employee, make sure you are aware of the true status of the employment relationship.

Express Contracts

The most obvious form of employment contract is the *express contract* (i.e., a contract where the terms are expressed by the parties). Express contracts include contracts where the terms of employment are set forth in writing and the document is signed by each party. However, an agreement does not have to be in writing to be enforceable as a contract. Oral agreements can also be valid contracts. Basically, the key is not whether the agreement was written down, but whether both parties understood that there was an agreement.

Collective bargaining agreements are a common example of an express contract that limits the employer's ability to fire an employee. These agreements frequently specify the misconduct for which an employee may be fired, or at the very least require good cause for termination. They also usually specify procedures that must be followed before the termination. Violation of the terms of a collective bargaining agreement can lead, at the very least, to a labor grievance against the employer. Under some agreements, the employee's collective bargaining rights may supersede his right to sue for breach of contract. Make sure to review the terms of any collective bargaining agreement and consult with an attorney before taking any adverse action against any employee who is protected by a collective bargaining agreement.

Implied Contracts

Even if there is no express employment contract, many states recognize that an implied contract may be created under certain circumstances. An *implied contract* arises out of the conduct of the parties, even though there is no formal written or oral agreement. If a court finds that an implied contract exists, then the employee who is a party to the contract can usually only be fired for good cause. As with express contracts, if an employee is operating under an implied contract, the company will need to document the employee's conduct so that it will be able to demonstrate that it had good cause to fire the employee.

The dangerous thing about implied contracts is that they can be found to exist even when the employer was not aware that there was a contract. This changes the rules midstream; the company thinks its employee is serving at-will, but later finds out that there is actually a contract and that the employee can only be fired for good cause. Of course, by the time the company finds out, the case is already in court and it is too late to do anything about it. Therefore, it is crucial to understand how implied contracts can be formed. Companies need to educate their managers and human resource departments about how implied contracts develop so that they can keep from accidentally dissolving the at-will relationship. If employers want to create an at-will relationship with the employee, an express contract signed as a condition of employment is the best way to provide evidence of this intention.

INFORMAL PROMISES

There are a number of cases in which courts have enforced an implied contract between an employee and his company based on an informal promise of continued employment by someone in authority. For example, suppose an employee is worried about his job security and asks his manager about his standing with the company. The manager tells him: "Don't worry, we never fire anybody unless they give us a good reason," or "As long as you do your job, you're not going to get fired." Some courts have held that statements like these amount to a promise that the employee will not be fired without good cause, thus creating an implied (or informal) contract.

To successfully sue under a theory of implied contract, the employee will have to show that he reasonably relied on this promise. Therefore, the promise will have to have been made by someone in authority, such as a manager or supervisor. (If a coworker or subordinate promises you that you will not be fired, it is not reasonable to rely on this since that person has no authority over your employment status). These cases also sometimes arise in the hiring process, where the person interviewing a candidate assures that candidate that he will have a job with the company as long as he performs well. It is a good idea to instruct your human resources personnel and all other individuals who conduct interviews not to make statements that could be construed as promises of "good cause" status for an employee.

EMPLOYEE HANDBOOKS AND MANUALS

Implied contracts can also be formed by the language in an employee handbook, particularly if the handbook describes the procedures that will be followed when discharging employees. For instance, many handbooks specify what kind of conduct is subject to discipline, as well as the range of discipline that is permitted for a particular kind of offense. In many cases, employee handbooks also use some form of good cause language in describing why employees might be disciplined or fired. They might also dictate the procedural steps to be followed before specific kinds of disciplinary action are taken (e.g., written notice to the employee of the proposed action or the employee's opportunity to refute the alleged misconduct). If not worded properly, these handbooks might amount to an implied contract in which the employer promises not to fire its employees except for good cause.

In addition, if the company does not adhere to the disciplinary procedures set forth in its employee manual, it might open itself up to claims of negligent discharge, wrongful termination, or unlawful discrimination. Accordingly, investigators should take care to know—and to comply with—handbook provisions and other relevant company policy when the time comes to decide what to do about an employee whose dishonest conduct has been established.

A company can avoid inadvertently creating an implied contract by including a disclaimer in any policy manuals or statements. The purpose of such a disclaimer is to prevent any employee from contending that he was misled into believing or relying on the policy statements of employee manuals as a term or condition of his employment. An example of such a disclaimer reads as follows:

> *Nothing in this manual, or in any of the policies or procedures set forth in this manual, is intended to create, nor should it be understood to create, a contract of any kind between the company and any employee. No promises of continued employment—express or implied—have been made or are intended by anything set forth in this manual. All employees of the company are at-will employees. The employment relationship between the company and any employee may be terminated by either the employee or the company at any time, with or without notice, and whether or not cause exists for the termination, at the absolute discretion of either the company or the employee.*

As was stated above, a company also faces potential liability for failing to follow the disciplinary procedures that are set forth in its employee handbook. It is a good idea for employers to include some language in the handbook that allows them to be flexible in how they discipline employees and to modify the disciplinary procedures if necessary. The following is an example of this type of clause:

> *The procedures and policies contained in this handbook are subject to change from time to time at the sole discretion of the company and do not confer any obligation on the company or right to employment. The company explicitly reserves the right to modify any of the provisions of these policies at any time and without notice. Furthermore, the company reserves the right to make use of any one of the disciplinary steps described in this handbook, in combination or alone, or immediately discharge an employee, at its discretion, depending upon the particular circumstances.*

Discharging Employees

These disclaimers should be clearly and noticeably displayed in the handbook to make sure that employees have read it. It may be advisable to put the disclaimers in bold type or all caps. This will insulate the employer against a claim by an employee that they thought the handbook amounted to a contract. To further strengthen the objective of the disclaimers, a company can require each employee to review and to sign them.

Statutory Violations

In addition to suits for wrongful termination and breach of contract, an employee who has been discharged may also claim that the firing and the process leading up to it violated various statutory rights and interests. Federal statutes protect those who have been terminated based on, among other things, their race, national origin, religion, sex, disability, or age. Even if the employer's reason for firing the employee is unbiased, the employer may be liable under these statutes if it relied on the report of an investigator who had discriminatory motives. There is also statutory whistleblower protection in many circumstances for employees who have been fired for reporting illegal conduct by their companies.

In addition, employees may find statutory protection based on the investigative methods used by the company, the procedures that led to termination, and the employer's investigation process. Concerning investigative methods, the employer may be liable under the Fair Credit Reporting Act if it obtained any credit, financial, or character information about the employee without obtaining prior written authorization from the employee. In addition, if the employer is a public agency or state actor, the employee could complain in a civil rights suit that the procedures leading to his firing violated his due process rights. Furthermore, in a matter within the jurisdiction of the National Labor Relations Board, he could complain that the investigation process violated the terms of a collective bargaining agreement or otherwise was an unfair labor practice.

Some statutory complaints can succeed even if there were legitimate grounds for terminating the employee. For instance, if due process was required but not observed, or if procedures under a collective bargaining agreement were not honored, then the employee's rights were violated regardless of whether the company had good cause to fire him. If the investigation that led up to the firing violated statutory employee rights, such as the Fair Credit Reporting Act, the employee still could recover damages against the employer. Notwithstanding other good and sufficient reasons for firing the employee, the company could be liable for illegal discrimination if a jury found that the discriminatory purpose was the primary motive for firing the employee.

EXAMPLE

A company's internal investigation determined that James, an African-American employee, was one of several employees who were pilfering company property. The other employees, all of whom were white, were disciplined, but not fired. James was fired even though his thefts were no more serious or damaging to the company. James alleged that he was fired primarily for racial reasons, notwithstanding the evidence that he had stolen from the company. Noting that no white employees were fired and that there was no substantial difference between James's misconduct and that of the white employees, the jury agreed and found the company guilty of illegal discrimination.

Thus, in addition to there being good grounds for firing an employee, it is important that all proper procedures be followed in investigating and imposing the discipline, and that there does not appear to be any ulterior motives for discharging him.

Common Law Causes of Action

Either because of complaints about how the internal investigation was handled, or because of disclosures to other employees or individuals outside of the company after having been fired, an employee may seek damages from the company and its investigators for violating one or more of his common law legal rights. These include:

- Defamation
- Intentional infliction of emotional distress
- Public disclosure of private facts
- False imprisonment

See Chapter 6 for a more detailed discussion of these causes of action.

Defamation

Once again, *defamation* refers to the publication of false statements that cause harm to another party. Because defamatory statements are false, truth is an absolute defense to a defamation action; therefore, if the investigation has a strong factual basis for termination, the company should be able to weather allegations that the employee was libeled. The common interest privilege also gives the company some cover from potential defamation claims, although investigators must be careful to limit information about the investigation to those who have a legitimate need to know it.

Intentional Infliction of Emotional Distress

To recover for *intentional infliction of emotional distress*, the plaintiff must prove that the defendant engaged in extreme and outrageous conduct that caused severe emotional distress. Similar to defamation claims, intentional infliction of emotional distress claims will likely fail if the investigation was properly conducted and the termination was factually well-founded.

Public Disclosure of Private Facts

Even if the facts supporting the employee's discharge are true, a company may still be liable for *public disclosure of private facts* if the employer makes public statements about an employee's private life, the information is not of public concern, and the disclosure of the information would be highly offensive to a reasonable person. Under this tort, a company might be liable for unreasonably disclosing private information about the employee to other employees or to members of the public. Truth is not a defense to public disclosure of private facts. The key is the reasonableness of the employer's conduct. For instance, it would probably be highly offensive to tell the friends and neighbors of a discharged employee that the employee was fired for theft.

Certainly not all disclosures to other employees or to outside individuals are unreasonable *per se*. An employer may have a legitimate need to inform other employees of the reason why a wrongdoer was terminated; in fact, there is some authority that the company has a qualified privilege to share with all of its employees the results of an internal investigation that was extensive and disruptive throughout the company. However, if the disclosure is overly broad (i.e., to people who do not really need to know) or if it is done in a particularly embarrassing and unreasonable manner (e.g., ambushing the employee by accusing him of theft and terminating him in front of a large gathering of his coworkers), the company could face liability.

> EXAMPLE
>
> *Following an internal investigation, the company told Hansen's supervisors that Hansen was to be fired because the investigation established that he was embezzling company funds to feed a gambling addiction. There is no necessarily right answer, but common sense would suggest that it is reasonable for employees in a managerial or supervisory position over Hansen to be told that he was being fired for embezzling from the company. This information is reasonably related to the exercise of their authority over Hansen, as well as the integrity of the work being performed under their supervision. However, it is less clear that these employees need to know about Hansen's gambling addiction in order to carry out their responsibilities.*
>
> *We can make the same observations about other prospective employers who call for a reference on Hansen when he applies for a position at another company. The prospective employer has a legitimate interest in knowing why Hansen was fired from this company (although many employers, out of concern for just this kind of liability, decline to share that information with later, prospective employers). Arguably, the prospective employer also has a legitimate interest in Hansen's gambling addiction, since it may lead to further misconduct at the new company, just as it did at his former one. Still, the addiction poses a closer question, involving, as it does, value judgments and an implied assessment of the seriousness and impact of Hansen's addiction (even the word addiction is value-laden). The safest course is for the employer to disclose only strictly factual matters that are not open to question.*

False Imprisonment

False imprisonment is the restraint by one person of the physical liberty of another without consent or legal justification. A company can avoid liability for false imprisonment by taking care to avoid an improper detention of the employee during any interview or interrogation.

Whistleblower Statutes

The company must take care that the employee's discharge is not perceived as retaliation for the employee's proper reporting of information to a government agency. An employee under internal investigation may well have given information to the government in an effort to obtain leniency or even immunity from prosecution. If that employee is then fired, he may claim it was for providing information that the government could use against the company.

Other Considerations

If the company is facing a parallel government investigation or potential civil or criminal liability arising out of the employee's conduct, discharging or otherwise disciplining the employee could have an adverse impact on the company's case. The act of disciplining the employee can be construed as evidence that the company was aware of the employee's offense. Where the discipline was severe—and especially if the employee was fired—it may be difficult for the company to attempt to minimize the severity of the employee's conduct or to challenge the government's contentions or evidence about the offense.

Conversely, disciplining an offending employee can stave off further regulatory or civil actions and enhance the company's public image. This may be particularly crucial for publicly traded companies and companies in highly regulated industries where the offense—and the company's response to the offense—are the subjects of mandatory reporting or disclosure requirements.

Prosecuting Employees

Of course, no matter what the results of a company's internal investigation, the company does not prosecute—or decide to prosecute—an employee. *Prosecution*—in the sense of charging and trying a person on criminal charges—is exclusively the right of the state. *Prosecutors* (i.e., the attorneys who represent the state or federal government) have the discretion to decide whether to file criminal charges against a person and with what crimes he will be charged. They typically do so based on their own investigations and standards.

Discharging Employees

However, complaints by victims and other citizens often initiate government criminal investigations and are factors in a government attorney's exercise of their prosecutorial discretion. Even where a government investigation is already ongoing, a company's internal investigation can influence a prosecutor by pointing at a particular employee or employees, or by providing information that tips the investigation in a particular direction.

Thus, the question for the employer is why should it use its internal investigation to try to cause or aid a government criminal investigation and prosecution, and what adverse consequences might result?

> **Video**
>
> In the video titled "Chapter VIII: Working with Prosecutors," fraud investigation expert Meric Bloch, J.D., CFE, explains how "gift-wrapping" your case increases the odds of a successful prosecution. (Go to www.acfe.com/internalinvestigations to view the video.)

Why Prosecute an Offending Employee?

In general, a company might want to prosecute an offending employee for a number of reasons. Prosecution of an offending employee punishes the employee and, hopefully, deters other employees from engaging in similar offenses.

Additionally, as discussed earlier, if the company itself is facing investigation and potential liability, voluntary disclosure and cooperation may put the company in a better light with the prosecutor.

Finally, prosecution of an employee may also help a company defray the losses suffered as a result of fraud. Following the conviction of an employee, the company may be able to recover some of its losses from the convicted employee through remedies that are available under federal and some state criminal laws. Similarly, prosecution may aid the complainant company in pursuing civil remedies against the employee.

The first two points need no further discussion here. The remainder of this section discusses recovering losses suffered as a result of fraud.

Recovery of Losses in Criminal Cases
Restitution as a Condition of Probation

As a condition of probation, a court can order a convicted employee to make restitution to the company or otherwise cooperate in the company's efforts to recover money or property. Restitution as a condition of probation can be ordered against both individual and corporate defendants, and may include a provision for installment payments over time to the victim. Usually, the court will take the defendant's ability to pay into account when ordering restitution so that the defendant has a reasonable chance of meeting the restitution condition.

A court-designated probation officer usually makes sentencing recommendations, including any special probationary terms to the court. If a prosecutor wishes to have a restitution order included in the perpetrator's sentence, he should present a request for a term of restitution to the probation officer as early in the pre-sentence investigation and evaluation process as possible. A request from the prosecuting attorney to include restitution as a term of probation also carries weight with the probation officer and with the court. For that reason, cooperation with the prosecutor and police during the criminal prosecution can pay dividends in their willingness to persuade the court to order restitution after a conviction.

Statutory Criminal Restitution

In addition to restitution as a condition of probation, federal law[16] and an increasing number of state statutes direct or permit judges to order convicted defendants to make restitution to victims of their crimes as part of their punishment after conviction. Statutory criminal restitution orders are in addition to any other penalties provided by law for the defendant's crimes and can apply whether or not the defendant receives probation.

Typically, statutory criminal restitution orders direct the return of the victim's property or its monetary equivalent if the property cannot be returned. Some orders also direct the return of the fruits of the crime or the victim's actual out-of-pocket expense caused by the crime. A criminal restitution order typically does not apply to a loss for which the victim has received, or will receive, compensation from another source (e.g., insurance).

Some statutes set a limit to the amount of restitution that can be ordered against a defendant who did not receive probation, although the limit usually does not apply to an order to return the victim's property or its equivalent value. The federal statute and other state statutes mandate full restitution, although the court may take the defendant's ability to pay into consideration in creating a payment schedule.

Unlike restitution that is ordered as a condition of probation, a criminal restitution order can be enforced against the defendant even after his discharge from probation or his release from prison. The federal statute (and some state statutes) permits a criminal restitution order to be enforced as a civil judgment by the victim against the defendant. Restitution orders also typically survive the death of the

---

[16] 18 U.S.C. §§ 3663A and 3664.

victim and may be enforced by his heirs or representatives. Criminal restitution orders are cumulative remedies and do not preclude the victim from pursuing a separate civil lawsuit against the defendant for the same conduct for which he was criminally convicted. However, any property or money received by the victim under a criminal restitution order will be credited against a civil judgment or restitution order.

Voluntary Restitution

Apart from mandatory restitution orders, the criminally convicted employee has an incentive to voluntarily make restitution. Voluntary restitution is a mitigating factor under federal and most state mandatory sentencing guidelines, meaning it can reduce the defendant's sentence if he is convicted of the fraud. Thus, the knowledge that a company will refer an employee offense for prosecution may aid in negotiations with the employee for restitution or recovery of misappropriated money or property. (A word of caution is in order, however. It is an ethical violation for an attorney to threaten criminal prosecution in order to gain an advantage in a civil dispute. Although there is no controlling authority on point, this conduct may also violate the Association of Certified Fraud Examiners' Code of Professional Ethics, as well as the codes of conduct for other professional organizations. If you intend to pursue prosecution, you can inform the employee of that fact and of his options to help himself if he is prosecuted. But do not conditionally link the decision to prosecute with the employee's cooperation.)

Aiding the Company's Civil Remedies and Litigation

If a company is planning to pursue civil remedies against an offending employee, referring the matter to a prosecutor has potential benefits to their investigation and to any planned civil litigation. The investigative powers of the government—both legally and in terms of resources—exceed those of most private companies. A state or federal prosecutor can use a grand jury to compel testimony and the production of records and documents from witnesses, and law enforcement officials can obtain court orders, including search warrants, to permit them to search for and obtain evidence from otherwise protected places, individuals, and institutions. Internal investigators have no such access to compulsory process unless and until a lawsuit is filed, and even then they cannot obtain search warrants.

Because of constitutional and statutory mandates, criminal cases are typically resolved more quickly than civil suits. It is also easier to recover losses through a criminal restitution order than to prove a damages case in civil litigation. The sole question for a criminal restitution order (which is entered after the defendant has been convicted) is the amount of the victim's losses that were caused by the defendant. A criminal defendant cannot bring additional parties into the action or assert cross-claims or counterclaims as he could in a civil suit. Having already been convicted, he can raise no substantive defenses against the restitution order. As noted above, in most jurisdictions, the criminal restitution order is enforceable as a civil judgment; therefore, the victim obtains a substantial equivalent of a civil judgment without the time and expense of a civil lawsuit.

Conversely, by deferring a civil claim for criminal prosecution, the victim company forfeits a great deal of control over the investigation and litigation. In a criminal case, the company has no real control over how to allocate investigative resources, whether and what to charge the employee with, the terms and conditions of any negotiated resolution (i.e., plea bargain), or the employee's sentence. These decisions are made by the prosecutor, the government investigators, and the judge.

Malicious Prosecution

If a company files a criminal complaint against an offending employee or otherwise instigates a criminal prosecution, the employee may retaliate with a malicious prosecution lawsuit. A malicious prosecution claim seeks recovery of damages for having to endure and defend a groundless lawsuit that the defendant filed, or caused to be filed, against the employee. Keep in mind that there is a strong social advantage in encouraging citizens to report criminal conduct and in having citizens resolve disputes through litigation. As a result, the law requires a claimant to show that a lawsuit was truly baseless and grounded in malice before he can win on a malicious prosecution claim. A company that makes a good faith report of illegal conduct by an employee is not liable for malicious prosecution, even if its report turns out to be wrong.

The elements of the cause of action for malicious prosecution may vary somewhat among jurisdictions, but in general, the employee must establish the following elements:
- The company instigated a criminal proceeding against the employee.
- The criminal proceeding was terminated in favor of the employee (i.e., the charges were dismissed or the employee was acquitted).
- There was no probable cause for the action, meaning that the company knew the action was groundless or had no reasonable basis to believe that the employee was guilty.
- The company acted with malice, meaning that the company used the prosecution for the purpose of gaining a private advantage (to collect a debt, to embarrass the employee, etc.) rather than the purpose of bringing a guilty person to justice.

As the second element states, an employee must show that the initial lawsuit was terminated in his favor if he is to succeed on a malicious prosecution claim. So if the employee is convicted, he cannot sustain a malicious prosecution suit against the complainant company. Even if he is not convicted, these lawsuits can usually be defended successfully, especially if the underlying investigation was careful and thorough. If the company can show that, based on the evidence it had gathered, there was a reasonable basis for believing the employee had committed the crime, this will effectively counter a malicious prosecution claim.

Discharging Employees

Review Questions

1. Which of the following statements is true?
   A. Term employees operate under the at-will doctrine.
   B. Employment contracts can be formed by the language in an employee handbook.
   C. There is no such thing as an implied contract.
   D. All of the above are true.

2. Which of the following can limit a company's ability to discipline or fire an employee?
   I. The terms of a collective bargaining agreement
   II. An informal promise to the employee of continued employment as long as he "does a good job"
   III. A description of the company's disciplinary procedures contained in an employee handbook

   A. I
   B. I and II
   C. I and III
   D. I, II, and III

3. An employment contract in which the terms of employment are set forth in writing and the document is signed by each party is known as an:
   A. Express contract
   B. Implied contract
   C. Informal contract
   D. None of the above

4. In addition to suits for wrongful termination and breach of contract, an employee who has been discharged may also claim that the termination violated various statutory rights and interests. Which of the following could be considered a statutory violation?
   A. The investigative methods used by the company
   B. Procedures used that led to termination
   C. The investigation process violated the terms of the collective bargaining agreement
   D. All of the above

5. In general, an employee's claim of malicious prosecution must establish that the company instigated a criminal proceeding against the employee, along with which of the following elements?
   A. The criminal proceeding was terminated in favor of the employee
   B. There was no probable cause for the action
   C. The company acted with malice
   D. All of the above

6. According to the text, which of the following is NOT true of statutory criminal restitutions?
   A. These orders only apply while the defendant is on probation.
   B. These orders are in addition to any other penalties provided by law for the defendant's crimes.
   C. These orders direct the return of the victim's property or its monetary equivalent if the property cannot be returned.
   D. None of the above are false statements.

IX. CONCLUSION

Conducting internal investigations is tedious, time-consuming, and filled with traps for the unwary. However, the alternative is simply to sit back and become the victim of fraud, or worse, the perpetrator of the fraud in the eyes of the government.

In the present legislative, administrative, and judicial climates, companies cannot simply sit back and claim ignorance. Accountants, auditors, officers, directors, attorneys, and managers are all being required to take a proactive role in assuring that fraud and other wrongdoing is prevented. If it occurs, then these individuals are required to find out what happened and to take steps to correct the problem both presently and in the future.

The purpose of this workbook has been to help you do a better job in conducting such investigations, and to make you aware of the potential legal liability that exists for those who are careless or unprepared. Hopefully this course has prompted you to take a hard look at the procedures you currently use and ask yourself, "What procedures are we currently following and how can they be improved?"

We hope you have enjoyed this course and have found it useful. We encourage you to now complete the practical exercises following this chapter. These exercises will test the theoretical concepts you have learned in real-life situations. Suggested answers are provided at the end of the workbook. Please take the time to write out your answers before you compare your answers with our suggestions.

X. PRACTICAL PROBLEMS

Devoslich, Inc. is a privately owned, mid-size company based on the eastern seaboard. It produces hypersensitive nautical navigational systems that are in use in most of the world's major shipping fleets. The company provides some systems to the U.S. Coast Guard, although the vast majority of its customers are private fleets.

Barrett Frasier is the chief executive officer for Devoslich. He has recently received reports that suggest the possibility of internal fraud. One of the company's auditors has detected a pattern of disbursements suggesting that someone is falsely billing the company. For the last fifteen months, on the tenth day of each month, the company shows a disbursement of between $9,500 and $9,999 to a company called "Quantic Components." Although invoices from Quantic are located in the accounts payable files, they provide no description as to the nature of the purchases. Furthermore, the invoices are all consecutively numbered, even though they were paid over the course of several months. Finally, it is noted that all of the invoices are in an amount just below $10,000. If an invoice is above $10,000, then a second authorization is required. If an invoice is below $10,000, it can be approved by any of the company's three procurement managers alone. Based on all these facts, Frasier believes the payments are fraudulent.

Frasier has contacted Susan Frost and Jack Crouch, the company's director and assistant director of security, respectively. Frasier has decided that the company should initiate an internal investigation of the matter.

Practical Problems

Practical Problem 1

The most likely suspect in the embezzlement scheme is Russ Taylor, one of the company's three procurement managers. Taylor has worked for Devoslich for three years. He signed off on nine of the fifteen invoices in question. The other six appear to have been approved by Frasier himself; although Frasier is sure he never approved these payments. He has never heard of Quantic Components.

In addition, Frasier has noticed that Taylor has been acting rather erratically as of late. He has been very irritable for several months and appears to be under a great deal of stress. Frasier approached Taylor once to see if he was all right, but Taylor assured him everything was fine. Nevertheless, Frasier remained convinced that Taylor was bothered about something.

Questions:

1. Based on the facts that have been presented, do you believe there is sufficient predication to begin an internal investigation?

2. Briefly explain the Fraud Examination Methodology and propose a hypothesis upon which you would begin the investigation.

Practical Problem 2

Frost and Crouch are of the opinion that Taylor is the most likely suspect. Their hypothesis is that Taylor is submitting false invoices using a shell company called "Quantic Components" to funnel cash out of the company.

Frost proposes that they check the business filings for Quantic Components. She hopes that this will help them identify the person or persons who own Quantic, and thereby help them determine the source of the billings and whether they are legitimate. Crouch suggests that they also check Taylor's criminal history. Devoslich does not generally perform a criminal history background check at the time of hire. Crouch wants to see if Taylor has a history of this kind of behavior. This might support a later action to terminate Taylor if he is found to have committed the fraud. Frost is not sure about this idea. Before proceeding, she wants to make sure they have a legal right to check Taylor's criminal records.

Questions:

1. Where can Frost and Crouch find Quantic's business filings, and what information will be contained in those filings?

2. Under what circumstances can the company perform a criminal background check on Taylor?

Practical Problems

Practical Problem 3

Crouch also proposes that they conduct a search of Taylor's office. It is located in the main building of the company's headquarters, on a publicly accessible floor. There is one door to that office and the door has a lock on it. During working hours, the door is rarely, if ever, locked. Taylor frequently leaves the office during work hours without locking the door. When he leaves at night, however, he always locks his office. Frost, as head of security, has a key to all offices in the building (a fact of which Taylor is aware). Security guards at the site also have a master key that permits entry into all areas of the facility. They accompany cleaning personnel into the offices after hours for general cleaning, trash pickup, etc.

Taylor has a desk, one file cabinet, some furniture, and a trash can in his office. The file cabinet is intended for Taylor's use, although other members of the purchasing department frequently retrieve files from it. Taylor is aware that these employees enter his office from time to time and retrieve files from the file cabinet. He has never expressed any complaint about this arrangement. The file cabinet has no locks on it.

Taylor's desk contains five drawers. One of the drawers contains a lock, the key to which is only held by two people, Taylor and Frasier. The desk was provided to Taylor by the company; in fact, it was used by his predecessor before Taylor was hired. At the time he took over the office, Frasier presented Taylor with the key to the "security drawer." Frasier informed Taylor that he also had a key to the drawer, in case Taylor ever lost his. Taylor is the only person who ever uses his desk or accesses any of the drawers. He generally keeps the security drawer locked.

From time to time, Taylor leaves his briefcase at the office. He purchased the briefcase himself and uses it to transport work papers to and from the office. The briefcase has a combination lock on it. Only Taylor knows the combination.

The company has no search policy.

Crouch says that a search should be conducted immediately after work (they want to avoid arousing suspicion in any possible culprits). Frost, on the other hand, believes they should obtain a warrant.

Questions:

1. If Crouch decides to conduct a search, what is the standard with which the company must comply to make sure the search is legal? Does the company need a warrant?

2. Are Frost and Crouch entitled to search the following areas: the office, the desk, the file cabinet, the trash can, and the briefcase? Explain your answers.

Practical Problems

Practical Problem 4

Crouch also suggests that the company tape-record and monitor all of Taylor's calls. Frost does not believe the company is legally entitled to take this action. The company has no policy regarding the monitoring of phone calls.

Question:

1. Who do you agree with and why?

Practical Problem 5

After reviewing the suspect invoices and interviewing other employees of the company, Frost and Crouch are convinced that Taylor is the culprit. They agree they are ready to interview him and hopefully obtain a confession. They schedule an interview time with Taylor, to be conducted in his office. At the scheduled time, Frost, Crouch, and McCant (the general counsel) arrive in Taylor's office. As they enter, Frost locks the door to ensure there will be no interruptions. Taylor's office has a large window that opens onto the hallway so that most of his office is visible to passersby. The shade on this window is left open. Frost, Crouch, and McCant take seats across the desk from Taylor. They are positioned between Taylor and the door.

Up until now, Taylor has not known what the purpose of the interview is to be. Frost had simply told him that he needed to talk to him about some "routine security issues in his department." However, after a few questions, Taylor becomes aware that he is under suspicion of embezzlement. At this point, he stops and says that he wants to speak to an attorney. Frost says, "Don't worry, that's why we've got the general counsel here." Questioning then resumes. At no time do any of the three questioners read Taylor his *Miranda* rights. At one point, Taylor says he needs to leave to get a drink of water. Frost says, "Just sit tight. We'll get you some water." Crouch promptly retrieves a glass of water for Taylor. At no time during the interview does Taylor leave the room.

Questions:

1. Based on these facts, do you think the company could be held liable for false imprisonment? Why or why not?

Practical Problems

2. Did Taylor have a right to have an attorney present at the interview? Did Frost respond properly to Taylor's request? Explain your answers.

3. Should the interviewers have given Taylor a *Miranda* warning? Why or why not?

4. Aside from the legal considerations discussed above, what other problems do you see with the way this interview was conducted?

Practical Problem 6

About halfway through the interview, Frost accuses Taylor of the crime, saying "We've been conducting an investigation of these invoices, and we know you're the one who's been stealing from the company. This amounts to fraud."

Taylor does not deny the crime outright. Instead, he makes a weak, qualified denial by claiming that he wasn't in the office on the day one of the invoices was approved for payment. Frost then repeats the accusation. In order to make it psychologically easier to admit to the crime, Frost adds the following: "Look, we understand that you didn't want to hurt anybody. You've been a good employee and you probably wouldn't have done this if you didn't really need the money. If the company had treated you better, you probably wouldn't have had to do this at all."

Eventually, Taylor confesses to the crime. He says he had amassed substantial gambling debts and he just needed the money on a short-term basis in order to pay off what he owed. He claims he intended to pay all the money back.

Questions:

1. Discuss Frost's treatment of Taylor. Specifically:

   A. Was it appropriate to accuse Taylor of the crime and, if so, was the accusation made in an appropriate manner?

   B. Was it appropriate for Frost to rationalize Taylor's behavior and, if so, was this done in an appropriate manner?

Practical Problems

2. Now that a benchmark admission has been reached, what information should Frost and Crouch seek to obtain from Taylor in his oral confession?

Practical Problem 7

At the conclusion of the interview, Crouch prepares a written confession for Taylor to sign. He includes the information that Taylor gave in his verbal confession. He also includes an excuse clause that reads: "I needed the money to pay off some pressing debts, which is why I borrowed these funds. I did not mean to commit a crime. I thought that as long as I paid the money back with interest, this was not illegal, and the company would not be hurt." Taylor reads the statement and signs it in the presence of all three interviewers.

Questions:

1. Was it appropriate for Crouch to prepare the statement, or should Taylor have written it?

2. Do you think the excuse clause in this signed statement is appropriate? Why or why not?

3. List nine key pieces of information that must be included in the signed statement.

Practical Problems

Practical Problem 8

Frost and Crouch prepare a report summarizing the findings from their investigation. They give no opinion as to the guilt or innocence of Taylor in the report, but they do summarize their reasonable conclusions about what happened based on the evidence and his confession. This report is presented to Frasier. Frasier immediately dismisses Taylor for theft and refers the case to the district attorney. Devoslich is a non-union company whose employees are regarded as at-will. Taylor never signed an employment contract and no promises of future employment were ever made to him.

He was, however, given an employee handbook at the time he was hired (as are all employees of Devoslich). The handbook sets forth specific procedures to be followed when allegations of misconduct are made against employees. It defines certain acts as being punishable by termination or suspension. *Fraud* and *theft* are both clearly defined and listed among the actions that shall justify termination, and Taylor's conduct fits under both definitions. The handbook also states that employees will be given a written warning concerning the allegations against them. It goes on to say that prior to any suspension or termination, employees will be entitled to a hearing before a three-member panel composed of the Devoslich managers. The handbook also states that management shall have the right to place an employee on administrative leave pending this hearing.

Question:

1. Based on this information, do you see any problems with Taylor's dismissal? Explain your answer.

XI: APPENDIX: VIDEO TRANSCRIPTS

Chapter I: Know Your Objective

INTERVIEWER: How important is it to know your goal?

MERIC BLOCH: Critical because you need to know your goal, also known as your investigation objective. Once you have that you can come up with the right strategy. How to develop the facts and the documents and the witnesses and also how you define the scope of the investigation. Without the objective in mind you can't do any of that. You'll just be wondering aimlessly and hope that the facts fall into your lap, which is not a way to investigate.

It's absolutely critical. To know the audience for your investigation is a key preparation step. The audience could be law enforcement. The audience could be business managers. it could be your company lawyers. But unless you know your audience, you will not know the ultimate use of the investigation, which affects your preparation and again affects your objective.

Chapter I: Fraud Awareness

INTERVIEWER: What steps can management and the board take to raise awareness of fraud within a company?

MERIC BLOCH: Well, one way they can do it is with a mandatory fraud reporting scheme, where that if people suspect there's fraud or abuse, they must report it upwards. That allows for it to be investigated. That sets a tone in the company that if you see something you must say something. Again, it's all about risk management. It's all about identifying the risks, investigating them, and making sure the holes get plugged. But it's more than just simply the platitudes about, " we really care and this shouldn't happen." It's more about saying, "we acknowledge that this happens, we certainly don't want it to happen too often."

INTERVIEWER: What role does monitoring policy play?

MERIC BLOCK: It keeps everybody honest. And what i mean by that is, if you work in a large company as I do, you may have some parts of the company with extensive reporting and some places with minimal reporting. And by monitoring it, not only are you looking at the volume of cases, you're looking at the dispersion of cases, you're also looking for trends in the same issue coming up, which may identify systemic weaknesses in the business. One of the problems in most big companies is that it's business processes and internal controls are designed by honest well intentioned people and they don't think like crooks. So, the unfortunate reality is that when you have a fraud case, it is shining a light on where you're vulnerable that most times, the people who designed your processes, never even imagined would be vulnerable.

Chapter I: Ethics Policy

MERIC BLOCH: I believe an ethics policy has two goals. One, to state the rules of the company, so they can be enforced. And the second is to reduce the taboo of making reports. I think the idea that an ethics policy makes people ethical is silly. I think otherwise it's just posturing. But I think what happens is it does serve the value, as I mentioned, of setting the rules down and really making people feel more comfortable reporting their concerns.

The purpose of the ethics policy is to state the company's rules, conflict of interests, respecting each other, things like that. And also in the ethics policy, to make people feel comfortable stepping forward and overcoming those taboos against tattling and reporting other people. Those are the two purposes I believe are an ethics policy. And I do agree with those who say it will not make an unethical person ethical or someone who wishes to be unethical is gonna' say, "well, the policy out there says I can't do it, so I don't."

Critical, is the company's expectation that you will report actual or suspected fraud or misconduct, as well as the acceptable avenues for reporting. For example, does the company want to direct all those reports to the hot-line. Do they want people to tell their manager or HR or legal and leave the hot-line as a last resort. You want to tell people essentially what your preferences are. However, if you do things other than the hot-line, you have to have mechanisms in your company that those reports people make to HR are gonna' find their way to compliance and somehow get recorded. So you want to state your expectation that reports will be made and you want to express your preference as to how best to make them.

Chapter I: Code of Ethics

JUSTIN PAPERNY: My name is Justin Paperny I was released from Taft Federal Prison Camp on August 17, 2009 after serving an 18 month prison term for securities fraud.
First off you can't say one thing and do another. Bear Stearns, Merrill Lynch, UBS we all had corporate codes of conduct. Merrill Lynch, we had nice stylish rooms decorated around the office. UBS, we had a nice code. You walk into the human resources room. Bear Stearns, we had a big binder. You would dust it off a little bit and open it up and you would see the big platitudes posted in big black font. The problems with these corporate codes was the culture always trumped the code. So I would ask management, I would ask my branch manager from UBS who got up and espoused the importance of

honesty and integrity at the sales meetings, and I would ask him why he behaved differently while creating a disclosure letter to protect the commissions from the hedge fund. So with management if you say one thing and you do another, do you hold all employees accountable. UBS let some brokers go who had ethical violations but they were low producing brokers. The brokers like a me, who were producing, we were treated differently because we produced. That's all it comes down to. Do you say one thing and do another? Are you prepared to deal with a moral dilemma? It's uncomfortable to talk about the limits. You fumble around for a little bit and you're not sure how to handle it. There is very little training and then when dilemma presents itself you expect an employee to handle it properly and there has been no training along the way. There's been no discussions or preparations to actually manage a dilemma. Most ways that dilemmas are dealt with, you just ignore it and you turn the other way, which in many ways is encouraging the behavior. So in short, if you're going to post the code use the code. It's only a start because when you have a code and don't use it employees know that it's a joke and they can get away with anything.

The value system of an auditor or compliance manager, in my sense their value should be different than the employees. My goal was to produce and generate commissions and bring assets under management. The compliance manager's job was to monitor these activities, protect and ensure the broker is doing it ethically and honestly and holding us accountable. That's the biggest key.

See salesmen are smart. Executives are smart. We will find a way, if given the opportunity to get around it. The key is are you thinking outside the box. I know that's an old cliché, but it's true. Are you investigating enough? How friendly are you with some of these people you may work with? Some of the stories I've shared in my newest book is when the CFO, who was once an auditor and then he's the CFO of a company and they are friends and by the way we're going to look at this and we're not going to look at that. There's got to be some separation and it takes real courage to dig deeper and dig deeper. That's the best advice that I would give. If you see something you have to address it.

We're smart and you need to become creative and think of all the ways that we could be committing crimes. Understanding how easily it can happen and looking for patterns. Sometimes the red flags are right in front of you. Those activity reports for the compliance manager with my client, millions in losses, millions in money coming in. I don't understand a ton about forensic accounting. I have a psychology degree from USC and I was a stockbroker turned convicted felon. I don't get all that. But I do know that if we had some better checks and balances, simply by looking at those monthly activity reports the fraud would have been stopped before I ever sent an email. Before I told him you have an elderly gentleman who can't get their $3 million in assets. I can't blame them but it's part of the problem.

Chapter I: Audit Committee

INTERVIEWER: What do you see as the role of the audit committee in fraud risk management fraud prevention?

MERIC BLOCH: Absolutely key. Both reactive and proactive. It's your audit committee that can mandate that the internal auditors do fraud risk assessments. And reactive, they're the ones who can track investigation findings and where investigations are being done, what's being investigated, what are the outcomes of the investigations, absolutely key.

Chapter I: Planning the Investigation

MERIC BLOCH: There are two types of documentation. One would be the material facts of the case and the things that you would obviously document would be investigation, excuse me, interview notes, interview summaries. The second type of thing that you would document in an investigation are your own notes, your own analyses. Those two things become critically important. The first part is your proof and the second part is your analysis, which together, when put into the report, make all the difference.

Most common challenges in case organization are identifying a full range of goals in the fraud examination. For example, is the goal to do the examination so that when you're done you're going to law enforcement. Is it to identify problems in the business. Is it to identify misconduct. Knowing that makes all the difference and can really help focus the case.

An investigation may break up into sub-parts. Are we going to the police. What are problems with our internal controls. Where did management make mistakes. But ultimately that all answers up into one common goal. So by knowing the common goal, you can still do an investigation in as many parts as you need to. The key also though, on a large scale investigation, is to know the relative strengths and weaknesses of the people who were involved. Internal auditors for example, are terrific at number crunching. HR people are terrific at interviewing. Your standard investigators may be good at both, but by knowing the skill sets of the people involved, it's like conducting an orchestra where you've brought all the strengths to bear and you know where the weaknesses are so you know you can compensate for them.

Chapter I: Working with Counsel

MERIC BLOCH: The attorney client privilege applies to a confidential communication between lawyer and client for the purposes of legal advice. The fraud investigations that we do in a corporate setting for example, the ones for example that I do are not done for the purposes of legal advice, but for a variety of business purposes. The work product privilege applies when it's done in preparation for defending litigation or carrying it out. Most of the time we're conducting our investigation before litigation has even entered the picture. As a best practice I operate under the presumption that neither of them apply. That would be my recommendation to others.

I have conducted internal investigations at the direction of counsel when the lawyers are trying to decide whether to sue someone or whether the company can be sued. The problem is that lawyers don't have the facts at their disposal. So that's when I will use my talents or my skills and go in and conduct the investigation to give them the facts that they need. And as an aside, in those cases it may be conducted under the attorney client privilege.

One of the most important things to realize is that the goals of the lawyers may not be the same as the goals that you have as an internal business advisor. For example, you retain an outside lawyer to protect your legal interests, but being sued or suing somebody is only one of the issues that confront your business leaders in your company. They may be worried about negative publicity. They may be worried about a market place threat. They may be worried about the next quarter's sales. Those things are not part of the reality of your outside lawyer. So your lawyers need to be carefully aligned with your business goals. But it should not be assumed that simply because they're your lawyers there's naturally going to be that alignment.

My advice would be to remember that the lawyers may be looking at a very narrow set of priorities and that's not a negative reflection on the lawyers, but to be sure that they understand your true goals. For example, you may be looking for the lawyers to assist you in having somebody prosecute you, somebody prosecute the wrongdoer. You may be looking for the lawyers to tell the perfect storm of factors that caused the fraud that has lead to the problem. Those are two very different goals that a good law firm can do either one, but you can't do both. If you're looking for a systemic investigation of the root causes of your fraud problem that is a good purpose for outside lawyers, but it is very different from when you engage them to say, "please find out who committed the fraud and amass the proof that i need to see those people prosecuted."

Chapter I: Predication

INTERVIEWER: How can a fraud examiner determine and document whether sufficient predication exists to support a full fraud examination?

MERIC BLOCH: The way I do it is I use the criminal justice concept of probable cause. Probable cause is based on two concepts: One, a reasonable belief that fraud or similar misconduct has occurred, and two, a reasonable belief that the person who is the target of the investigation is the one who committed it. That's how I develop the predication. You need some initial facts to point not only to the wrong doing, but to the person. Probable cause is a key predicate because otherwise you're investigating without a legitimate basis.

Fraud does not happen by accident. It is an intentional act. By attempting to prove that it didn't occur, what I believe you're trying to do is prove that the facts are capable of no other explanation than fraud. In other words, they can't be explained by misconduct, by negligence, to lack of training. That essentially it's capable of only one explanation and that's fraud occurred. Fraud does not happen by accident.

Chapter I: Corroborative Witnesses

JONATHAN TURNER: We know when we investigate fraud that we look at both documents and we talk to people. Documents can be forged, people can lie. So, as a result, we have to find subsidiary facts that support the truth, or falseness of a statement or a document. So, if I have an invoice, that's dated June first [1st], and I can find the accounts payable clerk. And she says, "I received this invoice, and that's my signature, and I coded it into the system." And then I can find a check request for the same amount, and a check for the same amount, those are corroborating documents, and a corroborating witness that support that that fact is true. So, it's vital that in a fraud scheme, I find corroborating witnesses that can support that facts are true. Or, that the witness has said is either true or false, and corroborating documents. Since I know that documents can be altered, and witnesses can lie, I can't rely on the one [1] document, or one [1] witness. I need a group. And since many people can lie, I need as many corroborating witnesses, and corroborating documents as possible, to assert the truth of something. I could end up with a situation where three [3] witnesses say he was tall. And three [3] witnesses say he was short. So, even though I have corroboration, I don't have clarification. I have to keep seeking corroboration, until I get clarification.

Chapter I: Co-Conspirators

JONATHAN TURNER: In order to know what happened in a fraud scheme, you have to either be the person that committed the scheme, or be closely involved with the scheme itself. So as you're interviewing people who appear to have direct knowledge or specific knowledge of the scheme, you have to become aware that they have also got jeopardy. They are at risk by being involved and telling you these things. And so you have to modify your investigation and interviewing technique in a way that calms their anxiety and convinces them to cooperate. When you deal with co-conspirators, when you deal with people who have guilty knowledge, you have to be aware that what they say is often designed to paint themselves in the best possible light. And so you have to listen for those evasions and protective mechanisms that may come out in those kinds of interviews.

Chapter II: Public Records

JONATHAN TURNER: Public Records are much more easily accessible than they used to be. Through various databases, that are commercially available. Uh, if you're in law enforcement, law enforcement databases. You can get access to a tremendous range of information very quickly, very easily, and very inexpensively. So, every case should involve a thorough public records examination. Now remember, what you get in computerized records is not public record, it's a computer version. Which may, or may not be accurate, and may or may not be complete, but it's a great starting place. So, if I run Secretary of State's Records to find all the companies you're involved in, I still have to go verify you are the person on that paperwork, and—and etcetera. But it's a great starting place.
So, in general, I want to know everything that's knowable about a subject of my Investigation. That includes things like Google Earth, where I can use a satellite picture of where you live, and the companies that you own. That includes marriage and divorce records, bankruptcy filings, criminal records, corporate records, all of which can be accessed by a "click of the button", through commercial data bases. If you don't have access to these data bases, use an Online Provider, or use a Records Provider, to do the work for you, but don't pass on Public Records Research. It's simply too easy, too inexpensive, and too valuable.

Chapter II: Real Property Records

JONATHAN TURNER: Real estate records, of course, are to show you the property that somebody owns. But more than that, they give you an insight into the Financial History. If you see, for example, that the person has purchased a property for a hundred thousand dollars [$100,000], with a ninety-seven thousand dollar [$97,000] mortgage on it, that tells you they didn't have a lot of cash available. Cause they had to qualify for that very small down payment mortgage. Or, you see a public record that shows they've owned the property for a long time, but, they've got building permits, clearly indicating that they improved this property over time, which might indicate that they spent a lot of money, especially, if there's no corresponding mortgages to go along with those expenditures. A third [3rd] indication is that maybe they've owned a piece of property, but it's now been transferred to a trust, or a corporate name. That gives you an idea to explore whether or not they have other vehicles that they have their assets in. So, while Real Estate Records might seem sort of basic, and boring, they can actually give you a great Snapshot into somebody's financial history and health.

Chapter V: Before the Interview

JONATHAN TURNER: Before you walk into an Interview, any Interview, you want to be as prepared as you can. You want to be as knowledgeable about your file, if there are steps you can take? If there are investigations you can do? If there are documents you can review? Do all of those things,

Appendix: Video Transcripts

before you walk into an Interview. You don't interview people, and then do research. You do your research, and then conduct your interview. In going into an Interview, you want to place, time, and location that's appropriate, so it needs to be a room that is neutral, but authoritative. A conference room is often a great place to do an Interview. A bedroom is a horrible place to do an Interview. You want a time. If your subject goes to lunch at eleven forty five [11:45], you don't start an interview at eleven thirty [11:30]. He will be looking at his watch the entire time. If your subject picks up her children, at three [3] forty five [3:45] in the afternoon, you don't start an Interview at three [3:00]. Again, you're not gonna be successful. All Interviews begin before you get to the subject. And, in the first [1st] place, every interview should start is, "What information you're looking for"?

Interviews, if you will, are a Google Search of a person. In other words, you sit down and you Google, and you type in what your query is, and you don't get the information you want, you refine your query. So, when I go into an Interview, whether it's a random individual, a cooperating person, a co-conspirator, or even the accused. I have to know what information I'm seeking, and I have to be willing to modify my questions, until I get the answers I'm looking for.

We don't have the ability to force cooperation. So, what we're really doing is persuading somebody that our view of their cooperation is a better choice than their view of self-protection. This is sometimes described as convincing them that the boat they're on is sinking, and that you're there to rescue them. Now in reality, nobody in an interview is looking for a new best friend. But if I can present to you, that the option I'm presenting is better than the path you're on, you're likely to take it. If I treat you with respect, if I am empathetic to your situation, if I recognize your humanity, I am more likely to be successful. If I am dismissive, derogatory, or condescending, I'm less likely to be successful. When I sit down across the table, to interview anybody, my goal is to get information. I use the Tools I have, language, tone, body language, to elicit their cooperation. Sometimes that means pounding the table, and being harsh. But most of the time, it means using, recognizing what elements they will reply best to and using those.

Chapter V: Proxemics

JONATHAN TURNER: This is really gonna be an individual style question. Because there is some theory that we can apply that is scientific. And, for example, if we put two [2] people across a table, that creates a barrier to communication. So, given the opportunity to remove that barrier, we will open up that flow of communication. So, where you sit, in relation to that person, will have a direct impact in how they respond. The level of closeness that you use physically will impact them. And everybody's comfort level is a little bit different. So, saying, you want to be eighteen [18] inches from the subject may be too close for some people, or may be too far for others.

When you get to a place where somebody is vulnerable almost everybody responds to somebody leaning into them. It's an empathetic gesture. You don't actually have to hug, but the gesture of coming closer creates that empathy. So, being aware of your body language, and your body's relation to theirs, allows you to move and respond in a way that says, when they lean back, you've created more stress. When they lean in, they're seeking comfort. So, there are a number of ways you can respond. I personally prefer to setup the room with as few barriers between me and the subject, as possible. I prefer to have the room setup comfortably. You know, the old cement walls, with the single pigtail light bulb hanging, it makes for good movies, but lousy interviews.

Chapter V: Asking Questions

JONATHAN TURNER: You should never prepare questions, before an interview. You don't want to have an outline of specific questions that you want to ask, before the Interview. Because you're too likely to use your questions as your guide instead of your subject. Now, you can have an outline of topics, you can have specific areas of inquiry. But a written list of questions stops you from hearing the subject, as well as you want to. When you ask a question in an Interview, your next question your next question is entirely dependent on what the subject says. So, if you already have your question defined, you don't listen. You just go to the next question. As an example, if I was to ask you, "whether you were involved in the theft?" And you said, "Not at first [1st]", that begs for a follow-up question that I could not have known, until you gave that answer. So, it's very important to outline topics, to list your evidence, and to have a framework, but is vital not to use pre prepared questions.

Chapter V: Establishing Rapport

JONATHAN TURNER: Rapport is one [1] of those very difficult to define places. It's not a thing; it's a state of being. And when you approach a person, that you have never met before, sometimes that rapport will be almost instant. Other times, you will have to work to create a comfort level between yourself and that person. And so, the "Steps of Rapport" are assessing the subject, making the initial comments, and assessing their response. And then revising your comments.

Realistically, sometimes that happens in a word. Other times, that takes ten [10] or fifteen [15] minutes to establish. So, it's not, as if there is a series of things you do, it's a place you get. Every one [1] of us has had this. We've all met somebody, in a random occurrence, and felt close to that person, or—or comfortable with that person very quickly. And other people, we never feel comfortable around. In an Interview, we don't get the option to develop rapport. We must do it. I can't make you do something different. So, I have to change myself, to create that "Level of Rapport" with you. Whether that means, my body language, my facial gestures, my tone, making it harder or softer, in order to get to that place of comfort. Rapport is not about the other person. It's about you. It's about your ability to change yourself, to make the other person comfortable.

Chapter V: Open and Closed Questions

JONATHAN TURNER: Open Questions are those that don't have a fixed answer. So, that the subject gets to define the answer himself. And they are vital, because you don't know the answer to an open question fully. In other words, if you were to ask a subject, "When did you begin stealing from the company?" You might know they began in October, but he might have begun in August. So, by un-asking an Open Question, you give them a chance to provide you information you didn't already know. As we said before, an Open Question is designed to give you information you didn't have. A Closed Question is designed to stop them from rambling. It's designed to stop them from exploring an area. So, if they start speculating about what happened at a meeting, you can then go, "Were you at the meeting?" Which is a yes, no question, and ties them to a position. Once you've tied them to a position, you can then expand upon that. "What happened at that meeting?" And get them to—to go on, in a broader way. But you're mix of Open and Closed Questions, controls the subject's response, the same way your use of specific language controls the response you get from Google. We don't like to think we're that easily programmed, but we are.

Chapter V: Question Sequence

JONATHAN TURNER: The most important thing about the "Order of the Questions" is that they should flow naturally. It should sound to the subject conversational, even though it's not a conversation. So, if you leap from topic to topic randomly, they won't understand what you're doing. And the confusion will be a barrier to communication. But, if you ask questions in a logical order, they're in a better position to understand, and participate in the process.

So, the approach that usually you want to go with is often described as, "Peeling an Onion." You're gonna talk about the issues at thirty thousand feet. And you're gonna talk about the issues at fifteen thousand feet. And then you're gonna talk about the issues at ten [10] thousand feet. And at each point, you're refining the information you're seeking a little bit more. If you probe too fast, too hard, into a sensitive area, you may shut them down. But by working at, layer by layer, they will get to a place where they have already cooperated so much, they almost can't stop themselves from continuing to cooperate.

Chapter V: Signs of Deception

JONATHAN TURNER: The biggest thing to know, about deception, is it causes stress. And, in response to stress, people will do something different. It might be more body gestures, it might be fewer body gestures, it might be that they give longer answers. It might be that they do inappropriate things, like laugh at the wrong time. Or, put their head in their—and lay it down on the table. Their response to stress is the deception indicator. And so, Accountants, who are trained to look for changes in numbers, this is the same thing. Investigators are trained to look for differences in behavior. What the difference is matters a lot less than the fact there is a difference.

Everybody's body language is different. Some people are very effusive, talk with their hands, get really excited. Other people are very stayed, and don't change your facial expression at all. You have to determine, in a very short period of time, what kind of person this is. So, by asking ordinary questions, you get an idea of how much head movement, the person has, and how much they move their arms when they speak. And how much animation their face shows. And then you can spot differences. So, the norming or calibrating process is about finding what's normal for that person. And then identifying differences, in the interview process.

Every change is potentially a—a sign of deception. So, if you have an individual, who speaks in a very educated way, and then starts speaking in a very uneducated way. Or, if you have somebody who uses first [1st] person, "I came to work. I opened the drawer. I put the money in." And then, "We did this, and then they did that, and then we did this, and then did that." What you're keying in on here is the change in the level of education, or the change in person of speech. Or, the change in viewpoint and perspective. People make a change, at a point that matters to them. I don't know if that point is significant for my Investigation, until I ask a question. But I want to find those changes to ask those questions.

There are answers that we expect, and in interviewing, there are categories of questions, where any answer but, yes, is no. And any answer but no, is yes. Think about it this way. When you ask somebody what time it is? They say, "Eleven forty five [11:45], or whatever time it is." They don't say, "I swear to God it's eleven forty five [11:45]." They don't say, "Well, it's a funny thing that you would ask me that, because just the other day I was" The things they don't do. So, qualified denial, when I ask you something, and instead of saying, no. You say something negative that isn't no. Did you take the money? "I'm not allowed in the safe." That's not, no. Did you take the money? "I would never have done that." That's not, no either. Did you take the money? "How could you question my ethics." Still not, no. And so, those kinds of Direct Accusations demand "Direct Yes or No" answers, because any answer but, no, is yes.

Chapter V: Admission Seeking Interview

JONATHAN TURNER: In an admission seeking interview is not an information gathering tool. I am not looking for them to tell me any new information that I don't already know. An admission seeking interview is a chance for the suspect to tell his side of the story. It is included only to tell his side of the story. I don't care, in an admission seeking interview, if you tell me the truth, or you lie to me, as long as I can tell the difference. So, the purpose of an admission seeking interview is to hear what the subject will say, in his own words, about the topic. I'm not interested in confronting him with documents, I will not call him a liar. I will not accuse him of improvable areas. I will simply tell him, that this is his opportunity to put his story on the record, and to let management consider his statement next to my report, when deciding what to do. All Interviews are built on the theory that you are gathering information, not giving it. This is most important in an Information Seeking Interview, excuse me. This is most important in an admission seeking interview, where you need the individual to be unaware of the depth of your knowledge, and the scope of your findings. They need to not be aware at the beginning. And that they have not learned anything all the way through. So, any information that you get from them benefits your case, and doesn't help them.

You don't ask them if they stole the money. You tell them that they stole the money. So, the—the direct accusation could be in the form of a declarative, "You embezzled from this company. All I want to know is why?" It can be in the form of a secondary question. For example, "When did you start embezzling from the company?" In other words, the accusation is implied, or implicit. But you want to ask them directly about their wrongdoing, not for the answer, now this is the important part. But for their response, because if this person believes that you know, they are very likely to make an Admission inadvertently, or intentionally. They may just give up. And there have been times; I did one [1] of these two [2] weeks ago. I interviewed a man, and the bet among management was that he would not confess to anything. And he walked in, and he looked at the stack of paper that I had in front of me, and I pushed it off to the side. And by my third [3rd] question, he said, "Look, I know you already know, so I've been taking money." He thought he would look better in the interview, by admitting, before he was confronted. So, the purpose of a direct accusation is to get the response, not a confession. The confession will come, or not, depending on the subject.

Chapter V: Saying Too Much

TOM HUGHES: the worst thing I ever did, as Bank Teller, is something that probably could not happen today. We had a daily deposit from a retailer down the street, who would send a deposit by armored car. We would sign for it, verify the deposit. One [1] day that deposit arrived, as the Teller next to me was proving her drawer, and tracing down the shortage of her own. So, the money, the bag of money was thrown in the drawer, and forgotten about. While the three [3] of us behind the line tried to help her, to work her with her shortage.

I found that bag of money in the—in the cabinet two [2] weeks later. People had lost track of it. Uh, a customer hadn't reconciled their statement yet. And, as far as anyone knew, nothing was—nothing was wrong. I actually opened the bag, and took a strap of twenties [20s] out of it, and brought it home. That was the last day before I went on vacation for a week. And it only occurred to me, after I got home, what a glitteringly stupid thing that was to do. Because now I was gonna be away for the Branch for a week. If someone found the bag, obviously, our customer wouldn't have made a two thousand dollar [$2,000] mistake. Someone would know that someone had been in that bag.

And while I was on vacation, the following week, because I had already spent all the money, of course. It occurred to me the only way for me to make this any better was to go to work, and take the rest of the money, so that the whole thing was missing. That way we can plausibly make the case that the money got thrown out, which happened on a fairly regular basis, money or tickets. Um, so when I went back after vacation, that's what I did. I went and bought three [3] dress shirts at a shop down the street. Put them in a shopping bag, went behind the line after lunch to show my buddy, the Head Teller. And then at the end of the day, I put "The Bag" in my bag, and walked out the front door with it. The crime was discovered about four [4] weeks later. And suddenly, internal security was all over our Branch. And they interviewed me fairly hard. But I realized in the course of the interview, that they had their details wrong. And there were guessing as to how I had committed the crime. Their mindset was that I had stolen the money the day it came in. And the voice in my head said, 'Relax dummy, if they're guessing, they don't know. And you're the only one [1] that knows. They don't know. So, I gritted my teeth, I denied, and nothing happened after that.

The gruffer of the Auditors explained to me in detail how I had committed the crime. It was my responsibility at the Branch to change the film in the camera every week. And I was consistently forgetting to change the film in the camera. Uh, partly cause of forgetfulness, laziness, and I didn't want to crawl up on the free standing vault to change the film every week. That was one [1] of the weeks I had not changed the film. And the Auditor took that to mean I had planned the crime. Although in another part of our Interview, he suggested that it was a "Crime of Opportunity", that I had not planned. So, I didn't think he had fully thought out his uh, his progression with me.
But when he told me the details of the crime, including at one [1] point, he suggested that I had hid the money under my coat, walked off the line, and passed our Assistant Manager, to the break room, hid it in the break room, so that at the end of the day, I could go back to the break room, retrieve the money, put it under my coat, walk past—past the Assistant Manager, and walk out. I thought, he clearly has no clue what really happened. Including what date the crime occurred. So, when that voice in my head said, "Relax, he doesn't know", that's the voice I listened to. The other Auditor was very engaging. He—he said he talked about Accelerated Rehabilitation. He said, "Give back the money you still have, and we can work this out. And I almost jumped. I almost said, "Maybe I can do this. Maybe I could turn this around." Until the other guy started talking.

    INTERVIEWER: It sounds to me like the other guy talked you out of confessing.

TOM HUGHES: He really did. Uh, it's my belief that if you're interviewing a suspect, don't give him your theory of the crime. Because if he's the criminal, he knows what happened. And if he knows that you're guessing, you've—you've handed him an advantage.

As I was being interviewed, I came to realize that speaking less was better. I—it wasn't my place to make a case for being honest. Because if someone's telling me they suspect me of being dishonest, all I can do is throw it back at them, and say. "Yes, I'm honest." No, you're not. Yes, I am. That doesn't go very far. I figured it would better just to let them talk. And, at one [1] point, I just said, "Guys, I'd love to help you out. I can't. I don't know what happened to the money. My belief is that we threw it out."

Chapter V: Rationalization

DIANN CATTANI: The first point that I crossed the line was actually very innocuous. We were traveling out west for the holidays, and I got my travel itinerary and I had noticed that they had put my personal travel onto my corporate profile American Express card. And it was not a big deal. It just, you know, a simple mistake. I went out west for the holidays and came back and thought okay I'll pay it back. I'll get that first paycheck and I'll pay the company back. But I get that first paycheck and I start weighing it out. Well you got all these bills from the holidays and the paycheck.

Well, next time, next paycheck I'll pay the company back. And in between there I crossed into that gray area, and started down that road of rationalization. The old Fraud Triangle, the opportunity, pressure, and rationalization. And I started to rationalize it. Well, we were out there for the holidays, with my family, voicemails, emails, constant interruption, we're trying to snow-ski, I had to come in for a conference call, very disruptive. Okay, we'll just call it a business trip. So once I crossed that line it became easier to rationalize more and more. It wasn't, I stole nearly five-hundred thousand dollars from this company, who not only gave me a wonderful career opportunity, fast track.

But making what I did more despicable was that they also treated me like family. As I said, it was a small company, and there was lot of personal, professional crossover in relationships. So in, it wasn't stroke a check to Diann Cattani for five hundred thousand. It was very incremental. It was an incremental descent into the bad behavior, to where the bad behavior became the norm. I started to justify going out with friends, we'd talk about business, the most recent client. So you throw out the corporate American Express because we call that networking.

As we were, the company continued to grow. And we were now in larger much fancy office space now, in downtown Atlanta. And when I started with the company, it took off quickly. And I was getting bonuses, quarterly bonuses of five thousand, eight thousand dollars, Christmas bonuses, ten, fifteen thousand dollars. As the company grew, and I started to not, took on more overhead, and all of the sudden my bonuses started to come down. Now I'm getting maybe a thousand to three thousand dollars in a quarterly bonus, maybe five thousand dollars at Christmas. And all this was taking place, and there was a little bit of that a, well wait a minute, I'm still working hard, working just as hard as I ever have. And all of the sudden now my salary's coming down. I'm working even harder and my bonuses have decreased. So there was, I think some, a little bit of disgruntlement.

I continually thought about it, but there was also, as I said, the rationalization process to it. And it's like, well wait a minute, I'm working hard, they're calling me in the middle of the night. And so, I guess a clear answer would be I thought about it, but yes I also put it out of my mind. I continued to rationalize more and more, and it was easy. There was not a lot of controls in place. There was not a lot of accountability. I cut the checks, I signed the checks, I reconciled the payroll accounts, the bank accounts. There was just not a lot of, there was not a lot of accountability. In fact, there was no accountability. And consultants, when you're in a consulting company, if you're in the office you're not making money. So, they were always on the road, and I don't know, I don't know that there was really a feeling of, "I can get away with it," as much as it was just rationalizing the wrong, and trying to make it right.

I learned to operate in a lot of shades of gray. There was a lot of rationalization for what I did and I was caught up in this fast life. And I felt like I should have everything that all of our peer group had. I didn't ever really step back and say, "Wait a minute. They are ten, twenty years older than you are." You know, they've worked ten, twenty years longer. I just thought I should, you know, have the same. I was, that competitive spirit, that competitive nature in me crossed over into a very ugly side of competitiveness. It was keeping up with the Joneses. And in order to do that, I stole. Stole money to support, sustain a lifestyle that I had become addicted to.

Chapter V: Ask for the Signature

JONATHAN TURNER: The thing that stops most statements from being signed is the examiner not asking for a signature. Too often, fraud examiners will think, "They will never sign this." And so, they don't ask. When I complete a statement with an individual, I put it in front of them, and I tell them, "Sign this." In fact, I keep in my briefcase, at all times, those little sticky notes that say, "Sign Here." And I stick it on the document, and slide it across the table. Almost always, if you're instructed to sign something, you will.

But if I apologize for asking, if I him and haw, if I act like there's something wrong with signing this document, you won't. In fact, I had somebody who dictated out a statement, and we wrote it up, and I put it in front of him, and he said. "My lawyer is not gonna want me to sign this." And I said, "I know, sign it." And he did. Had he refused to sign that document, I would be no worse off. But if I didn't try to get that signature, I wouldn't have gotten it. I equate getting signatures to baseball. If your job, as the hitter, is to get up at the plate, and swing at the pitch. If you don't swing, you will not hit the ball. If you swing, you might miss. But you cannot hit, if you don't swing. So, ask for the signature.

Chapter VII: Writing Reports

JONATHAN TURNER: This is probably the biggest challenge for Fraud Examiners. The purpose of the report is to inform the reader, is to provide the reader with the information they need to make the best decision possible. It's not to dazzle them with the depth of their Investigation. It's not to show them how many different ways you can parch the data. And it certainly isn't to drown them in detail. I recently ran across a report, which was described to me as a Management Overview. And it was sixty six [66] pages of minutia. Nobody at a senior level is going to read sixty six [66] pages. So, part of your job is to break down the information you've learned, into chunks that are appropriate for the audience. And here's the part that's hard for fraud examiners. You may have to create different reports for different audiences.

Law enforcement wants to know what the crime was, and what the proof is. Internal audit wants to know what control failures were, and what needs to be fixed. The Board of Directors wants to know what are the government issues, and what is the extent. Senior management wants to know how much is this going to cost? Each reader group has different questions that need different answers. And creating one [1] massive document, that tries to address all, actually doesn't address any.

The most important thing on writing reports is keep it short, and keep it simple. People tend to load with jargon, with acronyms, with extraneous information that simply isn't necessary. If you interviewed four hundred [400] witnesses, and they all say the same thing, you can say, "Four hundred [400] witnesses agree." You don't have to list all four hundred [400] witnesses. Keep it short, keep it simple. Remember, the purpose of your Report is so that the reader can make the correct decision. So, it has to be fair, it has to be balanced, it has to be accurate, and it has to be short.

Chapter VIII: Working with Prosecutors

MERIC BLOCH: The most important thing to realize with a prosecutor is limited resources. That most times when we make reports to police, any law enforcement agency, it goes nowhere. And we have to realize their reality of limited resources and priorities. The most important thing I could recommend to anybody who is investigating a case that is likely to go to law enforcement is to gift wrap the case. To have all the proof ready and admissible for them as possible and think, "what will it take to convince this agency to take this case, go to a prosecutor and see these people prosecuted." Is to put yourself in the mindset of that overworked agent with shifting priorities and say, "how do I sell my case on that guy?"

Excellent case preparation is key. Being able to hand it off to them essentially gift wrapped, where you've developed proof that would be legally admissible. So that literally all you would have to do is give it to them and they can take it and run. And that the only things they need to investigate would be things that you had not, things that you couldn't get access to, like bank records or things like that.

There's a tendency among people to bring in law enforcement too early, before it's done or expect them to significantly investigate the case. A good fraud examiner has the skills to do that investigation. And what I mean by gift wrapping is something very simple. A good forensic memo that lays out why fraud occurred, all the elements of it, how it would be proven, explains why it was fraud and not capable of any other explanation like incompetence, lack of training, or anything like that.

And in that gift wrap, frequently affidavits from key company employees and exhibits that contain the documentation that back that up, those would simply be records from your accounts payable department, checks from your treasury department showing that it went to the bad guy, things like that. That basically it is a self-contained package of not only a forensic explanation of what happened, but all the proof that supports that forensic explanation. And just like a good investigation report, it's self-contained. They don't need to go to anything else. They don't need supplementary documents. It's all there and all they have to do is get a cup of coffee and read it. And that's what I mean by gift wrapping it.

When I closed my biggest case I went to the FBI, I went to the U.S. Attorney, where people were prosecuted, they pleaded guilty, the last thing the FBI agent said to me was, "you know the case you gave me was 90% complete. Next time you have another one, please bring it to me." That's how you develop a good relationship, by respecting their priorities and quite realistically viewing those priorities. Saying, "you know, the best way I can help myself is to really help you get this case moving along." And that's how I found it to be the most effective.

XII. SOLUTIONS TO REVIEW QUESTIONS

I. Preparing for an Investigation

1. A company can be held liable for the illegal conduct of an employee if the employee was acting within the course and scope of his employment. Which of the following statements regarding course and scope is true?
    I. Any act an employee commits while on duty is considered to be within the course and scope of his employment.
    II. In order to be considered within the course and scope, the employee's acts must be of the kind the employee was authorized by the company to perform.
    III. Unless a company expressly authorizes illegal conduct by its employees, an illegal act will never be considered to be in the course and scope.
    IV. In order to be considered within the course and scope, the employee's acts must be intended to benefit the company.

    A. II and III
    B. I
    C. II, III, and IV
    D. II and IV

    A. *Incorrect: In order to be considered within the course and scope, the employee's acts must be of the kind the employee was authorized by the company to perform. However, it is not required that the company expressly authorizes illegal conduct.*
    B. *Incorrect: Within the course and scope does not apply to every act performed by an employee.*
    C. *Incorrect: The company does not have to expressly authorize the illegal conduct of the employee for the employee's actions to be in the course and scope of his employment.*
    D. *Correct: Generally, an employer is liable for any misconduct committed by an agent or employee in the course and scope of his employment. Within the course and scope means that the agent or employee performed acts of the kind he was authorized to perform and that his acts were intended, at least in some part, to benefit the company. The fact that the particular conduct was wrongful or criminal does not necessarily mean that it was outside of the course and scope of employment. Thus, a company can be liable for the illegal acts of its employees.*

Solutions to Review Questions

2. _____ covers the internal auditor's responsibilities to deter, detect, investigate, and report fraud.
   A. SIAS 1220
   B. AU 315
   C. SIAS 1210
   D. AU 210

   A. *Incorrect: SIAS 1220 deals with the internal auditor's due professional care requirements.*
   B. *Incorrect: AU 315 applies to external auditors, and it does not cover the internal auditor's responsibilities to deter, investigate, and report fraud.*
   C. *Correct: Internal auditors should be aware of IIA's Proficiency Standard 1210 for internal auditors. The practice advisory sub-standard 1210.A2-1: Auditor's Responsibilities Relating to Fraud Risk Assessment, Prevention, and Detection covers the internal auditor's responsibilities to deter, detect, investigate, and report fraud. In addition to the legal duties described therein, internal auditors should look to practice advisory 1210.A2-2: Auditor's Responsibilities Relating to Fraud Investigation, Reporting, Resolution, and Communication for guidance in dealing with fraud once evidence of it has been uncovered.*
   D. *Incorrect: AU 210 applies to external auditors, and it does not cover the internal auditor's responsibilities to deter, investigate, and report fraud.*

3. Fraud examination methodology is constructed so that all cases are handled in a uniform fashion. In general, what is the order in which an investigator should interview witnesses and suspects (from first to last)?
   I. The accused
   II. Neutral third-party witnesses
   III. Suspected co-conspirators
   IV. Corroborative witnesses

   A. I, II, III, IV
   B. II, IV, III, I
   C. IV, II, III, I
   D. IV, III, I, II

   A. *Incorrect: The accused should not be interviewed first in an investigation.*
   B. *Correct: Fraud examination methodology is designed so that the investigation moves from the general to the specific, gradually zeroing in on the perpetrator. Thus, witnesses should be interviewed in a logical fashion, starting from the least likely to be involved and proceeding to the most likely. Neutral third-party witnesses should be interviewed first, followed by witnesses who can corroborate known or suspected facts. Those suspected of complicity should be interviewed next, from the least culpable to the most culpable. This means that suspected co-conspirators*

should be interviewed before the primary suspect. If an investigator follows this method, he will have all of the relevant facts at his disposal by the time he interviews the suspect and attempts to obtain a confession.

C. *Incorrect: According to the steps in the fraud methodology, corroborative witnesses should be interviewed second in the interview process, not first.*

D. *Incorrect: According to the steps in the fraud methodology, corroborative witnesses should be interviewed second in the interview process, not first.*

4. Which of the following is NOT one of the three conditions of a fraud risk factor identified by AU 240?
    A. Incentives or pressures to commit fraud
    B. Opportunities to carry out fraud
    C. Attitudes or rationalizations to justify fraudulent conduct
    D. Fraudulent mindset of employee

    A. *Incorrect: Incentives or pressures to commit fraud is one of the conditions of a fraud risk factor identified by AU 240.*
    B. *Incorrect: Opportunities to carry out fraud is one of the conditions of a fraud risk factor identified by AU 240.*
    C. *Incorrect: Attitudes or rationalizations to justify fraudulent conduct are conditions of a fraud risk factor identified by AU 240.*
    D. *Correct: As described in AU 240, the auditor may identify events or conditions that indicate incentives or pressures to commit fraud, opportunities to carry out fraud, or attitudes or rationalizations to justify fraudulent conduct. These events and conditions are referred to as "fraud risk factors." The auditor should consider whether one or more of the fraud risk factors are present and should be considered in identifying and assessing the risks of material misstatement due to fraud.*

5. According to the text, internal auditors are often used to do which of the following?
    A. Provide assistance in technical areas of the company's operations
    B. Review internal documentary evidence
    C. Evaluate tips or complaints
    D. All of the above

    A. *Incorrect: While internal auditors are often used to provide assistance in technical areas of the company's operations, a better answer choice is available.*
    B. *Incorrect: While internal auditors are often used to review internal documentary evidence, a better answer choice is available.*
    C. *Incorrect: While internal auditors are often used to evaluate tips or complaints, a better answer choice is available.*
    D. *Correct: Internal auditors are often used to provide assistance in technical areas of the company's operations, review internal documentary evidence, and evaluate tips or complaints.*

Solutions to Review Questions

6. The totality of circumstances that would lead a reasonable, professionally trained, and prudent individual to believe a fraud has occurred, is occurring, or will occur is known as:
   A. Declaration
   B. Fraud Theory Approach
   C. Predication
   D. None of the above

   A. *Incorrect: Declaration is not the set of circumstances that would lead a reasonable person to believe fraud is occurring.*
   B. *Incorrect: The fraud theory approach comes about because the examiner must make certain assumptions to solve a fraud without complete evidence. Fraud theory begins with an assumption, based on known facts, of what might have occurred. Then that assumption is tested to determine whether it is provable.*
   C. *Correct: Predication is the totality of circumstances that would lead a reasonable, professionally trained, and prudent individual to believe a fraud has occurred, is occurring, or will occur.*
   D. *Incorrect: One of the above options is correct.*

7. Public disclosure of internal fraud can subject a company to:
   A. Loss of collateral business or trading partners
   B. Loss of government licenses necessary for certain regulated activities
   C. A decline in the value of publicly traded equities
   D. All of the above

   A. *Incorrect: Businesses that publicly disclose that they have been a victim of internal fraud might face a loss of collateral business or trading partners; however, according to the text, there is a better answer to this question.*
   B. *Incorrect: Loss of government licenses necessary for certain regulated activities might be another consequence of public disclosure; however, the reader should refer back to the section on the Employer's Duty to Investigate to determine what other ramifications from public disclosure there might be.*
   C. *Incorrect: Businesses might see a decline in the value of publicly traded equities; however, there is a better answer to this question.*
   D. *Correct: Public disclosure of internal fraud can subject a company to a number of additional adverse financial consequences, such as the loss of collateral business or trading partners, the loss of government licenses necessary for certain regulated activities, or a decline in the value of publicly traded equities. The directors of a corporation might face liability to their shareholders for the losses resulting from the misconduct or for any collateral consequences that result (e.g., fines or other civil liability imposed on the company). These are all factors that can incline a company toward avoiding knowledge of harmful facts.*

Solutions to Review Questions

8. Senior management and corporate counsel that fail to investigate certain instances of alleged misconduct and fail to establish appropriate procedures for limiting the prohibited conduct might be held liable for violating which of the following?
   A. Foreign Corrupt Practices Act
   B. Generally accepted accounting principles
   C. Private Securities Litigation Act
   D. None of the above

   A. Correct: The 1997 Foreign Corrupt Practices Act is aimed at detecting and disclosing specific wrongful conduct. This statute requires accurate recordkeeping concerning subject transactions, reporting of specific misconduct, and the establishment of appropriate procedures to prevent and limit the offending conduct.
   B. Incorrect: The generally accepted accounting principles are a framework of accounting standards.
   C. Incorrect: The Private Securities Litigation Act is an amendment to the 1934 Securities and Exchange Act.
   D. Incorrect: A correct answer choice is available.

9. While conducting a fraud investigation, it is NOT recommended that internal auditors:
   A. Assess the probable level and extent of complicity within the organization
   B. Design procedural methodology to identify the perpetrators, the extent of the fraud, the techniques used, and the cause of the fraud
   C. Call law enforcement in at the beginning of the investigation
   D. Be aware of the rights of the alleged perpetrators and personnel within the scope of the investigation and the reputation of the organization itself

   A. Incorrect: While conducting a fraud investigation, the internal auditor should access the probable level and extent of complicity within the organization.
   B. Incorrect: It is also recommended that internal auditors design procedural methodology to identify the perpetrators, the extent of the fraud, the techniques used, and the cause of the fraud.
   C. Correct: While it might be necessary to involve law enforcement at some point during the investigation, it generally should not be called in at the beginning.
   D. Incorrect: During an investigation, internal auditors need to be aware of the rights of the alleged perpetrators and personnel within the scope of the investigation and the reputation of the organization itself.

Solutions to Review Questions

10. When choosing an investigation team, it is critical to identify those who can legitimately assist in the investigation and those who have a legitimate interest in the outcome of the investigation. Why should these people be included on the investigation team and all other personnel be segregated?
    A. The more people involved in the investigation, the greater the chance that one of them might leak confidential information about the investigation
    B. The individuals involved in the investigation team might have to testify in legal proceedings
    C. Limiting the size of the team decreases the risk of tort claims
    D. All of the above

    A. *Incorrect: The risk of information being leaked is one reason why all extraneous personnel should be segregated from the investigation; however, according to the text, there is a better answer to this question.*
    B. *Incorrect: Knowing that the individuals involved in the investigation might have to testify in legal proceedings is another reason to keep only critical individuals on the investigative team; however, the reader should refer back to the section on Selecting the Investigative Team to determine what, if any, additional factors should also be considered.*
    C. *Incorrect: Any internal investigation, by its nature, can lead to harsh allegations against one or more suspects. This, in turn, can lead to charges of defamation and invasion of privacy, among others. These charges will be bolstered if it is found that the company spread information about the suspects to people who did not have a legitimate interest in that information. Therefore, by limiting the size of the investigation team, the company can limit its exposure to certain tort claims. However, there is a better answer to this question.*
    D. *Correct: When choosing an investigation team, it is critical to identify those who can legitimately assist in the investigation and those who have a legitimate interest in the outcome of the investigation. These individuals should be included on the investigative team, and all other personnel should be segregated. There are a number of reasons for this. First, the more people involved in the investigation, the greater the chance that one of these people might be somehow implicated in the fraud itself, or that one of them might leak confidential information about the investigation. Second, the individuals involved in the investigation team might have to testify in legal proceedings, or the documents that they generate might be subject to discovery if the investigation leads to civil litigation or criminal prosecution. By limiting the number of investigators, the company can limit its exposure to discovery. In addition, any internal investigation, by its nature, can lead to harsh allegations against one or more suspects. This, in turn, can lead to charges of defamation and invasion of privacy, among others. These charges will be bolstered if it is found that the company spread information about the suspects to people who did not have a legitimate interest in that information. Therefore, by limiting the size of the investigation team, the company can limit its exposure to certain tort claims.*

II. Collecting Documentary Evidence

1. The Freedom of Information Act (FOIA) provides for public access to which type of information?
   A. Trust records
   B. Divorce or probate suits
   C. Telephone records
   D. None of the above

   A. *Incorrect: The FOIA does not provide for public access to trust records.*
   B. *Correct: The FOIA provides for public access to divorce or probate records, as well as other public filings.*
   C. *Incorrect: Telephone records are not provided for under the FOIA.*
   D. *Incorrect: One of the above options is provided for by the FOIA.*

2. Most states require a doing business as (DBA) filing for which of the following business types?
   A. Limited partnerships
   B. Trust
   C. Joint ventures
   D. All of the above

   A. *Incorrect: Most states require a DBA filing for limited partnerships; however, according to the text, there is a better answer to this question.*
   B. *Incorrect: DBA information is also required by most states to be filed for trusts; however, the reader should refer back to the section on Fictitious Business Names and DBA to determine if any other of the above options is also correct.*
   C. *Incorrect: Most states require a DBA filing for joint ventures; however, there is a better answer to this question.*
   D. *Correct: DBA information for sole proprietorships (individuals) or partnerships is typically filed at the county level, although some states require filing at the state level as well. Most states also require limited partnerships, trusts, and joint ventures to file DBA information at the state or county level.*

3. All of the following information can be obtained through a UCC filings search EXCEPT:
   A. Name of the debtor or joint debtors
   B. Name of the financial lender
   C. Amount of debt incurred by the debtor
   D. Type of collateral pledged as security

Solutions to Review Questions

A. *Incorrect: The name of the debtor or joint debtors can be obtained through a UCC filing.*

B. *Incorrect: UCC filings will identify the name of the financial lender.*

C. *Correct: The amount of debt incurred by the debtor will not be revealed by a UCC filing.*

D. *Incorrect: The type of collateral pledged as security can be identified by a UCC filing.*

4. Each of the following is an online public records database EXCEPT:
   A. Factiva
   B. KnowX
   C. Accurint
   D. Hoover's

   A. *Correct: Factiva is a newspaper and media database.*
   B. *Incorrect: KnowX offers public records searches in various categories, including asset searches, adverse filings, property valuation, and people- and business-locator tools.*
   C. *Incorrect: Accurint is a LexisNexus service and one of the most widely used public records databases on the Internet.*
   D. *Incorrect: Hoover's provides comprehensive, up-to-date business information for professionals who need intelligence on U.S. and global companies, industries, and professionals.*

5. One of the most powerful people locator tools is the:
   A. Department of Motor Vehicles
   B. Credit bureau header
   C. Last name search
   D. Bankruptcy filings

   A. *Incorrect: Department of Motor Vehicles records were once thought to be good locator tools, but recent restrictions on the use of such data has reduced the effectiveness of these searches.*
   B. *Correct: Credit bureau header searches are among the most powerful locator tools. Nearly everyone has been involved in some credit activity either under their true names or an "a/k/a." However, make sure you comply with all rules governing the use of credit reports.*
   C. *Incorrect: Last name searches are available for those situations where precise past address information is not available. The searches seem to produce better results if the name is not common.*
   D. *Incorrect: Bankruptcy filings, tax liens, and court judgments have emerged in recent years as locator tools, because where such records exist on an individual, a valid Social Security number will be identified. However, these are not the most powerful locator tools.*

Solutions to Review Questions

6. The question of whether it is realistically possible to recover known assets may be partially answered by searching:
   A. Bankruptcy filings
   B. Tax liens
   C. Judgments
   D. All of the above

   A. *Incorrect: Searching bankruptcy filings can answer whether it is realistically possible to recover known assets; however, according to the text, there is a better answer to this question.*
   B. *Incorrect: Searching tax liens can also answer whether it is realistically possible to recover known assets; however, the reader should refer back to the section on Searches for Asset Potential to determine what other searches can be used to determine assets.*
   C. *Incorrect: Judgments can also be used to determine whether recovering known assets is possible; however, there is a better answer to this question.*
   D. *Correct: The question of whether it is realistically possible to recover known assets may be partially answered by searching bankruptcy filings, tax liens, and judgments.*

7. The Boolean operator symbol that designates a list of words that must appear together in an exact order is:
   A. +
   B. " "
   C. Near
   D. None of the above

   A. *Incorrect: The + Boolean operator designates words which must appear right next to each other.*
   B. *Correct: The Boolean operator symbol that designates a list of words that must appear together in the exact order is in quotation marks.*
   C. *Incorrect: The Boolean operator near designates words which appear within a certain number of words of each other.*
   D. *Incorrect: One of the above Boolean operators designates a list of words which must appear together.*

8. Specialized websites that collect the names of numerous other related websites, allowing the user to browse through a complete listing of possible sites to visit are known as:
   A. Search engines
   B. Directories
   C. Public records databases
   D. None of the above

Solutions to Review Questions

A. *Incorrect: Search engines are website tools that allow the user to type in keywords describing the subject in which he is interested.*

B. *Correct: As the name suggests, directories are specialized websites that collect the names of numerous other related websites, allowing the user to browse through a complete listing of possible sites to visit.*

C. *Incorrect: Public records databases provide online access, typically for a fee, to various types of public records such as business filings, archived periodicals, or criminal court records.*

D. *Incorrect: A correct answer choice is available.*

Solutions to Review Questions

III. Workplace Searches

1. The _____ is the principal constitutional limitation on investigative searches and surveillances by law enforcement, public employers, and other government representatives.
   A. Fourth Amendment
   B. Fifth Amendment
   C. Sixth Amendment
   D. Seventh Amendment

   A. *Correct: The Fourth Amendment is the principal constitutional limitation on investigative searches and surveillances by law enforcement, public employers, and other government representatives. It states: "The right of the people to be secure in their persons, houses, papers, and effects, against unreasonable searches and seizures, shall not be violated, and no warrants shall be issued, but upon probable cause, supported by oath or affirmation, and particularly describing the place to be searched, and the persons or things to be seized."*
   B. *Incorrect: The Fifth Amendment provides that a person cannot be compelled to give information which might incriminate him.*
   C. *Incorrect: The Sixth Amendment assures the right to an attorney and to confront the witnesses against the individual.*
   D. *Incorrect: The Seventh Amendment is not the principal constitutional limitation on investigative search and surveillance by law enforcement, public employers, and other government representatives.*

2. When a government employer searches an employee's workspace, the search must satisfy which two of the following conditions in order to be constitutionally valid?
   I. The search must be based on probable cause.
   II. The search must be reasonable in scope.
   III. The employer must obtain a warrant.
   IV. The search must be justified at its inception.

   A. I and II
   B. I and III
   C. I and IV
   D. II and IV

   A. *Incorrect: Workplaces searches are to be judged by a reasonableness standard. Criminal investigations are to be judged by a probable cause standard.*
   B. *Incorrect: When a public employer conducts an investigation of work-related misconduct, and when that investigation necessitates a search of the suspect's workspace, the employer is not generally required to obtain a*

Solutions to Review Questions

warrant to perform the search, nor is the employer required to make a showing of probable cause that the suspect has committed a crime.

C. *Incorrect: Workplaces searches are to be judged by a reasonableness standard. Criminal investigations are to be judged by a probable cause standard.*

D. *Correct: There is a two-part test to determine if a workplace search is reasonable.*
   1. *The search must be justified at its inception, meaning there must be reasonable grounds for suspecting that the search will turn up evidence that the employee is guilty of work-related misconduct.*
   2. *The search must be conducted in a way that is reasonably related in scope to the circumstances which justified the interference in the first place, meaning that the search must be no broader than necessary to serve the organization's legitimate, work-related purposes.*

3. ABC Corp., a private company, intentionally searched the purse of one of its employees. Assume that the employee had a reasonable expectation of privacy in the purse, and that the search was conducted in such a manner as to be highly offensive to a reasonable person. Also assume that there was no state action involved in the search. Which of the following statements is true?
   A. The employee can sue ABC for violating her Fourth Amendment rights
   B. The employee can sue ABC for common law invasion of privacy
   C. Both A and B are correct
   D. The employee has no grounds to sue ABC; only public employers can be sued for invasion of privacy

   A. *Incorrect: In general, the Fourth Amendment only limits the power of public employers to conduct internal investigations; it does not apply to private companies. Since ABC Corp. is not a public employer (and since there is no state action involved in the search) the Fourth Amendment would not apply in this scenario.*

   B. *Correct: In addition to constitutionally protected rights, employees also have common law privacy interests that limit an employer's right to search. These common law protections cover both public and private employees. In this case, the common law tort of invasion of privacy would apply. This tort actually consists of four separate causes of action: intrusion upon seclusion, public disclosure of private facts, false light invasion of privacy, and appropriation of likeness. Intrusion upon seclusion is the cause of action that is most frequently raised with regard to workplace searches.*

   To state a claim of intrusion upon seclusion, an employee must be able to prove that the employer (1) made an intentional intrusion, (2) into an area where an employee had a reasonable expectation of privacy, and (3) the intrusion would be highly offensive or objectionable to a reasonable person. All of these elements are present in this scenario.

   C. *Incorrect: Both A. and B. are not correct.*
   D. *Incorrect: Both public and private companies can be sued for common law invasion of privacy.*

Solutions to Review Questions

4. Which of the following is NOT true of reasonable expectations of privacy?
   A. The Fourth Amendment only applies to workplace searches where an employee has a reasonable expectation of privacy
   B. The employee has to have an ownership interest in the area to have a reasonable expectation of privacy
   C. If an employee has exclusive control over the area, that tends to show the employee had a reasonable expectation of privacy
   D. None of the above

   A. *Incorrect: The Fourth Amendment only applies to workplace searches where an employee has a reasonable expectation of privacy. Thus, in order to determine if a workplace search will violate the employee's Fourth Amendment rights, an employer must first determine if the employee has a reasonable expectation of privacy in the area to be searched.*
   B. *Correct: The employee does not have to have an ownership interest in the area to have a reasonable expectation of privacy in that area.*
   C. *Incorrect: If the employee has exclusive control over the area in question, this does tend to show that the employee has a reasonable expectation of privacy in that area.*
   D. *Incorrect: One of the above options is not true of reasonable expectations of privacy.*

5. Public employer workplace searches for investigations of work-related misconduct are to be judged on a:
   A. Reasonableness standard
   B. Probable cause standard
   C. Plain view standard
   D. All of the above

   A. *Correct: Public employer workplace searches for investigations of work-related misconduct are judged by a reasonableness standard.*
   B. *Incorrect: In criminal investigations, investigations of work-related misconduct are to be judged by a probable cause standard.*
   C. *Incorrect: Plain view refers to an exception to the warrant requirement of the Fourth Amendment.*
   D. *Incorrect: Only one of the available answer choices is correct.*

Conducting Internal Investigations

Solutions to Review Questions

6. Which of the following are recommended methods by which employers can reduce their liability for invasion of privacy claims?
    A. Lowering employees' expectations of privacy in the workplace
    B. Conducting a workplace search only with the government's involvement
    C. Adopting a written policy providing that, in order to maintain the security of its operations, the company retains the right to access and search all work areas and personal belongings
    D. Both A and C are correct

    A. *Incorrect: Lowering employees' expectations of privacy is one way for employers to reduce their liability for invasion of privacy claims; however, according to the text, there is a better answer to this question.*
    B. *Incorrect: Workplace searches can be conducted without the government's involvement, and the government's involvement does nothing to reduce an employer's liability for invasion of privacy claims.*
    C. *Incorrect: Adopting a written policy providing that, in order to maintain the security of its operations, the company retains the right to access and search all work areas and personal belongings is another way for employers to reduce their liability for invasion of privacy claims; however, there is a better answer to this question.*
    D. *Correct: Employers can reduce their potential liability for invasion of privacy claims by lowering employees' expectations of privacy in the workplace. If an employer puts employees on notice that their offices, desks, files, voice mail, etc. are not private, then logically, employees cannot assert that they have a reasonable privacy expectation in those areas. To lower the expectation of privacy in the workplace, employers should adopt a written policy providing that, in order to maintain the security of its operations, the company retains the right to access and search all work areas and personal belongings, including desks, file drawers, lockers, briefcases, handbags, pockets, and personal effects.*

7. The Electronic Communications Privacy Act (ECPA) does NOT cover:
    A. Audio-video surveillance
    B. Silent video surveillance
    C. Any video surveillance
    D. None of the above

    A. *Incorrect: If video surveillance is accompanied by audio recording, then this type of surveillance would be covered by Title I of the ECPA, which prohibits the interception of wire, electronic, or oral communication except in limited circumstances.*
    B. *Correct: The ECPA does not cover silent video surveillance.*
    C. *Incorrect: The ECPA covers some types of video surveillance.*
    D. *Incorrect: One of the above options is not covered by the ECPA.*

Solutions to Review Questions

8. Which of the following exceptions to the Electronic Communications Privacy Act (ECPA) allows suppliers of wire or electronic communications services to intercept electronic communications in the normal course of business?
   A. The ordinary course of business exception
   B. The consent exception
   C. The provider exception
   D. None of the above

   A. *Incorrect: Under the ordinary course of business exception, employers are permitted to monitor their employees' wire or electronic communications as long as the monitoring is done for a legitimate business purpose.*
   B. *Incorrect: The consent exceptions allow an entity to intercept an electronic communication if that entity is a party to the communication, or if one of the parties to the communication has given prior consent to the interception.*
   C. *Correct: The provider exception allows suppliers of wire or electronic communications services (e.g., telephone, voice mail, email, or Internet services) to intercept electronic communications in the normal course of business.*
   D. *Incorrect: A correct answer choice is available.*

Solutions to Review Questions

IV. Analyzing Documentary Evidence

1. Which of the following is the LEAST preferred method of organizing documentary evidence?
   A. By witness
   B. By date received
   C. By transaction
   D. None of the above are preferred methods of organizing documentary evidence

   A. *Incorrect: Preferred methods for organizing documentary evidence include assembling collected documents by witness or by grouping evidence of the same transaction together.*
   B. *Correct: Organizing documents obtained in an investigation by date is not recommended. Better methods include assembling collected documents by witness or by grouping evidence of the same transaction together.*
   C. *Incorrect: Preferred methods for organizing documentary evidence include assembling collected documents by witness or by grouping evidence of the same transaction together.*
   D. *Incorrect: A correct answer choice is available.*

2. _____ is a means of establishing that there has not been a material change to a piece of evidence.
   A. Evidence restoration
   B. Authentication
   C. Chain of custody
   D. None of the above

   A. *Incorrect: As part of the forensic document examination process, documentary evidence can be restored to reveal erasures, eradications, and faint indented writings; however, evidence restoration is not the term that is used to describe the means of establishing that there has not been a material change to a piece of evidence.*
   B. *Incorrect: Authentication refers to testimony from a person with first-hand knowledge that the evidence is what it purports to be.*
   C. *Correct: Chain of custody is a means of establishing that there has not been a material change or alteration to the evidence. From the moment evidence is collected, its chain of custody must be maintained for it to be accepted by the court. Chain of custody essentially refers to (1) who has had possession of an object and (2) what they've done with it.*
   D. *Incorrect: One of the above options is correct.*

Solutions to Review Questions

3. According to the text, which of the following is NOT true when seizing digital evidence?
   A. The fraud examiner should document the scene using photographs, diagrams, or video.
   B. If the computer is on, the fraud examiner should turn it off using the standard shutdown procedure.
   C. The fraud examiner should search near the computer's location for notes that appear to be passwords.
   D. When seizing a laptop computer, the fraud examiner should also recover all power supply cords and related components.

   A. Incorrect: The fraud examiner should document the scene (cubicle, office, room, etc.) with photographs or a diagram, depending on the complexity of the setup. It is also prudent to videotape the scene. In performing this step, painstaking attention to detail is critical.

   B. Correct: The first golden rule of securing and seizing digital evidence states: If the computer is on, don't turn it off. The converse of this rule is also true: If the computer is off, don't turn it on. Going through the computer's normal shutdown routine may cause a number of temporary files—some of which may be important to the investigation—to be deleted or overwritten. Instead, the investigator should simply unplug the computer if it's running.

   C. Incorrect: Many people have a habit of writing down or recording their passwords near their computers. With this in mind, the fraud examiner should look around for notes that appear to be passwords. This practice may aid in the discovery of passwords needed to access encrypted data in the event that the subject of the investigation is being uncooperative.

   D. Incorrect: When seizing a laptop computer, the fraud examiner should recover all of the components that belong to the laptop, such as CD- and DVD-ROMs and power supply cords. Often, laptop computers must be imaged with these components in use, and because of the proprietary nature of the laptops themselves, they will function with only their own components.

4. Which of the following is NOT a source of digital evidence?
   A. A printer
   B. A GPS navigation system
   C. A watch
   D. All of the above are sources of digital evidence

   A. Incorrect: Printers frequently have large hard drives installed that can contain important digital evidence. However, according to the text, this is not the best answer to this question.

   B. Incorrect: GPS navigation system technology can contain evidence regarding the whereabouts of a car or portable receiver. However, there is a better answer to this question.

   C. Incorrect: Some watches allow for the storage of contact information, notes, and telephone numbers within their memory. However, according to the text, this is not the best answer to this question.

Solutions to Review Questions

    D. *Correct: Sources of digital evidence include not only computer hardware, such as central processing units, flash drives, and external hard drives, but also printers, mobile phones, digital cameras, credit card readers, MP3 players, watches, and GPS navigation systems.*

5. According to the text, many counterfeited printed documents can be detected by:
    A. Shining a light across the paper surface at a low oblique angle or parallel to the surface
    B. Developing inconsistencies in the paper by shading or scratching on the surface with a pencil
    C. Making a side-by-side comparison with a corresponding genuine document
    D. None of the above

    A. *Incorrect: Shining a light across the paper surface at a low oblique angle or parallel to the surface is a method that can be used to develop indented writings.*
    B. *Incorrect: Developing inconsistencies in the paper by shading or scratching on the surface with a pencil should never be done.*
    C. *Correct: Many counterfeited printed documents can be detected by making a side-by-side comparison with a corresponding genuine document.*
    D. *Incorrect: One of the above options is correct.*

6. When organizing documentary evidence, the least preferred method is:
    A. By witness
    B. By evaluation
    C. Chronologically
    D. All of the above

    A. *Incorrect: When organizing documentary evidence, segregating documents by witness is one of the preferred methods.*
    B. *Incorrect: When organizing documentary evidence, segregating documents by transaction is one of the preferred methods.*
    C. *Correct: Chronological organization is the least preferred method in organizing documentary evidence.*
    D. *Incorrect: Only one of the above options is correct.*

7. Whenever possible, which of the following should be submitted to the forensic expert for examination?
    A. Original document
    B. Photocopy of document
    C. Photograph of document
    D. None of the above

A. Correct: When possible, the fraud examiner should obtain the original document for the document examiner and should not submit a photocopy. Photocopies do not permit the forensic expert to uncover clues such as indentations and erasures. As a result, the document examiner may not be able to determine features and reach conclusions that could have been made from the original document.

B. Incorrect: Fraud examiners and other investigators sometimes submit a copy of a document for examination because they do not wish to part with the original. As a result, the document examiner will probably not be able to determine features and reach conclusions that could have been made from the original document. When possible, the fraud examiner should obtain the original document for the document examiner and should not submit a copy.

C. Incorrect: Fraud examiners and other investigators sometimes submit a copy of a document for examination because they do not wish to part with the original. As a result, the document examiner will probably not be able to determine features and reach conclusions that could have been made from the original document. When possible, the fraud examiner should obtain the original document for the document examiner and should not submit a copy.

D. Incorrect: A correct answer choice is available.

8. The chain of custody is a process that memorializes which of the following?
   A. Who has had possession of an object
   B. What a person has done with an object
   C. Whether an object has been materially altered
   D. All of the above

   A. Incorrect: While the chain of custody does indeed memorialize who had possession of an object, a better answer choice is available.
   B. Incorrect: While the chain of custody does indeed memorialize what a person has done with an object, a better answer is available.
   C. Incorrect: While the chain of custody does indeed memorialize whether an object has been materially altered, a better answer is available.
   D. Correct: The chain of custody is both a process and a document that memorializes who has had possession of an object, and what they have done with it; it is simply a means of establishing that there has not been a material change or alteration to a piece of evidence.

Solutions to Review Questions

V. Interviewing Witnesses

1. Which of the following is NOT one of the purposes of an admission-seeking interview?
    A. Notify the suspect of his right to an attorney
    B. Distinguish the innocent from the culpable
    C. Obtain a valid confession
    D. Obtain a written statement acknowledging the facts

    A. *Correct: Notifying the suspect of his right to an attorney is not a purpose of an admission-seeking interview.*
    B. *Incorrect: Distinguishing the innocent from the culpable is one of the purposes of an admission-seeking interview.*
    C. *Incorrect: Obtaining a valid confession is another purpose of an admission-seeking interview.*
    D. *Incorrect: Obtaining a written statement acknowledging the facts is also a purpose of admission-seeking interviews.*

2. If the interviewer has reasonable cause to believe that a respondent is not being truthful, _____ questions can be asked.
    A. Informational
    B. Admission-seeking
    C. Closed
    D. Assessment

    A. *Incorrect: Informational questions are asked for the purpose of gathering unbiased factual information. These questions can be asked if the interviewer believes the respondent is not being truthful; however, they are not the best type of question to ask.*
    B. *Incorrect: If the interviewer decides with reasonable cause that the respondent is responsible for misdeeds, admission-seeking questions can be posed.*
    C. *Incorrect: Closed questions are those questions worded in a way which limits the respondent's answers to "yes" or "no." These types of questions would not be the type of question to use if one is trying to dig for a truthful response.*
    D. *Correct: If the interviewer has reasonable cause to believe that a respondent is not being truthful, assessment questions can be asked.*

3. Which of the following would be an appropriate excuse clause to include in a signed confession?
    A. "I didn't mean to do it."
    B. "I didn't mean to hurt anyone."
    C. "I didn't do it."
    D. None of the above—a confession should never contain an excuse by the confessor.

Solutions to Review Questions

   A. *Incorrect:* Instead of using language like "I didn't mean to do it," which implies lack of intent, the interviewer should focus on an excuse that provides only a moral explanation for the misconduct—"I wouldn't have done this if it had not been for pressing financial problems. I didn't mean to hurt anyone."
   B. *Correct:* The confessor's moral excuse should be mentioned in a signed confession. The interviewer should make sure that the confessor's excuse does not diminish his legal responsibility for his actions. This statement implies intent but still gives the subject a moral excuse.
   C. *Incorrect:* The subject would not claim "I didn't do it" in a confession; he would be admitting to the violation.
   D. *Incorrect:* One of the above options is an appropriate moral excuse to include in a signed confession.

4. *Proxemics* is a term used to describe:
   A. The environment of an interview
   B. The use of interpersonal space to convey meaning
   C. The subject's attitude
   D. None of the above

   A. *Incorrect:* Proxemics is not used to define the environment of the interview.
   B. *Correct:* Proxemics is a term used to define the use of interpersonal space to convey meaning. It is important for the interviewer to establish proxemic control over the interview. This requires paying attention to the relative positions of the interviewer and the subject within the interview room, and to the arrangement of furniture and other objects that might create barriers between the interviewer and the subject.
   C. *Incorrect:* The subject's attitude is not defined by proxemics.
   D. *Incorrect:* Proxemics is used to define one of the above options.

5. While taking notes during an interview, the interviewer should NOT:
   A. Take down verbatim as much of what the subject is saying as possible
   B. Concentrate on recording specific nouns, pronouns, verbs, and qualifiers that the subject uses
   C. Document his own opinions and conclusions about this respondent's guilt
   D. Maintain eye contact with the respondent as much as possible during note-taking

   A. *Incorrect:* According to the text, it is recommended that the interviewer take down verbatim as much of what the subject says as is possible. This includes repeated words and parenthetical comments. This practice allows the interviewer to later review what the subject actually said, as opposed to what the interviewer thought the subject said.
   B. *Incorrect:* When taking notes, the interviewer should concentrate on recording specific nouns, pronouns, verbs, and qualifiers that the subject uses.
   C. *Correct:* The interviewer should not document his own opinions and conclusions about the respondent's guilt while taking notes during an interview. Doing so will decrease the credibility of the interview findings.
   D. *Incorrect:* The interviewer should maintain eye contact with the respondent as much as possible during note-taking.

Solutions to Review Questions

6. In routine interview situations where the object is to gather information from neutral or corroborative witnesses, which of the following types of questions will generally NOT be used?
   A. Assessment
   B. Introductory
   C. Informal
   D. Closing

   A. *Correct: Assessment questions will generally not be used in routine interview situations. The purpose of assessment questions is to establish the credibility of the subject.*
   B. *Incorrect: Introductory questions should be used in routine interview situations. Introductory questions serve four primary purposes: to provide an introduction, to establish a rapport between the interviewer and the subject, to establish the theme of the interview, and to observe the subject's reactions.*
   C. *Incorrect: Informal questions should also be used in routine investigations. Informal questions should be non-confrontational and non-threatening, and should be asked for the purpose of gathering unbiased factual information.*
   D. *Incorrect: Closing questions are asked at the closing of the interview for the purpose of reconfirming the facts, gathering additional facts, concluding the interview, and maintaining goodwill.*

7. _____ questions are usually used to confirm facts that are already known.
   A. Closed
   B. Leading
   C. Complex
   D. Open

   A. *Incorrect: Closed questions are those which limit the possible responses by requiring a precise answer, usually "yes" or "no."*
   B. *Correct: Leading questions contain the answer as part of the question. They are usually used to confirm facts that are already known.*
   C. *Incorrect: Complex questions are not a type of question that interviewers will ask during an interview.*
   D. *Incorrect: Open questions are worded in a way that makes it difficult to answer "yes" or "no." During the informational phase of the interview, the interviewer should endeavor to ask primarily open questions. This is to stimulate conversation and allow the subject to convey as much information as possible.*

Solutions to Review Questions

8. A volatile interview is one that has the potential to bring about strong emotional reactions in the respondent. Which of the following is a method an investigator can used to control volatile interviews?
   A. Have two interviewers involved in the interview
   B. Conduct volatile interviews on a surprise basis
   C. Ask the order of questions out of sequence
   D. All of the above

   A. *Incorrect: There should be two interviewers involved in potentially volatile situations. This procedure provides psychological strength for the interviewers. Additionally, the second person can serve as a witness in the event that the subject later makes allegations of improper conduct. However, according to the text, there is a better answer to this question.*
   B. *Incorrect: Potentially volatile interviews should be conducted on a surprise basis, meaning that the subject should be given little or no advance notice of the interview. If the interview is not conducted by surprise, the interviewer runs the risk of the respondent not showing up, showing up with a witness, or being present with counsel. The reader should refer back to the section on Volatile Interviews to determine what additional steps can be taken to diffuse a volatile situation.*
   C. *Incorrect: In a potentially volatile interview, the order of questions should be out of sequence. This is to keep the volatile respondent from knowing the exact nature of the inquiry and where it is leading. However, there is a better answer to this question.*
   D. *Correct: To control volatile interviews, there should be two interviewers involved in potentially volatile situations. Volatile interviews should also be conducted on a surprise basis, and the order of questions should be out of sequence.*

9. In most people, lying produces stress. The human body will attempt to relieve this stress through verbal and nonverbal clues. A practiced interviewer will be able to draw information about the honesty of a subject's statements from his behavior. Which of the following is NOT considered a verbal clue to deception?
   A. Increasingly weaker denials
   B. Character testimony
   C. Comments regarding the interview
   D. A strong apparent concern regarding the accusations

Solutions to Review Questions

A. *Incorrect: Increasingly weaker denials are a verbal clue to deception. When confronted with an accusation, the dishonest person is likely to make a weak denial. Upon repeated accusations, the dishonest person's denial becomes weaker, to the point that the person becomes silent.*

B. *Incorrect: Character testimony is another verbal clue of deception. A liar will often request that the interviewer "Check with my wife." This is done to add credibility to the false statement.*

C. *Incorrect: Comments regarding the interview is also a verbal clue to deception. Deceptive people often will comment on the physical environment of the interview room, complaining that it is too hot, too cold, etc. As they come under increasing stress, they might frequently ask how much longer the interview will take.*

D. *Correct: The dishonest person will often try to appear casual and unconcerned, will frequently adopt an unnatural slouching posture, and might react to questions with nervous or false laughter or feeble attempts at humor. The honest person, conversely, will typically be very concerned about being suspected of wrongdoing, and will treat the interviewer's questions seriously.*

10. Probably the most common explanation for criminal activity, particularly internal fraud, is:
    A. Unfair treatment
    B. Inadequate recognition
    C. Financial problems
    D. Family problems

    A. *Correct: Probably the most common explanation for criminal activity, particularly internal fraud, is the accused's attempt to achieve equity. Studies have shown that counter-productive employee behavior—including stealing—is motivated primarily by job dissatisfaction.*
    B. *Incorrect: Inadequate recognition is not the most common explanation for internal fraud.*
    C. *Incorrect: Financial problems are not the most common explanation for internal fraud.*
    D. *Incorrect: Family problems are not the most common explanation for internal fraud.*

Solutions to Review Questions

11. According to the text, which of the following is true of benchmark admissions?
    A. Questions are structured so that the positive alternative is presented first, followed by the negative alternative
    B. Questions should be constructed so that the answer requires some type of explanation
    C. Questions should be constructed so that they can be answered "yes" or "no"
    D. All of the above

    A. *Incorrect: In benchmark admissions, there is not a set structure for wording questions. Investigators can put either the positive or negative alternative first, depending on the situation.*
    B. *Incorrect: The questions for the benchmark admission should not be constructed so that the answer requires some type of explanation.*
    C. *Correct: Questions for the benchmark admission should be constructed as leading questions, so they can be answered "yes" or "no."*
    D. *Incorrect: Not all of the above options are true of benchmark admissions.*

12. When preparing a written statement, how many unrelated offenses should be included?
    A. Only one offense should be included per written statement.
    B. At least two unrelated offenses should be included per written statement.
    C. A maximum of five unrelated offenses should be included per written statement.
    D. All offenses should be included in the same written statement.

    A. *Correct: When preparing a written statement, there should not be more than one written statement for each offense. If facts are inadvertently omitted, they can later be added to the original statement as an addendum.*
    B. *Incorrect: For legal purposes, the investigator should prepare separate statements for unrelated offenses. This rule applies because the target might be tried separately for each offense.*
    C. *Incorrect: For legal purposes, the investigator should prepare separate statements for unrelated offenses. This rule applies because the target might be tried separately for each offense.*
    D. *Incorrect: For legal purposes, the investigator should prepare separate statements for unrelated offenses. This rule applies because the target might be tried separately for each offense.*

Solutions to Review Questions

VI. Legal Considerations in Interviews

1. Green is an at-will employee of ABC Corporation, a private company. During an investigation of internal fraud, Green is interviewed by internal investigators about missing funds. Which of the following statements are correct? (Assume that there is no state action by ABC Corporation.)
   A. Green is entitled to have an attorney present at the interview
   B. The investigators must give *Miranda* warnings to Green
   C. Both of the above
   D. None of the above

   A. *Incorrect: The employee always has the right to consult an attorney, but there is typically no legal obligation to consult the employee's lawyer prior to the interview or to allow the employee's lawyer to sit in during an interview. Investigators should avoid giving advice to the employee as to whether he needs an attorney; that is the employee's choice, and the investigator should not risk misleading the employee about either his rights or his needs.*
   B. *Incorrect: Private employers do not have to give Miranda warnings, and both private and public employers may interview employees in non-custodial settings without giving Miranda warnings.*
   C. *Incorrect: Both of the above options are incorrect.*
   D. *Correct: If no state action is involved, a private employer can interview an employee without the presence of his attorney. Miranda warnings are only required after a person has been taken into custody or otherwise deprived of his freedom of action in any significant way by law enforcement. They also apply to questioning involving government personnel or employers.*

2. Under which cause of action can an investigator be held liable for a TRUE statement made about a suspect?
   A. Defamation
   B. Public disclosure of private facts
   C. Both of the above
   D. None of the above—investigators can never be held liable for true statements

   A. *Incorrect: Defamation applies only to false statements.*
   B. *Correct: A cause of action for public disclosure of private facts occurs when: (1) an employer makes public statements about an employee's private life; (2) the information is not of public concern; and (3) the disclosure of the information would be highly offensive to a reasonable person. This cause of action can arise even if the statements are true. The key is that the information is private in nature and that it is not a matter of public interest.*
   C. *Incorrect: An investigator cannot be held liable for a true statement under both the defamation and public disclosure of private facts causes of action.*
   D. *Incorrect: Investigators can be held liable for true statements.*

Solutions to Review Questions

3. As a result of a ruling by the National Labor Relations Board, an employer's request for confidentiality regarding an internal investigation must be accompanied by which of the following?
   A. *Miranda* warning
   B. Self-evaluation privilege
   C. Compelling need for secrecy
   D. All of the above

   A. Incorrect: Private employers do not have to give Miranda warnings, and both private and public employers may interview employees in non-custodial settings without giving Miranda warnings.

   B. Incorrect: The self-evaluation privilege is a qualified privilege that some state courts have used to protect self-investigative materials where confidentiality is essential to the purpose of the investigation and where the public policy interests in facilitating the self-investigation outweigh the needs of a third party for disclosure.

   C. Correct: In 2012, the National Labor Relations Board (NLRB) ruled that blanket confidentiality requests regarding employee complaints and internal investigations violate Section 7 of the National Labor Relations Act. In the past, it was common for employers to request confidentiality during an internal investigation; however, the NLRB has found that such requests must be accompanied by a compelling need for secrecy.

   D. Incorrect: Only one correct answer choice is available.

4. Employers are generally permitted to discipline or terminate an employee who refuses to cooperate with a reasonable request to provide information. However, employers are never permitted to terminate employees on these grounds if the employee:
   A. Has an employment contract
   B. Is employed under a collective bargaining agreement
   C. Both of the above
   D. None of the above

   A. Incorrect: If an employee has an employment contract, then the employer cannot terminate him for refusing to cooperate with a reasonable request to provide information until the employer can show good cause for termination.

   B. Incorrect: If an employee is employed under a collective bargaining agreement, then the employer cannot terminate him for refusing to cooperate with a reasonable request to provide information until the employer can show good cause for termination.

   C. Incorrect: If an employee has an employment contract or is employed under a collective bargaining agreement, then the employer cannot terminate him for refusing to cooperate with a reasonable request to provide information until the employer can show good cause for termination.

   D. Correct: If the employee has an employment contract or is employed under a collective bargaining agreement that requires the employer to have "good cause" to terminate employment, then the question will be whether the refusal to cooperate amounted to good cause for termination. If the employer can establish good cause to terminate, then the employer can terminate an employee even if he has an employment contract or a collective bargaining agreement.

Solutions to Review Questions

5. The Fifth Amendment's protections apply to:
   A. Civil offenses
   B. Criminal offenses
   C. Internal offenses
   D. All of the above

   A. Incorrect: The Fifth Amendment's protections do not apply to civil offenses. A suspect may also refuse to answer questions in a civil matter, but in this instance, his refusal can be held against him.

   B. Correct: The Fifth Amendment's protections only apply to criminal offenses. If a suspect refuses to answer questions in a criminal investigation, the refusal cannot be held against them.

   C. Incorrect: The Fifth Amendment's protections do not apply to internal offenses.

   D. Incorrect: The Fifth Amendment's protections do apply to one of the above options.

6. A suspect's right to leave a non-custodial interview or interrogation by law enforcement is provided by the:
   A. Fourth Amendment
   B. Fifth Amendment
   C. Sixth Amendment
   D. None of the above

   A. Correct: The Fourth Amendment's prohibition against unreasonable seizures limits the right of government officers and representatives to arrest or otherwise restrain an individual's freedom of movement. This includes law enforcement's right to detain a person for interview or interrogation if the person is not under arrest.

   B. Incorrect: The Fifth Amendment provides for a suspect's right against self-incrimination.

   C. Incorrect: The Sixth Amendment provides for a suspect's right to counsel.

   D. Incorrect: One of the given answer choices is correct.

7. For an individual to recover civil damages for intentional infliction of emotional distress, it must be proven that:
   A. A defendant's conduct must have been extreme and outrageous
   B. The defendant acted with the intent of causing severe emotional distress or with reckless disregard of whether his actions would cause severe emotional distress
   C. The plaintiff suffered severe distress
   D. All of the above

- A. *Incorrect: To recover civil damages for intentional infliction of emotional distress, it must be proven that the defendant's conduct was extreme and outrageous. However, according to the text, there is a better answer to this question.*
- B. *Incorrect: To recover civil damages, it has to be proven that the defendant acted with the intent of causing severe emotional distress. The reader should refer back to the section on Judicial Privilege to determine all of the elements that must be proven to recover civil damages.*
- C. *Incorrect: To recover civil damages, it will also need to be proven that the plaintiff suffered severe distress; however, there is a better answer to this question.*
- D. *Correct: Most jurisdictions recognize a right to recover civil damages for intentional infliction of emotional distress. This tort has three basic elements:*
  - *The defendant's conduct must have been extreme and outrageous.*
  - *The defendant must have acted with the intent of causing severe emotional distress, or with reckless disregard of whether his actions would cause severe emotional distress.*
  - *The plaintiff must have suffered severe distress.*

8. The attorney-client privilege can be applied to all of the following EXCEPT:
   A. Consulting experts
   B. Testifying experts
   C. Investigators working under the attorney's supervision
   D. Paralegals working under the attorney's supervision

   - A. *Incorrect: The attorney-client privilege also applies to consulting experts, outsiders who are retained to assist the lawyer in providing legal services or advice to the client.*
   - B. *Correct: The privilege does not apply to testifying experts.*
   - C. *Incorrect: The attorney-client privilege can be applied to secretaries, paralegals, law clerks, and investigators if the person is being used to facilitate legal advice and working directly under the lawyer's supervision.*
   - D. *Incorrect: The attorney-client privilege can be applied to secretaries, paralegals, law clerks, and investigators if the person is being used to facilitate legal advice and working directly under the lawyer's supervision.*

9. There is no single test for deciding whose communications with a corporation's lawyer will constitute privileged client communications. The two predominant tests that have been used for this end are the control group test and which of the following?
   A. The subject matter test
   B. The truthfulness test
   C. The polygraph test
   D. None of the above

Solutions to Review Questions

A. *Correct: There is no single test for deciding whose communications with a corporation's lawyers will constitute privileged client communications. The two predominant tests that have been used for this end are the control group test and the subject matter test. The subject matter test extends the privilege to other employees when the employee's communication is made at the direction of his superiors and when the subject matter of the communication concerns the employee's performance of his duties.*
B. *Incorrect: A truthfulness test is sometimes employed by an interviewer to test the truthfulness of an interview subject's responses.*
C. *Incorrect: A polygraph test is a controversial method of testing the veracity of a subject's statements by measuring physiological responses.*
D. *Incorrect: A correct answer choice is available.*

10. According to the text, which of the following is true of the attorney work product doctrine?
    A. Only protects materials that are prepared in anticipation of litigation
    B. Only protects the confidentiality of documents that are prepared by an attorney
    C. Only protects exhibits, documentary evidence, and witnesses' statements
    D. None of the above

    A. *Correct: The attorney work product doctrine is a discovery rule that prevents compelled disclosure of materials that have been collected, arranged, or prepared in anticipation of litigation.*
    B. *Incorrect: The attorney work product doctrine extends not only to information and documents prepared by a party or the party's attorneys, but also to materials prepared by consultants and experts who were hired by the attorney.*
    C. *Incorrect: Factual work product, rather than attorney work product, refers to exhibits, documentary and real evidence, witnesses' written or recorded statements, and other purely factual materials that were collected and organized in anticipation of litigation.*
    D. *Incorrect: One of the above is true of the attorney work product doctrine.*

11. Which of the following is NOT true of the self-evaluation privilege?
    A. Does not require the participation of a lawyer in the investigation
    B. Potentially protects more than just lawyer-client communications
    C. Only preserves the confidentiality of an internal investigation conducted in anticipation of litigation
    D. Protects self-investigative materials where confidentiality is essential to the purpose of the investigation

A. *Incorrect: The self-evaluation privilege differs from the attorney-client privilege in that it does not require the participation of a lawyer in the investigation.*

B. *Incorrect: The self-evaluation privilege potentially protects more than just lawyer-client communications.*

C. *Correct: The self-evaluation privilege differs from the work product doctrine in that it may apply even in the absence of anticipated litigation.*

D. *Incorrect: The self-evaluation privilege is a qualified privilege which the courts in some states have used to protect self-investigative materials where confidentiality is essential to the purpose of the investigation and where the public policy interest in facilitating the self-investigation outweighs the needs of a third party for disclosure.*

12. Since confidentiality is the cornerstone of any claim of privilege, investigators must identify and treat any interview record as confidential. Which of the following is a step investigators can take to try to ensure a document's confidentiality?
    A. Mark all pages of any contemporaneous notes and subsequent reports as "confidential"
    B. Write on the cover page and the top margin of each following page that its distribution is limited to specific individuals and that any other distribution or disclosure is unauthorized and prohibited
    C. Ensure that restricted distribution is observed
    D. All of the above

A. *Incorrect: To ensure a document's confidentiality, the investigator should mark all pages of any contemporaneous notes and subsequent reports as "confidential." However, according to the text, there is a better answer to this question.*

B. *Incorrect: Investigators should also write on the cover page and the top margin of each following page that its distribution is limited to specific individuals and that any other distribution or disclosure is unauthorized and prohibited. The reader should refer back to the section on Identify and Treat the Record as Confidential to determine what other steps might need to be taken to ensure a document's confidentiality.*

C. *Incorrect: No matter how the record is marked, it will lose its confidentiality if it is not handled as a confidential document. Those in the control group must ensure that the restricted distribution is observed. However, there is a better answer to this question.*

D. *Correct: Since confidentiality is the cornerstone of any claim of privilege, investigators must identify and treat any interview record as confidential. All pages of any contemporaneous notes and subsequent reports must be prominently marked as "confidential." The confidentiality of the document can be further underscored by writing on the cover page and the top margin of each following page that its distribution is limited to specific individuals and that any other distribution or disclosure is unauthorized and prohibited. The individuals to whom distribution is authorized should be strictly limited to the company's directors or managing officers who have a need to know the information and who have authority to direct an action by the company in response to the information. These are the individuals who are most likely to be regarded as the company's alter ego for purposes of the privilege.*

Solutions to Review Questions

VII. Writing Reports

1. What information should be included in an investigation report?
   A. All relevant facts
   B. Only those facts that support the fraud theory
   C. Only those facts that show culpability
   D. Only those facts that are not confidential

   A. Correct: Everything relevant should be included regardless of which side it favors or what it proves or disproves. At the outset of an internal fraud investigation, the examiner should carefully determine what information would be needed to prove the case, and attempt to include only this information.
   B. Incorrect: All facts should be reported without bias, not only those facts that support the fraud theory.
   C. Incorrect: All facts should be reported without bias, not those only facts that show culpability.
   D. Incorrect: All facts should be reported without bias. The investigator should not promise confidentiality of the interview to the respondent.

2. Green, an internal investigator, has prepared a report for his supervisor. The report summarizes the results of an internal investigation Green conducted. The report contains several facts that are harmful to the reputation of Blue, an employee. Some of the facts turn out to be false. Blue sues the company for libel. In order to successfully defend itself, the company will have to prove the following:
   I. The report was made in good faith.
   II. Green had a legitimate interest in the subject of the report.
   III. Green was working under the direct supervision of an attorney.
   IV. The report was only communicated to individuals with legitimate interests in the subject of the report.

   A. I
   B. I and IV
   C. I and III
   D. I, II, and IV

   A. Incorrect: To protect itself from a libel action, the company must show that the report or statement was made in good faith; however, there are additional steps that have to be taken by a company to protect itself from a libel action.
   B. Incorrect: Showing that a report or statement was made in good faith and that the internal investigator had a legitimate interest in the subject of the report are two points that must be proven for the internal investigator to

have common interest privilege. However, there is one other point that must be proven for the internal investigator to have common interest privilege.

C. *Incorrect: The common interest privilege is available to anyone with a legitimate interest in the investigation. It is not related to the attorney-client privilege or the work-product doctrine; therefore, it is not necessary that an attorney be involved at all.*

D. *Correct: Aside from the truth, the most important defense to a libel action for internal investigators is the common interest privilege. Under the common interest privilege, if a person makes a statement (1) in good faith; (2) regarding a subject in which the person making the statement has a legitimate interest or duty; (3) to another person with a corresponding interest or duty, then that statement is exempt from a libel claim. This privilege extends to communications (reports, oral statements, etc.) about internal investigations among individuals with a legitimate interest in the investigation. Statements made in good faith among these interested people are privileged from libel suits. Keep in mind, however, that malice defeats the privilege. If the person who made the communication knew that it was false or had a reckless disregard for whether it was true, then this statement is not privileged, meaning that the speaker can potentially be held liable.*

3. A good written report should only convey:
   A. Subjective facts
   B. Objective facts
   C. Editorial judgments
   D. All of the above

   A. *Incorrect: It is inappropriate to editorialize or give judgments in a report.*
   B. *Correct: Reports should only convey objective facts. If complex or technical terms must be used, the investigator should make sure they are used in their proper contexts, and, where necessary, the meaning of the complex terms should be explained.*
   C. *Incorrect: When writing an investigation report, it is inappropriate to editorialize or give judgments.*
   D. *Incorrect: Both subjective and objective facts will not be found in a good written report.*

4. According to the text, an attorney's internal report to controlling management may NOT be protected by the attorney-client privilege if the courts find that:
   A. The attorney acted as an investigator, and the report's purpose was therefore to analyze and advise the company about factual circumstances
   B. The report's purpose was to provide business advice
   C. The report's purpose was to provide legal advice
   D. Both A and B

Solutions to Review Questions

    A. *Incorrect: If the courts find that an attorney acted as an investigator and that the report's purpose was to analyze and advise the company about factual circumstances, then the information is no longer privileged. However, this is not the only correct answer to this question.*

    B. *Incorrect: If the courts find that the report's purpose was to provide business advice, then the information will no longer be privileged. However, this is not the only correct answer to this question.*

    C. *Incorrect: If it is found that the investigator's report was to provide legal advice, then this information will remain privileged.*

    D. *Correct: An attorney's internal report to controlling management might not be privileged if a court finds that the attorney acted as an investigator, and that the report's purpose was therefore to analyze and advise the company about factual circumstances or to provide business advice.*

5. A characteristic of a good report is:
   A. Accuracy
   B. Clarity
   C. Impartiality and relevance
   D. Timeliness
   E. All of the above

    A. *Incorrect: Accuracy is one of the characteristics of a good report. Each contact an investigator makes during the course of an internal investigation should be recorded in a timely basis in a memorandum of interview. The investigator should include all facts of possible relevance. However, according to the text, there is a better answer to this question.*

    B. *Incorrect: Clarity is another characteristic of a good report. Investigative reports on internal investigations should convey pertinent information in the clearest possible language. However, there is a better answer to this question.*

    C. *Incorrect: All good reports should show impartiality and relevance. All facts should be reported without bias. Everything relevant should be included regardless of which side it favors or what it proves or disproves. The reader should refer back to the section on Characteristics of a Good Report to determine what else should be included in a report to make it a good report.*

    D. *Incorrect: Timeliness is also a characteristic of a good report. Timeliness of reports is extremely important because it tends to enhance the accuracy of witness testimony. However, this is not the only characteristic of a good report.*

    E. *Correct: The text discusses four characteristics of a good report. They are: accuracy, clarity, impartiality and relevance, and timeliness.*

Solutions to Review Questions

VIII. Discharging Employees

1. Which of the following statements is true?
   A. Term employees operate under the at-will doctrine.
   B. Employment contracts can be formed by the language in an employee handbook.
   C. There is no such thing as an implied contract.
   D. All of the above are true.

   A. Incorrect: Employees who work under a contract are said to be term employees (because they have agreed under the provisions of the contract to work for a specified term). Term employees do not operate under the at-will doctrine; the employer does not have the right to terminate their employment at its discretion and without cause. The employer's right to fire an employee will be governed by the provisions of the employment contract. In most cases, this means that the employer can only fire the employee for good cause.

   B. Correct: Implied contracts can be formed by the language in an employee handbook, particularly if the handbook describes the procedures that will be followed when discharging employees. For instance, many handbooks specify what kind of conduct is subject to discipline, as well as the range of discipline that is permitted for a particular kind of offense. In many cases, employee handbooks also use some form of "good cause" language in describing why employees might be disciplined or fired. They might also dictate the procedural steps to be followed before specific kinds of disciplinary action can be taken—for example, written notice to the employee of the proposed action or the employee's opportunity to refute the alleged misconduct. If not worded properly, these handbooks might amount to an implied contract in which the employer promises not to fire its employees except for good cause.

   C. Incorrect: Employment contracts can be express or implied. Just because the company has not signed a written, formalized contract with an employee, this does not mean that there is no employment contract. Collective bargaining agreements, employee handbooks, and even oral promises can establish an employment contract and limit the company's ability to discipline or fire an employee.

   D. Incorrect: Only one of the above options is true.

2. Which of the following can limit a company's ability to discipline or fire an employee?
   I. The terms of a collective bargaining agreement
   II. An informal promise to the employee of continued employment as long as he "does a good job"
   III. A description of the company's disciplinary procedures contained in an employee handbook

   A. I
   B. I and II
   C. I and III
   D. I, II, and III

Solutions to Review Questions

- A. *Incorrect: The terms of a collective bargaining agreement can limit a company's ability to discipline or fire an employee; however, according to the text, there is a better answer to this question.*
- B. *Incorrect: The terms of a collective bargaining agreement and an informal promise to the employee of continued employment as long as he "does a good job" both limit a company's ability to discipline or fire an employee. However, the reader should refer back to the section on Types of Contracts to determine all of the contracts that can limit a company's ability to discipline or fire an employee.*
- C. *Incorrect: The terms of a collective bargaining agreement and a description of the company's disciplinary procedures contained in an employee handbook both limit a company's ability to discipline or fire an employee. However, there is a better answer to this question.*
- D. *Correct: Employment contracts can be express or implied. Just because the company has not signed a written, formalized contract with an employee does not mean that there is no employment contract. Collective bargaining agreements, employee handbooks, and even oral promises can establish an employment contract and limit the company's ability to discipline or fire an employee. Collective bargaining agreements are a common example of an express contract that limits the employer's ability to fire an employee. These agreements frequently specify the misconduct for which an employee may be fired, or at the very least require "good cause." They also usually specify procedures that must be followed before the termination. There are also a number of cases in which courts have enforced an implied contract between an employee and his company based on an informal promise of continued employment by someone in authority. For example, some courts have held that when a manager makes a statement like "as long as you do a job, you're not going to get fired," this amounts to a promise that the employee will not be fired without good cause, thus creating an implied (or informal) contract. Implied contracts can also be formed by the language in an employee handbook, particularly if the handbook describes the procedures that will be followed when discharging employees.*

3. An employment contract in which the terms of employment are set forth in writing and the document is signed by each party is known as an:
   A. Express contract
   B. Implied contract
   C. Informal contract
   D. None of the above

   - A. *Correct: The most obvious form of employment contract is one in which the terms of employment are set forth in writing and the document is signed by each party; this type of contract is known as an express contract.*
   - B. *Incorrect: An implied contract arises based on the conduct of the parties, even though there is no formal written or oral agreement.*
   - C. *Incorrect: An informal contract is often used to refer to an implied or oral contract, not a written contract.*
   - D. *Incorrect: One of the above options is an employment contract in which the terms of employment are set forth in writing and the document is signed by each party.*

Solutions to Review Questions

4. In addition to suits for wrongful termination and breach of contract, an employee who has been discharged may also claim that the termination violated various statutory rights and interests. Which of the following could be considered a statutory violation?
   A. The investigative methods used by the company
   B. Procedures used that led to termination
   C. The investigation process violated the terms of the collective bargaining agreement
   D. All of the above

   A. *Incorrect: One potential statutory violation is the investigative methods used by the company. For example, the employer may be in violation of the Fair Credit Reporting Act if it obtained any credit, financial, or character information about the employee without obtaining prior written authorization from the employee. However, according to the text, there is a better answer to this question.*
   B. *Incorrect: If the employer is a public agency or state actor, the employee could complain in a civil rights suit that the investigative procedures leading to his firing violated his due process rights. The reader should refer back to the section on Statutory Violations to determine what other statutes could be used to sue for wrongful termination.*
   C. *Incorrect: Within the jurisdiction of the National Labor Relations Board, the employee could complain that the investigative process violated the terms of a collective bargaining agreement or otherwise was an unfair labor practice. However, there is a better answer to this question.*
   D. *Correct: Employees may find statutory protection based on the investigative methods used by the company; the procedures that lead to termination; and the investigation process, which may have violated the terms of the collective bargaining agreement.*

5. In general, an employee's claim of malicious prosecution must establish that the company instigated a criminal proceeding against the employee along with which of the following elements?
   A. The criminal proceeding was terminated in favor of the employee
   B. There was no probable cause for the action
   C. The company acted with malice
   D. All of the above

   A. *Incorrect: While a claim of malicious prosecution must establish that the criminal proceeding was terminated in favor of the employee, a better answer choice is available.*
   B. *Incorrect: While a claim of malicious prosecution must establish that there was no probable cause for the action, a better answer choice is available.*
   C. *Incorrect: While a claim of malicious prosecution must establish that the company acted with malice, a better answer choice is available.*
   D. *Correct: The elements of the cause of action for malicious prosecution may vary somewhat among jurisdictions, but in general, the employee must establish the following elements:*
      - *The company instigated a criminal proceeding against the employee.*

Solutions to Review Questions

- *The criminal proceeding was terminated in favor of the employee (i.e., the charges were dismissed or the employee was acquitted).*
- *There was no probable cause for the action, meaning that the company knew the action was groundless or had no reasonable basis to believe that the employee was guilty.*
- *The company acted with malice, meaning that the company used the prosecution for the purpose of gaining a private advantage (e.g., to collect a debt, to embarrass the employee, etc.) rather than the purpose of bringing a guilty person to justice.*

6. According to the text, which of the following is NOT true of statutory criminal restitutions?
   A. These orders only apply while the defendant is on probation.
   B. These orders are in addition to any other penalties provided by law for the defendant's crimes.
   C. These orders direct the return of the victim's property or its monetary equivalent if the property cannot be returned.
   D. None of the above are false statements.

   A. *Correct: Unlike restitution that is ordered as a condition of probation, a criminal restitution order can be enforced against the defendant even after his discharge from probation or his release from prison.*
   B. *Incorrect: In addition to restitution as a condition of probation, federal law and an increasing number of state statutes direct or permit judges to order convicted defendants to make restitution to the victims of their crimes as part of their punishment after conviction. These restitution orders are in addition to any other penalties provided by law for the defendant's crimes.*
   C. *Incorrect: Typically, statutory criminal restitution orders direct the return of the victim's property or its monetary equivalent if the property cannot be returned. Some also direct the return of the fruits of the crime or the victim's actual out-of-pocket expense caused by the crime.*
   D. *Incorrect: One of the above options is not true of statutory criminal restitutions.*

XIII. SOLUTIONS TO PRACTICAL PROBLEMS

Practical Problem 1

1. Based on the facts that have been presented, do you believe there is sufficient predication to begin an internal investigation?

   Based on the facts presented, it appears that there is sufficient predication to begin an investigation. Predication *is the totality of circumstances that would lead a reasonable, professionally trained, and prudent individual to believe a fraud has occurred, is occurring, or will occur. Internal fraud investigations should not be conducted without proper predication.*

   In this case, there is certainly reason to believe a fraud has occurred and perhaps is still occurring. The company has detected a pattern of disbursements that occur once a month in consistent amounts just below the company's self-imposed review limit to a vendor about whom the owner of the company knows nothing. The invoices provide no description of what was purchased. The fact that the invoices are consecutively numbered also provides reason to suspect fraud, since the company has only paid one invoice a month for fifteen months. A legitimate vendor would have certainly sent out invoices to customers other than Devoslich. Finally, there is some evidence that Frasier's signature may have been forged on six of the invoices. All of these facts would certainly lead a reasonable person to suspect fraud. Thus, there is sufficient predication to begin an investigation.

2. Briefly explain the Fraud Examination Methodology and propose a hypothesis upon which you would begin the investigation.

   Fraud Examination Methodology establishes a uniform legal process for resolving fraud allegations on a timely basis. Assuming there is sufficient predication to conduct a fraud examination, specific examination steps are usually employed in an orderly manner. The fraud examination moves from the general to the specific, gradually zeroing in on the perpetrator through a process of careful acquisition and analysis of evidence. At each step of the examination, the evidence that has been obtained is assessed and compared to the overriding investigative theory. Where necessary, that theory is refined to direct the investigation at the most logical source of the fraud.

   To prove a fraud without complete evidence, the examiner must make certain assumptions. This is known as the fraud theory approach. Prior to the commencement of an interview or other overt investigation, the investigation team analyzes the available data to determine what facts are known. Based on these facts, investigators create a hypothesis of what might have happened. The hypothesis is invariably a "worst case" scenario; that is, after analyzing all the data, the investigator would determine the fraud(s) involved. The hypothesis is then tested to determine whether it is provable or not. As new evidence is gathered, the hypothesis is continuously refined and modified to conform to the known facts.

Solutions to Practical Problems

In this case, a logical hypothesis based on the known facts would be that Taylor is submitting fraudulent invoices to the company in the name of Quantic Components. It is not clear whether there are accomplices involved at this point; however, this cannot be ruled out.

Practical Problem 2

1. Where can Frost and Crouch find Quantic's business filings, and what information will be contained in those filings?

   In order to open a bank account or conduct business in a name other than one's own, the law requires the filing of documents showing ownership of that name. Whether Quantic is a legitimate company or a shell consisting of nothing more than a bank account, the company has probably filed a registration with some government office. Frost and Crouch will probably either find Quantic's business filings in the office of the secretary of state or at the county level.

   Corporations must be registered with the secretary of state (or state corporation bureau or corporate registry office) in the state in which the company does business. These corporate records will include: corporate name, ownership information, stock value, initial shareholders, directors and officers, registered agent, principal office, date of incorporation, and the corporation's standing and status.

   Some states also require foreign corporations (corporations which were incorporated in another state) to be registered with the state corporation office if the foreign corporation transacts business in that state. This application is also filed with the secretary of state and must include the date of incorporation, the principal office, the address of the registered agent, and the names of the officers and directors.

   Non-corporate business entities are generally required to make DBA (Doing Business As) filings in order to conduct business or to open a bank account. DBA information for sole proprietorships (individuals) or partnerships is typically filed at the county level, although some states require filing at the state level as well. Most states also require limited partnerships, trusts, and joint ventures to file DBA information at the state or county level. Very similar to corporate filings with the secretary of state, these records will allow investigators to identify the type of business entity, the date the business was started, and the owners or principals of the business.

   Corporate registrations and DBAs are public records that can easily be obtained by investigators and may help them identify the person or persons behind false billing schemes. However, in embezzlement schemes, the perpetrator will frequently use a false name when forming a shell company so that the fictitious business cannot be traced back to him. Therefore, even if Taylor is the person behind Quantic, the company's business filings might not show it.

2. Under what circumstances can the company perform a criminal background check on Taylor?

   If the investigators obtain the information directly from the source (i.e., the courthouse), then there is no restriction. However, if the company obtains the information from a third party, the Fair Credit Reporting Act (FCRA) may come into play.

Solutions to Practical Problems

Under ordinary circumstances, obtaining information from a third party requires notice to and the consent of the individual. However, there is an exception for workplace misconduct. An employer who uses a third party to conduct a workplace investigation no longer has to obtain the prior consent of an employee if the investigation involves suspected:

- *Misconduct*
- *Violation of law or regulations*
- *Violation of any pre-existing policy of the employer*

In order to qualify for this exception, the report from the third party must not be communicated to anyone other than the employer, an agent of the employer, or the government.

However, if "adverse action" is taken against the employee based on the results of the investigation, the FCRA still requires the employer to provide the employee with a summary of the report. "Adverse action" is broadly defined as any employment decision that adversely affects the employee. The summary must "contain the nature and substance of the communication upon which the adverse action is based." It does not, however, have to identify the individuals interviewed or the sources of the information.

Practical Problem 3

1. If Crouch decides to conduct a search, what is the standard with which the company must comply to make sure the search is legal? Does the company need a warrant?

The standard for the search will depend on the status of the company. If Devoslich is a public employer or state actor, it will have to comply with Fourth Amendment search standards. If, on the other hand, Devoslich is a private employer, then the U.S. Constitution is not implicated, and the only question will be whether the search violates Taylor's common law privacy interests.

In this case, Devoslich appears to be a private employer. The problem clearly states that Devoslich is a privately-owned company. In certain circumstances, private companies can still be state actors, such as when the company conducts a search at the direction of government authorities, or when the company conducts an investigation that is required by state or federal law. The key is that the private employer must be essentially acting as the government's agent in conducting the investigation. That does not appear to be the case here. While the company has some ties to the federal government in that it supplies navigational systems to the Coast Guard, there is no indication that the company is required by federal law to investigate the suspected wrongdoing, or that the company is in any way acting on behalf of the government. All of the facts presented show that the decision to investigate was made by company officials, and there is no indication that their actions were conducted on behalf of the state in any way. Thus, Devoslich is not a state actor.

Since Devoslich is not a public employer, its search will not be subject to Fourth Amendment standards. Therefore, there will be no requirement to obtain a warrant. Instead, the appropriate standard is to be determined by the common law standard for invasion of privacy. This can vary among jurisdictions, but in general, a common law invasion of privacy occurs when an employer (1) makes an intentional intrusion (2) into an area where an employee has a reasonable expectation of privacy and (3) the intrusion would be highly offensive or objectionable to a reasonable person.

Therefore, the first question to be asked is whether Taylor has a reasonable expectation of privacy in any of the contents of his office, or of his office itself. If so, then the search can only be conducted if it would not be highly offensive to a reasonable person.

An employer can reduce or eliminate its employees' privacy expectations in the workplace by adopting a search policy that puts employees on notice that their workspaces are subject to search at the company's discretion. However, Devoslich has no such policy. Therefore, the appropriateness of the search will have to be determined as to each area or item that Frost and Crouch want to search.

Solutions to Practical Problems

It should also be noted that some state constitutions may give employees more protection than that afforded by the U.S. Constitution. Devoslich's investigators should consult with their own state's constitutional standards before searching Taylor's office.

2. Are Frost and Crouch entitled to search the following areas: the office, the desk, the file cabinet, the trash can, and the briefcase? Explain your answers.

   Frost and Crouch must conduct their search in accordance with common law invasion of privacy standards. The first question to be asked under this standard is whether there is a reasonable expectation of privacy in the area to be searched. If not, then the investigators are free to search the area. If there is a reasonable expectation of privacy, a search can still be conducted as long as it is reasonable and would not be offensive to an ordinary person.

   ### The Office
   Taylor probably does not have a reasonable expectation of privacy in his office as a whole. The key to this analysis is whether Taylor has exclusive control of the office. In this case, Taylor's office is located in a publicly accessible area, and it is frequently unlocked during the day, even when Taylor is not present. We know that other members of the purchasing department frequently enter the office to retrieve files, and Taylor does not object to this behavior.

   It is true that Taylor locks the office at night, and given the fact that the search is planned for after hours, one might suppose that this heightens the expectation of privacy. However, Taylor is at least aware that Frost has a copy of the key to the office. He is therefore aware that others are able to enter the office after hours. Furthermore, the fact that cleaning personnel enter the office after hours demonstrates that others do, in fact, have access to the office even after Taylor has locked it. All of these facts tend to indicate that Taylor does not have a reasonable expectation of privacy in the office. Therefore, Frost and Crouch would be permitted to enter the office to conduct a search.

   ### The Desk
   The question of whether Taylor has a reasonable expectation of privacy in his desk is more complicated. First, it is obvious that there is no reasonable expectation of privacy in anything that is left in the open on top of Taylor's desk. Since there is no reasonable privacy expectation in the office as a whole, it follows that anything that is displayed in plain view within the office would not enjoy a privacy expectation.

   The real question is whether the contents of Taylor's desk drawers may be searched. We know that Taylor is the only person who ever uses the desk and that he keeps the "security drawer" locked. These facts would bolster a claim by Taylor that he had a reasonable expectation of privacy in the contents of the desk.

   On the other hand, the hypothetical tells us that the desk is the property of the company, not Taylor. In addition, we know that others regularly enter the office, sometimes when Taylor is not present. Since four of the drawers have no locks, it is reasonable to assume that others could access their contents, which tends to diminish the expectation of privacy. There is a stronger case to be made for Taylor's privacy interest in the "security drawer" since this is kept locked. However, Taylor is aware that Frasier keeps a key to that drawer, even though we are not told if Frasier ever opens the drawer.

The question of whether Taylor has a reasonable expectation of privacy in the contents of the desk is a close one, and it could depend on how the courts in a particular jurisdiction have interpreted the common law standard for invasion of privacy. Frost and Crouch should consult with McCant, the general counsel, about their state's law before searching the desk.

If it is found that Taylor has a reasonable expectation of privacy in the contents of the desk, a search can still be conducted as long as it is done in such a way that it would not be offensive to a reasonable person.

The File Cabinet

Taylor probably could not reasonably expect the contents of the file cabinet to be private. According to the facts, other employees frequently enter Taylor's office and retrieve files from the cabinet. In addition, there is no lock on the cabinet, and Taylor knows that other people frequently open it to retrieve files. These facts all tend to show that the file cabinet is not private. Therefore, Frost and Crouch are entitled to search the file cabinet.

The Trash

Similarly, Taylor probably has no legitimate privacy expectation in his office trash can. First, we know that others have access to his office. Assuming the trash can is in an open area, anybody who enters the office would have access to the trash. Thus, it would not be under Taylor's exclusive control. Furthermore, we know that office cleaning personnel empty the trash, and that they are accompanied by security personnel when they do so. These facts demonstrate that others have access to the trash; thus, it is unlikely that Taylor could make a reasonable claim that he thought the trash was under his exclusive control or that he considered it to be private.

The Briefcase

Taylor probably does have a reasonable expectation of privacy in his briefcase. The facts show that he purchased the briefcase and that he is the only one who knows the combination to the lock. This would tend to show that he has exclusive control over it.

The company could make an argument that the briefcase was used for work purposes and that it was left on work premises; therefore, Taylor could not reasonably expect it to be private. However, Taylor probably has the better argument here; the briefcase is his property, and by keeping the combination a secret, he has demonstrated that he considers the contents to be private. This is probably a reasonable assumption on his part.

A search of the briefcase can only be conducted if it would not be highly offensive to a reasonable person. Frost and Crouch probably will not be able to meet this standard if they search the briefcase. They are searching the office at *night, out of Taylor's presence, and without notifying him. It is reasonable to believe that he would be highly offended if they broke into his briefcase to search its contents.*

Practical Problem 4

1. Whom do you agree with and why?

Frost is correct in this regard. If the company records and monitors all of Taylor's phone calls, this will probably be found to violate the Electronic Communications Privacy Act of 1986 (ECPA). This statute applies to public and private employers; thus Devoslich is subject to its provisions.

In general, the ECPA makes it a federal crime for an individual to intentionally or willfully intercept, access, disclose, or use another person's electronic communication. This includes telephone conversations. There are, however, three statutory exceptions that permit employers to lawfully monitor phone calls in certain situations. They are: the provider exception, the consent exception, and the ordinary course of business exception.

The provider exception allows telephone company employees to intercept electronic communications in the normal course of business—for instance, to run quality control checks. This would not apply to Devoslich's monitoring of Taylor's phone calls.

Under the consent exception, the company would be able to monitor Taylor's calls if Taylor had given prior consent to the interception. The employee's consent must be express; it cannot be implied or inferred from the circumstances. There is nothing here to indicate that Taylor has consented to this type of monitoring. Therefore, the consent exception will not apply.

Under the ordinary course of business exception, employers are permitted to monitor their employees' phone calls as long as the monitoring is done for a legitimate business purpose. There is some authority which says that preventing business losses or employee misconduct qualifies as a legitimate business purpose. Therefore, limited monitoring might be permissible if it is legitimately related to the company's efforts to minimize fraud losses or investigate internal misconduct.

However, blanket monitoring of the type Crouch suggests will probably be found to violate the Act. Even where there is a legitimate business purpose for monitoring employee phone calls, the method used to intercept and monitor the calls must not be any more intrusive than is necessary to achieve the employer's purpose. For instance, it would be impermissible to listen to personal calls that are not related to the investigation. Tape recording and listening to all calls would probably be regarded as overly broad.

In addition to the ECPA, the company's efforts to monitor Taylor's phone calls could also give rise to an invasion of privacy claim. The company would not be permitted to monitor calls in which Taylor had a reasonable expectation of privacy if the monitoring was done in such a way as to be highly offensive to a reasonable person.

Solutions to Practical Problems

Practical Problem 5

1. Based on these facts, do you think the company could be held liable for false imprisonment? Why or why not?

From the facts that are presented, it is possible that the company could be liable for false imprisonment. False imprisonment is the restraint by one person of the physical liberty of another without consent or legal justification. A claim of false imprisonment arises if an employee is detained against his will for any appreciable time, however short, in any way. Actual force is not required; threat or other words, gestures, or acts that create an apprehension of force may suffice.

Potential liability for false imprisonment arises any time the employee is involuntarily detained for an interview, interrogation, or to conduct a search. Generally, an employer may question an employee at work about a violation of company policy without incurring liability as long as the employee submits to the questioning voluntarily; that is, not as a result of threats or force. However, the actual length, nature, and manner of the interview may determine whether liability arises.

To determine if there has been a false imprisonment, investigators should consider factors such as whether the employee's presence or continued presence was required by force or threats of force, or whether investigators refused to allow the employee to leave the room, such as by locking the door.

In this case, there are a couple of factors that could support a claim for false imprisonment. First, the three interviewers locked the door during the interview, an act that could easily create the impression in Taylor's mind that he was not permitted to leave. In addition, all three interviewers placed themselves between Taylor and the door, another indicator that Taylor was being detained. In an interview situation, the door to the interview room should never be locked, and there should never be a physical barrier between the subject and the exit. Finally, when Taylor attempted to leave the room, Frost told him to remain in the room. This is probably not illegal, as long as Taylor was not threatened or forced to remain in the room. On the other hand, combined with the other facts, this could create the appearance that Taylor was being detained against his will.

None of these factors conclusively proves that there was a false imprisonment, but they certainly could support such a claim. Therefore, investigators should be careful not to create an atmosphere in which the subject has reason to believe he is not free to leave the interview.

2. Did Taylor have a right to have an attorney present at the interview? Did Frost respond properly to Taylor's request? Explain your answers.

Taylor did not have a right to have an attorney present at the interview. The right to counsel is provided by the Sixth Amendment to the U.S. Constitution. Constitutional protections only apply where state action is involved. Since Devoslich is a private company, its employees do not enjoy the constitutional right to counsel in connection with an internal investigation. (The employee always has the right to consult an attorney, but there is typically no legal obligation to consult the employee's lawyer prior to the interview or to allow the employee's lawyer to sit in during an interview.)

Furthermore, even if this investigation had been conducted at a government agency, where there was clearly state action, it is unlikely that Taylor would have had the right to have an attorney present. The Sixth Amendment right to counsel only applies at what the courts call crucial *stages in the criminal proceeding. Investigative questioning is not generally considered such a* crucial *stage. Therefore, it is clear that Taylor was not entitled to have an attorney present during the interview.*

Despite this fact, Frost's response was still inappropriate. When Taylor asked to speak to an attorney, Frost replied "Don't worry, that's why we've got the general counsel here." It is inappropriate for investigators to give advice to an employee as to whether he needs an attorney; that is the employee's choice and the investigator should not risk misleading the employee about either his rights or his needs. In addition, as general counsel, McCant serves as the legal representative of Devoslich, not Taylor. Her exclusive purpose is to represent the company's interests and to advise the company. Frost's statement, "that's why we've got the general counsel here," implied that McCant may have been representing Taylor's interests, something that is clearly false.

3. Should the interviewers have given Taylor a *Miranda* warning? Why or why not?

The interviewers were not required to give Taylor a Miranda *warning prior to questioning him.* Miranda *warnings are only required after a person has been taken into custody or otherwise deprived of his freedom or action in any significant way by law enforcement. They also apply to questioning involving government personnel or employers. Private employers do not have to give* Miranda *warnings, and both private and public employers may interview employees in non-custodial settings without giving* Miranda *warnings. Since Devoslich is a private employer, there is no* Miranda *requirement in this case.*

4. Aside from the legal considerations discussed above, what other problems do you see with the way this interview was conducted?

A couple of problems are apparent from the information provided above. First, the investigators conducted the interview in Taylor's office, while Taylor sat at his desk. It is never advisable to interview a subject in his office or at his desk.

Solutions to Practical Problems

A desk can be a physical barrier, as well as a psychological one; it creates a symbol of authority for the person seated behind it. The interviewer does not want to confer a sense of authority upon the subject.

Second, the shade on the window to Taylor's office was left open. This may or may not be a problem, depending on the circumstances. In general, it is important for an interview to be conducted in a private area where distractions are not likely to occur. Since the window shade was left open, the interview will be visible to passersby in the hallway. This diminishes the privacy of the interview and may inhibit communication. In addition, Taylor will be able to observe people passing by, which may be distracting to him. Finally, Taylor's office is presumably the place where he conducts most of his business. By conducting the interview in this location, the investigators are increasing the chances of work-related distractions.

Practical Problem 6

1. Discuss Frost's treatment of Taylor. Specifically:

    A. Was it appropriate to accuse Taylor of the crime and, if so, was the accusation made in an appropriate manner?

    During an admission-seeking interview such as this one, the interviewer must at some point make a direct accusation of the subject. Thus, it was appropriate and probably necessary for Frost to accuse Taylor of the crime.

    However, interviewers should avoid using emotive words such as steal *and* fraud *during the accusatory process. Strong words like this make it harder for the subject to admit to the wrongdoing. Frost should have phrased the accusation with softer language, such as "our investigation shows that you're responsible for the losses" or "we have established that you have been submitting false invoices."*

    B. Was it appropriate for Frost to rationalize Taylor's behavior and, if so, was this done in an appropriate manner?

    Assuming the subject does not confess to the misconduct when faced with direct accusations, it is appropriate for the interviewer to establish a morally acceptable rationalization that will allow the accused to square the misdeed with his conscience. Thus, it was appropriate for Frost to offer the rationalization. It is acceptable for the accused to explain away the moral consequences of the action by seizing on any plausible explanation other than being a "bad person."

    The key is that the rationalization may explain away the moral consequences of the misdeed, but it cannot dismiss the legal consequences of the accused's actions. Interviewers must not make any statements that would lead the accused to believe he will be excused from legal liability by cooperating. In this case, Frost's rationalization focused only on the moral aspect of Taylor's embezzlement, pointing out that he needed the money and asserting that the company had not treated Taylor well. Thus, the rationalization was offered in an appropriate manner.

    If Frost had suggested that Taylor had not meant to commit the crime, this excuse would have gone to Taylor's intent. This would have been inappropriate, since it would have had a bearing on Taylor's legal liability.

Solutions to Practical Problems

2. Now that a benchmark admission has been reached, what information should Frost and Crouch seek to obtain from Taylor in his oral confession?

Once a benchmark admission of guilt has been obtained, it is the interviewer's job to gently probe for additional details—preferably those that would be known only to the perpetrator. During the verbal confession, Frost and Crouch should focus on obtaining the following items of information:

- *That Taylor knew the conduct was wrong*
- *Facts known only to the person who committed the crime*
- *An estimate of the number of instances or amounts*
- *A motive for the offense*
- *When the misconduct began*
- *When or if the misconduct was terminated*
- *Others involved*
- *The location of any physical evidence*
- *How and where Taylor disposed of the proceeds*
- *Location of assets*
- *Specifics of each offense*

Solutions to Practical Problems

Practical Problem 7

1. Was it appropriate for Crouch to prepare the statement, or should Taylor have written it?

   It was appropriate for Crouch to prepare the statement. There is no legal requirement that a statement must be in the handwriting or wording of the declarant. In fact, it is generally not a good idea to let a confessor draft the statement. It is preferable for the investigator to prepare the statement for the confessor to sign.

2. Do you think the excuse clause in this signed statement is appropriate? Why or why not?

   This excuse clause should have been drafted more carefully. When preparing a signed statement, the confessor's moral excuse should be mentioned; however, the interviewer should make sure that the confessor's excuse does not diminish his legal responsibility for the actions. Instead of using language like "I didn't mean to do this," which implies lack of intent, the interviewer should focus on an excuse that provides only a moral explanation for the misconduct: "I wouldn't have done this if it had not been for pressing financial problems. I didn't mean to hurt anyone."

   The excuse clause in this statement implies that Taylor did not intend to commit a crime. While it does not completely eliminate Taylor's responsibility for the misdeed (he still intended to submit phony invoices and he still cashed the checks), it is not as effective as it could be. Crouch should have focused solely on Taylor's moral excuses—that he had large debts due to a gambling problem and needed the money. The excuse clause should not address Taylor's legal responsibility for the misconduct in any way.

3. List nine key pieces of information that must be included in the signed statement.

   The information to be included in the signed statement is essentially the same as that which the interviewer should obtain in an oral confession. There are, however, a few extra inclusions that should be made in a written confession. They are:
   1. *Voluntariness of the Confession: The statement should contain language expressly stating that the confession is being made voluntarily.*
   2. *Intent: The statement must include language demonstrating that the confessor knew the conduct was wrong and intended to commit the act.*
   3. *Dates of Offense: Unless the exact dates of the offense are known, the word* approximately *must precede any dates of the offense.*
   4. *Approximate Amounts of Losses: Approximate losses should be included. Unless the exact amount has been determined, care must be taken that the amounts are labeled as* approximate. *It is appropriate to include a range ("probably no less than $____ or more than $____).*
   5. *Approximate Number of Instances: Ranges are also satisfactory for the number of instances if the exact amount is not known.*

Solutions to Practical Problems

6. *Willingness to Cooperate:* It makes it easier for the confessor to sign a written statement when he perceives that the statement includes language portraying him in a more favorable light. The confessor can convert that natural tendency by emphasizing cooperation and willingness to make amends

7. *Excuse Clause:* The confessor's moral—but not legal—excuse should be included.

8. *Acknowledgement:* The statement should contain a sentence that acknowledges that the confessor has read the statement and that it is correct. Also, the confessor should initial all the pages of the statement.

9. *Truthfulness of Statement:* The written statement should state specifically that it is true. However, the language also should allow for mistakes. Typical language reads: "This statement is true and complete to the best of my current recollection."

Practical Problem 8

1. Based on this information, do you see any problems with Taylor's dismissal? Explain your answer.

   The hypothetical states that Devoslich employees are regarded as at-will. This means that either party—Taylor or the company—is free to terminate the relationship at any time, for any reason. Just as an employee has the right to leave his job whenever he wants, an employer also has a right to fire an employee for any reason or for no reason at all. Thus, it might appear that Frasier had an absolute right to fire Taylor.

   However, under some circumstances, the language in an employee handbook can create an implied contract between the company and its employees. This can happen, for instance, when the handbook describes the procedures for discharging employees. In this case, the handbook clearly specified the kind of conduct that was subject to discipline, and the procedural steps to be followed before an employee could be suspended or terminated. If these promises are found to have created a contract between the company and Taylor, then the company is liable for breach of contract. Frasier clearly did not follow the company's procedures for dealing with fraud and theft; Taylor never got a written warning or a hearing as was provided for in the handbook.

   In addition, by failing to adhere to the disciplinary procedures set forth in its employee manual, Devoslich may have opened itself up to claims of negligent discharge, wrongful termination, or unlawful discrimination.

XIV. CONDUCTING INTERNAL INVESTIGATIONS FINAL EXAMINATION

For instructions on how to take this exam online, please visit ACFE.com/OnlineCPEgrading. (Important note: due to occasional corrections or clarifications in exam questions, slight variations might exist between the questions in the online exam and the questions printed below. The online exam always provides the most current and accurate final exam questions, so the ACFE strongly recommends completing the exam online if possible.)

1. In order to solve a fraud without complete evidence, an investigator begins with an assumption, based on the known facts, of what might have occurred. Then he tests that assumption to determine whether it is provable. As new evidence is gathered, the hypothesis is continuously refined and modified to conform to known facts. This method of investigation is known as _____.

    A. The predication approach
    B. The fraud theory approach
    C. Forensic distillation
    D. Qualitative analysis

2. Fraud examination methodology is constructed so that all cases are handled in a uniform fashion. In general, which of the following investigative steps should be performed FIRST in an investigation?
    A. Document examination
    B. Interviews of third-party witnesses
    C. Interviews of corroborative witnesses
    D. Interview of the primary suspect

3. Common law imposes duties of care and loyalty on directors and officers of corporations. Which of the following statements about the common law duties of care and loyalty are true?
    I. Directors and officers must use the same reasonable care in conducting the affairs of a company that they would in their own affairs.
    II. Under the common law duties of care and loyalty, directors or officers may be required to conduct an internal investigation of suspected employee fraud.
    III. The common law duties of care and loyalty only relate to business dealings and therefore have no bearing on the investigation of fraud.
    IV. A director or officer who refuses to investigate a known case of employee fraud may be personally liable to the company for the losses caused by the fraud.

    A. I and II
    B. I, II, and III
    C. I, II, and IV
    D. II and IV

Final Examination

4. Blue is the CEO of Acme Inc. Blue recently received an anonymous call alleging that Green, a sales director for Acme, has been overbilling the company's major customers for the last two years. Blue is concerned because she knows that a company can be held liable for an employee's misconduct if the misconduct occurred in the course and scope of his employment. Which of the following statements about course and scope is true?
   A. An employee's actions are within the course and scope of his employment only if they occurred while the employee was on duty and on the company's premises.
   B. An employee's actions are within the course and scope of his employment if they were the kinds of acts he was authorized to perform and if they were intended, at least in some part, to benefit the company.
   C. Unless a company expressly authorizes illegal conduct by its employees, an illegal act cannot be considered in the course and scope of employment.
   D. An employee's actions are considered within the course and scope of his employment as long as he identifies himself as a representative of the company.

5. Because the investigation of fraud deals with the individual rights of others, an investigation must be conducted only with adequate cause or predication. *Predication* is defined as:
   A. Documentary evidence, corroborated by at least two sources, that proves fraud has occurred, is occurring, or will occur
   B. Any allegation of serious wrongdoing
   C. The totality of circumstances that would lead a reasonable, professionally trained, and prudent individual to believe a fraud has occurred, is occurring, or will occur
   D. None of the above

6. Corporations are formed by filing articles of incorporation with the secretary of state in the state where the company does business. The filing is a public record and can be a valuable source of information to fraud investigators. Which of the following information is typically NOT included in a corporation's articles of incorporation?
   A. The location of the corporation's principal office
   B. The names of the corporation's directors and officers
   C. The tax returns and quarterly reports for the corporation
   D. The date of incorporation

7. Able is an investigator for XYZ Corporation. He wants to conduct a criminal history check on Baker, one of the company's employees. Will this search come under the Fair Credit Reporting Act (FCRA)?
   A. Yes, if Able hires a third party to check Baker's criminal history.
   B. Yes, if Able personally goes to the courthouse to check Baker's criminal history.
   C. Both A and B are correct.
   D. Neither A nor B is correct.

8. Able is investigating a suspected embezzlement by one of XYZ Corporation's employees. As part of this investigation, he is assembling a financial profile of the suspect. Among other things, he wants to see if the suspect has made any significant real estate purchases since the embezzlement scheme began. Information on real estate transactions such as deeds, grants, transfers, and mortgages is located:
   A. With the state tax assessor
   B. With the secretary of state
   C. With the U.S. Department of Land Management
   D. With the county recorder

9. The Freedom of Information Act makes certain records open to the public. Which of the following types of records are NOT available to the general public?
   A. Tax rolls
   B. Banking records
   C. Real property records
   D. Assumed name records

10. Which of the following statements regarding the Fair Credit Reporting Act (FCRA) is FALSE?
    A. The FCPA applies to consumer credit reports.
    B. The FCRA applies even if the person or organization seeking the information gathers it directly from the source.
    C. The FCRA applies to consumer reports bearing on a person's character or general reputation.
    D. The FCRA applies to consumer reports bearing on a person's mode of living.

11. The _____ is the primary statute that governs the availability of government records to the general public. The Act sets very specific guidelines on which government records are open to the public and which are not.
    A. Fair Credit Reporting Act
    B. Right to Financial Privacy Act
    C. Privacy Act of 1974
    D. Freedom of Information Act

12. Green is a corporate security officer for XYZ Corp., a private company. During an internal fraud investigation, Green searched the briefcase of Blue, an XYZ employee. Assume Blue had a reasonable privacy expectation in the briefcase, and that the search was performed in a highly offensive manner. Also assume that there was no state action involved in the investigation. Which of the following statements is true?
    A. Blue can sue XYZ for violating his Fourth Amendment Rights.
    B. Blue can sue XYZ for common law invasion of privacy.
    C. Blue can sue Green for invasion of privacy, but XYZ is not liable for Green's actions because his conduct was illegal.
    D. Blue has no grounds to sue XYZ because only state actors can be sued for unlawful searches.

Final Examination

13. Which of the following is a TRUE statement regarding the installation by employers of video surveillance cameras anywhere on the company premises?
    A. Generally, an employer may install video cameras in a restroom as long as they don't point toward toilet stalls or urinals.
    B. Video surveillance generally is not permissible in areas where employees have a legitimate expectation of privacy.
    C. In most circumstances, an employer may install cameras in a dressing room so long as the video footage is properly secured.
    D. In most circumstances, an employer may use video surveillance that is accompanied by audio recording.

14. When a government employer searches an employee's workspace, there is a two-part test to determine if the search is legal. Which of the following are the two standards that must be satisfied?
    I. The employer must obtain a warrant.
    II. The search must be justified at its inception.
    III. The search must be reasonable in scope.
    IV. The search must be based on probable cause.

    A. I and IV
    B. I and III
    C. II and III
    D. II and IV

15. Beta is conducting an internal investigation of suspected fraud on behalf of ABC Company. Beta wants to intercept and monitor the phone calls of one of ABC's employees to determine if the employee is involved in the scheme, but he is not sure if this is legal. Which federal law governs the interception of electronic communications?
    A. The Electronic Communications Privacy Act
    B. The Freedom of Information Act
    C. The Pen Register Prohibition Act
    D. The Privacy Act of 1974

16. Which of the following is a TRUE statement regarding invasion of employee privacy?
    A. If an employee does not have a reasonable expectation of privacy in an area, his employer can search that area without violating the employee's common law right to privacy.
    B. Common law protections of employees' privacy cover private employees, but not public employees, unless the public employees work for the federal government.
    C. Common law protections of employees' privacy take precedence over Fourth Amendment protections.
    D. Common law protections of employees' privacy cover public employees, but not private employees.

17. If government investigators seize evidence in violation of the Fourth Amendment, that evidence will be inadmissible in a prosecution of the defendant. This is known as _____.
    A. The exclusionary rule
    B. The due process exception
    C. The *Miranda* rule
    D. Whistleblower protection

18. Beta, an employee of ABC, is suspected of work-related misconduct. ABC's investigators want to search Beta's workspace. Which of the following statements is true?
    A. If ABC is a government agency, the investigators will have to obtain a warrant before they conduct the search.
    B. If ABC is a private employer, the investigators will have to obtain a warrant before they conduct the search.
    C. Both A and B are correct.
    D. Neither A nor B is correct.

19. Which of the following statements regarding employer monitoring of employee phone calls is FALSE?
    A. Generally, an employer is permitted to monitor employee phone calls for purposes of quality control.
    B. Generally, an employer is permitted to monitor employee phone calls if the employee provided implied consent.
    C. Generally, an employer is permitted to monitor employee phone calls in order to prevent employee misconduct.
    D. Generally, an employer is permitted to monitor employee phone calls if the employee expressly consented to the monitoring.

20. You work for ABC Company, which has recently suffered a large loss due to internal fraud. The company's investigators suspect Baker of the fraud and want to search his office. His desk has a locked drawer on it, and they ask you if they can search inside that drawer. Which of the following responses is most accurate?
    A. Yes, because a company can search anywhere on its premises.
    B. No, because locked containers are private and cannot be searched except by the police.
    C. Yes, because a crime has been committed and the company has a duty to identify the perpetrator.
    D. Maybe; it depends on the circumstances.

21. _____ refers to (1) who has had possession of an object and (2) what they've done with it. It consists of establishing, as to each person who had control or custody of a piece of tangible evidence, how and when the object was received; how it was maintained or stored while in each person's possession; what changes, if any, it underwent in that person's custody; and how it left that person's custody.
    A. Authentication
    B. Chain of custody
    C. Forensic examination
    D. None of the above

22. Which of the following statements about handling and storing documentary evidence is true?
    A. Documents should be stored in sealed, initialed, and dated folders or envelopes
    B. The original document should be preserved for forensic examinations
    C. The documents should never be stapled or paper-clipped
    D. All of the above

Final Examination

23. Under the rules of evidence, tangible evidence cannot be admitted in a legal proceeding unless a competent witness testifies as to its identity. Essentially, the witness must confirm that the evidence is what it purports to be. This process is known as _____.
    A. Authentication
    B. Chain of custody
    C. Forensic examination
    D. None of the above

24. Blue, an internal investigator for ABC Corp., is seizing computer components in connection with an investigation into forgery of company checks. Which of the following statements about seizing digital evidence is true?
    I. Blue should document the scene of the seizure using photographs, diagrams, or video.
    II. If the computer is on, Blue should simply unplug it.
    III. Blue may need a search warrant to seize the suspect's personal flash drive as evidence.

    A. I and II
    B. I and III
    C. II and III
    D. I, II, and III

25. Which of the following statements regarding the confidentiality of tangible evidence collected by investors is FALSE?
    A. The work product privilege cannot be waived, even if the contents of documentary evidence are indiscriminately published.
    B. It is important that investigators treat any tangible evidence they collect as confidential.
    C. Documents should be stored securely and logged under a reliable classification and retrieval system.
    D. Memoranda or reports that summarize and evaluate documentary evidence are likely to be regarded as opinion work product and should be privileged from discovery by outside parties.

26. _____ questions are worded in a way that makes it difficult to answer "yes" or "no." These questions call for a monologue response and can be answered in several different ways. Interviewers should primarily use this type of question during the informational phase of an interview.
    A. Closed
    B. Leading
    C. Complex
    D. Open

27. Red is an internal investigator for ABC Corporation. Based on his investigation, Red is reasonably certain that Green, an ABC employee, was involved in a recent embezzlement scheme. Red is now prepared to conduct an admission-seeking interview of Green. Which of the following are valid goals of this interview?
    I. To clear Green if he is innocent
    II. To encourage Green to confess if he is culpable
    III. To make sure Green does not discuss the investigation with government investigators
    IV. To obtain a signed statement of the facts

    A. II and IV
    B. I, II, and IV
    C. II, III, and IV
    D. I, II, III, and IV

28. Which of the following statements regarding note-taking during an investigative interview is FALSE?
    A. The interviewer can enhance his credibility by making sure to document his impressions about the subject's guilt.
    B. Most subjects in a professional setting understand the critical value of notes.
    C. If the subject is opposed to note-taking, the interviewer should attempt to find out why and then try to alleviate the subject's concerns.
    D. The interviewer should note of any indicators of responsibility, innocence, or guilt by the subject.

29. All of the following statements about written confessions are true EXCEPT:
    A. A written confession should include precise language that clearly describes the misconduct.
    B. In order to be admissible in a court of law, the entire written confession must be in the confessor's handwriting.
    C. A written confession should include an express statement that the confession is being made voluntarily.
    D. A written confession may contain a moral excuse for the confessor's misconduct.

30. Green is an investigator who is interviewing several of Acme Co.'s employees as part of an internal fraud examination. Which of the following statements is false?
    A. Green should conduct the interviews in private.
    B. Green should not interview more than one person at a time.
    C. Green should promise the employees that anything said in the interviews will be confidential.
    D. Green should conduct the interviews in a room that is comfortably lit and well-ventilated.

31. Which of the following statements regarding an admission-seeking interview is FALSE?
    A. Any accusation should be made in the form of a statement, not a question.
    B. Emotive words, such as *steal, fraud,* and *crime,* must be used during the accusatory process.
    C. Any accusation should be phrased as though the accused's guilt has already been established.
    D. The interviewer must accuse the subject of wrongdoing.

Final Examination

32. It is important to choose the appropriate venue for an investigative interview. Which of the following statements about interview locations is NOT true?
    A. The interview room should be located where the subject will feel a sense of privacy.
    B. The interview room should be locked during the interview.
    C. The interview room should be comfortably lit and well-ventilated.
    D. The interview room should be quiet and free from distractions.

33. Which constitutional amendment protects people from having to give self-incriminating testimony?
    A. First Amendment
    B. Fourth Amendment
    C. Fifth Amendment
    D. Sixth Amendment

34. Able is an auditor who works for XYZ, a private company. Able suspects Beta, an XYZ employee, of having embezzled several thousand dollars. Able plans to interview Beta about the missing funds. Which of the following statements is true?
    A. Beta has a right to have an attorney present at the interview.
    B. Able must give *Miranda* warnings to Beta before the interview.
    C. Beta has a duty to cooperate with the investigation.
    D. None of the above statements are true.

35. There is a qualified privilege that protects internal investigators from defamation lawsuits under certain situations. It applies to statements that investigators make (1) in good faith; (2) regarding a subject in which the investigator has a legitimate interest or duty; (3) to another person with a corresponding interest or duty. This qualified privilege is known as the _____.
    A. Self-interrogatory privilege
    B. *Miranda* privilege
    C. Judicial proceeding privilege
    D. Common interest privilege

36. Which of the following statements regarding employees' duty to cooperate during an internal investigation is FALSE?
    A. Employees' duty to cooperate does not exist in employer-employee relationships in which the federal government is the employer.
    B. Employees have a duty to cooperate during an internal investigation if what is requested from them is reasonable.
    C. Employers are generally permitted to discipline or terminate an employee who refuses to cooperate with a reasonable request to provide information.
    D. At-will employees can be fired without any specific cause, so the employer generally does not have to justify firing an at-will employee who refuses to cooperate.

37. The restraint by one person of the physical liberty of another without consent or legal justification is known as _____. It can occur if an employee is detained against his will for any appreciable time, however short, in any way.
    A. Negligent incarceration
    B. Intentional infliction of emotional distress
    C. Wrongful prosecution
    D. False imprisonment

38. Which of the following statements about the attorney work product doctrine is true?
    A. It protects the confidentiality of all documents or reports prepared as part of any internal investigation.
    B. It only protects the confidentiality of documents that are prepared by an attorney.
    C. Both A and B are true.
    D. Neither A nor B is true.

39. Which of the following is a TRUE statement regarding defamation?
    A. A statement cannot be defamatory if it is never communicated to a third party.
    B. A statement of pure opinion can give rise to a defamation claim.
    C. Truth is not a defense to a charge of defamation.
    D. Spoken remarks cannot give rise to a defamation claim.

40. Able, a security officer for XYZ Company, has recently completed an investigation of internal theft. Based on the facts, Able believes that Baker, a warehouse clerk for XYZ, was responsible for the crime. Able is now preparing an investigation report for the company's management team. What information should Able include in the investigation report?
    A. Only those facts that tend to show Baker is responsible for the crime
    B. Only those facts that support Able's fraud theory
    C. All facts that are relevant to the investigation
    D. All facts that were gathered, regardless of whether they were relevant to the investigation

41. The potential of being sued for libel is one of the primary legal concerns that accompany the preparation of an investigative report. In order to sue for libel and recover damages, a person must prove which of the following?
    I. The defendant made a false written statement about him.
    II. The false statement was communicated to a third party.
    III. The person suffered harm as a result of the false communication.

    A. I only
    B. I and II
    C. I and III
    D. I, II, and III

42. Which of the following statements regarding internal investigative reports is FALSE?
    A. Internal investigative reports will not be read by the general public.
    B. If internal investigative reports are prepared properly, their readers should not have to refer to other documents to understand the issues.
    C. Internal investigative reports should adequately answer the classic questions of who, what, when, where, why, and how.
    D. Internal investigative reports might be read by adverse third parties.

Final Examination

43. Investigative reports frequently contain private or embarrassing information about people. If the company is not careful in how it handles and distributes investigative reports, it could face an invasion of privacy lawsuit. In general, investigative reports should only be distributed to:
    A. Individuals within the company
    B. The primary suspect and his manager
    C. Those who have a legitimate interest in the investigation
    D. The police

44. Employers and employees may enter into contracts that govern the length and terms of employment and the grounds upon which an employee may be fired. Employees who work under this type of contract are known as _____ employees.
    A. Term
    B. At-will
    C. Transient
    D. Temporary

45. Which of the following statements is true?
    A. At-will employees can only be fired for "good cause."
    B. There is no such thing as an implied employment contract.
    C. Statements in an employee handbook can be sufficient to create an implied employment contract.
    D. None of the above are true.

46. Under the at-will doctrine, an employer has a right to fire an employee for any reason. However, many states now recognize some form of public policy exception to the at-will doctrine. Under this exception, companies are not allowed to fire employees if the firing would undermine a fundamental public policy. Which of the following examples would NOT come under the public policy exception?
    A. An employee is fired for missing work to serve on a jury.
    B. An employee is fired for taking company money to pay personal medical bills.
    C. An employee is fired for refusing to falsify the company's financial statements.
    D. An employee is fired because he filed a workers' compensation claim.

47. Which of the following statements regarding the enforceability of an employment contract is TRUE?
    A. In order for an employment contract to be enforceable, it must be in writing.
    B. An employment contract can be enforceable even if it doesn't expressly state that it is a "contract for employment."
    C. In order for an employment contract to be enforceable, it must be signed by both the employee and the employer.
    D. An employment contract isn't enforceable unless it includes an express termination provision that is initialed by both the employee and the employer.

48. Generally, term employees can only be fired for "good cause." All of the following would tend to demonstrate that an employee was fired for good cause EXCEPT:
    A. The company conducted a fair investigation and found that the employee had violated company rules.
    B. The level of discipline was reasonably related to the seriousness of the offense.
    C. The company had significant evidence that the employee had committed a rules violation.
    D. The company immediately fired the employee after receiving an anonymous tip that he had violated company rules.

49. Which of the following statements regarding officers' and directors' duties of loyalty and reasonable care in overseeing company operations is FALSE?
    A. Failure to investigate reliable allegations of misconduct can subject the directors or officers to criminal liability for any damages that the company incurs as a result of the failure to investigate.
    B. Failure to investigate reliable allegations of misconduct can amount to a violation of officers' and directors' duties of loyalty and reasonable care.
    C. Officers and directors must act in the best interests of their company and take reasonable steps to prevent harm that the company might suffer as a result of employee misconduct.
    D. Failure to investigate reliable allegations of misconduct can subject the directors or officers to civil liability for any damages that the company incurs as a result of the failure to investigate.

50. Which of the following is true of the Private Securities Litigation Reform Act of 1995?
    A. An external auditor who learns of material illegal acts by his client company or its employees may be required to inform the SEC of those acts if management fails to take corrective action after it is notified of the illegal acts
    B. A company's duty to disclose typically pertains to facts that are material to the financial statement or other public record
    C. All of the above
    D. None of the above

51. If a company is found liable, the company is eligible to have its base fine reduced under the Organizational Sentencing Guidelines if it:
    A. Has an effective compliance program in place
    B. Self-reports violations to appropriate government agencies
    C. Cooperates with the government investigation of the misconduct
    D. All of the above

52. Which of the following statements regarding auditor communication about fraud is FALSE?
    A. Possible fraud that is inconsequential should be reported directly to those charged with governance.
    B. Possible fraud involving senior management should be reported directly to those charged with governance.
    C. Possible fraud that causes a material misstatement should be reported directly to those charged with governance.
    D. Possible fraud should be brought to the attention of an appropriate level of management.

Final Examination

53. The _____ expressly prohibits financial institutions from disclosing financial information about individual customers to government agencies without the consent of the customer or a search warrant, subpoena, court order, or other formal demand.
    A. Right to Financial Privacy Act
    B. Freedom of Information Act
    C. Gramm-Leach Bliley Act
    D. Fair Credit Reporting Act

54. Which of the following searches CANNOT be used to aid in the decision-making process to hire a potential employee?
    A. Bankruptcy filings
    B. Tax liens
    C. Workers' compensation records
    D. Judgments

55. Which of the following can be used to locate information on the Internet?
    A. Search engines
    B. Web directories
    C. All of the above
    D. None of the above

56. Information concerning a corporation's name, ownership, stock value, initial shareholders, directors, and officers is registered and maintained at the:
    A. Federal level
    B. State level
    C. Local level
    D. All of the above

57. Which of the following statements regarding workplace searches by public employers is TRUE?
    A. Public employers are held to a standard of "reasonableness under all the circumstances."
    B. Public employers are required to obtain a search warrant to conduct workplace searches.
    C. To conduct workplace searches, public employers are required to show probable cause that the suspect employee committed a crime.
    D. Public employers may not search areas in which an employee has a reasonable expectation of privacy.

58. Which of the following is a separate cause of action of the tort of invasion of privacy?
    A. Intrusion upon seclusion
    B. Public disclosure of private facts
    C. False light invasion of privacy
    D. Appropriation of likeness
    E. All of the above

59. Employers generally need to obtain what type of consent to monitor their employees' email?
    A. Oral or written consent
    B. Express written consent
    C. Express or implied consent
    D. None, no consent is needed

60. The ordinary course of business exception under the Electronic Communications Privacy Act does NOT state:
    A. That employers are permitted to monitor their employees' phone calls under certain circumstances as long as the monitoring is done for a legitimate business purpose
    B. That the method used to intercept and monitor the call must be no more intrusive than necessary
    C. That personal calls may be monitored if it is being done for a legitimate purpose
    D. All of the above

61. There are a few non-scientific means that fraud examiners can use to help identify certain document features that could be suspicious. These means could include which of the following?
    A. Side-by-side comparisons
    B. Holding the document up in front of a bright light
    C. Reducing the light from the room
    D. All of the above

62. Which of the following is NOT true of digital evidence?
    A. Digital evidence is especially vulnerable to alteration or destruction if handled improperly.
    B. The term *digital evidence* is limited to data recovered from a computer hard drive.
    C. Digital evidence is used to establish the same types of details—who, what, when, where, why, and how—as documentary evidence.
    D. All of the above are true.

63. Which of the following is a TRUE statement regarding the abilities of digital forensic specialists?
    A. They are able to determine whether a seized flash drive was ever inserted into a computer and, if it was, what files were accessed while the drive was inserted.
    B. They are able to determine whether a seized flash drive was ever inserted into a computer, but not what files might have been accessed.
    C. They are unable to determine whether a seized flash drive was ever inserted into a computer.
    D. They are able to conduct a link-file analysis on a seized flash drive to determine how many different computers it has been inserted into.

64. When organizing documentary evidence, it is recommended that investigators keep:
    A. Chronologies
    B. To-do lists
    C. Both of the above
    D. None of the above

65. According to the text, the majority of communication between individuals is:
    A. Spoken
    B. Non-spoken
    C. Verbally
    D. None of the above

Final Examination

66. When asking informational questions, the investigator should NOT:
    A. Ask the questions in a manner that will develop the facts in the order of their occurrence, or in some other systematic order.
    B. Be sure that he understands the subject's answers, and if they are not perfectly clear, have the subject interpret them at that time instead of saving this for later.
    C. Stop the subject's narrative to clarify facts that are difficult to understand instead of saving them for later.
    D. Ask only one question at a time, and frame the question so that only one answer is required.

67. Which of the following question types is used to establish the respondent's credibility?
    A. Assessment
    B. Introductory
    C. Informational
    D. Closing

68. Motions such as picking lint from clothing, playing with objects such as pencils, or holding one's hands while talking are known as:
    A. Illustrators
    B. Anatomical physical responses
    C. Manipulators
    D. Fleeing positions

69. Which of the following methods can be used to diffuse an alibi?
    A. Display physical evidence
    B. Discuss witnesses
    C. Discuss deceptions
    D. All of the above

70. _____ is an essential element in all criminal actions involving fraud.
    A. Understanding
    B. Intent
    C. Rationalization
    D. None of the above

71. Which of the following statements about at-will employees is TRUE?
    A. At-will employees have a duty to cooperate during an internal investigation.
    B. At-will employees are under an employment contract for a specified term.
    C. At-will employees cannot be fired without any specific cause.
    D. At-will employees cannot be fired for refusal to cooperate during an internal investigation.

72. Which of the following statements about the Fifth Amendment is NOT correct:
    A. The Fifth Amendment prohibits the federal government from depriving individuals of life, liberty, or property without due process of law.
    B. In general, the Fifth Amendment does not protect the records and documents of a collective entity, such as a corporation.
    C. The Fifth Amendment applies to both state and private action.
    D. The Fifth Amendment prevents the state from punishing a public employee for refusing to provide incriminating evidence against himself.

73. Defamation that appears in written form is known as:
    A. Libel
    B. Slander
    C. Both A and B
    D. Neither A nor B

74. The attorney-client privilege can be waived by:
    A. The client
    B. The attorney
    C. A third party
    D. Both A and B

75. When summarizing the results of an interview, the investigator should try to write the report on the interview or interrogation in a way that preserves the elements of the:
    A. Attorney-client privilege
    B. Work product doctrine
    C. Self-evaluation privilege
    D. All of the above

76. Disclosing an investigator's report to government personnel MAY:
    A. Convince prosecutors or regulators that the company has no liability in the matter under investigation
    B. Show such a high degree of cooperation and good faith that prosecutors or regulators may be convinced to decline to prosecute or pursue enforcement actions within the company
    C. Mitigate punishment or discipline as a result of a voluntary disclosure
    D. All of the above

77. The _____ is a discovery rule that prevents compelled disclosure of documents and materials that have been collected, arranged, or prepared in anticipation of litigation.
    A. Work-product doctrine
    B. Attorney-client privilege
    C. Self-evaluation privilege
    D. Litigation-document privilege

78. An _____ may arise based on the conduct of the parties, even though there is no formal written or oral agreement.
    A. Express contract
    B. Implied contract
    C. Explicit contract
    D. None of the above

79. The decision to prosecute—in the sense of charging and trying a person on criminal charges—is generally made by:
    A. The company who initiated the internal investigation
    B. The investigator who conducted the internal investigation
    C. Prosecutors
    D. All of the above

Final Examination

80. If a company is planning to pursue civil remedies against an offending employee, referring the matter to a prosecutor has potential benefits to the investigation and to any planned civil litigation. Which of the following would be considered a benefit of referring the matter to a prosecutor?
    A. Criminal cases are typically resolved more quickly than civil suits
    B. It is easier to recover losses through a criminal restitution order than to prove a damages case in civil litigation
    C. The company can obtain a substantial equivalent of a civil judgment without the time and expense of a civil lawsuit
    D. All of the above

XV. INDEX

A

Accurint, 99, 107, 306
admission-seeking questions, 158, 176
Americans with Disability Act, 82
Anti-Kickback Act, 9
articles of incorporation, 79
Ask.com, 103, 106
assessment questions, 158, 167, 172, 320
attorney work product doctrine, 223, 239, 328
attorney-client privilege, 49, 218, 219, 220, 221, 222, 226, 233, 234, 235, 238, 244, 246, 248, 327, 329, 331
at-will doctrine, 251, 252, 264, 333
AU 200, *Responsibilities and Functions of the Independent Auditor*, 36
AU 240, *Consideration of Fraud in a Financial Statement Audit*, 35
audit committee financial expert, 20, 21
Auditing Standard No. 5, 25, 35, 44, 45, 46
authentication, 137, 138, 145, 146

B

benchmark admission, 186, 187, 278, 323, 350
Bing, 103, 106
black boxes, 69
Boolean operators, 104
Bureau of Public Debt, 92
bureau of vital statistics, 83

C

calibrating, 167
Certified Fraud Examiner, 48
chain of custody, 137
clarity, 241, 249, 332
closed questions, 162, 318, 320
closing questions, 158, 320
code of ethics, 17, 18, 19
collective bargaining agreement, 128, 197, 202, 206, 207, 237, 253, 256, 264, 325, 333, 334, 335
collective bargaining agreements, 253, 333, 334
Committee of Sponsoring Organizations, 16
common law, 29
common-interest privilege, 213
compliance program, 30, 32
confidential communications, 200, 220, 244
confidentiality, 2, 31, 35, 43, 49, 139, 151, 154, 166, 207, 217, 218, 219, 220, 222, 226, 227, 228, 229, 231, 232, 233, 236, 239, 241, 242, 244, 246, 247, 328, 329, 330
consent exception, 123, 124, 125, 133, 313, 345
consulting experts, 219, 327
consumer reporting agency, 64, 65

Index

control group test, 221, 238, 327, 328
Customs and Border Protection Service, 89

D

D&B, 99, 100
DBA, 72, 79, 80, 107, 305, 339
DCS, 100
defamation, 48, 98, 122, 211, 212, 213, 214, 242, 247, 257, 304, 324
Department of Defense, 32, 77, 86
Department of Homeland Security, 89, 92
Department of Justice, 32, 87
Department of Labor, 88
Department of Motor Vehicles, 83, 94, 107, 306
Department of the Treasury, 88, 89
Department of Veterans Affairs, 89
Dialog, 91, 99
digital evidence, 138, 142, 147, 148, 149, 231, 315, 316
directories, 102, 104, 105, 106, 308
Dogpile, 106
Driver's Privacy Protection Act, 68, 69
Drug Enforcement Administration, 90
due diligence, 96
Due Process clause, 198
duty to cooperate, 109, 197, 198
duty to investigate, 6, 8, 9, 27, 28

E

EDGAR, 91
Electronic Communications Privacy Act, 123, 133, 312, 313, 345
emotive words, 179
employee handbook, 215, 254, 255, 264, 280, 333, 334, 353
Employee Polygraph Protection Act, 208
Employee Retirement Income Security Act, 88
Epilepsy, 208
evidence in plain view, 117
exclusionary rule, 119
exclusive control, 111, 112, 113, 127, 133, 311, 342, 343
Experian, 100
express contracts, 253

F

Factiva, 101, 107, 306
factual work product, 224, 233
Fair and Accurate Credit Transactions Act, 65
Fair Credit Reporting Act, 63, 64, 66, 256, 335, 339
Fair Labor Standards Act, 208
false imprisonment, 97, 122, 151, 215, 216, 259, 275, 346
false light, 120, 122, 210, 211, 310

Family Educational Rights and Privacy Act, 72, 76
Federal Aviation Administration, 90
Federal Bureau of Investigation, 87
Federal Energy Regulatory Commission, 90
Federal Maritime Commission, 90
Fifth Amendment, 7, 132, 198, 200, 201, 202, 203, 205, 237, 238, 251, 309, 326
Financial Crimes Enforcement Network, 7, 89
firewalls, 145
flash drive, 145
Foreign Corrupt Practices Act, 5, 28, 200, 234, 303
forensic document examiners, 136, 139
Fourth Amendment, 109, 111, 112, 113, 114, 115, 116, 117, 118, 119, 120, 122, 132, 133, 198, 199, 205, 238, 309, 310, 311, 326, 341
Freedom of Information Act, 62, 107, 305
fruad theory approach, 51, 302

G
G.A. Public Records Services, 100
General Services Administration, 90
Generally Accepted Accounting Principles, 10
good cause, 28, 130, 197, 198, 252, 253, 254, 255, 256, 325, 333, 334
good faith and fair dealing, 122, 215
Google, 103, 106, 125, 143
Gossmeyer v. McDonald, 118
Gramm-Leach-Bliley Act, 66

H
hardware, 112, 142, 144, 145, 316
Health Insurance Portability and Accountability Act, 69
Hewlett-Packard, 67
HighBeam, 101
Hoover's, 100, 107, 306
HUD, 86
hypothesis, 51, 52, 270, 271, 337, 338
hypothetical questions, 158

I
ICOFR, 15, 16, 17, 44, 45, 46, 47
illustrators, 171
implied contracts, 253
improper disclosure of private information, 122
informational questions, 158, 162, 318
infoUSA, 99
Institute of Internal Auditors, 33
Integrated Automated Fingerprint Identification System, 87
intent, 188, 190, 351
intentional infliction of emotional distress, 122, 214, 216, 238, 257, 326, 327
intentional spoliation, 231

Index

Internal Control—Integrated Framework, 16
Internal Revenue Service, 88
International Standards for the Professional Practice of Internal Auditing, 33, 35
Internet Archive, 105
Internet Public Library, 105
introductory questions, 158, 159, 320
intrusion into seclusion, 210
investigative consumer report, 65

J
judicial privilege, 213, 214

K
KnowX, 98, 107, 306

L
Labor-Management Reporting and Disclosure Act, 88
laptop computers, 147
leading questions, 163, 320
LexisNexis, 91, 98, 101
libel, 211, 242
link file analysis, 145
Lowe v. City of Macon, 118

M
malicious prosecution, 247, 263
Mamma, 106
manipulators, 171
memorandum of interview, 241, 332
Metacrawler, 106
Miranda warnings, 177, 203, 204, 237, 324, 347
misleading conduct, 229
misprision of felony, 232
motive, 188

N
National Labor Relations Act, 126, 204, 206, 207, 229
National Labor Relations Board, 126, 207, 229, 256, 335
negligent spoliation, 231
NLRB v. Weingarten, 207
non-public records, 62
non-union employees, 207
norming, 167

O
O'Connor v. Ortega, 113, 118
objective facts, 241, 331
obstruction of justice, 230

off-balance sheet transactions, 23
Office of Labor-Management Standards, 88
on-site court records searches, 95
open questions, 162, 320
opinion work product, 225, 233
Organizational Sentencing Guidelines, 5, 30

P

pen registers, 124
perjury, 231
predication, 50, 51, 58, 302, 337
Private Securities Litigation Reform Act, 10, 11
probable cause, 109, 113, 114, 115, 116, 117, 118, 132, 205, 263, 309, 310, 311
ProQuest, 99, 101
provider exception, 125, 133, 313, 345
proxemics, 152, 194, 319
proxy, 145
Public Company Accounting Oversight Board, 11, 12, 25, 44
public disclosure of private facts, 120, 210, 243, 258, 310, 324
public policy exception, 251, 252
public records, 49, 62, 64, 70, 71, 73, 76, 78, 90, 93, 96, 98, 99, 100, 107, 140, 306, 339
publication, 211, 212, 257

R

rapport, 159, 160, 320
rationalization, 181, 183, 185, 187, 188, 349
reasonable expectation of privacy, 111, 112, 113, 114, 120, 125, 126, 127, 128, 132, 133, 147, 210, 310, 311, 341, 342, 343, 345
reasonableness standard, 112, 113, 118, 309, 310, 311
respondeat superior doctrine, 97
restitution, 260, 261, 262, 336
Right to Financial Privacy Act, 68

S

Sarbanes-Oxley Act, 8, 11, 12, 13, 15, 23, 25, 44
search engines, 102, 103, 104, 106
Securities and Exchange Act, 10
Securities and Exchange Commission, 5, 68, 90
Securities Exchange Act, 200
self-evaluation privilege, 218, 226, 227, 233, 235, 239, 244, 328, 329
self-reporting, 32
sensitive questions, 161
Sixth Amendment, 30, 132, 198, 204, 238, 309, 326, 347
slander, 211
social media, 126
Social Security Administration, 85
spoliation of evidence, 231
state action, 110, 119, 120, 132, 198, 199, 200, 201, 202, 204, 237, 310, 324, 347

Index

Stored Communications Act, 125
subject matter test, 221, 222, 238, 328
subpoenas, 70, 75, 129, 130, 202, 203, 217

T

Telephone Records and Privacy Protection Act, 67
theme, 159, 160, 166, 167, 180, 181, 182, 185, 187, 189, 320
top-down approach, 46
tort law, 210
TransUnion, 100
trespass, 119, 122

U

U.S. Citizenship and Immigration Services, 92
U.S. Secret Service, 89
U.S. Small Business Administration, 92
Uniform Commercial Code, 78, 89, 94
union contract, 128, 206
Upjohn decision, 222

V

venue, 151
vicarious liability, 29
Victim and Witness Protection Act, 229
video surveillance, 127, 133, 312
Violent Crime Control and Law Enforcement Act, 97
Virtual Library, 105
volatile interview, 157, 158, 195, 321
voluntary disclosure programs, 32, 247

W

whistleblowers, 208
Wiretap Act, 123, 127
work product doctrine, 218, 227, 233, 234, 244, 245, 246, 329
workers' compensation, 82, 98, 252
wrongful termination, 122, 206, 214, 215, 219, 251, 255, 256, 264, 335, 353

Y

Yahoo!, 103, 105, 106, 125

ASSOCIATION OF CERTIFIED FRAUD EXAMINERS

SELF-STUDY COURSE EVALUATION
Conducting Internal Investigations

Please take a few moments to fill out this important survey to help us better serve you.
Please return the completed survey to ACFE using the enclosed envelope.

1. Overall, how satisfied or dissatisfied are you with this self-study course?
   - ❏ Not at all satisfied
   - ❏ Not very satisfied
   - ❏ Somewhat satisfied
   - ❏ Satisfied
   - ❏ Extremely satisfied

2. Why do you say this?
   _____
   _____
   _____
   _____

3. Would you recommend this course to colleagues?
   - ❏ Definitely not recommend
   - ❏ Probably not recommend
   - ❏ Probably recommend
   - ❏ Definitely recommend

4. Please tell us how much this course will help you in your daily job responsibilities.
   - ❏ Help a lot
   - ❏ Help a little
   - ❏ Help not at all

5. What did you like best about the course (please be specific)?
   _____
   _____
   _____
   _____

6. What did you like least about the course (please be specific)?
   _____
   _____
   _____
   _____
   _____

7. How strongly do you agree or disagree with the following statements?

   The stated learning objectives of this course were met.
   ❏ Strongly Agree ❏ Agree ❏ Disagree ❏ Strongly Disagree

   The time allocated for this course was appropriate.
   ❏ Strongly Agree ❏ Agree ❏ Disagree ❏ Strongly Disagree

   Prerequisite requirements, if any, were appropriate.
   ❏ Strongly Agree ❏ Agree ❏ Disagree ❏ Strongly Disagree

8. How many hours did it take you to complete this course?
   _____

9. How strongly do you agree or disagree with the following: "The course materials (packets, worksheets, exercises, etc.)..."

   Were accurate:
   ❏ Strongly Agree ❏ Agree ❏ Disagree ❏ Strongly Disagree

   Were relevant:
   ❏ Strongly Agree ❏ Agree ❏ Disagree ❏ Strongly Disagree

   Contributed to achievement of learning objectives:
   ❏ Strongly Agree ❏ Agree ❏ Disagree ❏ Strongly Disagree

10. What is the main reason you took this self-study course (choose one)?
    - ❏ Employer wanted me to gain additional training
    - ❏ I could do it at my own pace (nights, weekends, etc.)
    - ❏ I did not have to travel
    - ❏ Subjects covered are applicable to my current work
    - ❏ I could start it at any time
    - ❏ To gain CPE credits
    - ❏ I am working toward becoming a CFE
    - ❏ Other (please specify):
    _____
    _____
    _____
    _____
    _____

Continued on other side ▶

◀ Continued from other side

11. How did you hear about this course (choose all that apply)?
    - ❏ ACFE Catalog (Quarterly Resource Guide)
    - ❏ ACFE Bookstore catalog
    - ❏ Recommended by a friend/colleague
    - ❏ Received announcement in the mail
    - ❏ ACFE.com
    - ❏ Email announcement/newsletter
    - ❏ *Fraud Magazine*
    - ❏ Other (please specify):

    _____

12. What is your preferred method for obtaining CPE credit hours?
    - ❏ Attend chapter meetings
    - ❏ Self-study products
    - ❏ Seminars
    - ❏ Annual conferences
    - ❏ Instruct an event
    - ❏ Author articles
    - ❏ *Fraud Magazine* quizzes
    - ❏ Online/Web-based
    - ❏ Other (please specify):

    _____

13. How many ACFE self-study courses have you completed in the past three years (excluding this one)?

    _____

14. Have you purchased any CPE self-study courses from other organizations in the past three years? If yes, please list the organization.
    - ❏ Yes
    - ❏ No

    _____

15. Are you a CFE?
    - ❏ Yes
    - ❏ No

16. What other professional designations do you hold?

    _____

17. How many years have you been in the anti-fraud profession?

    _____

18. Please provide any additional comments (suggestions for future topics, errors, general feedback, etc.)

    _____
    _____
    _____
    _____
    _____

OPTIONAL. Please provide your contact information.

Name _____

Employer _____

Phone Number _____

Email Address _____

For questions regarding this survey or any other comments regarding self-study products, contact the ACFE Bookstore at +1 (512) 478-9000 / (800) 245-3321 or visit **ACFE.com/Shop**

The survey is complete. Thank you for your feedback.

ACFE
Association of Certified Fraud Examiners

Global Headquarters
The Gregor Building
716 West Ave
Austin, TX 78701-2727
USA